CLYMER™

SUZUKI

VS700-800 INTRUDER TWINS
1985-1994

The world's finest publisher of mechanical how-to manuals

INTERTEC® PUBLISHING CORPORATION

P.O. Box 12901, Overland Park, Kansas 66282-2901

Copyright ©1995 Intertec Publishing Corporation

FIRST EDITION
First Printing January, 1995

Printed in U.S.A.

ISBN: 0-89287-629-8

Library of Congress: 94-75183

MOTORCYCLE INDUSTRY COUNCIL

Technical photography by Ed Scott.

Photographic assistance by Randy Stephens.

Technical illustrations by Mitzi McCarthy and Robert Caldwell.

COVER: Photographed by Mark Clifford, Mark Clifford Photography, Los Angeles, California.

778001

Chapter One
General Information | 1

Chapter Two
Troubleshooting | 2

Chapter Three
Lubrication, Maintenance and Tune-up | 3

Chapter Four
Engine | 4

Chapter Five
Clutch | 5

Chapter Six
Transmission and Gearshift Mechanisms | 6

Chapter Seven
Fuel, Emission Control and Exhaust Systems | 7

Chapter Eight
Electrical System | 8

Chapter Nine
Liquid Cooling System | 9

Chapter Ten
Front Suspension and Steering | 10

Chapter Eleven
Rear Suspension and Final Drive | 11

Chapter Twelve
Brakes | 12

Chapter Thirteen
Body and Frame | 13

Index | 14

Wiring Diagrams | 15

The following books and guides are published by Intertec Publishing Corp.

CLYMER™ SHOP MANUALS
Boat Motors and Drives
Motorcycles and ATVs
Snowmobiles
Personal Watercraft

ABOS®/INTERTEC BLUE BOOKS® AND TRADE-IN GUIDES
Recreational Vehicles
Outdoor Power Equipment
Agricultural Tractors
Lawn and Garden Tractors
Motorcycles and ATVs
Snowmobiles
Boats and Motors
Personal Watercraft

AIRCRAFT BLUEBOOK-PRICE DIGEST®
Airplanes
Helicopters

I&T SHOP SERVICE™ MANUALS
Tractors

INTERTEC SERVICE MANUALS
Snowmobiles
Outdoor Power Equipment
Personal Watercraft
Gasoline and Diesel Engines
Recreational Vehicles
Boat Motors and Drives
Motorcycles
Lawn and Garden Tractor

CONTENTS

QUICK REFERENCE DATA IX

CHAPTER ONE
GENERAL INFORMATION 1
Manual organization   Expendable supplies
Notes, cautions and warnings   Basic hand tools
Safety first   Precision measuring tools
Service hints   Special tools
Torque specifications   Cleaning solvent
Fasteners   Mechanic's tips
Lubricants   Ball bearing replacement
RTV gasket sealant   Oil seals
Threadlock   Riding safety
Gasket remover

CHAPTER TWO
TROUBLESHOOTING 34
Operating requirements   Clutch
Troubleshooting instruments   Transmission
Troubleshooting   Excessive vibration
Engine performance   Carburetor troubleshooting
Engine noises   Front suspension and steering
Engine lubrication   Brake problems

CHAPTER THREE
LUBRICATION, MAINTENANCE AND TUNE-UP 44
Routine checks   New battery installation
Pre-checks   Battery electrical cable connectors
Service intervals   Periodic lubrication
Tires and wheels   Periodic maintenance
Battery   Tune-up

CHAPTER FOUR
ENGINE **91**

Engine principles
Servicing engine in frame
Engine
Front cylinder head cover
  and camshaft
Rear cylinder head cover
  and camshaft
Camshaft
Cylinder head and cylinder

Valves and valve components
Pistons and piston rings
Oil pump
Primary drive gear
Secondary gear assembly
Crankcase
Crankshaft and connecting rods
Break-in

CHAPTER FIVE
CLUTCH **172**

Clutch
Clutch hydraulic system
Master cylinder

Slave cylinder
Bleeding the system

CHAPTER SIX
TRANSMISSION AND GEARSHIFT MECHANISMS **198**

External gearshift mechanism

Transmission

CHAPTER SEVEN
FUEL, EMISSION CONTROL AND EXHAUST SYSTEMS **219**

Carburetor operation
Carburetor service
Carburetor assembly
Carburetor service
Carburetor adjustments
Throttle cable replacement
Fuel tank

Fuel shutoff valve and filter
Fuel pump
Crankcase breather system
  (U.S. only)
Evaporative emission control system
  (California models only)
Exhaust system

CHAPTER EIGHT
ELECTRICAL SYSTEM **250**

Electrical connectors
Battery negative terminal
Charging system
Voltage regulator/rectifier
Alternator
Transistorized ignition system
Starter system
Electric starter

Starter clutch and gears
Starter relay
Lighting system
Switches
Electrical components
Fuses
Circuit breaker
Wiring diagrams

CHAPTER NINE
LIQUID COOLING SYSTEM 309

Hoses and hose clamps
Cooling system check
Pressure check
Cooling fan, shroud and fan duct

Thermostat and housing
Water pump
Hoses

CHAPTER TEN
FRONT SUSPENSION AND STEERING 323

Front hub
Wheels
Tire changing
Tire repairs

Handlebar
Steering head and stem
Front forks

CHAPTER ELEVEN
REAR SUSPENSION AND FINAL DRIVE 361

Rear wheel
Rear hub
Final drive unit, drive shaft and universal joint

Swing arm
Shock absorbers

CHAPTER TWELVE
BRAKES 381

Disc brakes
Front brake pad replacement
Front brake caliper
Front brake hose replacement

Front brake disc
Bleeding the system
Rear drum brake
Rear brake pedal and linkage

CHAPTER THIRTEEN
BODY AND FRAME 411

Seats
Frame side covers
Frame head side covers
Footpegs

Sidestand
Front fender
Frame

INDEX 420

WIRING DIAGRAMS 423

QUICK REFERENCE DATA

TIRE INFLATION PRESSURE (COLD)*

	Tire Pressure				
	Front			Rear	
Load	psi	kPa		psi	kPa
Solo riding	28	200		32	225
Dual riding	32	225		36	250

* Tire inflation pressure for factory equipped tires. Aftermarket tires may require different inflation pressure.

RECOMMENDED LUBRICANTS AND FLUIDS

Fuel	Regular unleaded
U.S. and Canada	87 [(R + M)/2 method] or 91 octane or higher
U.K. and all others	85-95 octane
Engine oil	SAE 10W-40 API grade SE or SF
Capacity	
Change	2.4 ml (2.5 U.S. qt./2.1 Imp. qt.)
Change and filter	2.8 ml (3.0 U.S. qt./2.5 Imp. qt.)
At overhaul	3.3 ml (3.5 U.S. qt./2.9 Imp. qt.)
Coolant	Ethylene glycol
Capacity at change	1.7 ml (1.8 U.S. qt./1.5 Imp. qt.)
Final drive oil	SAE 90 hypoid gear oil with GL-5 under API classification
Capacity at change	2-2.2 ml (6.8-7.0 U.S. qt./7.4-7.7 Imp. qt.)
Brake fluid	DOT 4
Clutch hydraulic fluid	DOT 3 or DOT 4
Battery refilling	Distilled water
Fork oil	SAE 10W
Capacity per leg	
1985-1986	3.37 ml (11.4 U.S. oz./11.9 Imp. oz.)
1987	3.55 ml (12.0 U.S. oz./12.5 Imp. oz.)
1988-on	4.13 ml (14.0 U.S. oz./14.5 Imp. oz.)
Oil level each leg	
1985-1986	144 mm (5.67 in.)
1987	117.4 mm (4.62 in.)
1988-on	124.3 mm (4.89 in.)
Cables and pivot points	Cable lube or SAE 10W/30 motor oil

MAINTENANCE AND TUNE UP TIGHTENING TORQUES

Item	N·m	ft.-lb.
Oil drain plug	18-23	13-16.5
Valve adjuster locknut	13-16	9.5-11.5
Cylinder head side cover bolts (side opposite spark plug)	21-25	15-18

TUNE-UP SPECIFICATIONS

Valve clearance	
Intake and exhaust	0.08-0.13 mm (0.003-0.005 in.)
Spark plug type	
1985-1988	NGK DP8EA-9, ND X24EP-U9
1989-on	NGK DPR8EA-9, ND X24EPR-U9
Spark plug gap	0.8-0.9 mm (0.03-0.04 in.)
Idle speed	1,000 ±100 rpm

REPLACEMENT BULBS

U.S. and Canadian Models

Item	Voltage/wattage
Headlight (high/low beam)	12V 60/55W
Taillight/brakelight	
1986-1987	12V 8/23W
1988-on	12V 5/21W
Directional signal	
1986-1987	
Front	12V 8/23W
Rear	12V 23W
1988-on	
Front	12V 5/21W
Rear	12V 21W
License plate light	12V 8W
High beam indicator light	12V 1.7 W
Instrument and all other indicator lights	12V 3W

Other than U.S. and Canadian Models

Item*	Voltage/wattage
Headlight (high/low beam)	12V 60/55W
Parking light	
E-02, E-24	12V 3.4W
E-15, E-16, E-18, E-22	12V 4W
Taillight/brakelight	
E-02, E-15, E-16, E-18, E-22	12V 5/21W
E-24	12V 8/23W
License plate light	
E-02, E-15, E-16, E-18, E-22	12V 5W
E-24	12V 8W
Directional signal	
E-02, E-15, E-16, E-18, E-22	12V 21W
E-24	12V 23W
Speedometer light	12V 21W
High beam indicator light	12V 1.7W
All other indicator lights	12V 3W

* E-02= England, E-15= Finland, E-16 Norway, E-18= Switzerland, E-22= West Germany, E-24= Austria

CLYMER™

SUZUKI

VS700-800 INTRUDER TWINS
1985-1994

INTRODUCTION

This detailed, comprehensive manual covers the U.S. and U.K. models of the Suzuki Intruder 700-800 cc V-twins from 1985-1994.

The expert text gives complete information on maintenance, tune-up, repair and overhaul. Hundreds of photos and drawings guide you through every step. The book includes all you will need to know to keep your Suzuki running right. Throughout this book where differences occur among the models, they are clearly identified.

A shop manual is a reference. You want to be able to find information fast. As in all Clymer books, this one is designed with you in mind. All chapters are thumb tabbed. Important items are extensively indexed at the rear of the book. All procedures, tables, photos, etc., in this manual are for the reader who may be working on the bike for the first time or using this manual for the first time. All the most frequently used specifications and capacities are summarized in the *Quick Reference Data* pages at the front of the book.

Keep the book handy in your tool box. It will help you better understand how your bike runs, lower repair costs and generally improve your satisfaction with the bike.

1

CHAPTER ONE

GENERAL INFORMATION

This detailed, comprehensive manual covers the U.S. and the U.K. models of the Suzuki Intruder 700-800 cc V-twins from 1985-1994. **Table 1** lists the chassis numbers (VIN) for models covered in this manual.

Troubleshooting, tune-up, maintenance and repair are not difficult, if you know what tools and equipment to use and what to do. Step-by-step instructions guide you through jobs ranging from simple maintenance to complete engine and suspension overhaul.

This manual can be used by anyone from a first time do-it-yourselfer to a professional mechanic. Detailed drawings and clear photographs give you all the information you need to do the work right.

Some procedures will require the use of special tools. The resourceful mechanic can, in many cases, think of acceptable substitutes for special tools, there is always another way. This can be as simple as using a few pieces of threaded rod, washers and nuts to remove or install a bearing or fabricating a tool from scrap material. However, using a substitute for a special tool is not recommended as it can be dangerous to and may damage the part. If you find that a tool can be designed and safely made, but will require some type of machine work, you may want to search out a local community college or high school that has a machine shop curriculum. Some shop teachers welcome outside work that can be used as practical shop applications for advanced students.

Table 1 lists model coverage with VIN and frame serial numbers. Metric and U.S. standards are used throughout this manual and U.S. to metric conversion is given in **Table 2**.

Tables 1-5 are located at the end of this chapter.

MANUAL ORGANIZATION

This chapter provides general information and discusses equipment and tools useful both for preventive maintenance and troubleshooting.

Chapter Two provides methods and suggestions for quick and accurate diagnosis and repair of problems. Troubleshooting procedures discuss typical symptoms and logical methods to pinpoint the trouble.

Chapter Three explains all periodic lubrication and routine maintenance necessary to keep your Suzuki operating well and competitive. Chapter Three also includes recommended tune-up procedures, eliminating the need to constantly consult other chapters on the various assemblies.

Subsequent chapters describe specific systems such as the engine top end, engine bottom end, clutch, transmission, fuel, exhaust, electrical, cooling, suspension, drive train, steering and brakes. Each chapter provides disassembly, repair and assembly procedures in simple step-by-step form. If a repair is impractical for a home mechanic, it is so indicated. It is usually faster and less expensive to take such repairs to a Suzuki dealer or competent repair shop. Specifications concerning a particular system are included at the end of the appropriate chapter.

NOTES, CAUTIONS AND WARNINGS

The terms NOTE, CAUTION and WARNING have specific meanings in this manual. A NOTE provides additional information to make a step or procedure easier or clearer. Disregarding a NOTE could cause inconvenience, but would not cause damage or personal injury.

A CAUTION emphasizes an area where equipment damage could occur. Disregarding a CAUTION could cause permanent mechanical damage; however, personal injury is unlikely.

A WARNING emphasizes an area where personal injury or even death could result from negligence. Mechanical damage may also occur. WARNINGS *are to be taken seriously*. In some cases, serious injury and death has resulted from disregarding similar warnings.

SAFETY FIRST

Professional mechanics can work for years and never sustain a serious injury. If you observe a few rules of common sense and safety, you can enjoy many safe hours servicing your own machine. If you ignore these rules you can hurt yourself or damage the equipment.

1. *Never* use gasoline as a cleaning solvent.

2. *Never* smoke or use a torch in the vicinity of flammable liquids, such as cleaning solvent, in open containers.

3. If welding or brazing is required on the machine, remove the fuel tank and rear shock to a safe distance, at least 50 feet away.

4. Use the proper sized wrenches to avoid damage to fasteners and injury to yourself.

5. When loosening a tight or stuck nut, be guided by what would happen if the wrench should slip. Be careful; protect yourself accordingly.

6. When replacing a fastener, make sure to use one with the same measurements and strength as the old one. Incorrect or mismatched fasteners can result in

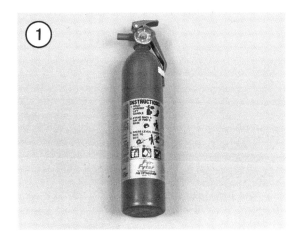

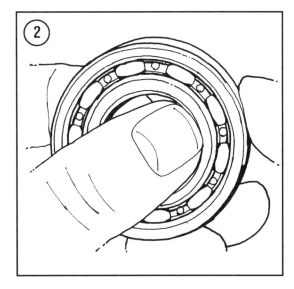

damage to the bike and possible personal injury. Beware of fastener kits that are filled with cheap and poorly made nuts, bolts, washers and cotter pins. Refer to *Fasteners* in this chapter for additional information.

7. Keep all hand and power tools in good condition. Wipe greasy and oily tools after using them. They are difficult to hold and can cause injury. Replace or repair worn or damaged tools.

8. Keep your work area clean and uncluttered.

9. Wear safety goggles during all operations involving drilling, grinding, the use of a cold chisel or anytime you feel unsure about the safety of your eyes. Safety goggles should also be worn anytime solvent and compressed air is used to clean a part.

10. Keep an approved fire extinguisher nearby (**Figure 1**). Be sure it is rated for gasoline (Class B) and electrical (Class C) fires.

11. When drying bearings or other rotating parts with compressed air, never allow the air jet to rotate the bearing or part. The air jet is capable of rotating them at speeds far in excess of those for which they were designed. The bearing or rotating part is very likely to disintegrate and cause serious injury and

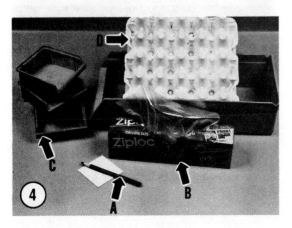

damage. To prevent bearing damage when using compressed air, hold the inner bearing race by hand (**Figure 2**).

SERVICE HINTS

Most of the service procedures covered are straightforward and can be performed by anyone reasonably handy with tools. It is suggested, however, that you consider your own capabilities carefully before attempting any operation involving major disassembly of the engine or transmission.

Take your time and do the job right. Do not forget that a newly rebuilt engine must be broken-in the same way as a new one. Keep the rpm within the limits given in your owner's manual when you get back on the road or out in the dirt.

1. "Front," as used in this manual, refers to the front of the bike; the front of any component is the end closest to the front of the bike. The "left-" and "right-hand" sides refer to the position of the parts as viewed by a rider sitting on the seat facing forward. For example, the throttle control is on the right-hand side. These rules are simple, but confusion can cause a major inconvenience during service.

2. Whenever servicing the engine or clutch, or when removing a suspension component, the bike should be secured in a safe manner.

> *WARNING*
> *Never disconnect the positive (+) battery cable unless the negative (–) cable has first been disconnected. Disconnecting the positive cable while the negative cable is still connected may cause a spark. This could ignite hydrogen gas given off by the battery, causing an explosion.*

3. Disconnect the negative battery cable (**Figure 3**) when working on or near the electrical, clutch, or starter systems and before disconnecting any electrical wires. On most batteries, the negative terminal will be marked with a minus (–) sign and the positive terminal with a plus (+) sign.

4. Tag all similar internal parts for location and mark all mating parts for position (A, **Figure 4**). Record number and thickness of any shims as they are removed. Small parts such as bolts can be identified by placing them in plastic sandwich bags (B, **Figure 4**). Seal and label them with masking tape.

5. Place parts from a specific are of the engine (e.g. cylinder head, cylinder, clutch, shift mechanism, etc.) into plastic boxes (C, **Figure 4**) to keep them separated.

6. When disassembling transmission shaft assemblies, use an egg flat (the type that restaurants get their eggs in) (D, **Figure 4**) and set the parts from the shaft in one of the depressions in the same order in which is was removed.

NOTE
Some of the procedures or service specifications listed in this manual may not be applicable if your Suzuki has been modified or if it has been equipped with non-stock equipment. When modifying or installing non-stock equipment, file all printed instruction or technical information regarding the new equipment in a folder or notebook for future reference. If your Suzuki was purchased second hand, the previous owner may have installed non-stock parts. If necessary, consult with your dealer or the accessory manufacturer on components that may affect tuning or repair procedures.

7. Wiring should be tagged with masking tape and marked as each wire is removed. Again, do not rely on memory alone.

8. Finished surfaces should be protected from physical damage or corrosion. Keep gasoline and brake fluid off painted surfaces.

9. Use penetrating oil on frozen or tight bolts, then strike the bolt head a few times with a hammer and punch (use a screwdriver on screws). Avoid the use of heat where possible, as it can warp, melt or affect the temper of parts. Heat also ruins finishes, especially paint and plastics.

10. No parts removed or installed (other than bushings and bearings) in the procedures given in this manual should require unusual force during disassembly or assembly. If a part is difficult to remove or install, find out why before proceeding.

11. Cover all openings after removing parts or components to prevent dirt, small tools, etc. from falling in.

12. Read each procedure *completely* while looking at the actual parts before starting a job. Make sure you *thoroughly* understand what is to be done and then carefully follow the procedure, step-by-step.

13. Recommendations are occasionally made to refer service or maintenance to a Suzuki dealer or a specialist in a particular field. In these cases, the work will be done more quickly and economically than if you performed the job yourself.

14. In procedural steps, the term "replace" means to discard a defective part and replace it with a new or exchange unit. "Overhaul" means to remove, disassemble, inspect, measure, repair or replace defective parts, reassemble and install major systems or parts.

15. Some operations require the use of a hydraulic press. Unless you have a press, it would be wiser to have these operations performed by a shop equipped for such work, rather than to try to do the job yourself with makeshift equipment that may damage your machine.

16. Repairs go much faster and easier if your machine is clean before you begin work. There are many special cleaners on the market, like Simple Green or Bel-Ray Degreaser, for washing the engine and related parts. Follow the manufacturer's directions on the container for the best results. Clean all oily or greasy parts with cleaning solvent as you remove them.

WARNING
Never *use gasoline as a cleaning agent. It presents an extreme fire hazard. Be sure to work in a well-ventilated area when using cleaning solvent. Keep a fire extinguisher, rated for gasoline fires, handy in any case.*

CAUTION
If you use a car wash to clean your bike, don't direct the high pressure water hose at steering bearings, carburetor hoses,

1

suspension linkage components, wheel bearings and electrical components. The water will flush grease out of the bearings or damage the seals.

17. Much of the labor charges for repairs made by dealers are for the time involved during in the removal, disassembly, assembly, and reinstallation of other parts in order to reach the defective part. It is frequently possible to perform the preliminary operations yourself and then take the defective unit to the dealer for repair at considerable savings.

18. If special tools are required, make arrangements to get them before you start. It is frustrating and time-consuming to get partly into a job and then be unable to complete it.

19. Make diagrams (or take a Polaroid picture) wherever similar-appearing parts are found. For instance, crankcase bolts are often not the same length. You may think you can remember where everything came from—but mistakes are costly. There is also the possibility that you may be sidetracked and not return to work for days or even weeks—in which the time carefully laid out parts may have become disturbed.

20. When assembling parts, be sure all shims and washers are replaced exactly as they came out.

21. Whenever a rotating part butts against a stationary part, look for a shim or washer. Use new gaskets if there is any doubt about the condition of the old ones. A thin coat of oil on non-pressure type gaskets may help them seal more effectively.

22. High spots may be sanded off a piston with sandpaper, but fine emery cloth and oil will do a much more professional job.

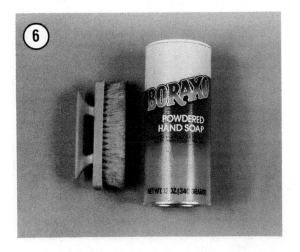

23. Carbon can be removed from the head, the piston crowns and the exhaust ports with a dull screwdriver. Do *not* scratch machined surfaces. Wipe off the surface with a clean cloth when finished.

24. A baby bottle makes a good measuring device for adding oil to the front forks. Get one that is graduated in fluid ounces and cubic centimeters. After it has been used for this purpose, do *not* let a small child drink out of it as there will always be an oil residue in it.

25. If it is necessary to make a clutch cover or ignition cover gasket and you do not have a suitable old gasket to use as a guide, you can use the outline of the cover and gasket material to make a new gasket. Apply engine oil to the cover gasket surface. Then place the cover on the new gasket material and apply pressure with your hands. The oil will leave a very accurate outline on the gasket material that can be cut around.

CAUTION
When purchasing gasket material to make a gasket, measure the thickness of the old gasket and purchase gasket material with the same approximate thickness.

26. Heavy grease can be used to hold small parts in place if they tend to fall out during assembly. However, keep grease and oil away from electrical and brake components.

27. The carburetor is best cleaned by disassembling it and soaking the parts in a commercial cleaning solvent. Never soak gaskets and rubber parts in these cleaners. Never use wire to clean out jets and air passages. They are easily damaged. Use compressed air to blow out the carburetor only if the float has been removed first.

28. There are many items available that can be used on your hands before and after working on your bike. A little preparation prior to getting "all greased up" will help when cleaning up later. Before starting out, work Vaseline, soap or a product such as Invisible Glove (**Figure 5**) onto your forearms, into your hands and under your fingernails and cuticles. This will make cleanup a lot easier. For cleanup, use a waterless hand soap such as Sta-Lube and then finish up with powdered Boraxo and a fingernail brush (**Figure 6**).

PARTS REPLACEMENT

When you order parts from the dealer or other parts distributor, always order by frame and engine serial numbers. Refer to **Table 1**. Compare new parts to old before purchasing them. If they are not alike, have the parts manager explain the difference to you.

TORQUE SPECIFICATIONS

Torque specifications throughout this manual are given in Newton-meters (N•m) and foot-pounds (ft.-lb.).

Existing torque wrenches calibrated in meter kilograms can be used by performing a simple conversion. All you have to do is move the decimal point one place to the right; for example, 3.5 mkg = 35 N•m. This conversion is accurate enough for mechanical work even though the exact mathematical conversion is 3.5 mkg = 34.3 N•m.

Refer to **Table 3** for general torque specifications for various size screws, bolts and nuts that may not be listed in the respective chapters. To use the table, first determine the size of the bolt or nut. Use a vernier caliper and measure the inside dimension of the threads of the nut (**Figure 7**) and across the threads for a bolt (**Figure 8**).

FASTENERS

The materials and designs of the various fasteners used on your Suzuki are not arrived at by chance or accident. Fastener design determines the type of tool required to work the fastener. Fastener material is carefully selected to decrease the possibility of physical failure.

Nuts, bolts and screws are manufactured in a wide range of thread patterns. To join a nut and bolt, the diameter of the bolt and the diameter of the hole in the nut must be the same. It is just as important that the threads on both be properly matched.

The best way to tell if the threads on 2 fasteners are matched is to turn the nut on the bolt (or the bolt into the threaded hole in a piece of equipment) with fingers only. Be sure both pieces are clean. If much force is required, check the thread condition on each fastener. If the thread condition is good but the fasteners jam, the threads are not compatible. A thread pitch gauge (**Figure 9**) can also be used to determine pitch. Suzuki motorcycles are manufac-

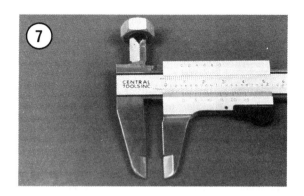

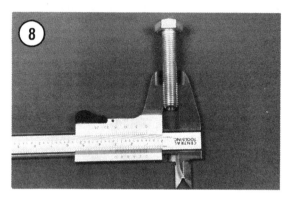

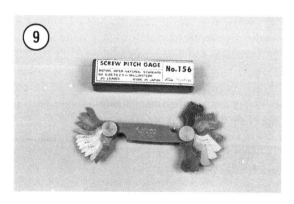

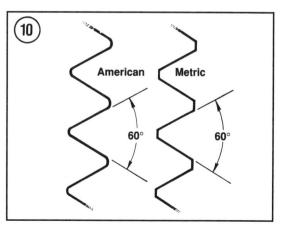

tured with ISO (International Organization for Standardization) metric fasteners. The threads are cut differently than that of American fasteners (**Figure 10**).

Most threads are cut so that the fastener must be turned clockwise to tighten it. These are called right-hand threads. Some fasteners have left-hand threads; they must be turned counterclockwise to be tight-

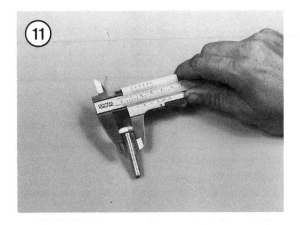

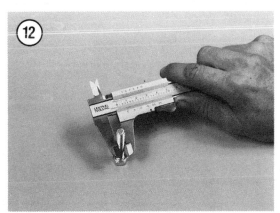

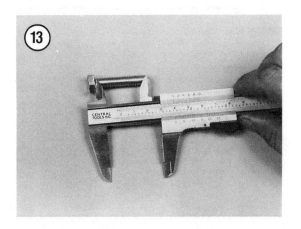

ened. Left-hand threads are used in locations where normal rotation of the equipment would tend to loosen a right-hand threaded fastener.

ISO Metric Screw Threads

ISO (International Organization for Standardization) metric threads come in 3 standard thread sizes: coarse, fine and constant pitch. The ISO coarse pitch is used for most all common fastener applications. The fine pitch thread is used on certain precision tools and instruments. The constant pitch thread is used mainly on machine parts and not for fasteners. The constant pitch thread, however, is used on all metric thread spark plugs.

ISO metric threads are specified by the capital letter M followed by the diameter in millimeters and the pitch (or the distance between each thread) in millimeters separated by the sign ×. For example a M8 × 1.25 bolt is one that has a diameter of 8 millimeters with a distance of 1.25 millimeters between each thread. The measurement across 2 flats on the head of the bolt (**Figure 11**) indicates the proper wrench size to be used. **Figure 12** shows how to determine bolt diameter.

> *NOTE*
> *When purchasing a bolt from a dealer or parts store, it is important to know how to specify bolt length. The correct way to measure bolt length is by measuring the length starting from underneath the bolt head to the end of the bolt (**Figure 13**). Always measure bolt length in this manner to avoid purchasing bolts that are too long or too short.*

Machine Screws

There are many different types of machine screws. **Figure 14** shows a number of screw heads requiring different types of turning tools. Heads are also designed to protrude above the metal (round) or to be slightly recessed in the metal (flat). See **Figure 15**.

Bolts

Commonly called bolts, the technical name for these fasteners is cap screws. Metric bolts are described by the diameter and pitch (or the distance between each thread). For example a M8 × 1.25 bolt is one that has a diameter of 8 millimeters and a distance of 1.25 millimeters between each thread. The measurement across 2 flats on the head of the bolt (**Figure 11**) indicates the proper wrench size to be used. Use a vernier caliper and measure across the threads (**Figure 12**) to determine the bolt diameter and to measure the length (**Figure 13**).

Nuts

Nuts are manufactured in a variety of types and sizes. Most are hexagonal (6-sided) and fit on bolts, screws and studs with the same diameter and pitch.

Figure 16 shows several types of nuts. The common nut is generally used with a lockwasher. Self-locking nuts have a nylon insert which prevents the nut from loosening; no lockwasher is required. Wing nuts are designed for fast removal by hand. Wing nuts are used for convenience in non-critical locations.

To indicate the size of a metric nut, manufacturers specify the diameter of the opening and the thread pitch. This is similar to bolt specifications, but without the length dimension. The measurement across 2 flats on the nut indicates the proper wrench size to be used (**Figure 17**).

Self-locking Fasteners

Several types of bolts, screws and nuts incorporate a system that develops an interference between the bolt, screw, nut or tapped hole threads. Interference is achieved in various ways: by distorting threads, coating threads with dry adhesive or nylon, distorting the top of an all-metal nut, using a nylon insert in the center or at the top of a nut, etc.

Self-locking fasteners offer greater holding strength and better vibration resistance. Some prevailing torque fasteners can be reused if in good condition. Others, like the nylon insert nut, form an initial locking condition when the nut is first in-

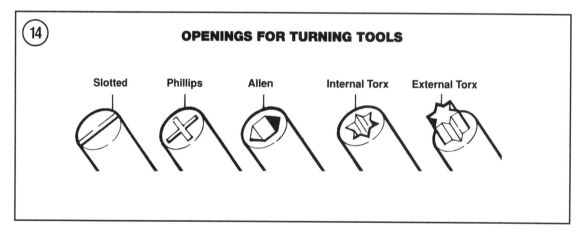

(14) **OPENINGS FOR TURNING TOOLS**

Slotted   Phillips   Allen   Internal Torx   External Torx

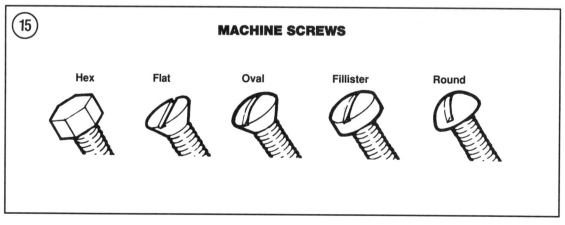

(15) **MACHINE SCREWS**

Hex   Flat   Oval   Fillister   Round

Common nut   Self-locking nut

Wing nut

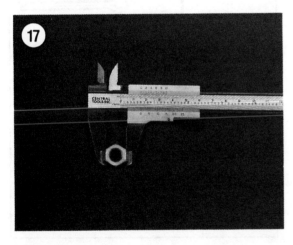

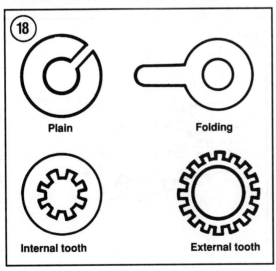

Plain   Folding

Internal tooth   External tooth

stalled; the nylon forms closely to the bolt thread pattern, thus reducing any tendency for the nut to loosen. When the nut is removed, the locking efficiency is greatly reduced. For greatest safety, it is recommended that you install new self-locking fasteners whenever they are removed.

Washers

There are 2 basic types of washers: flat washers and lockwashers. Flat washers are simple discs with a hole to fit a screw or bolt. Lockwashers are designed to prevent a fastener from working loose due to vibration, expansion and contraction. **Figure 18** shows several types of washers. Washers are also used in the following functions:

a. As spacers.
b. To prevent galling or damage of the equipment by the fastener.
c. To help distribute fastener load during torquing.
d. As seals.

Note that flat washers are often used between a lockwasher and a fastener to provide a smooth bearing surface. This allows the fastener to be turned easily with a tool.

Cotter Pins

Cotter pins (**Figure 19**) are used to secure fasteners in a special location. The threaded stud, bolt or axle must have a hole in it. Its nut or nut lock piece has castellations around its upper edge into which the cotter pin fits to keep it from loosening. When properly installed, a cotter pin is a positive locking device.

The first step in properly installing a cotter pin is to purchase one that will fit snugly when inserted through the nut and the mating thread part. This should not be a problem when purchasing cotter pins through a Suzuki dealer; you can order them by their respective part numbers. However, when you purchase them at a hardware or automotive store, keep this in mind. The cotter pin should not be so tight that you have to drive it in and out, but you do not want it so loose that it can move or float after it is installed.

Before installing a cotter pin, tighten the nut to the recommended torque specification. If the castellations in the nut do not line up with the hole in the bolt or axle, tighten the nut until alignment is achieved. Do not loosen the nut to make alignment. Insert a new cotter pin through the nut and hole, then tap the head lightly to seat it. Bend one arm over the flat on the nut and the other against the top of the axle or bolt. Cut the arms to a suitable length to prevent them from snagging on clothing, or worse, your hands, arms or legs; the exposed arms will cut flesh easily. When the cotter pin is bent and its arms cut to length, it should be tight. If you can wiggle the cotter pin, it is improperly installed.

Cotter pins should not be reused as their ends may break and allow the cotter pin to fall out and perhaps the fastener to unscrew itself.

Circlips

Circlips can be internal or external design. They are used to retain items on shafts (external type) or within bores (internal type). In some applications, circlips of varying thicknesses are used to control the end play of parts assemblies. These are often called selective circlips. Circlips should be replaced during installation, as removal weakens and deforms them.

Two basic styles of circlips are available: machined and stamped circlips. Machined circlips (**Figure 20**) can be installed in either direction (shaft or housing) because both faces are machined, thus creating two sharp edges. Stamped circlips (**Figure 21**) are manufactured with one sharp edge and one rounded edge. When installing stamped circlips in a thrust situation (transmission shafts, fork tubes, etc.), the sharp edge must face away from the part producing the thrust. When installing circlips, observe the following:

    a. Compress or expand circlips only enough to install them.

    b. After the circlip is installed, make sure it is completely seated in its groove.

Transmission circlips become worn with use and increase side play. For this reason, always use new circlips when ever a transmission is to be reassembled.

LUBRICANTS

Periodic lubrication assures long life for any type of equipment. The *type* of lubricant used is just as important as the lubrication service itself, although in an emergency the wrong type of lubricant is better than none at all. The following paragraphs describe the types of lubricants most often used on motorcycle equipment. Be sure to follow the manufacturer's recommendations for lubricant types.

Generally, all liquid lubricants are called "oil." They may be mineral-based (including petroleum bases), natural-based (vegetable and animal bases), synthetic-based or emulsions (mixtures). "Grease" is an oil to which a thickening base has been added so that the end product is semi-solid. Grease is often classified by the type of thickener added; lithium soap is commonly used.

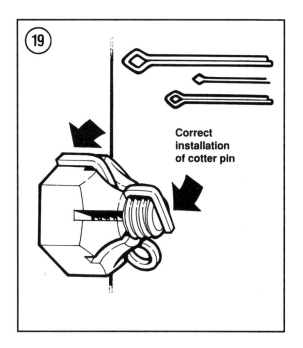

(19) Correct installation of cotter pin

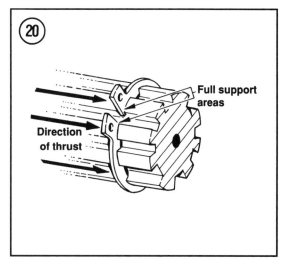

(20) Direction of thrust — Full support areas

Engine Oil

Four-cycle oil for motorcycle and automotive engines is graded by the American Petroleum Institute (API) and the Society of Automotive Engineers (SAE) in several categories. Oil containers display these ratings on the top or label.

API oil grade is indicated by letters; oils for gasoline engines are identified by an "S". Suzuki models described in this manual require SE or SF graded oil.

Viscosity is an indication of the oil's thickness. The SAE uses numbers to indicate viscosity; thin oils have low numbers while thick oils have high numbers. A "W" after the number indicates that the viscosity testing was done at low temperature to simulate cold-weather operation. Engine oils fall into the 5 to 50 range.

Multi-grade oils (for example 10W-40) are less viscous (thinner) at low temperatures and more viscous (thicker) at high temperatures. This allows the oil to perform efficiently across a wide range of engine operating conditions. The lower the number, the better the engine will start in cold climates. Higher numbers are usually recommended for engine running in hot weather conditions.

Grease

Greases are graded by the National Lubricating Grease Institute (NLGI). Greases are graded by number according to the consistency of the grease; these range from No. 000 to No. 6, with No. 6 being the most solid. A typical multipurpose grease is NLGI No. 2. For specific applications, equipment manufacturers may require grease with an additive such as molybdenum disulfide (MOS2) (**Figure 22**).

RTV GASKET SEALANT

Room temperature vulcanizing (RTV) sealant is used on some pre-formed gaskets and to seal some components. RTV is a silicone gel supplied in tubes and can be purchased in a number of different colors.

Moisture in the air causes RTV to cure. Always place the cap on the tube as soon as possible when using RTV sealants. RTV has a shelf life of one year and will not cure properly when the shelf life has expired. Check the expiration date on RTV tubes before using and keep partially used tubes tightly sealed.

Applying RTV Sealant

Clean all gasket residue from mating surfaces. Surfaces should be clean and free of oil and dirt. Remove all RTV gasket material from blind attaching holes, as it can cause a "hydraulic" effect and affect bolt torque.

Apply RTV sealant in a continuous bead. Circle all mounting holes unless otherwise specified. Torque mating parts within 10 minutes after application.

THREADLOCK

A chemical such as "Loctite." A locking compound will lock fasteners against vibration loosening and seal against leaks. Loctite 242 (blue) and 271

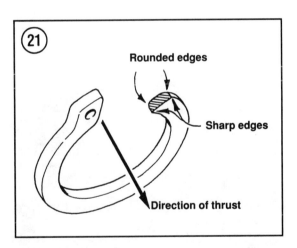

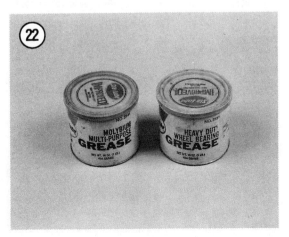

(red) are recommended for many threadlock requirements described in this manual.

Loctite 242 (blue) is a medium strength threadlock and component disassembly can be performed with normal hand tools. Loctite 271 (red) is a high strength threadlock and heat or special tools, such as a press or puller, may be required for component disassembly.

Applying Threadlock

Surfaces should be clean and free of oil, grease, dirt and other residue; clean threads with an aerosol electrical contact cleaner before applying the Loctite. When applying Loctite, use a small amount. If too much is used, it may work its way into parts not meant to be stuck together.

GASKET REMOVER

Stubborn gaskets can present a problem during engine service as they can take a long time to remove. Consequently, there is the added problem of secondary damage occurring to the gasket mating surfaces from the incorrect use of gasket scraping tools. To quickly and safely remove stubborn gaskets, use a spray gasket remover. Spray gasket remover can be purchased through automotive parts houses. Follow the manufacturer's directions for use.

EXPENDABLE SUPPLIES

Certain expendable supplies are required during maintenance and repair work. These include grease, oil, gasket cement, wiping rags and cleaning solvent. Ask your dealer for the special locking compounds, silicone lubricants and other products (**Figure 23**) which make bike maintenance simpler and easier. Cleaning solvent or kerosene is available at some service stations, paint or hardware stores.

> *WARNING*
> *Having a stack of clean shop rags on hand is important when performing engine and suspension service work. However, to prevent the possibility of fire damage from spontaneous combustion from a pile of solvent soaked rags, store*

them in a lid sealed metal container until they can be washed or discarded.

> *NOTE*
> *To avoid absorbing solvent and other chemicals into your skin while cleaning parts, wear a pair of petroleum-resistant rubber gloves. These can be purchased through industrial supply houses or well-equipped hardware stores.*

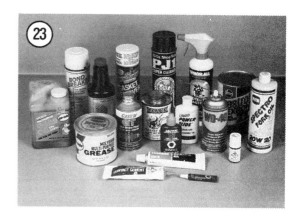

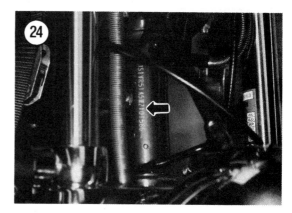

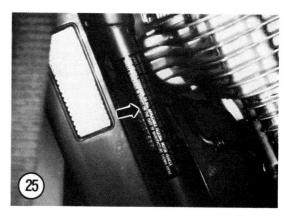

PARTS REPLACEMENT

Suzuki makes frequent changes during a model year, some minor, some relatively major. When you order parts from the dealer or other parts distributor, always order by frame and engine numbers. The frame number serial number is stamped on the right-hand side of the steering head (**Figure 24**). The vehicle identification number (VIN) plate is attached to the left-hand side of the frame down tube (**Figure 25**). The engine number is stamped on a raised pad on the right-hand side of the crankcase (**Figure 26**) behind the starter motor cover. The carburetor number (**Figure 27**) is on the side of the carburetor body below the top cover.

Write the numbers down and carry them with you. Compare new parts to old before purchasing them. If they are not alike, have the parts manager explain the difference to you. **Table 1** lists engine and frame serial numbers for the models covered in this manual.

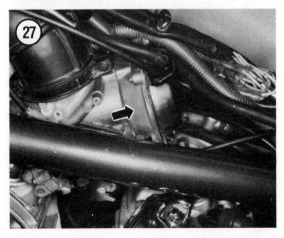

NOTE
If your Suzuki was purchased second-hand and you are not sure of its model year, use the bike's VIN and frame serial numbers and the information listed in **Table 1**. *Read your bike's serial number. Then compare the numbers listed in* **Table 1**. *If your bike's serial number is listed in* **Table 1**, *cross-reference the number with the adjacent model number and year.*

BASIC HAND TOOLS

Many of the procedures in this manual can be carried out with simple hand tools and test equipment familiar to the average home mechanic. Keep your tools clean and in a tool box. Keep them organized with the sockets and related drives together, the open-end combination wrenches together, etc. After using a tool, wipe off dirt and grease with a clean cloth and return the tool to its correct place.

Top quality tools are essential; they are also more economical in the long run. If you are now starting to build your tool collection, stay away from the "advertised specials" featured at some parts houses, discount stores and chain drug stores. These are usually a poor grade tool that can be sold cheaply and that is exactly what they are—*cheap*. They are usually made of inferior material, and are thick, heavy and clumsy. Their rough finish makes them difficult to clean and they usually don't last very long. If it is ever your misfortune to use such tools, you will probably find out that the wrenches do not fit the heads of bolts and nuts correctly and damage the fastener.

Quality tools are made of alloy steel and are heat treated for greater strength. They are lighter and better balanced than cheap ones. Their surface is smooth, making them a pleasure to work with and easy to clean. The initial cost of good quality tools may be more but they are cheaper in the long run. Don't try to buy everything in all sizes in the beginning; do it a little at a time until you have the necessary tools.

The following tools are required to perform virtually any repair job on a bike. Each tool is described and the recommended size given for starting a tool collection. **Table 4** includes the tools that should be on hand for simple home repairs and/or major overhaul as shown in **Figure 28**. Additional tools and some duplicates may be added as you become more familiar with the bike. Almost all motorcycles and vehicles (with the exception of the U.S. built Harley Davidson and some English motorcycles) use metric size bolts and nuts. If you are starting your collection now, buy metric sizes.

Screwdrivers

The screwdriver is a very basic tool, but if used improperly it will do more damage than good. The slot on a screw has a definite dimension and shape. A screwdriver must be selected to conform with that shape. Use a small screwdriver for small screws and a large one for large screws or the screw head will be damaged.

Two basic types of screwdrivers are required: common (flat-blade) screwdrivers (**Figure 29**) and Phillips screwdrivers (**Figure 30**).

Note the following when selecting and using screwdrivers:

a. The screwdriver must always fit the screw head. If the screwdriver blade is too small for the screw slot, damage may occur to the screw slot and screwdriver. If the blade is too large, it cannot engage the slot properly and will result in damage to the screw head.

b. Standard screwdrivers are identified by the length of their blade. A 6-inch screwdriver has a blade six inches long. The width of the screwdriver blade will vary, so make sure that the blade engages the screw slot the complete width of the screw.

c. Phillips screwdrivers are sized according to their point size. They are numbered one, two, three and four. The degree of taper determines the point size; the No. 1 Phillips screwdriver will be the most pointed. The points become more blunt as their number increases.

> *NOTE*
> *You should also be aware of another screwdriver similar to the Phillips, and that is the Reed and Prince tip. Like the Phillips, the Reed and Prince screwdriver tip forms an "X" but with one major exception, the Reed and Prince tip has a much more pointed tip. The Reed and Prince screwdriver should never be used on Phillips screws and*

vise versa. Intermixing these screwdrivers will cause damage to the screw and screwdriver. If you have both types in your tool box and they are similar in appearance, you may want to identify them by painting the screwdriver shank underneath the handle.

d. When selecting screwdrivers, note that you can apply more power with less effort with a longer

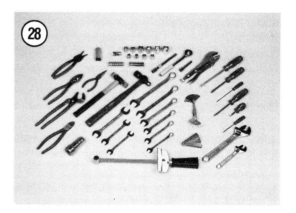

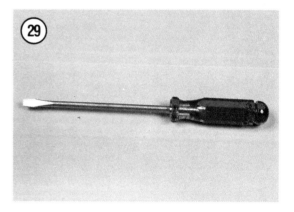

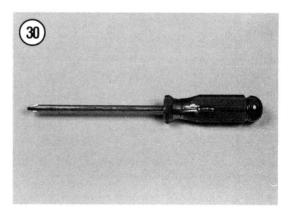

screwdriver than with a short one. Of course, there will be situations where only a short handle screwdriver can be used. Keep this in mind though, when having to remove tight screws.

e. Because the working end of a screwdriver receives quite a bit of abuse, you should purchase screwdrivers with hardened-tips. The extra money will be well spent.

Screwdrivers are available in sets which often include an assortment of common and Phillips blades. If you buy them individually, buy at least the following:

a. Common screwdriver—5/16 × 6 in. blade.

b. Common screwdriver—3/8 × 12 in. blade.

c. Phillips screwdriver—size 2 tip, 6 in. blade.

d. Phillips screwdriver—size 3 tip, 6 and 8 in. blade.

Use screwdrivers only for driving screws. Never use a screwdriver for prying or chiseling metal. Do not try to remove a Phillips, Torx or Allen head screw with a standard screwdriver (unless the screw has a combination head that will accept either type); you can damage the head so that the proper tool will be unable to remove it.

Keep screwdrivers in the proper condition and they will last longer and perform better. Always keep the tip of a standard screwdriver in good condition. **Figure 31** shows how to grind the tip to the proper shape if it becomes damaged. Note the symmetrical sides of the tip.

Pliers

Pliers come in a wide range of types and sizes. Pliers are useful for cutting, bending and crimping. They should never be used to cut hardened objects

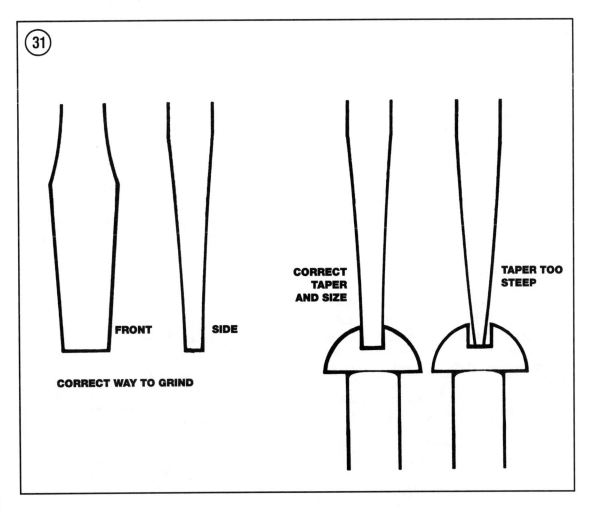

(31)

CORRECT
TAPER
AND SIZE

TAPER TOO
STEEP

FRONT   SIDE

CORRECT WAY TO GRIND

or to turn bolts or nuts. **Figure 32** shows several pliers useful in repairing your Suzuki.

Each type of pliers has a specialized function. Slip-joint pliers are general purpose pliers and are used mainly for holding things and for bending. Needlenose pliers are used to hold or bend small objects. Water pump pliers can be adjusted to hold various sizes of objects; the jaws remain parallel to grip around objects such as pipe or tubing. There are many more types of pliers.

> *CAUTION*
> *Pliers should not be used for loosening or tightening nuts or bolts. The pliers' sharp teeth will grind off the nut or bolt corners and damage it.*

> *CAUTION*
> *If slip-joint or water pump pliers are going to be used to hold an object with a finished surface, wrap the object with tape or cardboard for protection.*

Vise-grip Pliers

Vise-grip pliers (**Figure 33**) are used to hold objects very tightly while another task is performed on the object. While vise-grip pliers work well, caution should be followed with their use. Because vise-grip pliers exert more force than regular pliers, their sharp jaws can permanently scar the object. In addition, when vise-grip pliers are locked into position, they can crush or deform thin wall material.

Vise-grip pliers are available in many types for more specific tasks.

Circlip (Snap Ring) Pliers

Circlip pliers (**Figure 34**) are special in that they are only used to remove circlips from shafts or within engine or suspension housings. When purchasing circlip pliers, there are two kinds to distinguish from. External pliers (spreading) are used to remove circlips that fit on the outside of a shaft. Internal pliers (squeezing) are used to remove circlips which fit inside a gear or housing.

> *WARNING*
> *Because circlips can sometimes slip and "fly off" during removal and installation, always wear safety glasses.*

Box-end, Open-end and Combination Wrenches

Box-end, open-end and combination wrenches are available in sets or separately in a variety of sizes. On open- and box-end wrenches, the number stamped near the end refers to the distance between 2 parallel flats on the hex head bolt or nut. On combination wrenches, the number is stamped near the center.

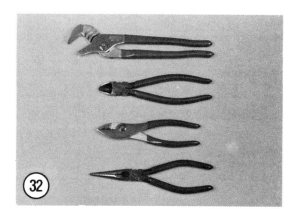

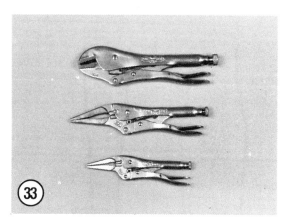

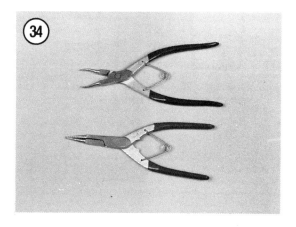

Box-end wrenches require clear overhead access to the fastener but can work well in situations where the fastener head is close to another part. They grip on all six edges of a fastener for a very secure grip. They are available in either 6-point or 12-point. The 6-point gives superior holding power and durability but requires a greater swinging radius. The 12-point works better in situations with limited swinging radius.

Open-end wrenches are speedy and work best in areas with limited overhead access. Their wide flat jaws make them unstable for situations where the bolt or nut is sunken in a well or close to the edge of a casting. These wrenches grip only two flats of a fastener so if either the fastener head or the wrench jaws are worn, the wrench may slip off.

Combination wrenches (**Figure 35**) have open-end on one side and box-end on the other with both ends being the same size. These wrenches are favored by professionals because of their versatility.

Adjustable (Crescent) Wrenches

An adjustable wrench (sometimes called crescent wrench) can be adjusted to fit nearly any nut or bolt head which has clear access around its entire perimeter. Adjustable wrenches (**Figure 36**) are best used as a backup wrench to keep a large nut or bolt from turning while the other end is being loosened or tightened with a proper wrench.

Adjustable wrenches have only two gripping surfaces which make them more subject to slipping off the fastener, damaging the part and possibly injuring your hand. The fact that one jaw is adjustable only aggravates this shortcoming.

These wrenches are directional; the solid jaw must be the one transmitting the force. If you use the adjustable jaw to transmit the force, it will loosen and possibly slip off.

Adjustable wrenches come in all sizes but something in the 6 to 8 in. range is recommended as an all-purpose wrench.

Socket Wrenches

This type is undoubtedly the fastest, safest and most convenient to use. Sockets which attach to a ratchet handle (**Figure 37**) are available with 6-point or 12-point openings and 1/4, 3/8 and 3/4 in. drives. The drive size indicates the size of the square hole which mates with the ratchet handle (**Figure 38**).

Allen Wrenches

Allen wrenches (**Figure 39**) are available in sets or separately in a variety of sizes. These sets come in SAE and metric size, so be sure to buy a metric set. Allen bolts are sometimes called socket bolts. Sometimes the bolts are difficult to reach and it is suggested that a variety of Allen wrenches be pur-

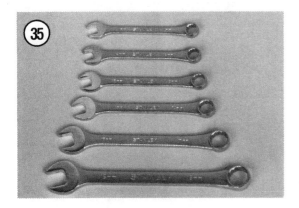

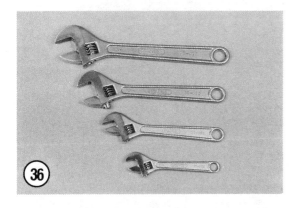

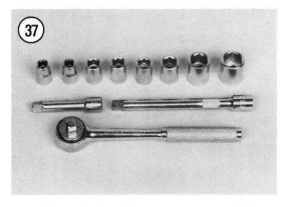

chases (e.g. socket driven, T-handle and extension type) as shown in **Figure 40**.

Torque Wrench

A torque wrench is used with a socket to measure how tightly a nut or bolt is installed. They come in a wide price range and with either 3/8 or 1/2 in. square drive (**Figure 41**). The drive size indicates the size of the square drive which mates with the socket. Purchase one that measures 0-280 N•m (0-200 ft.-lb.).

Impact Driver

This tool might have been designed with the bike in mind. This tool makes removal of fasteners easy and minimizes damage to bolts and screw slots. Impact drivers and interchangeable bits (**Figure 42**) are available at most large hardware, motorcycle and auto parts stores. Don't purchase a cheap one as they do not work as well and require more force (the "use a larger hammer" syndrome) than a moderately priced one. Sockets can also be used with a hand impact driver. However, make sure that the socket is designed for use with an impact driver or air tool. Do not use regular hand sockets, as they may shatter during use.

Hammers

The correct hammer (**Figure 43**) is necessary for repairs. A hammer with a face (or head) of rubber or plastic or the soft-faced type that is filled with buckshot is sometimes necessary in engine tear downs. Never use a metal-faced hammer on engine or suspension parts, as severe damage will result in most cases. Ball-peen or machinist's hammers will be required when striking another tool, such as a punch or impact driver. When striking a hammer against a punch, cold chisel or similar tool, the face of the hammer should be at least 1/2 in. larger than the head of the tool. When it is necessary to strike hard against a steel part without damaging it, a brass hammer should be used. A brass hammer can be used because brass will give when striking a harder object.

When using hammers, note the following:

   a. Always wear safety glasses when using a hammer.

   b. Inspect hammers for damaged or broken parts. Repair or replace the hammer as required. Do not use a hammer with a taped handle.

   c. Always wipe oil or grease off of the hammer before using it.

   d. The head of the hammer should always strike the object squarely. Do not use the side of the hammer or the handle to strike an object.

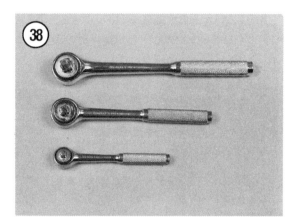

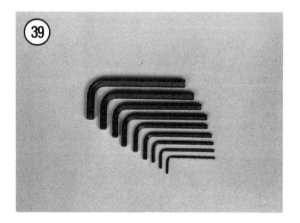

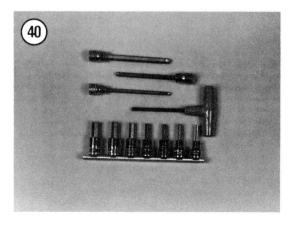

e. Always use the correct hammer for the job.

Tap and Die Set

A complete tap and die set is a relatively expensive tool. But when you need a tap or die to clean up a damaged thread, there is really no substitute. Be sure to purchase one for metric threads when working on your Suzuki.

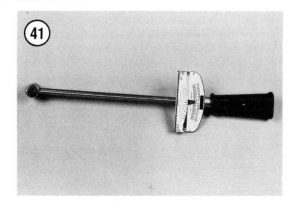

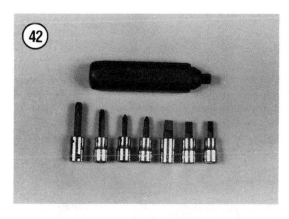

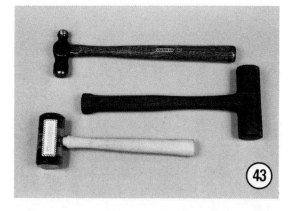

Tire Levers

When changing tires, use a good set of tire levers. Never use a screwdriver in place of a tire lever; refer to Chapter Ten for tire changing procedures using these tools. Before using the tire levers, check the working ends of the tool and remove any burrs. Don't use a tire lever for prying anything but tires. For better leverage when changing tires on your Suzuki, you may want to invest in a set of 16 in. long tire irons. These can be ordered through your dealer.

Drivers and Pullers

These tools are used to remove and install oil seals, bushings, bearings and gears. These will be called out during service procedures in later chapters as required.

PRECISION MEASURING TOOLS

Measurement is an important part of motorcycle service. When performing many of the service procedures in this manual, you will be required to make a number of measurements. These include basic checks such as valve clearance, engine compression and spark plug gap. As you get deeper into engine disassembly and service, measurements will be required to determine the size and condition of the piston and cylinder bore, valve and guide wear, camshaft wear, crankshaft runout and so on. When making these measurements, the degree of accuracy will dictate which tool is required. Precision measuring tools are expensive. If this is your first experience at engine or suspension service, it may be more worthwhile to have the checks made at a Suzuki dealer or machine shop. However, as your skills and enthusiasm increase for doing your own service work, you may want to begin purchasing some of these specialized tools. The following is a description of the measuring tools required during engine and suspension overhaul.

Feeler Gauge

Feeler gauges come in assorted sets and types (**Figure 44**). The feeler gauge is made of either a piece of a flat or round hardened steel of a specified thickness. Wire gauges are frequently recommended to measure spark plug gap. Flat gauges are used for all other measurements. Feeler gauges are also de-signed for specialized uses, such as for measuring valve clearances. On these gauges, the gauge end is usually small enough and angled so as to make checking valve clearances easier.

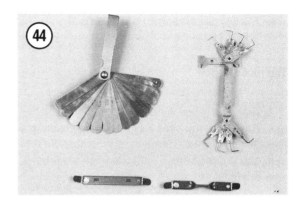

Vernier Caliper

This tool (**Figure 45**) is invaluable when reading inside, outside and depth measurements to within close precision. It can be used to measure clutch spring length and the thickness of clutch plates, shims and thrust washers.

Outside Micrometers

One of the most reliable tools used for precision measurement is the outside micrometer (**Figure 46**). Outside micrometers will be required to measure valve shim thickness, piston diameter and valve stem diameter. Outside micrometers are also used with other tools to measure the cylinder bore and the valve guide inside diameters. Micrometers can be purchased individually or as a set.

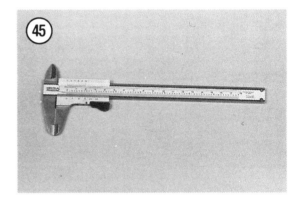

Dial Indicator

Dial indicators (**Figure 47**) are precision tools used to check dimension variations on machined parts such as transmission shafts and axles and to check crankshaft and axle shaft end play. Dial indi-cators are available with various dial types for dif-ferent measuring requirements.

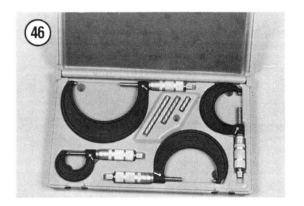

Cylinder Bore Gauge

The cylinder bore gauge is a very specialized precision tool. The gauge set shown in **Figure 48** is comprised of a dial indicator, handle and a number of length adapters to adapt the gauge to different bore sizes. The bore gauge can be used to make cylinder bore measurements such as bore size, taper and out-of-round. Depending on the bore gauge, it can sometimes be used to measure brake caliper and master cylinder bore sizes. An outside micrometer must be used together with the bore gauge to deter-mine bore dimensions.

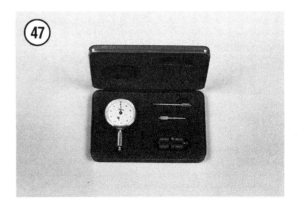

Small Hole Gauges

A set of small hole gauges allow you to measure a hole, groove or slot ranging in size up to 13 mm (0.500 in.). A small hole gauge will be required to measure valve guide, brake caliper and brake master cylinder bore diameters. An outside micrometer

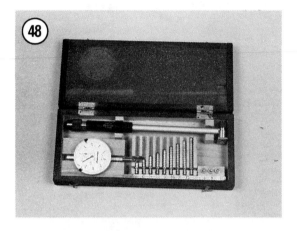

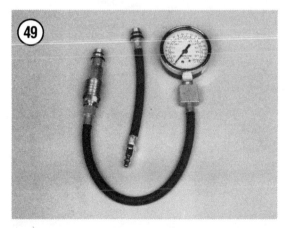

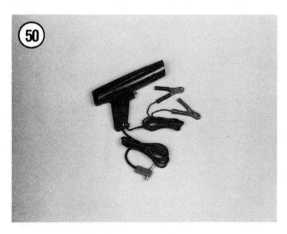

must be used together with the small hole gauge to determine bore dimensions.

Compression Gauge

An engine with low compression cannot be properly tuned and will not develop full power. A compression gauge (**Figure 49**) measures engine compression. The one shown has a flexible stem with an extension that can allow you to hold it while kicking the engine over. Open the throttle all the way when checking engine compression. See Chapter Three.

Cylinder Leak Down Tester

By positioning a cylinder on its compression stroke so that both valves are closed and then pressurizing the cylinder, you can isolate engine problem areas (e.g. leaking valve, damaged head gasket, broken, worn or stuck piston rings) by listening for escaping air through the carburetors, exhaust pipe, cylinder head mating surface, etc. To perform this procedure, a leak down tester and an air compressor are required. This procedure is described in Chapter Three. Cylinder leak down testers can be purchased through Suzuki dealers, accessory tool manufacturers and automotive tool suppliers.

Strobe Timing Light

This instrument is useful for checking ignition timing. By flashing a light at the precise instant the spark plug fires, the position of the timing mark can be seen. The flashing light makes a moving mark appear to stand still opposite a stationary mark.

Suitable lights range from inexpensive neon bulb types to powerful xenon strobe lights (**Figure 50**). A light with an inductive pickup is recommended to eliminate any possible damage to ignition wiring. Use according to manufacturer's instructions.

Multimeter or VOM

This instrument (**Figure 51**) is invaluable for electrical system troubleshooting. See *Electrical Troubleshooting* in Chapter Eight for its use.

Screw Pitch Gauge

A screw pitch gauge (**Figure 52**) determines the thread pitch of bolts, screws, studs, etc. The gauge is made up of a number of thin plates. Each plate has a thread shape cut on one edge to match one thread pitch. When using a screw pitch gauge to determine a thread pitch size, try to fit different blade sizes onto the bolt thread until both threads match (**Figure 53**).

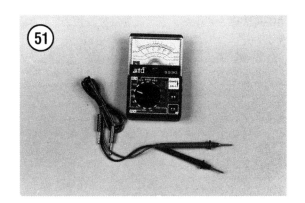

Magnetic Stand

A magnetic stand (**Figure 54**) is used to securely hold a dial indicator when checking the runout of a round object or when checking the end play of a shaft.

V-Blocks

V-blocks (**Figure 55**) are precision ground blocks used to hold a round object when checking its runout or condition. In motorcycle repair, V-blocks can be used when checking the runout of such items as valve stems, camshaft, balancer shaft, crankshaft, wheel axles and fork tubes.

Surface Plate

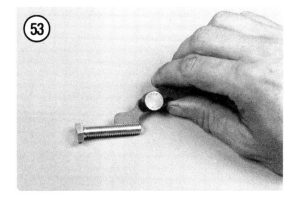

A surface plate can be used to check the flatness of parts or to provide a perfectly flat surface for minor resurfacing of cylinder head or other critical gasket surfaces. While industrial quality surface plates are quite expensive, the home mechanic can improvise. A thick metal plate can be put to use as a surface plate. The metal surface plate with a piece of sandpaper or dry wall surface sanding sheets glued to its surface can be used for cleaning and smoothing cylinder head and crankcase mating surfaces.

> *NOTE*
> *Check with a local machine shop on the availability and cost of having a metal plate resurfaced for use as a surface plate.*

SPECIAL TOOLS

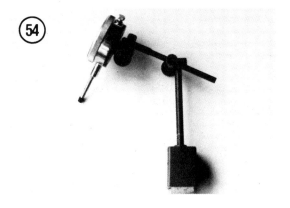

A few special tools may be required for major service. These are described in the appropriate chapters and are available either from a Suzuki dealer or other manufacturers as indicated.

This section describes special tools unique to this type of bike's service and repair.

Spoke Wrench

This special wrench is used to tighten wheel spokes (**Figure 56**). Always use the correct size wrench to avoid rounding out and damaging the spoke nipple.

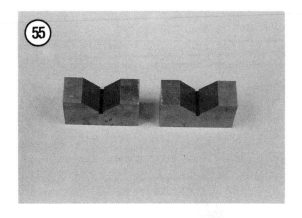

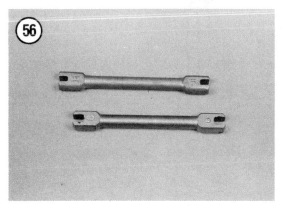

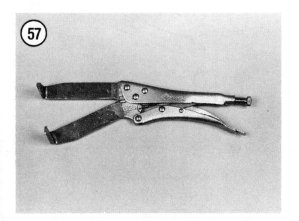

The Grabbit

The Grabbit (**Figure 57**) is a special tool used to hold the clutch boss when removing the clutch nut and to secure the drive sprocket when removing the sprocket nut.

Other Special Tools

A few other special tools may be required for major service. These are described in the appropriate chapters and are available from Suzuki dealers or other manufacturers as indicated.

CLEANING SOLVENT

With the environmental concern that is prevalent today concerning the disposal of hazardous solvents, the home mechanic should select a water soluble, biodegradable solvent. These solvents can be purchased through dealers, automotive parts houses and large hardware stores.

Selecting a solvent is only one of the problems facing the home mechanic when it comes to cleaning parts. You need some type of tank to clean parts as well as to store the solvent. There are a number of manufacturers offering different types and sizes of parts cleaning tanks. While a tank may seem a luxury to the home mechanic, you will find that it will quickly pay for itself through its efficiency and convenience. When selecting a parts washer, look for one that can recycle and store the solvent, as well as separate the sludge and contamination from the clean solvent. Most important, check the warranty, if any, as it pertains to the tank's pump. Like most tools, when purchasing a parts washer, you get what you pay for.

> *WARNING*
> *Having a stack of clean shop rags on hand is important when performing engine work. However, to prevent the possibility of fire damage from spontaneous combustion from a pile of solvent-soaked rags, store them in a lid-sealed metal container until they can be washed or discarded.*

> *NOTE*
> *To avoid absorbing solvent and other chemicals into your skin while cleaning parts, wear a pair of petroleum-resistant*

rubber gloves. These can be purchased through industrial supply houses or well-equipped hardware stores.

MECHANIC'S TIPS

Removing Frozen Nuts and Screws

When a fastener rusts and cannot be removed, several methods may be used to loosen it. First, apply penetrating oil such as Liquid Wrench or WD-40 (available at hardware or auto supply stores). Apply it liberally and let it penetrate for

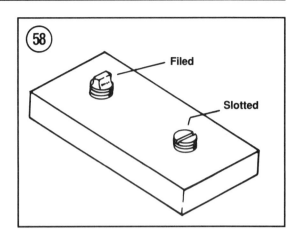

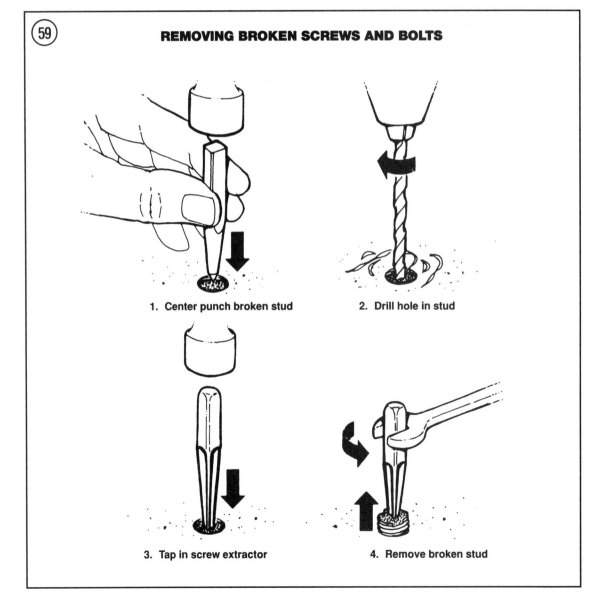

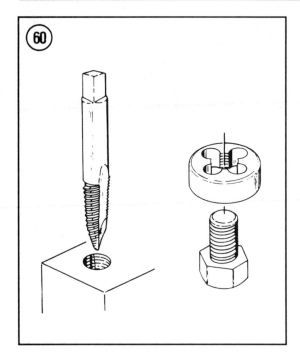

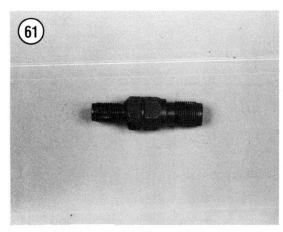

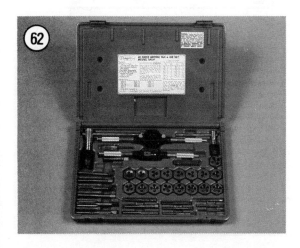

10-15 minutes. Rap the fastener several times with a small hammer; do not hit it hard enough to cause damage. Reapply the penetrating oil if necessary.

For frozen screws, apply penetrating oil as described, then insert a screwdriver in the slot and rap the top of the screwdriver with a hammer. This loosens the rust so the screw can be removed in the normal way. If the screw head is too chewed up to use this method, grip the head with vise-grip pliers and twist the screw out.

Avoid applying heat unless specifically instructed, as it may melt, warp or remove the temper from parts.

Removing Broken Screws or Bolts

When the head breaks off a screw or bolt, several methods are available for removing the remaining portion.

If a large portion of the remainder projects out, try gripping it with vise-grips. If the projecting portion is too small, file it to fit a wrench or cut a slot in it to fit a screwdriver. See **Figure 58**.

If the head breaks off flush, use a screw extractor. To do this, center punch the exact center of the remaining portion of the screw or bolt. Drill a small hole in the screw and tap the extractor into the hole. Back the screw out with a wrench on the extractor. See **Figure 59**.

Remedying Stripped Threads

Occasionally, threads are stripped through carelessness or impact damage. Often the threads can be cleaned up by running a tap (for internal threads on nuts) or die (for external threads on bolts) through the threads. See **Figure 60**. To clean or repair spark plug threads, a spark plug tap can be used (**Figure 61**).

NOTE
*Tap and dies can be purchased individually or in a set as shown in **Figure 62**.*

If an internal thread is damaged, it may be necessary to install a Helicoil (**Figure 63**) or some other type of thread insert. Follow the manufacturer's instructions when installing their insert.

Removing Broken or Damaged Studs

If a stud is broken or the threads severely damaged, perform the following. A tube of red Loctite
(No. 271), 2 nuts, 2 wrenches and a new stud will be
required during this procedure. Studs that are
stripped or damaged will require the use of a stud
remover.

1. Thread two nuts onto the damaged stud. Then
tighten the 2 nuts against each other so that they are
locked.

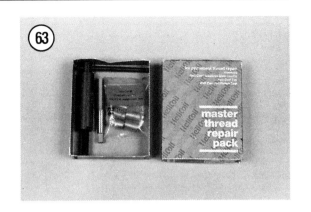

> *NOTE*
> *If the threads on the damaged stud do*
> *not allow installation of the 2 nuts,*
> *you will have to remove the stud with*
> *a stud remover.*

2. Turn the bottom nut counterclockwise and unscrew the stud.

3. Threaded holes with a bottom surface should be
blown out with compressed air as dirt buildup in the
bottom of the hole may prevent the stud from being
torqued properly. If necessary, use a bottoming tap
to true up the threads and to remove any deposits.

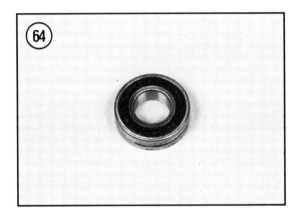

4. Install 2 nuts on the top half of the new stud as in
Step 1. Make sure they are locked securely.

5. Coat the bottom half of a new stud with red
Loctite (No. 271).

6. Turn the top nut clockwise and thread the new
stud securely.

7. Remove the nuts and repeat for each stud as
required.

8. Follow Loctite's directions on cure time before
assembling the component.

BALL BEARING REPLACEMENT

Ball bearings (**Figure 64**) are used throughout
your Suzuki's engine and chassis to reduce power
loss, heat and noise resulting from friction. Because
ball bearings are precision made parts, they must be
maintained by proper lubrication and maintenance.
When a bearing is found to be damaged, it should be
replaced immediately. However, when installing a
new bearing, care should be taken to prevent damage
to the new bearing. While bearing replacement is
described in the individual chapters where applicable, the following can be used as a guideline.

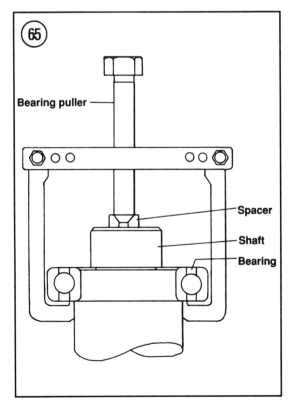

NOTE
Unless otherwise specified, install bearings with the manufacturer's mark or number on the bearing facing outward.

Bearing Removal

While bearings are normally removed only when damaged, there may be times when it is necessary to

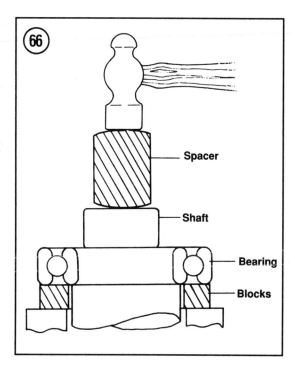

remove a bearing that is in good condition. Depending on the situation, you may be able to remove the bearing without damaging it. However, bearing removal in some situations, no matter how careful you are, will cause bearing damage. Care should always be given to bearings during their removal to prevent secondary damage to the shaft or housing. Note the following when removing bearings.

1. When using a puller to remove a bearing from a shaft, care must be taken so that shaft damage does not occur. Always place a piece of metal between the end of the shaft and the puller screw. In addition, place the puller arms next to the inner bearing race. See **Figure 65**.

2. When using a hammer to remove a bearing from a shaft, do not strike the hammer directly against the shaft. Instead, use a brass or aluminum spacer between the hammer and shaft (**Figure 66**). In addition, make sure to support both bearing races with wood blocks as shown in **Figure 66**.

3. The most ideal method of bearing removal is with a hydraulic press. However, certain procedures must be followed or damage may occur to the bearing, shaft or case half. Note the following when using a press:

   a. Always support the inner and outer bearing races with a suitable size wood or aluminum spacer ring (**Figure 67**). If only the outer race is supported, the balls and/or the inner race will be damaged.

   b. Always make sure the press ram (**Figure 67**) aligns with the center of the shaft. If the ram is not centered, it may damage the bearing and/or shaft.

   c. The moment the shaft is free of the bearing, it will drop to the floor. Secure or hold the shaft to prevent it from falling.

Bearing Installation

1. When installing a bearing in a housing, pressure must be applied to the outer bearing race (**Figure 68**). When installing a bearing on a shaft, pressure must be applied to the inner bearing race (**Figure 69**).

2. When installing a bearing as described in Step 1, some type of driver will be required. Never strike the bearing directly with a hammer or the bearing will be damaged. When installing a bearing, a piece of pipe or a socket with an outer diameter that matches

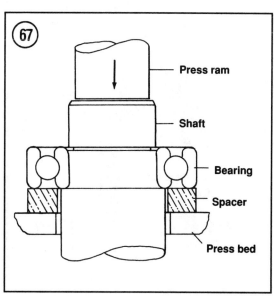

the bearing race will be required. **Figure 70** shows the correct way to use a socket and hammer when installing a bearing over a shaft.

3. Step 1 describes how to install a bearing in a case half and over a shaft. However, when installing a bearing over a shaft and into a housing at the same time, a snug fit will be required for both outer and inner bearing races. In this situation, a spacer must be installed underneath the driver tool so that pressure is applied evenly across both races. See **Figure 71**. If the outer race is not supported as shown in **Figure 71**, the balls will push against the outer bearing track and damage it.

Shrink Fit

1. Installing a bearing over a shaft: When a tight fit is required, the bearing inside diameter will be smaller than the shaft. In this case, driving the bearing on the shaft using normal methods may cause bearing damage. Instead, the bearing should be heated before installation. Note the following:

   a. Secure the shaft so that it can be ready for bearing installation.

   b. Clean the bearing surface on the shaft of all residue. Remove burrs with a file or sandpaper.

   c. Fill a suitable pot or beaker with clean mineral oil. Place a thermometer (rated higher than 248° F [120° C]) in the oil. Support the thermometer so that it does not rest on the bottom or side of the pot.

   d. Remove the bearing from its wrapper and secure it with a piece of heavy wire bent to hold

it in the pot. Hang the bearing in the pot so that it does not touch the bottom or sides of the pot.

   e. Turn the heat on and monitor the thermometer. When the oil temperature rises to approximately 248° F (120° C), remove the bearing from the pot and quickly install it. If necessary, place a socket on the inner bearing race and tap the bearing into place. As the bearing chills, it will tighten on the shaft so you must work

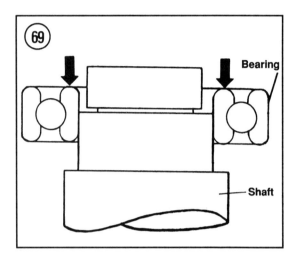

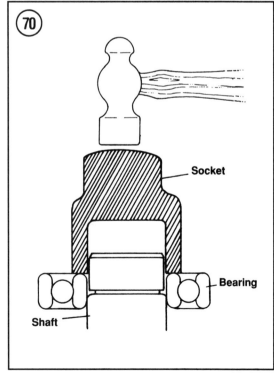

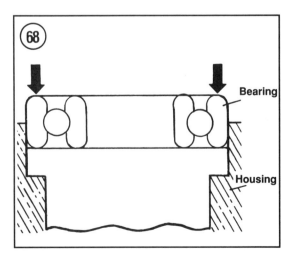

quickly when installing it. Make sure the bearing is installed all the way.

2. Installing a bearing in a housing: Bearings are generally installed in a housing with a slight interference fit. Driving the bearing into the housing using normal methods may damage the housing or cause bearing damage. Instead, the housing should be heated before the bearing is installed. Note the following:

CAUTION
Before heating the crankcases in this procedure to remove the bearings, wash the cases thoroughly with detergent and water. Rinse and rewash the cases as required to remove all traces of oil and other chemical deposits.

a. The housing must be heated to a temperature of about 212° F (100° C) in an oven or on a hot plate. An easy way to check to see that it is at the proper temperature is to drop tiny drops of water on the case as it heats up; if they sizzle and evaporate immediately, the temperature is correct. Heat only one housing at a time.

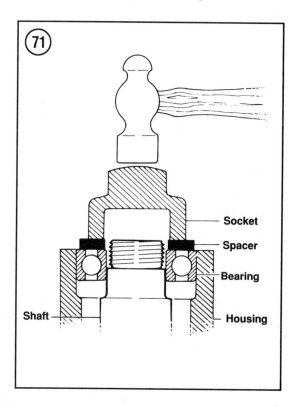

Socket

Spacer

Bearing

Shaft

Housing

CAUTION
Do not heat the housing with a torch (propane or acetylene). Never bring a flame into contact with the bearing or housing. The direct heat will destroy the case hardening of the bearing and will likely warp the housing.

b. Remove the housing from the oven or hot plate and hold onto the housing with a kitchen pot holder, heavy gloves or heavy shop cloths—it is hot.

NOTE
A suitable size socket and extension works well for removing and installing bearings.

c. Hold the housing with the bearing side down and tap the bearing out. Repeat for all bearings in the housing.

d. Before installing new bearings, heat the housing halves and place the new bearings in a freezer, if possible. Chilling the bearings will slightly reduce their overall diameter while the hot housing assembly is slightly larger due to heat expansion. This will make installation much easier.

NOTE
Always install bearings with the manufacturer's mark or number facing outward.

e. While the housing is still hot, install the new bearing(s) into the housing. Install the bearings by hand, if possible. If necessary, lightly tap the bearing(s) into the housing with a socket placed on the outer bearing race. Do not install new bearings by driving on the inner bearing race. Install the bearing(s) until it seats completely.

OIL SEALS

Oil seals (**Figure 72**) are used to prevent leakage of oil, water, grease or combustion gasses from between a housing and a shaft. Improper removal of a seal can damage the housing or shaft. Improper installation of the seal can damage the seal. Note the following:

a. Prying is generally the easiest and most effective method of removing a seal from a housing.

However, always place a rag underneath the pry tool to prevent damage to the housing.

b. Grease should be packed in the seal lips before the seal is installed.

c. Oil seals should always be installed so that the manufacturer's numbers or marks face out.

d. Oil seals should be installed with a socket placed on the outside of the seal as shown in **Figure 73**. Make sure the seal is driven squarely into the housing. Never install a seal by hitting against the top of the seal with a hammer.

RIDING SAFETY

General Tips

1. Read your owner's manual and know your machine.

2. Check the throttle and brake controls before starting the engine.

3. Know how to make an emergency stop.

4. Never add fuel while anyone is smoking in the area or when the engine is running.

5. Never wear loose scarves, belts or boot laces that could catch on moving parts.

6. Always wear eye and head protection and protective clothing to protect your *entire* body. Today's riding apparel is very stylish and you will be ready for action as will as being well protected.

7. Riding in the winter months requires a good set of clothes to keep your body dry and warm, otherwise your entire trip may be miserable. If you dress properly, moisture will evaporate from your body. If you become too hot and if your clothes trap the moisture, you will become cold. Even mild temperatures can be very uncomfortable and dangerous when combined with a strong wind or traveling at high speed. See **Table 5** for wind chill factors. Always dress according to what the wind chill factor is, not the ambient temperature.

8. Never allow anyone to operate the bike without proper instruction. This is for their bodily protection and to keep your bike from damage or destruction.

9. Never attempt to repair your bike with the engine running except when necessary for certain tune-up procedures.

10. Check all of the machine components and hardware frequently, especially the wheels and the steering.

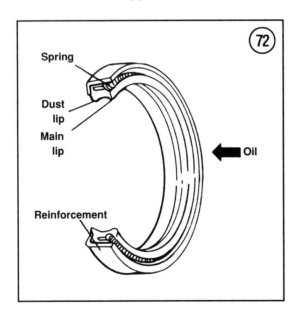

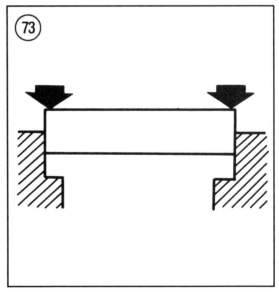

1

Table 1 FRAME SERIAL NUMBERS

Year/model	U.S. Models Frame number
1986 VS700G	JS1VP51A-G2100001-on
1987 VS700H	JS1VP51A-H2100001-on
1988 VS750J	JS1VR51A-J2100001-on
1989 VS750K	JS1VR51A-K2100001-on
1990 VS750L	JS1VR51A-L2100001-on
1991 VS750M	JS1VR51A-M2100001-on
1992 VS800N	JS1VS52A-N2100001-on
1993 VS800P	JS1VS52A-P2100001-on
1994 VS800R	JS1VS52A-R2100001-on
Year/model	U.K. Models Frame number
1985 VS750F	VR51A-100912-on
1986 VS750G	VR51A-102696-on
1987 VS750H	VR51A-106527-on
1988 VS750J	VR51A-108001-on
1989 VS750K	VR51A-108331-on
1990 VS750L	VR51A-108460-on
1991 VS750M	VR52A-109300-109309, 109434-on
1992 VS800N	VR52A-100001-on
1993 VS800P	VR52A-102741-on
1994 VS800R	VR52A-106743-on

Table 2 DECIMAL AND METRIC EQUIVALENTS

Fractions	Decimal in.	Metric mm	Fractions	Decimal in.	Metric mm
1/64	0.015625	0.39688	33/64	0.515625	13.09687
1/32	0.03125	0.79375	17/32	0.53125	13.49375
3/64	0.046875	1.19062	35/64	0.546875	13.89062
1/16	0.0625	1.58750	9/16	0.5625	14.28750
5/64	0.078125	1.98437	37/64	0.578125	14.68437
3/32	0.09375	2.38125	19/32	0.59375	15.08125
7/64	0.109375	2.77812	39/64	0.609375	15.47812
1/8	0.125	3.1750	5/8	0.625	15.87500
9/64	0.140625	3.57187	41/64	0.640625	16.27187
5/32	0.15625	3.96875	21/32	0.65625	16.66875
11/64	0.171875	4.36562	43/64	0.671875	17.06562
3/16	0.1875	4.76250	11/16	0.6875	17.46250
13/64	0.203125	5.15937	45/64	0.703125	17.85937
7/32	0.21875	5.55625	23/32	0.71875	18.25625
15/64	0.234375	5.95312	47/64	0.734375	18.65312
1/4	0.250	6.35000	3/4	0.750	19.05000
17/64	0.265625	6.74687	49/64	0.765625	19.44687
9/32	0.28125	7.14375	25/32	0.78125	19.84375
19/64	0.296875	7.54062	51/64	0.796875	20.24062
5/16	0.3125	7.93750	13/16	0.8125	20.63750
21/64	0.328125	8.33437	53/64	0.828125	21.03437
11/32	0.34375	8.73125	27/32	0.84375	21.43125
23/64	0.359375	9.12812	55/64	0.859375	22.82812
3/8	0.375	9.52500	7/8	0.875	22.22500
25/64	0.390625	9.92187	57/64	0.890625	22.62187
13/32	0.40625	10.31875	29/32	0.90625	23.01875
27/64	0.421875	10.71562	59/64	0.921875	23.41562
7/16	0.4375	11.11250	15/16	0.9375	23.81250
29/64	0.453125	11.50937	61/64	0.953125	24.20937
15/32	0.46875	11.90625	31/32	0.96875	24.60625
31/64	0.484375	12.30312	63/64	0.984375	25.00312
1/2	0.500	12.70000	1	1.00	25.40000

Table 3 STANDARD TIGHTENING TORQUES

Conventional or "4" Marked bolt*		
Bolt diameter (mm)	N·m	ft.-lb.
4	1-2	0.7-1.5
5	2-4	1.5-3.0
6	4-7	3-5
8	10-16	7-11.5
10	22-35	16-25.5
12	35-55	25.5-40
14	50-80	36-58
16	80-130	58-94
18	130-190	94-137.5
"7" Marked bolt*		
Bolt diameter (mm)	N·m	ft.-lb.
4	1.5-3	1-2
5	3-6	2-4.5
6	8-12	6-8.5
8	18-28	13-20
10	40-60	29-43.5
12	70-100	50.5-72.5
14	110-160	79.5-115.5
16	170-250	123-181
18	200-280	144-202

* Number is marked on top of Suzuki bolt head. These are Suzuki numbers and do not appear on aftermarket bolts.

Table 4 WORKSHOP TOOLS

Tool	Size or specification
Screwdriver	
Common	1/8 × 4 in. blade
Common	5/16 × 8 in. blade
Common	3/8 × 12 in. blade
Phillips	Size 2 tip, 6 in. overall
Pliers	
Slip joint	6 in. overall
Vise Grips	10 in. overall
Needlenose	6 in. overall
Channel lock	12 in. overall
Snap ring	Assorted
Wrenches	
Box-end set	Assorted
Open-end set	Assorted
Crescent	6 in. and 12 in. overall
Socket set	1/2 in. drive ratchet with assorted metric sockets
Socket drive extensions	1/2 in. drive, 2 in., 4 in. and 6 in.
Socket universal joint	1/2 in. drive
Allen	Socket driven (long and short), T-handle driven and 90°
Hammers	
Soft faced	—
Plastic faced	—
Metal faced	—
Other special tools	
Impact driver	1/2 in. drive with assorted bits
Torque wrench	1/2 in. driver (ft.-lb.)
Flat feeler gauge	Metric set

Table 5 WINDCHILL FACTORS

Estimated wind speed in mph	Actual thermometer reading (°F)											
	50	40	30	20	10	0	−10	−20	−30	−40	−50	−60
	Equivalent temperature (°F)											
Calm	50	40	30	20	10	0	−10	−20	−30	−40	−50	−60
5	48	37	27	16	6	−5	−15	−26	−36	−47	−57	−68
10	40	28	16	4	−9	−21	−33	−46	−58	−70	−83	−95
15	36	22	9	−5	−18	−36	−45	−58	−72	−85	−99	−112
20	32	18	4	−10	−25	−39	−53	−67	−82	−96	−110	−124
25	30	16	0	−15	−29	−44	−59	−74	−88	−104	−118	−133
30	28	13	−2	−18	−33	−48	−63	−79	−94	−109	−125	−140
35	27	11	−4	−20	−35	−49	−67	−82	−98	−113	−129	−145
40	26	10	−6	−21	−37	−53	−69	−85	−100	−116	−132	−148
*	Little danger (for properly clothed person)			Increasing danger			• Danger from freezing of exposed flesh •		Great danger			

*Wind speeds greater than 40 mph have little additional effect.

CHAPTER TWO

TROUBLESHOOTING

Every motorcycle engine requires an uninterrupted supply of fuel and air, proper ignition and adequate compression. If any of these are lacking, the engine will not run.

Diagnosing mechanical problems is relatively simple if you use orderly procedures and keep a few basic principles in mind.

The troubleshooting procedures in this chapter analyze typical symptoms and show logical methods of isolating causes. These are not the only methods. There may be several ways to solve a problem, but only a systematic approach can guarantee success.

Never assume anything. Do not overlook the obvious. If you are riding along and the bike suddenly quits, check the easiest, most accessible problem spots first. Is there gasoline in the tank? Has a spark plug wire fallen off?

If nothing obvious turns up in a quick check, look a little further. Learning to recognize and describe symptoms will make repairs easier for you or a mechanic at the shop. Describe problems accurately and fully. Saying that "it won't run" isn't the same thing as saying "it quit at high speed and won't start," or that "it sat in my garage for 3 months and then wouldn't start."

Gather as many symptoms as possible to aid in diagnosis. Note whether the engine lost power gradually or all at once. Remember that the more complicated a machine is, the easier it is to troubleshoot because symptoms point to specific problems.

After the symptoms are defined, areas which could cause problems are tested and analyzed. Guessing at the cause of a problem may provide the solution, but it can easily lead to frustration, wasted time and a series of expensive, unnecessary parts replacements.

You do not need fancy equipment or complicated test gear to determine whether repairs can be attempted at home. A few simple checks could save a large repair bill and lost time while the bike sits in a dealer's service department. On the other hand, be

2

realistic and don't attempt repairs beyond your abilities. Service departments tend to charge heavily for putting together a disassembled engine that may have been abused. Some won't even take on such a job—so use common sense and don't get in over your head.

OPERATING REQUIREMENTS

An engine needs 3 basics to run properly: correct fuel/air mixture, compression and a spark at the correct time. If one or more are missing, the engine will not run. Four-stroke engine operating principles are described under *Engine Principles* in Chapter Four. The electrical system is the weakest link of the 3 basics. More problems result from electrical breakdowns than from any other source. Keep that in mind before you begin tampering with carburetor adjustments and the like.

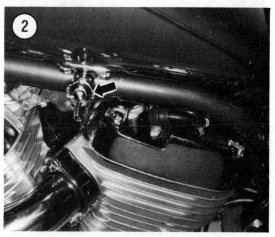

If the machine has been sitting for any length of time and refuses to start, check and clean the spark plugs and then look to the gasoline delivery system. This includes the fuel tank, fuel pump, fuel filter, fuel shutoff valve and fuel lines to the carburetors. Gasoline deposits may have formed and gummed up the carburetor jets and air passages. Gasoline tends to lose its potency after standing for long periods. Condensation may contaminate the fuel with water. Drain the old fuel (fuel tank, fuel lines and carburetors) and try starting with a fresh tankful.

TROUBLESHOOTING INSTRUMENTS

Chapter One lists the instruments needed and instruction on their use.

TROUBLESHOOTING

When the bike is difficult to start, or won't start at all, it doesn't help to wear down the battery using the electric starter. Check for obvious problems even before getting out your tools. Go down the following list step-by-step. Do each one; you may be embarrassed to find the engine stop switch off, but that is better than wearing down the battery.

Engine Fails to Start

If the bike will not start, perform the following checks in order:

    a. Fuel system check.
    b. Compression check.
    c. Battery check.
    d. Ignition system check.

Fuel system check

> **WARNING**
> *Do not use an open flame to check in the tank. A serious explosion is certain to result.*

1. Is there fuel in the tank? Remove or open the filler cap (**Figure 1**) and rock the bike. Listen for fuel sloshing around.
2. Is the fuel shutoff valve in the ON position (**Figure 2**) and on models so equipped, is the vacuum line to the valve from the engine still connected?

3. Make sure the engine stop switch (**Figure 3**) is not in the OFF position.

4. Is the choke in the correct position? The choke knob should be pulled *out* (**Figure 4**) for a cold engine and pushed *in* (**Figure 5**) for a warm engine.

Compression check

A compression test shows how much pressure builds in a cylinder during starting. If the compression falls below specified levels, the engine will become difficult to start or will not start. Refer to *Compression Testing* in Chapter Three. Interpret results as follows:

    a. Normal: Perform the *Ignition Check* in this chapter.

    b. Abnormal: If the engine compression is low, perform the procedures listed under *Compression Testing* in Chapter Three.

Ignition check

Perform the following spark test to determine if the ignition system is operating properly.

1. Remove one of the spark plugs as described in Chapter Three.

2. Attach the spark plug wire connector to the spark plug and touch the spark plug base to a good ground like the engine cylinder head. Position the spark plug so you can see the electrodes.

> *WARNING*
> *During the next step, do not hold the spark plug, wire or connector with fingers or a serious electrical shock may result. If necessary, use a pair of insulated pliers to hold the spark plug or wire. The high voltage generated by the ignition system could produce serious or fatal shocks.*

3. Crank the engine over with the starter. A fat blue spark should be evident across the spark plug electrodes.

> *NOTE*
> *If the starter does not operate or if the starter motor rotates but the engine does not turn over, refer to* **Engine Will Not Crank** *in this section.*

4. If the spark is good, recheck the fuel and compression systems.

5. If the spark is not good, check for one or more of the following:

    a. Loose electrical connections.

    b. Dirty electrical connections.

    c. Loose or broken ignition coil ground wire.

    d. Broken or shorted high tension lead to the spark plug(s).

    e. Ignition unit malfunction.

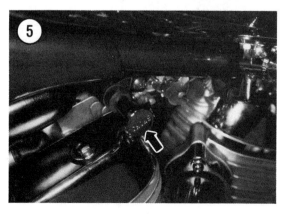

f. Clutch or sidestand switch malfunction.

g. Ignition or engine stop switch malfunction.

h. Blown fuse.

Battery check

If ignition system tests okay, but the starter turns slowly, service the battery as described under *Battery* in Chapter Three.

Engine is Difficult to Start

Check for one or more of the following possible malfunctions:

a. Fouled spark plug(s).

b. Improperly adjusted choke.

c. Intake tube(s) air leak.

d. Contaminated fuel system.

e. Improperly adjusted carburetor(s).

f. Weak ignitor unit.

g. Weak ignition coil(s).

h. Poor compression.

i. Engine and transmission oil too heavy.

Engine Will Not Crank

Check for one or more of the following possible malfunctions:

a. Blown fuse.

b. Discharged battery.

c. Defective starter motor and/or starter clutch.

d. Seized piston(s).

e. Seized crankshaft bearings.

f. Broken connecting rod(s).

g. Sidestand, neutral or clutch safety switch(s) malfunction.

h. Engine stop switch malfunction.

i. Defective starter motor button and contact.

ENGINE PERFORMANCE

In the following check list, it is assumed that the engine runs, but is not operating at peak performance. This will serve as a starting point from which to isolate a performance malfunction.

Engine Will Not Idle

a. Carburetor(s) incorrectly adjusted.

b. Fouled or improperly gapped spark plug(s).

c. Leaking head gasket.

d. Obstructed fuel line or fuel shutoff valve.

e. Obstructed fuel filter.

f. Ignition timing incorrect due to defective ignition component(s).

g. Valve clearance incorrect.

Engine Misses at High Speed

a. Fouled or improperly gapped spark plugs.

b. Improper carburetor main jet selection.

c. Ignition timing incorrect due to defective ignition component(s).

d. Weak ignition coil(s).

e. Obstructed fuel line or fuel shutoff valve.

f. Obstructed fuel filter.

g. Clogged carburetor jets.

h. Dirty air filter element.

Engine Overheating

a. Incorrect carburetor adjustment or jet selection.

b. Ignition timing retarded due to defective ignition component(s).

c. Improper spark plug heat range.

d. Cooling system malfunction.

e. Incorrect coolant level.

f. Oil level low.

g. Oil not circulating properly.

h. Valves leaking.

i. Heavy engine carbon deposits.

j. Dragging brake(s).

k. Clutch slipping.

Engine Overheating

a. Clogged radiator.

b. Damaged thermostat.

c. Worn or damaged radiator cap.

d. Water pump worn or damaged.

e. Thermostatic switch malfunction.

f. Damaged fan blades.

Smoky Exhaust and Engine Runs Roughly

a. Clogged air filter element.

b. Carburetor adjustment incorrect—mixture too rich.

c. Choke not operating correctly.

d. Water or other contaminants in fuel.

e. Clogged fuel line.

f. Spark plug(s) fouled.

g. Ignition coil(s) defective.

h. Ignitor unit or pickup coil defective.

i. Loose or defective ignition circuit wire(s).

j. Short circuit from damaged wire insulation.

k. Loose battery cable connection.

l. Valve timing incorrect.

m. Intake tube(s) or air filter(s) air leak.

Engine Loses Power at Normal Riding Speed

a. Carburetor incorrectly adjusted.

b. Engine overheating.

c. Ignition timing incorrect due to defective ignition component(s).

d. Incorrectly gapped spark plugs.

e. Obstructed muffler.

f. Dragging brake(s).

Engine Lacks Acceleration

a. Carburetor mixture too lean.

b. Clogged fuel line.

c. Ignition timing incorrect due to defective ignition component(s).

d. Dragging brake(s).

e. Slipping clutch.

ENGINE NOISES

Often the first evidence of an internal engine problem is a strange noise. That knocking, clicking or tapping sound which you never heard before may be warning you of impending trouble.

While engine noises can indicate problems, they are difficult to interpret correctly; inexperienced mechanics can be seriously misled by them.

Professional mechanics often use a special stethoscope (which looks like a doctor's stethoscope) for isolating engine noises. You can do nearly as well with a "sounding stick" which can be an ordinary piece of doweling, a length of broom handle or a section of small hose. By placing one end in contact with the area to which you want to listen and the other end near your year, you can hear sounds emanating from that area. The first time you do this, you may be horrified at the strange sounds coming from even a normal engine. If you can, have an experienced friend or mechanic help you sort out the noises.

Consider the following when troubleshooting engine noises:

1. *Knocking or pinging during acceleration*— Caused by using a lower octane fuel than recommended. May also be caused by poor fuel. Pinging can also be caused by a spark plug of the wrong heat range or carbon build-up in the combustion chamber. Refer to *Correct Spark Plug Heat Range* and *Compression Test* in Chapter Three.

2. *Slapping or rattling noises at low speed or during acceleration*— May be caused by piston slap, i.e., excessive piston-cylinder wall clearance.

3. *Knocking or rapping while decelerating*— Usually caused by excessive rod bearing clearance.

4. *Persistent knocking and vibration*— Usually caused by worn main bearing(s).

5. *Rapid on-off squeal*— Compression leak around cylinder head gasket or spark plug(s).

6. *Valve train noise*— Check for the following:

a. Valves adjusted incorrectly.

b. Valve sticking in guide.

c. Low oil pressure.

ENGINE LUBRICATION

An improperly operating engine lubrication system will quickly lead to engine seizure. The engine oil level should be checked weekly and topped up, as described in Chapter Three. Oil pump service is described in Chapter Four.

Oil Consumption High or Engine Smokes Excessively

a. Worn valve guides.

b. Worn or damaged piston rings.

Excessive Engine Oil Leaks

a. Clogged air filter breather hose(s).

b. Loose engine parts.

c. Damaged gasket sealing surfaces.

Black Smoke

a. Clogged air filter element.
b. Incorrect carburetor fuel level (too high).
c. Choke stuck open.
d. Incorrect main jet (too large).

Gray Smoke

a. Worn valve guide.
b. Worn valve oil seal.
c. Worn piston ring oil ring.
d. Excessive cylinder and/or piston wear.

CLUTCH

The four basic clutch troubles are:
a. Clutch noise.
b. Clutch slipping.
c. Improper clutch disengagement or dragging.
d. Low hydraulic level in master cylinder or air in hydraulic fluid line.

All clutch troubles, except adjustments, require partial clutch disassembly to identify and cure the problem. The troubleshooting chart in **Figure 6** lists clutch troubles and checks to make. Refer to Chapter Five for clutch service procedures.

TRANSMISSION

The basic transmission troubles are:
a. Excessive gear noise.
b. Difficult shifting.
c. Gears pop out of mesh.
d. Incorrect shift lever operation.

Transmission symptoms are sometimes hard to distinguish from clutch symptoms. The troubleshooting chart in **Figure 7** lists transmission troubles and checks to make. Refer to Chapter Six for transmission service procedures. Be sure that the clutch is not causing the trouble before working on the transmission.

ELECTRICAL PROBLEMS

If bulbs burn out frequently, the cause may be excessive vibration, loose connections that permit

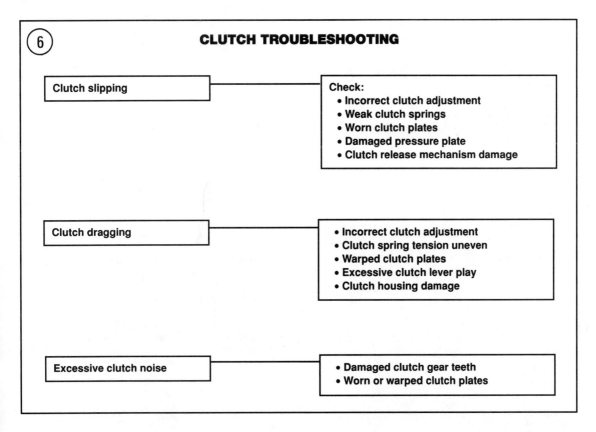

(6) CLUTCH TROUBLESHOOTING

Clutch slipping	Check: • Incorrect clutch adjustment • Weak clutch springs • Worn clutch plates • Damaged pressure plate • Clutch release mechanism damage
Clutch dragging	• Incorrect clutch adjustment • Clutch spring tension uneven • Warped clutch plates • Excessive clutch lever play • Clutch housing damage
Excessive clutch noise	• Damaged clutch gear teeth • Worn or warped clutch plates

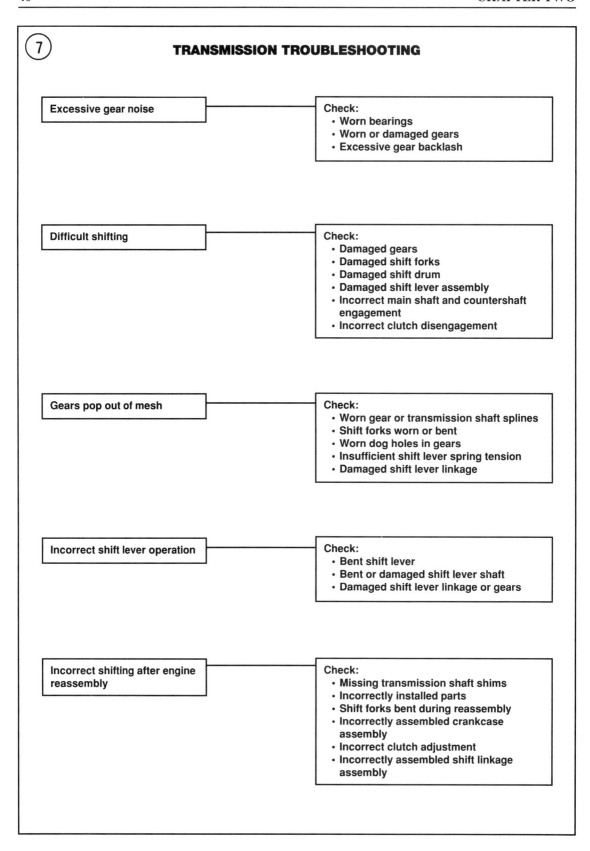

⑦   **TRANSMISSION TROUBLESHOOTING**

Excessive gear noise ————————————— Check:
- Worn bearings
- Worn or damaged gears
- Excessive gear backlash

Difficult shifting ————————————— Check:
- Damaged gears
- Damaged shift forks
- Damaged shift drum
- Damaged shift lever assembly
- Incorrect main shaft and countershaft engagement
- Incorrect clutch disengagement

Gears pop out of mesh ————————————— Check:
- Worn gear or transmission shaft splines
- Shift forks worn or bent
- Worn dog holes in gears
- Insufficient shift lever spring tension
- Damaged shift lever linkage

Incorrect shift lever operation ————————————— Check:
- Bent shift lever
- Bent or damaged shift lever shaft
- Damaged shift lever linkage or gears

Incorrect shifting after engine reassembly ————————————— Check:
- Missing transmission shaft shims
- Incorrectly installed parts
- Shift forks bent during reassembly
- Incorrectly assembled crankcase assembly
- Incorrect clutch adjustment
- Incorrectly assembled shift linkage assembly

sudden current surges, or the installation of the wrong type of bulb.

Most light and ignition problems are caused by loose or corroded ground connections. Check these prior to replacing a bulb or electrical component.

EXCESSIVE VIBRATION

Usually this is caused by loose engine mounting hardware. If not, it can be difficult to find without disassembling the engine. High speed vibration may be due to a bent axle shaft or loose or faulty suspension components. Vibration can also be caused by the following conditions:
  a. Broken frame.
  b. Worn drive chain.
  c. Improperly balanced wheels.
  d. Defective or damaged wheels.
  e. Defective or damaged tires.
  f. Internal engine wear or damage.

CARBURETOR TROUBLESHOOTING

Basic carburetor troubleshooting procedures are found in **Figure 8**.

FRONT SUSPENSION AND STEERING

Poor handling may be caused by improper tire pressure, a damaged or bent frame or front steering components, worn wheel bearings or dragging brakes. Possible causes of suspension and steering malfunctions are listed in the following.

Irregular or Wobbly Steering

  a. Loose wheel axle nuts.
  b. Loose or worn steering head bearings.
  c. Excessive wheel hub bearing play.
  d. Damaged wheel.
  e. Unbalanced wheel assembly.
  f. Worn hub bearings.
  g. Incorrect wheel alignment.
  h. Loose or bent spoke.
  i. Bent or damaged steering stem or frame (at steering neck).
  j. Tire incorrectly seated on rim.

  k. Excessive front end loading from non-standard equipment.
  l. Damaged fairing assembly.
  m. Loose fairing mounts or brackets.

Stiff Steering

  a. Low front tire air pressure.
  b. Bent or damaged steering stem or frame (at steering neck).
  c. Loose or worn steering head bearings.

Stiff or Heavy Fork Operation

  a. Incorrect fork springs.
  b. Incorrect fork oil viscosity.
  c. Incorrect fork adjustment.
  d. Excessive amount of fork oil.
  e. Bent fork tubes.

Poor Fork Operation

  a. Worn or damage fork tubes.
  b. Fork oil level low due to leaking fork seals.
  c. Incorrect fork adjustment(s).
  d. Bent or damaged fork tubes.
  e. Contaminated fork oil.
  f. Worn fork springs.
  g. Heavy front end loading from non-standard equipment.

Poor Rear Shock Absorber Operation

  a. Damper unit leaking.
  b. Incorrect rear shock adjustment.
  c. Heavy rear end loading from non-standard equipment.
  d. Incorrect loading.

BRAKE PROBLEMS

Sticking disc brakes may be caused by a stuck piston(s) in a caliper assembly, warped pad shim(s) or improper rear brake adjustment. See **Figure 9** for disc brake troubles and checks to make. Sticking brake shoes may be caused by an out-of-round brake drum.

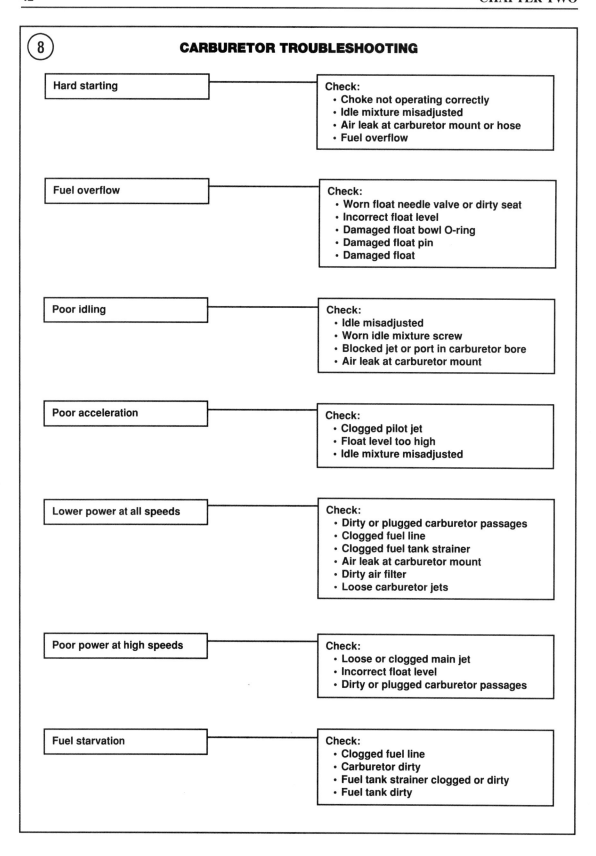

8 **CARBURETOR TROUBLESHOOTING**

Hard starting

Check:
- Choke not operating correctly
- Idle mixture misadjusted
- Air leak at carburetor mount or hose
- Fuel overflow

Fuel overflow

Check:
- Worn float needle valve or dirty seat
- Incorrect float level
- Damaged float bowl O-ring
- Damaged float pin
- Damaged float

Poor idling

Check:
- Idle misadjusted
- Worn idle mixture screw
- Blocked jet or port in carburetor bore
- Air leak at carburetor mount

Poor acceleration

Check:
- Clogged pilot jet
- Float level too high
- Idle mixture misadjusted

Lower power at all speeds

Check:
- Dirty or plugged carburetor passages
- Clogged fuel line
- Clogged fuel tank strainer
- Air leak at carburetor mount
- Dirty air filter
- Loose carburetor jets

Poor power at high speeds

Check:
- Loose or clogged main jet
- Incorrect float level
- Dirty or plugged carburetor passages

Fuel starvation

Check:
- Clogged fuel line
- Carburetor dirty
- Fuel tank strainer clogged or dirty
- Fuel tank dirty

⑨   **DISK BRAKE TROUBLESHOOTING**

2

| Disc brake fluid leakage | **Check:**
• Loose or damaged line fittings
• Worn caliper piston seals
• Scored caliper piston and/or bore
• Loose banjo bolts
• Damaged sealing washers
• Leaking master cylinder diaphragm
• Leaking master cylinder secondary seal
• Cracked master cylinder housing
• Too high brake fluid level
• Loose master cylinder cover |

| Brake overheating | **Check:**
• Warped brake disc
• Incorrect brake fluid
• Caliper piston and/or brake pads
  hanging up
• Riding brakes during riding |

| Brake chatter | **Check:**
• Warped brake disc
• Loose brake disc
• Incorrect caliper alignment
• Loose front axle nut and/or clamps
• Worn wheel bearings
• Damaged front hub
• Restricted brake hydraulic line
• Contaminated brake pads |

| Brake locking | **Check:**
• Incorrect brake fluid
• Plugged passages in master cylinder
• Incorrect front brake adjustment
• Caliper piston and/or brake pads
  hanging up
• Warped brake disc |

| Insufficient brakes | **Check:**
• Air in brake lines
• Worn brake pads
• Low brake fluid level
• Incorrect brake fluid
• Worn brake disc
• Worn caliper piston seals
• Glazed brake pads
• Leaking primary cup seal in
  master cylinder
• Contaminated brake pads and/or disc |

| Brake squeal | **Check:**
• Contaminated brake pads and/or disc
• Dust or dirt collected behind brake pads
• Loose parts |

CHAPTER THREE

LUBRICATION, MAINTENANCE AND TUNE-UP

A motorcycle, even in normal use, is subjected to tremendous heat, stress and vibration. When neglected, any bike becomes unreliable and actually dangerous to ride.

To gain the utmost in safety, performance and useful life from the Suzuki Intruder, it is necessary to make periodic inspections and adjustments. Frequently minor problems are found during these inspections that are simple and inexpensive to correct at the time. If they are not found and corrected at this time they could lead to major and more expensive problems later on.

Start out by doing simple tune-up, lubrication and maintenance. Tackle more involved jobs as you become more acquainted with the bike.

Table 1 is a suggested factory maintenance schedule. Tables 1-6 are located at the end of this chapter.

NOTE
Where differences occur relating to the United Kingdom (U.K.) models they are identified. If there is no (U.K.) designation relating to a procedure, photo or illustration it is identical to the United States (U.S.) models.

ROUTINE CHECKS

The following simple checks should be performed at each stop at a service station for gas.

3

Engine Oil Level

Refer to *Engine Oil Level Check* under *Periodic Lubrication* in this chapter.

Fuel

All Intruder engines are designed to use gasoline that has a pump octane number (R+M)/2 of 85 or higher or a gasoline with a research octane number of 89 or higher. The pump octane number is normally displayed at service station gas pumps. Using a gasoline with a lower octane number can cause pinging or spark knock, both conditions of which can lead to engine damage. Unleaded fuel is recommended because it reduces engine and spark plug deposits.

When choosing gasoline and filling the fuel tank, note the following:

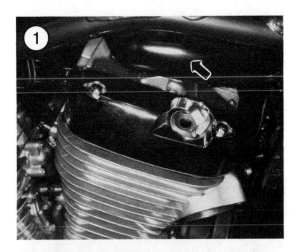

a. When filling the tank, do not overfill it. Fuel expands in the tank due to engine heat or heading by the sun. Stop adding fuel when the fuel level reaches the bottom of the filler tube inside the fuel tank.

b. To help meet clean air standards in some areas of the United States and Canada, oxygenated fuels are being used. Oxygenated fuels are conventional gasolines that are blended with an alcohol or ether compound to increase the gasoline's octane. When using an oxygenated fuel, make sure that it meets the minimum octane rating as previously specified.

c. Because oxygenated fuels can damage plastic and paint, make sure not to spill fuel onto the fuel tank during fuel stops.

d. An ethanol (ethyl or grain alcohol) gasoline that contains more than 10 percent ethanol by volume may cause engine starting and performance related problems.

e. A methanol (methyl or wood alcohol) gasoline that contains more than 5 percent methanol by volume may cause engine starting and performance related problems. Gasoline that contains methanol must have corrosion inhibitors to protect the metal, plastic and rubber parts in the fuel system from damage.

f. Suzuki states that you can use a gasoline containing no more than 15 percent MTBE (Methyl Tertiary Butyl Ether) by volume.

g. If your bike is experiencing fuel system damage or performance related problems from the use of oxygenated fuels, consult with a mechanic in an area where this type of fuel is widely sold and used.

Coolant Level

Check the coolant level in the radiator only when the engine is **COOL**. Preferable prior to the first ride of the day. The coolant reserve tank (**Figure 1**) is not transparent and therefore cannot be used to check coolant level in the system. The only visual inspection possible is by removing the radiator cap and looking into the filler neck.

1. Remove the screws securing the radiator cover (**Figure 2**) and remove the cover.

WARNING
*Do not remove the radiator cap when the engine is **HOT**. The coolant is under pressure and scalding and severe burns could result.*

2. Slowly turn the radiator cap (**Figure 3**) *counterclockwise* to release any residual pressure.
3. Remove the radiator cap completely.
4. Hold the bike vertical and observe the level in the radiator. The coolant should be up to the bottom of the radiator cap inlet fitting on the upper tank of the radiator.

NOTE
*If the coolant level is very low, there may be a leak in the cooling system. If this condition exists, refer to **Cooling System Inspection** in this chapter.*

NOTE
Never add just water to the system as this will dilute the coolant-to-water mixture to an unsafe level.

5. Insert a small funnel (**Figure 4**) into the radiator filler neck and add a 50:50 mixture of distilled water and antifreeze into the radiator to bring the level to the cap inlet fitting on the upper tank of the radiator.
6. Install the radiator cap and turn it *clockwise* until it stops turning and is locked in place.
7. Install the radiator cover and tighten the screws securely.

General Inspection

1. Quickly inspect the engine for signs of oil or fuel leakage.
2. Check the tires for embedded stones. Pry them out with a suitable small tool.
3. Make sure all lights work.

NOTE
At least check the brake light. It can burn out at any time. Motorists cannot stop as quickly as you and need all the warning you can give.

Tire Pressure

Tire pressure must be checked with the tires cold. Correct tire pressure varies with the load you are carrying or if you have a passenger. See **Table 2**.

Brake Operation

Check that both brakes operate with full hydraulic (front) or mechanical (rear) advantage. Check the front brake fluid level as described under *Disc Brake Fluid Level Inspection* in this chapter. Check that there is no brake fluid leakage from the front master cylinder, front caliper or brake lines.

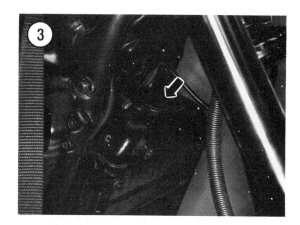

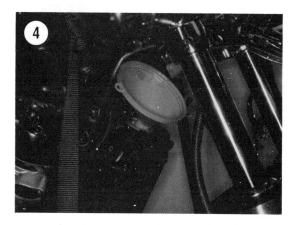

Battery

Remove the inspection cover (**Figure 5**) on the right-hand side of the battery case. The electrolyte level must be between the upper and lower level marks on the case.

> *NOTE*
> *This inspection window area shows the electrolyte level in the one cell next to the window only. It is suggested that the battery be removed so the level can be checked in all 6 cells.*

For complete details see *Battery Removal, Installation and Electrolyte Level Check* in this chapter.

Check the level more frequently in hot weather; electrolyte will evaporate rapidly as ambient heat increases.

Throttle

Sitting on the bike, with the brake ON, the transmission in NEUTRAL and with the engine idling, move the handlebars from side to side, making sure

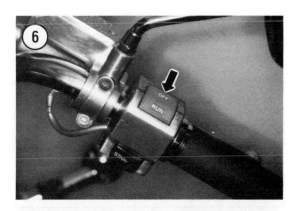

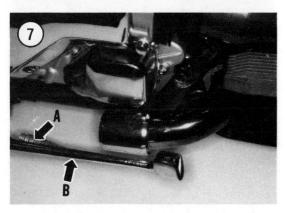

the idle does not increase or decrease by itself. Check that the throttle opens and closes smoothly in all steering positions. Shut off the engine.

Engine Stop Switch

The engine stop switch (**Figure 6**) is designed primarily as an emergency switch. It is part of the right-hand switch assembly next to the throttle housing and it has 2 operating positions: OFF and RUN. When the switch is in the OFF position, the engine will not start or run. In the RUN position, the engine should start and run with the ignition switch on, the clutch lever pulled in, while pressing the starter button. With the engine idling, move the switch to OFF. The engine should turn off.

Sidestand Check Switch System Inspection (1987-on Models)

1. Place wood block(s) under the engine to support the bike securely with the rear wheel off the ground.

2. Check the sidestand spring (A, **Figure 7**). Make sure the spring is in good condition and has not lost tension.

3. Swing the sidestand (B, **Figure 7**) down and up a few times. The sidestand should swing smoothly and the spring should provide proper tension in the raised position.

4. While sitting on the motorcycle, shift the transmission into NEUTRAL and move the sidestand up.

5. Start the engine and allow it to warm up. Then pull in the clutch lever and shift the transmission into gear.

6. Lower the sidestand with your foot. The engine should stop as the sidestand is lowered.

7. If the sidestand check switch did not operate as described, inspect the sidestand check switch as described in Chapter Eight.

Crankcase Breather Hose

Inspect the hose for cracks and deterioration and make sure that the hose clamps are tight.

Evaporative Emission Control System (California Models)

Inspect the hoses to make sure they are not kinked or bent and that they are securely connected to their respective parts.

Lights and Horn

With the engine running, check the following.
1. Pull the front brake lever on and check that the brake light comes on.
2. Push the rear brake pedal down and check that the brake light comes on soon after you have begun depressing the pedal.
3. With the engine running, check to see that the headlight and taillight are on.
4. Move the dimmer switch up and down between the HI and LO positions and check to see that the headlight elements are working in the headlight(s).
5. On U.K. models, move turn the switch on and off and check to see that the headlight elements are working in the headlight.
6. Push the turn signal switch to the left and right positions and check that all 4 turn signals are working.
7. Push the horn button and make sure that the horn blows loudly.
8. If during the test, the rear brake pedal traveled too far before the brake light came on, adjust the rear brake light switch as described in Chapter Eight.
9. If the horn or any of the lights failed to operate properly, refer to Chapter Eight.

PRE-CHECKS

The following checks should be performed prior to the first ride of the day.
1. Inspect all fuel lines and fittings for wetness.
2. Make sure the fuel tank is full of fresh gasoline.
3. Make sure the engine oil level is correct. Add oil if necessary.
4. Make sure the final drive unit oil level is correct. Add oil if necessary.
5. Check the operation of the front brake. Add hydraulic fluid to the front brake master cylinder if necessary.
6. Check the operation of the rear brake. Adjust the rear brake pedal free play as described in this chapter.

7. Check the operation of the clutch. Add hydraulic fluid to the clutch master cylinder if necessary.
8. Check the throttle and the rear brake pedal. Make sure they operate properly with no binding.
9. Inspect the front and rear suspension; make sure they have a good solid feel with no looseness.
10. Check tire pressure. Refer to **Table 2**.
11. Check the exhaust system for damage.
12. Check the tightness of all fasteners, especially engine mounting hardware.

SERVICE INTERVALS

The services and intervals shown in **Table 1** are recommended by the factory. Strict adherence to these recommendations will ensure long service from the Suzuki. If the bike is run in an area of high humidity, the lubrication services must be done more frequently to prevent possible rust damage.

For convenience when maintaining your motorcycle, most of the services shown in these tables are described in this chapter. However, some procedures which require more than minor disassembly or adjustment are covered elsewhere in the appropriate

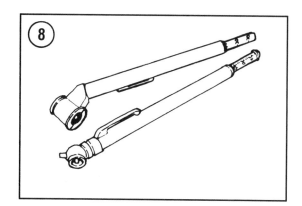

chapter. The *Table of Contents* and *Index* can help you locate a particular service procedure.

TIRES AND WHEELS

Tire Pressure

Tire pressure should be checked and adjusted to maintain the tire profile, good traction and handling and to get the maximum life out of the tire. A simple, accurate gauge (**Figure 8**) can be purchased for a few dollars and should be carried in your motorcycle tool kit. Tire pressure should be checked when the tires are cold. The appropriate tire pressures are shown in **Table 2**.

> *NOTE*
> *After checking and adjusting the air pressure, make sure to install the air valve cap (**Figure 9**). The cap prevents small pebbles and dirt from collecting in the valve stem; this could allow air leakage or result in incorrect tire pressure readings.*

> *NOTE*
> *A loss of air pressure may be due to a loose or damaged valve core. Put a few drops of water on the top of the valve core. If the water bubbles, tighten the valve core and recheck. If air is still leaking from the valve after tightening it, replace the valve stem assembly.*

Tire Inspection

The tires take a lot of punishment so inspect them periodically for excessive wear. Inspect the tires for the following:

a. Deep cuts and imbedded objects (i.e., stones, nails, etc.). If you find a nail or other object in a tire, mark its location with a light crayon prior to removing it. This will help to locate the hole for repair. Refer to Chapter Ten for tire changing and repair information.
b. Flat spots.
c. Cracks.
d. Separating plies.
e. Sidewall damage.

Tire Wear Analysis

Abnormal tire wear should be analyzed to determine its causes. The most common causes are the following:

a. Incorrect tire pressure: Check tire pressure as described in this chapter.
b. Overloading.
c. Incorrect wheel balance: The tire/wheel assembly should be balanced when installing a new tire and or tube and then re-balanced each time the tire is removed and reinstalled.
d. Worn or damaged wheel bearings.

Incorrect tire pressure is the biggest cause of abnormal tire wear **Figure 10**. Under-inflated tires will result in higher tire temperatures, hard or imprecise steering and abnormal tire wear. Overinflated tires will result in a hard ride and abnormal tire wear. Examine the tire tread, comparing wear in the center

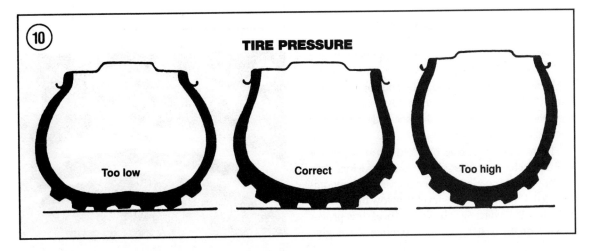

10

TIRE PRESSURE

Too low   Correct   Too high

of the contact patch with tire wear at the edge of the contact patch. Note the following:

a. If a tire shows excessive wear at the edge of the contact patch, but the wear at the center of the contact patch is okay, the tire has been under-inflated.

b. If a tire shows excessive wear in the center of the contact patch, but the wear at the edge of the contact patch is okay, the tire has been overinflated.

Tread Depth

Check local traffic regulations concerning minimum tread depth. Measure the tread depth at the center of tire and to the center of the tire tread (**Figure 11**) using a tread depth gauge (**Figure 12**) or a small ruler. Suzuki recommends that original equipment tires be replaced when the front tire tread depth is 1.5 mm (1/16 in.) or less, when the rear tread depth is 2.0 mm (3/32 in.) or less or when tread wear indicators appear at the designated area on the tire indicating the minimum tread depth.

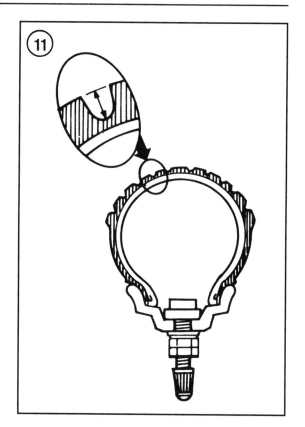

Rim Inspection

Frequently inspect the wheel rims (**Figure 13**). If a rim has been damaged it might have been enough to knock it out of alignment. Improper wheel alignment can cause severe vibration and result in an unsafe riding condition. If the rim portion of a wire wheel is damaged it can be replaced. If the rim portion of an alloy wheel is damaged the wheel must be replaced as it cannot be serviced or repaired.

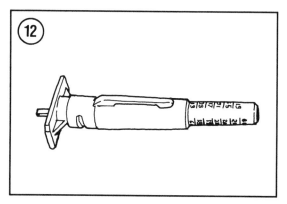

BATTERY

The battery is an important component in the electrical system. It is also the one most frequently neglected. In addition to checking and correcting the battery electrolyte level on a weekly basis, the battery should be cleaned and inspected at periodic intervals listed in **Table 1**.

The battery should be checked periodically for electrolyte level, state of charge and corrosion. During hot weather periods, frequent checks are recommended. If the electrolyte level is below the fill line, add distilled water as required. To assure proper mixing of the water and acid, operate the engine

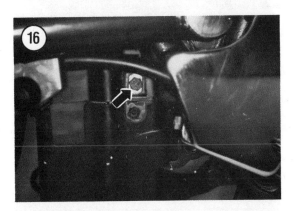

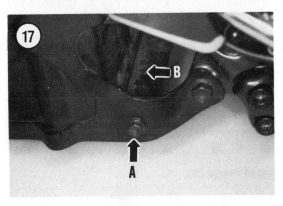

immediately after adding water. *Never* add battery acid instead of water; this will shorten the battery's life.

> *CAUTION*
> *If it becomes necessary to remove the battery breather tube when performing any of the following procedures, make sure to route the tube correctly during installation to prevent electrolyte or gas from spewing onto the battery case or any other component. Incorrect breather tube routing can cause structural and/or cosmetic damage.*

Removal, Installation and Electrolyte Level Check

1. Place the bike on the sidestand.
2. Remove the bolt and disconnect the battery negative (−) lead (**Figure 14**).
3. Remove the screw (A, **Figure 15**) securing the battery positive (+) cable terminal protector, remove the protector (B, **Figure 15**).
4. Remove the bolt and disconnect the battery positive (+) lead (**Figure 16**).
5. Remove one of the front lower bolts (A, **Figure 17**) securing the battery case floor (B, **Figure 17**) in place.
6. Either hold onto the battery case floor or place wood block(s) under it to support the floor when the other bolt is removed.
7. Remove the front lower bolt from the other side of the case.
8. Lower the battery case floor (A, **Figure 18**) and slide the battery (B, **Figure 18**) out of the case. Remove the battery.

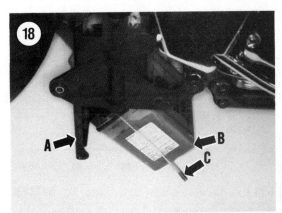

9. The electrolyte level should be maintained between the 2 marks on the battery case (A, **Figure 19**).

WARNING
Protect your eyes, skin and clothing. If electrolyte gets into your eyes, flush your eyes thoroughly with clean water and get prompt medical attention.

CAUTION
Be careful not to spill battery electrolyte on plastic, painted or plated surfaces. The liquid is highly corrosive and will damage the finish. If it is spilled, wash it off immediately with soapy water and thoroughly rinse with clean water.

10. Rinse the battery off with clean water and wipe dry.
11. Remove the caps from the battery cells (**Figure 20**) and add distilled water to correct the level. Never add electrolyte (acid) to correct the level.

NOTE
If distilled water has been added, reinstall the battery caps and gently shake the battery for several minutes to mix the existing electrolyte with the new water.

12. After the fluid level has been corrected and the battery allowed to stand for a few minutes, remove the battery caps and check the specific gravity of the electrolyte with a hydrometer (**Figure 21**). See *Battery Testing* in this chapter.

CAUTION
*If distilled water has been added to a battery in freezing or near freezing weather, add it to the battery, dress warmly and then ride the bike for a **minimum of 30 minutes**. This will help mix the water thoroughly into the electrolyte in the battery. Distilled water is lighter than electrolyte and will float on*

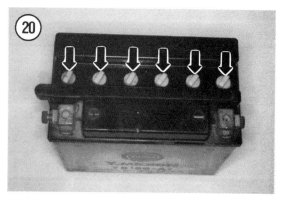
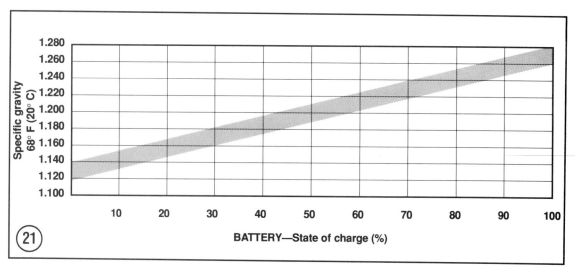

top of the electrolyte if it is not mixed in properly. If the water stays on the top, it may freeze and fracture the battery case, ruining the battery.

13. After the battery has been refilled, recharged or replaced, install it as follows:

   a. Clean the battery terminals (B, **Figure 19**) of all corrosion and/or oxidation. After a thorough cleaning, coat the terminals with a thin layer of dielectric grease to retard corrosion and decomposition of the terminals.

   b. Position the battery on the ground with the negative (–) terminal (A, **Figure 22**) toward the *left-hand* side of the bike. The positive (+) terminal and the breather outlet are on the *right-hand* side (B, **Figure 22**).

   c. Make sure the breather tube (C, **Figure 18**) is in place on the battery prior to installing the battery.

   d. Carefully move the battery (B, **Figure 18**) up into the battery case and hinge the case floor (A, **Figure 18**) up into position. Install one of the bolts (A, **Figure 17**) only finger tight at this time.

   e. Install the bolt on the other side and tighten securely. Then tighten the first bolt securely.

   f. Attach the red positive (+) cable and bolt (**Figure 16**) first then the black negative (–) cable (**Figure 14**). Tighten the bolts securely.

   g. Install the battery positive (+) cable terminal protector, (B, **Figure 15**) and tighten the screw securely.

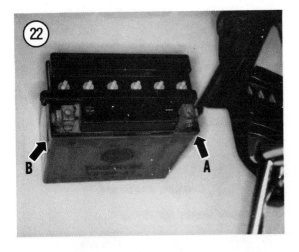

Testing

Hydrometer testing is the best way to check battery condition. Use a hydrometer with numbered graduations from 1.100 to 1.300 rather than one with color-coded bands. To use the hydrometer, squeeze the rubber ball, insert the tip into the cell and release the pressure on the ball. Draw enough electrolyte to float the weighted float inside the hydrometer. Note the number in line with the surface of the electrolyte; this is the specific gravity for this cell. Squeeze the rubber ball again and return the electrolyte to the cell from which it came.

The specific gravity of the electrolyte in each battery cell is an excellent indication of that cell's condition. A fully charged cell will read from 1.265-1.280, while a cell in good condition reads from 1.225-1.265 and anything below 1.225 is practically dead.

NOTE
Specific gravity varies with temperature. For each 10° the electrolyte temperature above 27° C (80° F), add 0.004 to readings indicated on the hydrometer. Subtract 0.004 for each 10° below 27° C (80° F).

If the cells test in the poor range, the battery requires recharging. The hydrometer is useful for checking the progress of the charging operation. **Table 3** shows approximate state of charge.

Charging

WARNING
During the charging process, highly explosive hydrogen gas is released from the battery. The battery should be charged only in a well-ventilated area away from any open flames (including pilot lights on home gas appliances). Do not allow any smoking in the area. Never check the charge by arcing (connecting pliers or other metal objects) across the terminals; the resulting spark can ignite the hydrogen gas.

CAUTION
Always remove the battery from the bike's frame before connecting the battery charger. Never recharge a battery in the bike's frame; the corrosive mist that is

emitted during the charging process will corrode all surrounding surfaces.

1. Connect the positive (+) charger lead to the positive (+) battery terminal and the negative (–) charger lead to the negative (–) battery terminal.

2. Remove all vent caps from the battery, set the charger to 12 volts and switch the charge ON. If the output of the charger is variable, it is best to select a low setting—1 1/2 to 2 amps. Normally, a battery should be charged at a slow charge rate of 1/10 its given capacity.

> *CAUTION*
> *The electrolyte level must be maintained at the upper level during the charging cycle; check and refill as necessary.*

3. The charging time depends on the discharged condition of the battery. The chart in **Figure 23** can be used to determine approximate charging times at different specific gravity readings. For example, if the specific gravity of your battery is 1.180, the approximate charging time would be 6 hours.

4. After the battery has been charged for about 6 hours, turn the charger OFF, disconnect the leads and check the specific gravity of each cell. It should be within the limits specified in **Table 3**. If it is, and remains stable for 1 hour, the battery is considered charged.

5. To ensure good electrical contact, cables must be clean and tight on the battery's terminals. If the cables terminals are badly corroded, even after performing the above cleaning procedures, the cables should be disconnected, removed from the bike and cleaned separately with a wire brush and a baking soda solution. After cleaning, apply a very thin coating of dielectric grease, petroleum jelly (Vaseline) or silicone spray to the battery terminals before reattaching the cables.

NEW BATTERY INSTALLATION

When replacing the old battery with a new one, be sure to charge it completely (specific gravity 1.260-1.280) before installing it in the bike. Failure to do so or using the battery with a low electrolyte level will permanently damage the new battery.

> *NOTE*
> *Recycle your old battery. When you replace the old battery, be sure to turn in*

*the old battery at that time. The lead plates and the plastic case can be recycled. Most motorcycle dealers will accept your old battery in trade when you purchase a new one, but if they will not, many automotive supply store certainly will. **Never** place an old battery in your household trash since it is illegal, in most states, to place any acid or lead (heavy metal) contents in landfills. There is also the danger of the battery being crushed in the trash truck and spraying acid on the truck operator.*

BATTERY ELECTRICAL CABLE CONNECTORS

To ensure good electrical contact between the battery and the electrical cables, the cables must be clean and free of corrosion.

1. If the electrical cable terminals are badly corroded, disconnect them from the bike's electrical system.

2. Thoroughly clean each connector with a wire brush and then with a baking soda solution. Rinse thoroughly with clean water and wipe dry with a clean cloth.

3. After cleaning, apply a thin layer of dielectric grease to the battery terminals before reattaching the cables.

4. If disconnected, attach the electrical cables to the bike's electrical system.

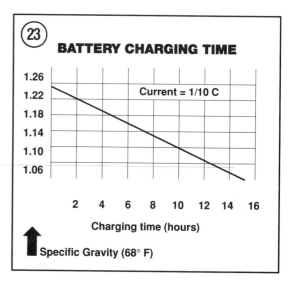

(23) **BATTERY CHARGING TIME**

Current = 1/10 C

Charging time (hours)

Specific Gravity (68° F)

5. After connecting the electrical cables, apply a light coating of dielectric grease to the electrical terminals (B, **Figure 19**) of the battery to retard corrosion and decomposition of the terminals.

PERIODIC LUBRICATION

Oil

Oil is graded according to its viscosity, which is an indication of how thick it is. The Society of Automotive Engineers (SAE) system distinguishes oil viscosity by numbers. Thick oils have higher viscosity numbers than thin oils. For example, an SAE 5 oil is a thin oil while an SAE 90 oil is relatively thick. If the oil has been tested in cold weather it is denoted with a "W" after the number as "SAE 10W."

Grease

A good quality grease (preferably waterproof) should be used. Water does not wash grease from parts as easily as it washes off oil. In addition, grease

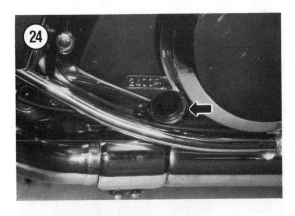

maintains its lubricating qualities better than oil on long and strenuous rides. In a pinch, though, the wrong lubricant is better than none at all. Correct the situation as soon as possible.

Engine Oil Level Check and Adding Oil

Engine oil level is checked with the oil level inspection window, located at the right-hand side of the engine on the clutch cover.
1. Place the bike on the sidestand on level ground.
2. Start the engine and let it idle for 1-2 minutes.
3. Shut off the engine and let the oil settle for 1-2 minutes.
4. Hold the bike in the true vertical position. A false reading will be given if the bike is tipped to either side.
5. Look at the oil level inspection window. The oil level should be between the 2 lines (**Figure 24**). If the level is below the lower "F" line, add the recommended weight engine oil to correct the level.
6. Remove the oil filler cap (**Figure 25**).
7. Insert a funnel into the oil fill hole and fill the engine with the correct viscosity and quantity of oil. Refer to **Table 4**.
8. Install the oil filler cap and tighten securely.
9. Repeat Steps 2-5 and recheck the oil level.

Engine Oil and Oil Filter Change

Change the engine oil and the oil filter at the same time at the factory-recommended oil change interval indicated in **Table 1**. This assumes that the motorcycle is operated in moderate climates. In extreme climates, oil should be changed every 30 days. The time interval is more important than the mileage interval because acids formed by combustion blowby will contaminate the oil even if the motorcycle is not run for several months. If the motorcycle is operated under dusty conditions, the oil will get dirty more quickly and should be changed more frequently.

Suzuki recommends the use of Suzuki Performance 4 Motor Oil that is a very high performance motor oil which has a special friction modifier added. If this type of oil is not used, use only a high-quality detergent motor oil with an API rating of SE or SF. The API rating is stamped on top of the can or printed on the label on the plastic bottle

(**Figure 26**). Try to use the same brand of oil at each change. Use of any oil additive is not recommended as it may cause clutch slippage. Refer to **Figure 27** for correct oil viscosity to use under anticipated ambient temperatures (not engine oil temperature).

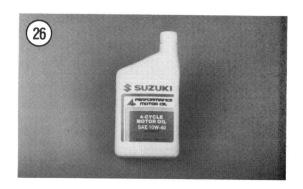

To change the engine oil and filter you will need the following:

a. Drain pan.
b. Funnel.
c. Open-end wrench (drain plug).
d. Suzuki oil filter wrench or equivalent.
e. Oil (refer to **Table 4** for quantity).
f. New oil filter element.

There are a number of ways to discard the old oil safely. Some service stations and oil retailers will accept your used oil for recycling; some may even give you money for it. Never drain the oil onto the ground nor place it in your household trash.

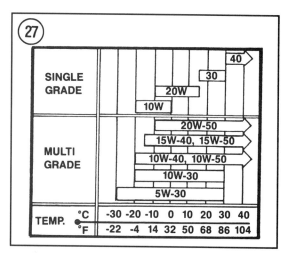

> *NOTE*
> *If you are going to recycle the oil, do not add any other type of chemical (fork oil, brake fluid, etc) to the oil as the oil recycler will probably not accept the oil. Final drive gear oil is acceptable.*

1. Start the engine and let it reach operating temperature; 15-20 minutes of stop-and-go riding is usually sufficient.

2. Turn the engine off and place the bike on level ground on the sidestand.

3. Place a drain pan under the left-hand rear portion of the crankcase and remove the drain plug (**Figure 28**). Remove the oil filler cap (**Figure 25**) this will speed up the flow of oil.

4. Inspect the sealing washer on the crankcase drain plug. Replace if its condition is in doubt.

5. Install the drain plug and washer and tighten to the torque specification listed in **Table 5**.

> *NOTE*
> *Before removing the oil filter, clean off all road dirt and any oil residue around it (**Figure 29**).*

6. Move the drain pan under the oil filter at the front of the engine.

> *NOTE*
> *Because the front exhaust pipe and the radiator lower hose outlet are so close to the oil filter there is very little working room for oil filter removal and in-*

*stallation. The easiest way to remove the oil filter is to use a Suzuki "cap type" oil filter wrench (**Figure 30**) (part No. 09915-47320) and a box wrench.*

7. Use the special tool and socket wrench and unscrew the oil filter (**Figure 31**) from the engine. Place the old filter in a reclosable plastic bag and close it to prevent residual oil from draining out. Discard the used oil filter properly.

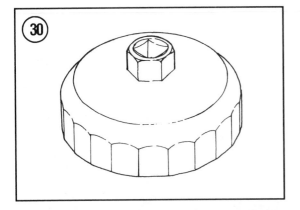

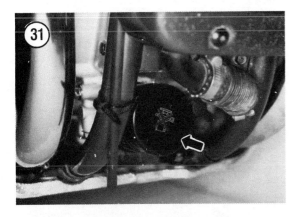

8. Clean off the oil filter mating surface of the crankcase with a shop rag and cleaning solvent. Remove any sludge or road dirt. Wipe it dry with a clean, lint-free cloth.

9. Apply a light coat of clean engine oil to the O-ring seal on the new oil filter (**Figure 32**).

10. Screw on the new oil filter by hand until the O-ring seal contacts the crankcase mating surface.

11. Make a mark on the face of the oil filter wrench with a permanent marker pen so it can be easily seen. Position this mark at the 12 o'clock position and install the wrench on the oil filter. Tighten the oil filter 2 full turns, then stop. The filter is now tight enough.

12. During oil filter removal, some oil may get onto the exhaust pipe. Prior to starting the engine, wipe off any spilled oil with a shop cloth. If necessary, spray some aerosol electrical contact cleaner on the pipe to remove the oil residue. If the oil is not cleaned off it will smoke once the engine is started and the exhaust pipe gets hot.

NOTE
Approximately every 3rd or 4th time the engine oil is changed it's a good idea to remove the oil sump plate and clean and inspect the inlet screen as described in the following procedure.

13. Insert a funnel into the oil fill hole and fill the engine with the correct viscosity and quantity of oil. Refer to **Table 5**.

14. Install the oil filler cap (**Figure 25**) and tighten securely.

15. Start the engine, let it run at idle speed and check for leaks.

16. Turn the engine off and check for correct oil level as described in this chapter; adjust as necessary.

Engine Oil Sump

Approximately every 3rd or 4th time the engine oil is changed it's a good idea to remove the oil sump plate and clean and inspect the sump inlet screen. If the bike is ridden in dusty areas it's a good idea to remove and clean it more often.

1. Drain the engine oil as described in this chapter.

2. Move the drain pan under the oil sump cover plate.

3. Remove the screws securing the oil sump cover plate (**Figure 33**).

> *NOTE*
> *Figure 34 is shown with the engine removed from the frame for clarity. It is not necessary to remove the engine for this procedure.*

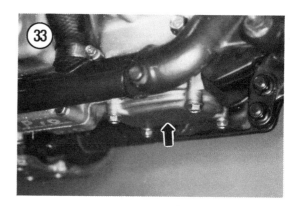

4. Remove the screws (A, **Figure 34**) securing the oil sump filter screen and remove the screen (B, **Figure 34**).

5. Clean the cover and screen in solvent and thoroughly dry.

6. Inspect the screen (A, **Figure 35**) for any broken areas or damage. Replace if necessary.

7. Inspect the O-ring seal (**Figure 36**) in the cover for hardness or deterioration; replace if necessary.

8. Position the screen with the flush side of the edging (B, **Figure 35**) facing toward the crankcase and install the screen.

9. Install the cover (**Figure 37**) and tighten the screws securely.

10. Refill the engine oil as described in this chapter.

Final Drive Oil Level Check

The final drive case should be cool. If the bike has been run, allow it to cool down (minimum of 10 minutes), then check the oil level. When checking or changing the final drive oil, do not allow any dirt or foreign matter to enter the case opening.

1. Place the bike on the sidestand on a level surface.

2. Wipe the area around the oil filler cap clean and unscrew the oil filler cap (**Figure 38**).

3. The oil level is correct if the oil is up to the lower edge of the filler cap hole. If the oil level is low, add hypoid gear oil until the oil level is correct. Refer to **Table 4** for correct oil viscosity and type to use under anticipated ambient temperatures.

4. Inspect the O-ring seal on the oil filler cap. If it is deteriorated or starting to harden it must be replaced.

5. Install the oil filler cap and tighten securely.

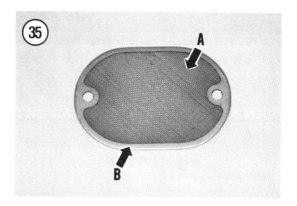

Final Drive Oil Change

The factory-recommended oil change interval is listed in **Table 1**.

To drain the oil you will need the following:

a. Drain pan.

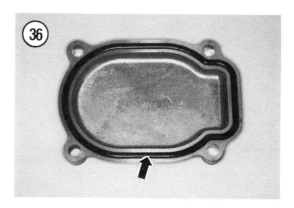

b. Funnel.

c. Approximately 200 ml (6.8 oz.) of hypoid gear oil.

Discard old oil as outlined under *Engine Oil and Filter Change* in this chapter.

1. Ride the bike until normal operating temperature is obtained. Usually 15-20 minutes of stop-and-go riding is sufficient.

2. Place the bike on the centerstand.

3. Place a drain pan under the drain plug.

4. Remove the oil filler cap (**Figure 38**) and the drain plug (**Figure 39**).

5. Let the oil drain for at least 15-20 minutes to ensure that the majority of the oil has drained out.

6. Inspect the sealing washer on the drain plug; replace the sealing washer if necessary.

7. Install the drain plug and tighten it securely.

8. Insert a funnel into the oil filler cap hole.

9. Add hypoid gear oil until the oil level is correct. Refer to **Table 4** for correct oil viscosity and type to use under anticipated ambient temperatures.

NOTE
In order to measure the correct amount of fluid, use a plastic baby bottle. These have measurements in milliliters (ml) and fluid ounces (oz.) on the side.

10. Install the oil filler cap (**Figure 38**).

11. Test ride the bike and check for oil leaks. After the test ride recheck the oil level as described in this chapter and readjust if necessary.

Front Fork Oil Change

It is a good practice to change the fork oil at the interval listed in **Table 1** or once a year. If it becomes contaminated with dirt or water, change it immediately.

The front forks are not equipped with a drain screw. In order to change the fork oil, the forks must be removed from the bike and partially disassembled.

1. Remove the fork assemblies as described under *Front Forks* in Chapter Ten.

2. Remove the fork spring.

3. Turn the fork assembly upside down and drain the fork oil into a suitable container. Pump the fork several times by hand to expel most of the remaining oil (**Figure 40**). Dispose of the fork oil properly.

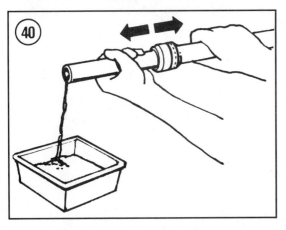

NOTE
*If you recycle your engine oil, do **not**
add the fork oil to the oil as the oil
recycler will probably not accept the oil.*

NOTE
*Suzuki recommends that the fork oil
level be measured, if possible, to ensure
a more accurate filling.*

NOTE
*To measure the correct amount of fluid,
use a plastic baby bottle. These bottles
have measurements in milliliters (ml) on
the side.*

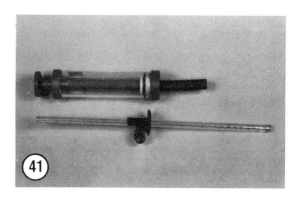

4. Hold the fork assembly in a vertical position and compress the fork completely.

5. Add the recommended amount of SAE 10W fork oil to the fork assembly listed in **Table 4**.

6. Hold the fork assembly as close to perfect vertical as possible.

7. Use an accurate ruler or the Suzuki oil level gauge (part No. 09943-74111), or equivalent (**Figure 41**), to achieve the correct oil level listed in **Table 4**. Refer to **Figure 42**.

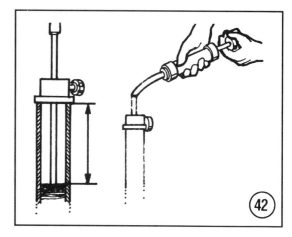

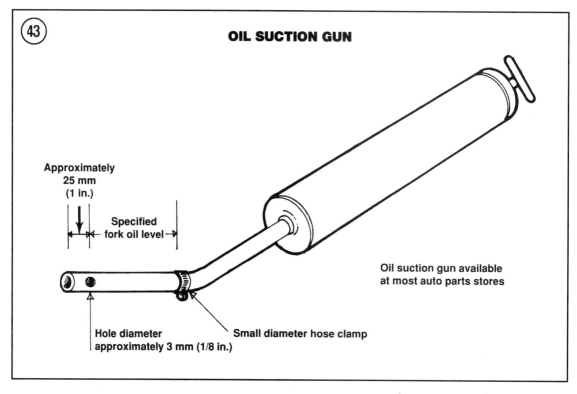

OIL SUCTION GUN

Approximately
25 mm
(1 in.)

Specified
fork oil level

Oil suction gun available
at most auto parts stores

Hole diameter
approximately 3 mm (1/8 in.)

Small diameter hose clamp

NOTE
*An oil level measuring device can be made as shown in **Figure 43**. Position the lower edge of the hose clamp the specified oil level distance up from the small diameter hole. Fill the fork with a few ml's more than the required amount of oil. Position the hose clamp on the top edge of the fork tube and draw out the excess oil. Oil is sucked out until the level reaches the small diameter hole. A precise oil level can be achieved with this simple device.*

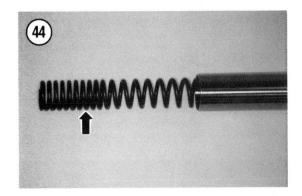

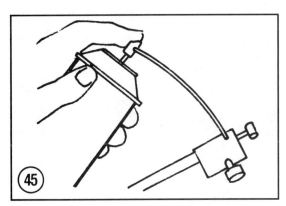

8. Allow the oil to settle completely and recheck the oil level measurement. Adjust the oil level if necessary.

9. Install the fork spring with the closer wound coils (**Figure 44**) going in last.

10. Hold the fork assembly in a vertical position (the upper end is open) and install the fork assemblies as described in Chapter Ten.

Throttle Cable

The throttle control cable should be lubricated at the cable inspection intervals specified in **Table 1** or when it has become stiff or sluggish. At this time, it should also be inspected for fraying, and the cable sheath should be checked for chafing. The cables are relatively inexpensive and should be replaced when found to be faulty.

The cable should be lubricated with a cable lubricant and a cable lubricator (**Figure 45**).

CAUTION
*If the stock cable has been replaced with nylon-lined cables, do **not** oil them as described in the following procedure. Oil and most cable lubricants will cause the liner to expand, pinching the liner against the cable. Nylon lined cables are normally used dry. When servicing nylon-lined cables, follow the cable manufacturer's instructions.*

NOTE
The main cause of cable breakage or cable stiffness is improper lubrication. Maintaining the cables as described in this section will assure long service life.

1. Remove the screws securing the right-hand switch assembly (**Figure 46**) together to gain access to the throttle cable end.

2. Disconnect the throttle cable from the grip assembly and the upper portion of the switch assembly (**Figure 47**).

3. Remove the fuel tank as described under *Fuel Tank Removal/Installation* in Chapter Seven.

4. Attach a lubricator following the manufacturer's instructions (**Figure 45**).

5. Place a clean shop cloth at the other end of the cable to catch the excess lubricant as it exits the cable end.

6. Insert the nozzle of the lubricant can in the lubricator, press the button on the can and hold down until the lubricant begins to flow out of the other end of the cable.

7. Remove the lubricator, reconnect the cable and adjust the cable.

8. Install the fuel tank.

Brake System

The following brake components should be lubricated with silicone grease (specified for brake use) whenever the components are removed for service:

a. Master cylinder rubber boots (inside).

b. Brake caliper boots (inside).

c. Brake caliper pin bolt sliding surface.

**Rear Brake Pedal Rod
(Models So Equipped)**

Whenever the rear brake pedal is adjusted or when the pedal feels stiff, lubricate the points shown in **Figure 48** with clean engine oil.

**Brake Pedal
Pivot Shaft Lubrication**

The brake pedal should be removed, as described in Chapter Twelve, periodically and the pivot shaft lubricated with grease.

Speedometer Cable Lubrication

The inner speedometer cable should be lubricated periodically or whenever needle operation is erratic. At the same time, check the outer cable for damage.

1. Unscrew the knurled speedometer cable ring at the left-hand side of the speedometer case

2. At the front wheel, remove the speedometer cable (**Figure 49**) from the speedometer gear housing.

3. Attach a cable lubricator (**Figure 45**) to the cable following the manufacturer's instructions.

4. Insert the nozzle of the lubricant can into the lubricator, press the button on the can and hold it down until the lubricant begins to flow out of the other end of the cable. If the lubricant flows out from the cable lubricator, the lubricator is not installed properly onto the end of the cable. You may have to install the lubricator a few times to get it to seal

properly. Place a shop cloth at the base of the speedometer cable to catch all excess lubricant that will flow out.

NOTE
If lubricant does not flow out the end of the cable, check the entire cable for fraying, bending or other damage.

5. Remove the lubricator and wipe off all excess lubricant from the cable.

6. Install the speedometer cable into the speedometer gear housing at the front wheel.

7. Reconnect the upper end of the speedometer cable to the speedometer housing.

Steering Stem Lubrication

The retainer-type ball bearings used in the steering system should be removed, cleaned and lubricated with bearing grease as described in Chapter Ten.

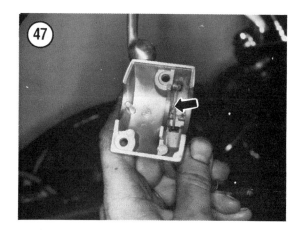

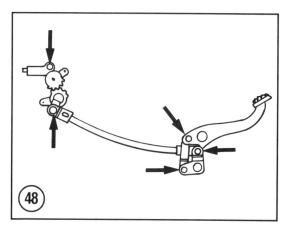

Miscellaneous Lubrication Points

Lubricate the clutch lever, front brake lever, sidestand pivot point and the footpeg pivot points. Use SAE 10W-40 engine oil.

PERIODIC MAINTENANCE

Disc Brake Fluid Level

The fluid level should be up between the upper and lower mark within the reservoir. If the brake fluid level reaches the lower level mark (**Figure 50**)

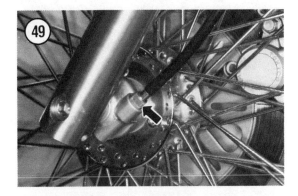

on the side of the master cylinder reservoir, the fluid level must be corrected by adding fresh brake fluid.

1. Place the bike on level ground and position the handlebars so the front master cylinder reservoir is in its normal riding position.

2. Clean the top of the master cylinder of all dirt and foreign matter.

3. Remove the screws securing the cover (**Figure 51**). Remove the cover and the diaphragm.

4. Add brake fluid until the level is to the upper level line within the master cylinder reservoir. Use fresh brake fluid from a sealed brake fluid container.

> *WARNING*
> *Use brake fluid from a sealed container clearly marked DOT 3 or DOT 4 only (specified for disc brakes). Others may vaporize and cause brake failure. Do not intermix different brands or types of brake fluid as they may not be compatible. Do not intermix a silicone based (DOT 5) brake fluid as it can cause brake component damage leading to brake system failure.*

> *CAUTION*
> *Be careful when handling brake fluid. Do not spill it on painted or plated surfaces or plastic parts as it will destroy the surface. Wash the area immediately with soapy water and thoroughly rinse it off.*

5. Reinstall the diaphragm and the top cover (**Figure 51**). Tighten the screws securely.

Front Disc Brake Line

Check hydraulic brake line (**Figure 52**) between the front master cylinder and the front brake caliper. If there is any leakage, tighten the connections and bleed the brakes as described under *Bleeding the System* in Chapter Twelve. If this does not stop the leak or if a brake line is obviously damaged, cracked or chafed, replace the brake line and bleed the system.

Clutch Fluid Level Check

The clutch is hydraulically operated and requires no routine adjustment.

The hydraulic fluid in the clutch master cylinder should be checked as listed in **Table 1** or whenever the level drops, whichever comes first. Bleeding the clutch system and servicing clutch components are covered in Chapter Five.

> *CAUTION*
> *If the clutch operates correctly when the engine is cold or in cool weather, but operates erratically (or not at all) after the engine warms-up or when riding in hot weather, there is air in the hydraulic line and the clutch system must be bled. Refer to **Bleeding the System** in Chapter Five.*

The fluid level in the reservoir should be up to the upper mark within the reservoir. This upper level mark is only visible when the master cylinder top cover is removed. If the fluid level reaches the lower level mark (**Figure 53**), visible through the viewing port in the master cylinder reservoir, the fluid level must be corrected by adding fresh hydraulic (brake) fluid.

1. Place the bike on level ground and position the handlebars so the master cylinder reservoir is in its normal riding position.

2. Clean any dirt from the area around the top cover prior to removing the cover.

3. Remove the screws securing the top cover and remove the top cover (**Figure 54**) and the diaphragm.

> *WARNING*
> *Use hydraulic fluid from a sealed container clearly marked DOT 3 or DOT 4 only. Do not intermix different brands or types of hydraulic fluid as they may not be compatible. Do not intermix a silicone based (DOT 5) hydraulic fluid as it can cause clutch component damage leading to clutch release system failure.*

> *CAUTION*
> *Be careful when handling hydraulic fluid. Do not spill it on painted or plated surfaces as it will destroy the surface. Wash the area immediately with soapy water and thoroughly rinse it off.*

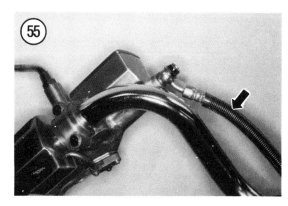

4. Add clutch fluid until the level is to the upper level line within the master cylinder body. Use fresh

hydraulic fluid from a sealed hydraulic fluid container.

5. Reinstall the diaphragm and the top cover (**Figure 54**). Tighten the screws securely.

Clutch Hydraulic Line

Check clutch line (**Figure 55**) between the master cylinder and the clutch slave cylinder. If there is any leakage, tighten the connections and bleed the clutch as described under *Bleeding the System* in Chapter

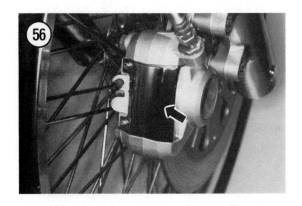

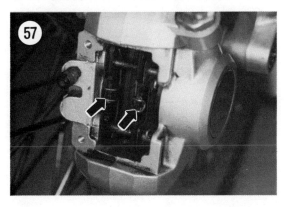

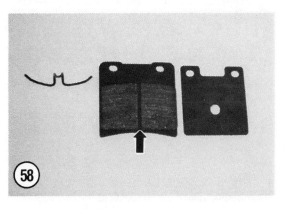

Five. If this does not stop the leak or if a clutch line is obviously damaged, cracked or chafed, replace the clutch line and bleed the system as described in Chapter Five.

Disc Brake Pad Wear

Inspect the brake pads for excessive or uneven wear, scoring and oil or grease on the friction surface.

1. Remove the dust cover (**Figure 56**) from the brake caliper.
2. Look into the caliper assembly (**Figure 57**) and check the wear lines on the brake pads.

> *NOTE*
> ***Figure 58*** *is shown with the brake pads removed from the caliper for clarity. The wear line is visible without removing the pads.*

3. Replace both pads if the wear line (**Figure 58**) on the pads reaches the brake disc.
4. If this condition exist, replace the pads as described in Chapter Twelve.

Disc Brake Fluid Change

Every time the reservoir cap is removed, a small amount of dirt and moisture enters the brake fluid. The same thing happens if a leak occurs or any part of the hydraulic system is loosened or disconnected. Dirt can clog the system and cause unnecessary wear. Water in the brake fluid vaporizes at high temperature, impairing the hydraulic action and reducing the brake's stopping ability.

To maintain peak performance, change the brake fluid as indicated in **Table 1**. To change brake fluid, follow the *Bleeding the System* procedure in Chapter Twelve. Continue adding new fluid to the master cylinder and bleeding out at the caliper until the fluid leaving the caliper is clean and free of contaminants.

> *WARNING*
> *Use brake fluid from a sealed container clearly marked DOT 3 or DOT 4 only (specified for disc brakes). Others may vaporize and cause brake failure. Do not intermix different brands or types of brake fluid as they may not be compatible. Do not intermix a silicone based (DOT 5) brake fluid as it can cause*

brake component damage leading to brake system failure.

Rear Drum Brake Lining Wear Indicator

The rear drum brake is equipped with a brake lining wear indicator. This enables you to check the brake lining condition without removing the rear wheel and brake assembly for inspection purposes.

1. Apply the rear brake fully.

2. Observe where the line on the brake camshaft (A, **Figure 59**) falls within the embossed wear range (B, **Figure 59**) on the brake panel.

3. If the lines falls within this range the brake lining thickness is within specification and do not require any service.

4. If the lines falls outside of this range (**Figure 60**) the brake linings are worn to the point that they require replacement.

5. If necessary, replace the rear brake linings as described under *Rear Drum Brake* in Chapter Twelve.

Rear Brake Pedal
Height and Freeplay Adjustment

The rear brake pedal height should be adjusted at the interval listed in **Table 1**. The pedal height will change with brake lining wear from use. The top of the brake pedal should be positioned above the top surface of the footpeg (**Figure 61**) 40 mm (1.6 in.). The pedal freeplay should be 20-30 mm (0.8-1.2 in.).

1. Make sure the brake pedal is in the at-rest position.

NOTE
Figure 62 is shown with the footpeg assembly removed from the frame for clarity. It is not necessary to remove the footpeg assembly to adjust the brake pedal.

2. To change height position, loosen the locknut (A, **Figure 62**) and turn the adjust bolt (B, **Figure 62**) until the correct height is achieved. Tighten the locknut (A) securely.

3. To change the freeplay adjustment, turn the adjust nut (**Figure 63**) at the end of the brake rod, or cable. Turn the adjust nut in either direction until the correct amount of freeplay is achieved.

Throttle Cable Adjustment

The throttle cable should have 0.5-1.0 mm (0.02-0.04 in.) of free play. If adjustment is necessary, perform the following.

1. At the throttle assembly end of the throttle cable, loosen the locknut (A, **Figure 64**) and turn the adjuster (B, **Figure 64**) in either direction until the correct amount of free play is achieved.

2. Tighten the locknut (A).

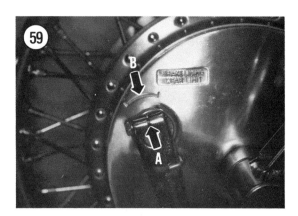

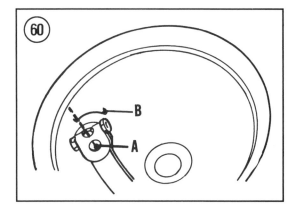

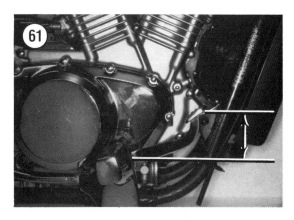

3. If the proper amount of adjustment cannot be achieved using this procedure, the cable has stretched to the point where it needs replacing. Refer to *Throttle Cable Replacement* in Chapter Seven.

4. Check the throttle cable from the throttle grip to the throttle cable joint above the front carburetor. Also check from the cable joint to each carburetor. Make sure they are not kinked or chafed. Replace as necessary.

5. Make sure the throttle grip rotates freely from a fully closed to fully open position. Check with the

(62)

(63)

(64)

handlebar at center, at full right and at full left. If necessary, remove the throttle grip and apply a lithium base grease to the rotating surfaces.

> *WARNING*
> *With the engine idling, move the handlebar from side to side.*

If idle speed increases during this movement, the throttle cable may need adjusting or may be incorrectly routed through the frame. Correct this problem immediately. Do **not** ride the bike in this unsafe condition.

Camshaft Chain Tensioner Adjustment

There is *no* provision for cam chain tensioner adjustment on this engine. Camshaft chain tension is maintained automatically.

Exhaust System

Check for leakage at all fittings. Tighten all bolts and nuts; replace any gaskets as necessary. Refer to *Exhaust System* in Chapter Seven.

Air Filter Elements

The front and rear air filter elements should be removed and cleaned at the interval listed in **Table 1**. Always replace both air filter elements at the same time and they should be replaced sooner if soiled, severely clogged or broken in any area.

The air filter element removes dust and abrasive particles from the air before the air enters each carburetor and the engine. Without the air filter, very fine particles could enter into the engine and cause rapid wear of the piston rings, cylinders and bearings and might clog small passages in the carburetors. Never run the bike without both air filter elements installed.

Proper air filter servicing can do more to ensure long service from your engine than almost any other single item.

The air filter elements are a dry-element type; no oiling is required.

Front Air Filter
Removal/Installation

Refer to **Figure 65** for this procedure:

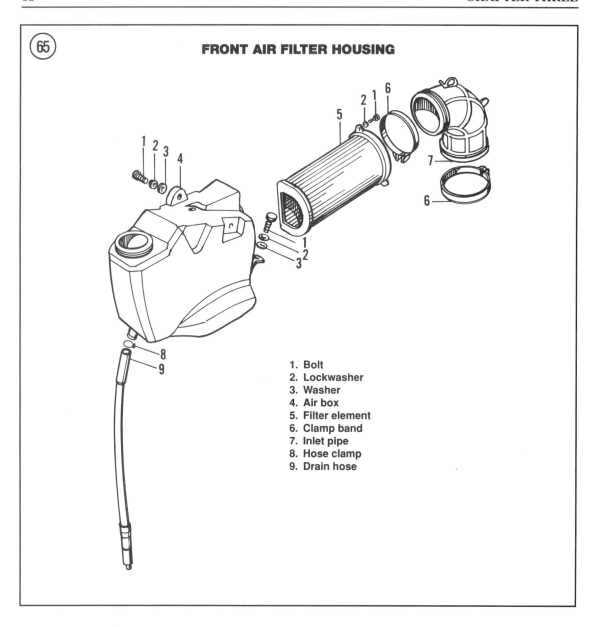

FRONT AIR FILTER HOUSING

1. Bolt
2. Lockwasher
3. Washer
4. Air box
5. Filter element
6. Clamp band
7. Inlet pipe
8. Hose clamp
9. Drain hose

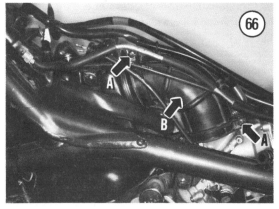

1. Remove the rider's seat as described under *Seat Removal/Installation* in Chapter Thirteen.

2. Remove the fuel tank as described in Chapter Seven.

3. Disconnect the battery negative (–) lead as described in this chapter.

4. Loosen the screws (A, **Figure 66**) on the clamping bands on each end of front air filter inlet pipe. Slide the clamping bands onto the inlet pipe.

5. Remove the cable bands from the inlet pipe and move the cables out of the way.

6. Remove the inlet pipe (B, **Figure 66**) from the front air filter element and the carburetor inlet. Remove the front inlet pipe.

7. Remove the 3 bolts securing the air filter element (**Figure 67**) to the air filter case and remove the element from the air box.

8. Inspect the element as described in this chapter.

9. Install the air filter element and make sure it is correctly seated into the air box so there is no air leak, then install the bolts. Tighten the screws securely.

10. Install all items removed.

Rear Air Filter Removal/Installation

Refer to **Figure 68** for this procedure:

1. Remove the rider's seat as described under *Seat Removal/Installation* in Chapter Thirteen.

2. Remove the fuel tank as described in Chapter Seven.

3. Disconnect the battery negative (–) lead as described in this chapter.

4. Remove the tiewrap bands from the inlet pipe and move the hose (A, **Figure 69**) out of the way.

5. Loosen the screws (B, **Figure 69**) on the clamping bands on each end of rear air filter inlet pipe. Slide the clamping bands onto the inlet pipe.

6. Remove the inlet pipe (C, **Figure 69**) from the rear air filter case and the carburetor inlet. Remove the rear inlet pipe.

7. Loosen the mounting bolts on the right-hand ignition coil (A, **Figure 70**) and move the coil toward the outside.

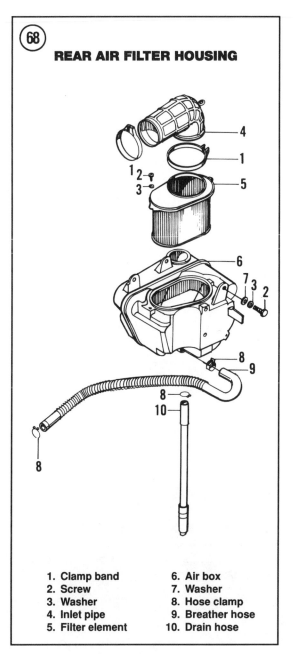

REAR AIR FILTER HOUSING

1. Clamp band	6. Air box
2. Screw	7. Washer
3. Washer	8. Hose clamp
4. Inlet pipe	9. Breather hose
5. Filter element	10. Drain hose

8. Remove the screws securing the air filter element (B, **Figure 70**) to the air filter case and remove the element from the case.

9. Inspect the element as described in this chapter.

10. Install the air filter element and make sure it is correctly seated into the air box so there is no air leak, then install the screws. Tighten the screws securely.

11. Install all items removed.

**Inspection
(Front and Rear)**

1. Wipe out the interior of both air boxes with a shop rag dampened with cleaning solvent. Remove any foreign matter that may have passed through a broken element.

2. Gently tap the air filter element to loosen the dust.

> *CAUTION*
> *In the next step, do not direct compressed air toward the outside surface of the element. If air pressure is directed to the outside surface it will force the dirt and dust into the pores of the element thus restricting air flow. Also use low pressure, if high pressure is used a good element may be damaged.*

3. Gently apply *low* compressed air toward the *inside surface* of the element (**Figure 71**) to remove all loosened dirt and dust from the element.

4. Inspect the element (**Figure 72**); if it is torn or damaged in any area it must be replaced. Do not *run* the bike with a damaged element as it may allow dirt to enter the engine. Also if the filter is severely soiled, replace it with a new one.

5. Make sure the foam gasket (**Figure 73**) is in place and is not broken or damaged. This gasket cannot be replaced separately, if damaged; replace the air filter element.

Fuel Line Inspection

Inspect the fuel line from the fuel shutoff valve to the carburetors (**Figure 74**) and the fuel lines attached to the fuel pump (**Figure 75**). If any are cracked or starting to deterioration they must be replaced. Make sure the hose clamps are in place and holding securely.

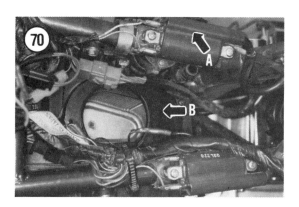

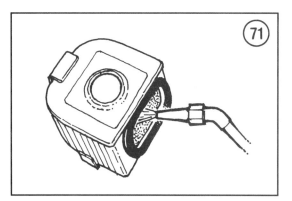

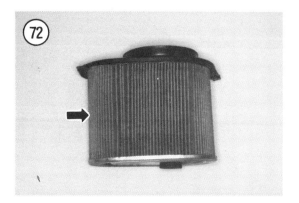

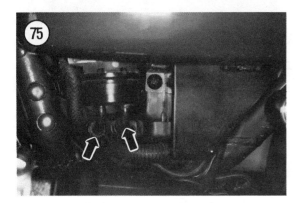

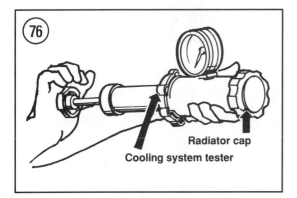

Radiator cap
Cooling system tester

3

Vacuum Line Inspection

Inspect the condition of all vacuum lines for cracks or deterioration; replace if necessary. Make sure the hose clamps are in place and holding securely.

Cooling System Inspection

At the interval indicated in **Table 1**, the following items should be checked. If you do not have the test equipment, the tests can be done by a Suzuki dealer, automobile dealer, radiator shop or service station.

1. Have the radiator cap pressure tested (**Figure 76**). The specified radiator cap relief pressure is 75-105 kPa (10.7-14.9 psi). The cap must be able to sustain this pressure for a minimum of 10 seconds. Replace the radiator cap if it does not hold pressure or if the relief pressure is too high or too low.

CAUTION
Do not exceed the indicated test pressure. If test pressure exceeds the specifications the radiator may be damaged.

2. Leave the radiator cap off and have the entire cooling system pressure tested. The entire cooling system should be pressurized up to, but not exceeding, 100 kPa (14.2 psi). The system must be able to sustain this pressure for 10 seconds. Replace or repair any components that fail this test.

3. Test the specific gravity of the coolant with an anti-freeze tester to ensure adequate temperature and corrosion protection. The system must have at least a 50:50 mixture of anti-freeze and distilled water. Never let the mixture become less than 40% anti-freeze or corrosion protection will be impaired.

4. Check all cooling system hoses for damage or deterioration. Refer to **Figure 77**, **Figure 78** and **Figure 79**. Replace any hose that is questionable. Make sure all hose clamps are tight.

5. Carefully clean any road dirt, bugs, mud, etc. from the front surface of the radiator core (A, **Figure 80**). Use a whisk broom, compressed air or low-pres-

sure water. If the radiator has been hit by a small rock
or other item, carefully straighten out the fins with a
screwdriver.

> *NOTE*
> *If the radiator has been damaged*
> *across approximately 20% or more of*
> *the frontal area, the radiator should*
> *be re-cored or replaced as described*
> *under **Radiator Removal/Installation***
> *in Chapter Nine.*

Coolant Change

The cooling system should be completely drained
and refilled at the interval indicated in **Table 1**.

It is sometimes necessary to remove the radiator
or drain the coolant from the system on order to
perform a service procedure on some parts of the
bike. If the coolant is still in good condition (not time
to replace the coolant), the coolant can be reused if
it is kept clean. Drain the coolant into a clean drain
pan and pour it into a clean sealable container like a
plastic milk or bleach bottle. This coolant can then
be reused if it is still clean.

> *CAUTION*
> *Antifreeze is poisonous and may at-*
> *tract animals. Do not leave the*
> *drained coolant where it is accessible*
> *to children or animals.*

> *CAUTION*
> *Use only a high quality ethylene glycol*
> *anti-freeze specifically labeled for use*
> *with aluminum engines. Do not use an*
> *alcohol-based anti-freeze.*

In areas where freezing temperatures occur, add a
higher percentage of anti-freeze to protect the system to temperatures far below those likely to occur.
Table 4 lists the recommended amount of anti-freeze
for protection at various ambient temperatures.

The following procedure must be performed when
the engine is cool.

> *CAUTION*
> *Be careful not to spill anti-freeze on*
> *painted surfaces as it will destroy the*
> *surface. Wash immediately with*
> *soapy water and rinse thoroughly*
> *with clean water.*

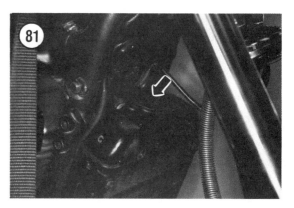

1. Place the bike on the sidestand.

2. Remove the screws securing the radiator cover (B, **Figure 80**) and remove the cover.

3. Remove the radiator cap (**Figure 81**). This will speed up the draining process.

4. Place a drain pan under left-hand frame rail below the water pump cover. Remove the drain bolt (**Figure 82**).

5. Remove the air bleeder bolt (**Figure 83**) on the left-hand upper frame rail. This will allow additional

air into the system to aid in the complete draining of the coolant.

6. Do not install the drain bolt or air bleeder bolts yet.

7. Take the bike off the sidestand and tip the bike from side to side to drain any residual coolant from the cooling system. Place the bike back onto the sidestand.

8. Install the air bleeder bolt and tighten securely. Do not over tighten as this bolt will be loosened later in the procedure.

9. If the drained coolant was contaminated or very dirty; flush the cooling system with freshwater. Allow the water to run through the cooling system for approximately 5 minutes. Shut off the water and allow the water to drain out.

10. Take the bike off the sidestand and tip the bike from side to side to drain all residual water from the cooling system. Place the bike back onto the sidestand.

11. Install the drain bolt and washer to the frame rail and tighten securely.

NOTE
An anti-leak solution is added at the factory to the cooling system to help prevent possible leakage. Suzuki recommends adding 2 packs of Bar's Leak anti-leakage material, or equivalent, to the coolant solution at every coolant change.

12. Refill the cooling system as follows:

   a. Loosen the air bleeder bolt (**Figure 83**) on the left-hand upper frame rail

   b. Insert a small funnel (**Figure 84**) into the radiator filler neck.

CAUTION
*Do not use a higher percentage of coolant-to-water than recommended for the ambient temperature. A higher concentration of coolant (60% or greater) will actually **decrease** the performance of the cooling system.*

   c. Add a 50:50 mixture of distilled water and antifreeze into the radiator to bring the level to the cap inlet fitting on the radiator upper tank.

   d. Tighten the air bleeder bolt securely.

   e. Do not install the radiator cap at this time.

f. Lean the bike from side to side to bleed out as much air from the system as possible.

13. Start the engine and let it run at idle speed until the engine reaches normal operating temperature. Make sure there are no air bubbles in the coolant and that the coolant level stabilizes at the correct level. Add coolant as necessary.

14. Shut off the engine.

15. Install the radiator cap and turn it *clockwise* until it is on securely and will turn no farther.

16. Test ride the bike and readjust the coolant level if necessary after the cooling system has cooled down.

17. Install the radiator cover.

Crankcase Breather
(U.S. Only)

Inspect the breather hose from the cylinder head cover breather cover to the air filter air case. If it is cracked or starting to deteriorate it must be replaced. Make sure the hose clamps are in place and holding securely.

Evaporative Emission Control System
(California Models Only)

Fuel vapor from the fuel tank is routed into a charcoal canister when the engine is stopped. When the engine is started these vapors are drawn, through the vacuum controlled valves, into the carburetors and into the engine to be burned. Make sure all vacuum hoses are correctly routed and attached. Inspect the hoses and replace any if necessary.

Refer to Chapter Seven for detailed information on the *Evaporative Emission Control System* and for vacuum hose routing.

Wheel Bearings

There is no factory-recommended mileage interval for cleaning and repacking the wheel bearings. They should be inspected and serviced, if necessary, every time the wheel is removed or whenever there is a likelihood of water contamination. The correct service procedure are covered in Chapter Ten and Chapter Eleven.

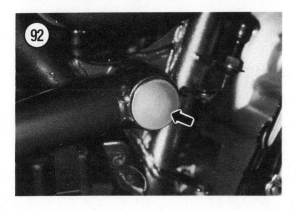

Front Suspension Check

1. Apply the front brake and pump the forks up and down as vigorously as possible. Check for smooth operation and check for any fork oil leaks around the oil seal area on each fork leg.

2. Make sure the fork cap bolt (**Figure 85**) and the lower fork bridge bolt (**Figure 86**) are tight on both fork assemblies.

3. Remove the trim caps (**Figure 87**) and make sure the bolts securing the handlebar holders to the upper fork bridge are tight.

4. On 1992-on models, make sure the screws securing the handlebar balancer weight end caps are tight and secure.

5. On 1987-on models, remove the front axle trim cap (**Figure 88**) from each fork leg.

6. On 1985 and 1986 models, remove the cotter pin and check the tightness of the front axle nut on the right-hand side.

7. Make sure the front axle pinch bolt (**Figure 89**) and front axle (**Figure 90**) are tight.

CAUTION
If any of the previously mentioned bolts and nuts are loose, refer to Chapter Nine for correct procedures and torque specifications.

8. On 1985 and 1986 models, install a new cotter pin through the axle nut and bend the ends over completely.

Rear Suspension Check

1. Place a wood block(s) under the engine to support the bike securely with the rear wheel off the ground.

2. Push hard on the rear wheel (sideways) to check for side play in the rear swing arm bearings. Remove the wood block(s).

3. Remove the trim cap from the upper bolt, then check the tightness of the shock absorber's upper and lower mounting bolts and nuts (**Figure 91**).

4. On the right-hand side, remove the trim cap (**Figure 92**) covering the swing arm pivot bolt nut.

5. Make sure the nut (**Figure 93**) on the swing arm pivot bolt is tight.

6. On the right-hand side, remove the trim cap (**Figure 94**) covering the rear axle bolt nut.

7. Make sure the nut (**Figure 95**) on the rear axle bolt is tight.

8. Make sure the 3 nuts (**Figure 96**) securing the final drive unit to the swing arm are tight. Only 2 of the nuts are visible, be sure to check all 3 nuts for tightness.

9. Remove the rubber cap (**Figure 97**) from the rear brake torque arm nut.

10. Remove the cotter pin and check the tightness of the rear brake torque arm nut (**Figure 98**). Reinstall the cotter pin.

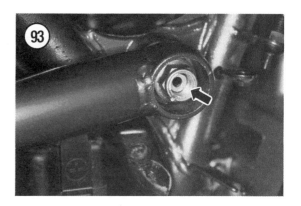

> *CAUTION*
> *If any of the previously mentioned bolts and nuts are loose, refer to Chapter Ten for correct procedures and torque specifications.*

11. Install all trim caps removed.

Nuts, Bolts and Other Fasteners

Constant vibration can loosen many of the fasteners on the motorcycle. Check the tightness of all fasteners, especially those on:

    a. Engine mounting hardware.
    b. Engine crankcase covers.
    c. Handlebar and front forks.
    d. Gearshift lever.
    e. Brake pedal and lever.
    f. Final drive unit nuts.
    g. Exhaust system.
    h. Lighting equipment.

Steering Head Adjustment Check

Check the steering head bearings for looseness at the interval listed in **Table 1**.

1. Place wood block(s) under the engine to support the bike securely with the front wheel off the ground.

2. Hold onto the front fork tube and gently rock the fork assembly back and forth. If you feel looseness, refer to Chapter Ten.

TUNE-UP

Perform a complete tune-up at the interval listed in **Table 1** of normal riding. More frequent tune-ups may be required if the bike is ridden in stop-and-go traffic. The purpose of the tune-up is to restore the

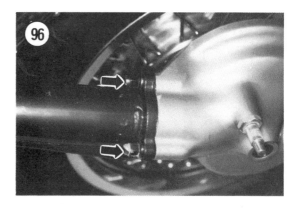

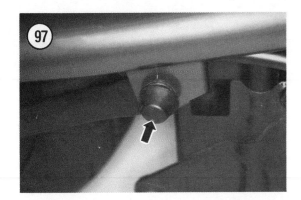

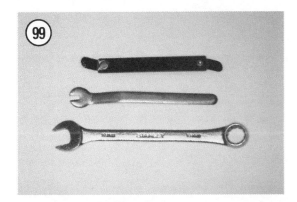

performance lost due to normal wear and deterioration of parts.

The spark plugs should be routinely replaced at every other tune-up or if the electrodes show signs of erosion. In addition, this is a good time to clean the air filter elements. Have all known new parts on hand before you begin.

Because the different systems in an engine interact, the procedures should be done in the following order:

a. Adjust valve clearances.

b. Run a compression test.

c. Change spark plugs.

c. Synchronize the carburetors.

d. Set the idle speed.

Table 6 summarizes tune-up specifications.

To perform a tune-up on your Suzuki, you will need the following tools and equipment:

a. 18 mm (5/8 in.) spark plug wrench.

b. Socket wrench and assorted sockets.

c. Flat feeler gauge and valve adjuster wrenches (**Figure 99**).

d. Compression gauge.

e. Spark plug wire feeler gauge and gapper tool.

f. Carburetor synchronization tool—to measure manifold vacuum.

Valve Clearance Measurement and Adjustment

The correct valve clearance for all models is listed in **Table 6**. The exhaust valves are located at opposite ends of the engine adjacent to the exhaust pipes and the intake valves are located at the center V-portion of the engine adjacent to the carburetors. There are 2 intake valves and 2 exhaust valves per cylinder.

The valves in the rear cylinder are to be adjusted first and then the valves in the front cylinder.

NOTE
This procedure must be performed with the engine cool, at room temperature (below 35° C [95° F]).

1. Remove the carburetor from the front cylinder head as described in Chapter Seven. Perform only the steps necessary to move the front carburetor away from the front cylinder head in order to gain access to the intake valve inspection cap on the front cylinder head.

2. Place a clean shop cloth into the front cylinder's intake pipe (**Figure 100**) to prevent the entry of foreign matter.

3. Remove both spark plugs as described in this chapter. This will make it easier to rotate the engine.

4. Remove the bolts securing the cylinder head side cover (**Figure 101**). Remove all 4 side covers and the cushions from the spark plug side.

> *NOTE*
> *Either use a wide flat-tipped screw-driver or a special tool made by Suzuki. This special tool (**Figure 102**) is made specifically for this purpose and if carefully used, will not mar nor damage the surface on the rotor bolt cover.*

5. On the alternator cover, remove the timing inspection hole cap (A, **Figure 103**) and the rotor bolt cover (B, **Figure 103**).

> *NOTE*
> *The following steps are shown with the engine removed from the frame for clarity. It is not necessary to remove the engine to adjust the valves.*

> *NOTE*
> *Prior to removing the valve adjuster covers, mark each with the cylinder letter "F" (front) or "R" (rear) and front and rear location on the cylinder head so they will be reinstalled in the correct location.*

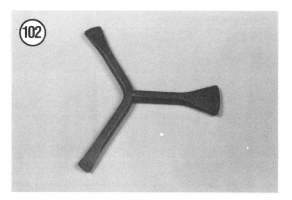

6. Remove the bolts securing both valve adjuster covers (**Figure 104**) on the cylinder head. Remove both covers on each cylinder head.

> *NOTE*
> *A cylinder at TDC will have free play in **both** sets of intake and exhaust valve rocker arms indicating that all of the valves are closed.*

7. Use a socket and wrench on the alternator rotor bolt. Rotate the engine clockwise, as viewed from the left-hand side, until the rear cylinder is at top dead center (TDC) on the compression stroke. Align the "R/F T" mark with the center of the inspection hole in the alternator rotor (**Figure 105**).

8. With the "R/F T" mark aligned with the center of the inspection hole in the alternator rotor, jiggle both rocker arms and make sure both have free play. If one of rocker arms (either intake or exhaust) is still under tension, rotate the engine an additional 360° until both rocker arms have free play.

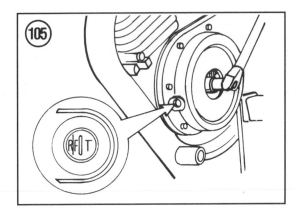

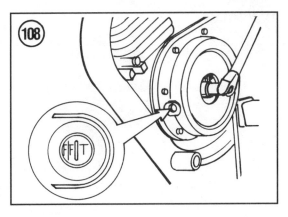

9. Again check that the "R/F T" mark is still aligned with the center of the inspection hole in the alternator rotor (**Figure 105**).

10. With the engine in this position, check the clearance of the intake and exhaust valves. The clearance measurement for both the intake and exhaust valves are the same.

11. Check the clearance by inserting a flat feeler gauge between the adjusting screw and each valve stem (**Figure 106**). When the clearance is correct, there will be a slight drag on the feeler gauge when it is inserted and withdrawn.

12. To correct the clearance, perform the following:

   a. Loosen the adjuster 10 mm locknut (A, **Figure 107**) on one of the intake valve adjusters.

   b. Screw the adjuster (B, **Figure 107**) in or out so there is a slight resistance felt on the feeler gauge (C, **Figure 107**).

   c. Hold the adjuster to prevent it from turning further and tighten the locknut securely.

   d. Recheck the clearance to make sure the adjuster did not turn after the correct clearance was achieved. Readjust if necessary.

CAUTION
Adjust both the right- and left-hand valve clearance as close to each other as possible.

   e. Repeat this step for the adjuster of the other intake valve.

13. Repeat Step 12 for the exhaust valves.

14. Use a socket and wrench on the alternator rotor bolt. Rotate the engine clockwise, as viewed from the left-hand side 450° (1 1/4 turns), until the front cylinder is at top dead center (TDC) on the compression stroke. Align the "F/F T" mark with the center of the inspection hole in the alternator rotor (**Figure 108**).

15. With the "F/F T" mark aligned with the center of the inspection hole in the alternator rotor, jiggle both rocker arms and make sure all 4 have free play. If one of the rocker arms (either intake or exhaust) is still under tension, rotate the engine an additional 360° until both rocker arms have free play.

16. Again check that the "F/F T" mark is still aligned with the center of the inspection hole in the alternator rotor (**Figure 108**).

17. Repeat Steps 10-13 for the intake and exhaust valves on the front cylinder.

18. Rotate the engine several complete revolutions and recheck the valve clearances. Readjust if necessary.

19. Inspect the O-ring seal (**Figure 109**) on the valve adjuster covers, replace if necessary. Install the covers in the correct location and tighten the bolts securely.

20. Inspect the seal on the timing inspection hole cap (A, **Figure 110**) and the rotor bolt cover (B, **Figure 110**) for wear or damage. Replace as necessary. Install the cap and cover and tighten securely.

21. On the spark plug side of the cylinder head, install the cushion (**Figure 111**) on the cylinder head prior to installing the cylinder head side cover.

22. Install the cylinder head side cover (**Figure 101**) and bolts. Tighten the bolts, on the side opposite the spark plug, to the torque specification listed in **Table 5**. Tighten the bolts on the other side securely.

23. Install the spark plug and reconnect the spark plug lead.

24. Remove the clean shop cloth from the front cylinder's intake pipe.

25. Install the front cylinder's carburetor as described in Chapter Seven.

Compression Test

Check the cylinder compression at the interval indicated in **Table 1**. Record the results and compare them to the results at the next interval. A running record will show trends in deterioration so that corrective action can be taken before complete failure.

The results when properly interpreted, can indicate general cylinder, piston ring and valve condition.

1. Warm the engine to normal operating temperature, then shut it off. Make sure the choke valves are completely open.

2. Remove both spark plugs as described in this chapter.

3. Connect the compression tester to one cylinder following the manufacturer's instructions.

4. Crank the engine over until there is no further rise in pressure.

5. Remove the tester and record the reading. Repeat for the other cylinder.

6. When interpreting the results, actual readings are not as important as the difference between the read-

ings. The recommended cylinder compression pressure and the maximum allowable difference between cylinders are listed in **Table 6**. Greater differences than that listed in **Table 6** indicate broken rings, leaky or sticking valves, a blown head gasket or a combination of all.

If the compression readings between the cylinders differ less than 10 psi, the rings and valves are in good condition.

If a low reading (10% or more) is obtained it indicates valve or ring trouble. To determine which, pour about a teaspoon of engine oil through the spark plug hole onto the top of the piston. Turn the engine over once to clear the oil, then take another compression test and record the reading. If the compression returns to normal, the valves are good but the rings are defective. If the compression does not increase, the valves require servicing. A valve(s) could be hanging open but not burned or a piece of carbon could be on a valve seat.

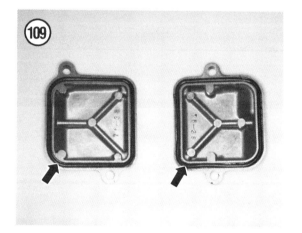

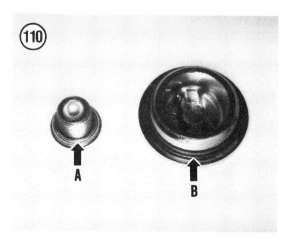

Spark Plug Selection

Select plugs in a heat range designed for the loads and temperature conditions under which the engine will operate. Using incorrect heat ranges, however, can cause piston seizure, scored cylinder walls or damaged piston crowns.

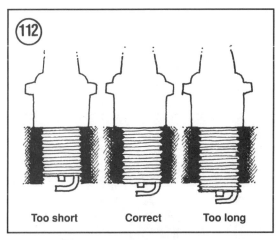

Too short   Correct   Too long

In general, use a hotter plug for low speeds, low loads and low temperatures. Use a colder plug for high speeds, high engine loads and high temperatures.

> *NOTE*
> *In areas where seasonal temperature variations are great, the factory recommended "two-plug system"—a cold plug for hard summer riding and a hot plug for slower winter operation—may prevent spark plug and engine problems. The plug should operate hot enough to burn off unwanted deposits, but not so hot that it is damaged or causes preignition.*

A spark plug of the correct heat range will show a light tan color on the portion of the insulator within the cylinder after the plug has been in service.

The reach (length) of a plug is also important (**Figure 112**). A longer than normal plug could interfere with the valves and pistons, causing permanent and severe damage. The recommended spark plugs are listed in **Table 6**.

Spark Plug Removal/Cleaning

1. Grasp each spark plug lead (**Figure 113**) and carefully pull it off the plug. If the boot is stuck to the plug, twist it slightly to break it loose.

> *CAUTION*
> *If any dirt falls into the cylinder when the plugs are removed, it could cause serious engine damage.*

2. Use compressed air and blow away any dirt that may have passed by the rubber boot on the spark plug lead and accumulated in the spark plug well.
3. Remove spark plugs with an 18 mm spark plug wrench. Keep the spark plugs in the order that they were removed. If anything turns up during the inspection step, you will then know which cylinder it came from.

> *NOTE*
> *If plugs are difficult to remove, apply penetrating oil around base of plugs and let it soak in about 10-20 minutes.*

4. Inspect the spark plug carefully. Look for a plug with broken center porcelain, excessively eroded

electrodes and excessive carbon or oil fouling. Replace such a plug. If deposits are light, the plug may be cleaned in solvent with a wire brush or in a special spark plug sandblast cleaner. Regap the plug as explained in this chapter.

NOTE
Spark plug cleaning with the use of a sand-blast type device is not recommended. While this type of cleaning is thorough, the plug must be perfectly free of all abrasive cleaning material when done. If not, it is possible for the cleaning material to fall into the engine during operation and cause damage.

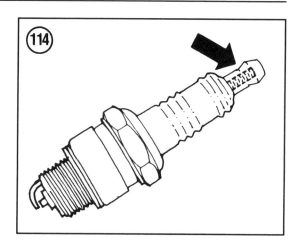

Spark Plug Gapping and Installation

A new plug should be carefully gapped to ensure a reliable, consistent spark. You must use a special spark plug gapping tool with a wire feeler gauge.

1. Remove the new plug from the box. Do not *screw* on the small piece (**Figure 114**) that is sometimes loose in the box, they are not to be used.

2. Insert a wire feeler gauge between the center and each side electrode of each plug (**Figure 115**). The correct gap is listed in **Table 6**. If the gap is correct, you will feel a slight drag as you pull the feeler gauge through. If there is no drag or the gauge won't pass through, bend the side electrode(s) with the gapping tool (**Figure 116**) to set the proper gap.

3. Put a *small* drop of oil or aluminum anti-seize compound on the threads of the spark plug.

4. Screw each spark plug in by hand until it seats. Very little effort is required. If force is necessary, you have the plug cross-threaded; unscrew it and try again.

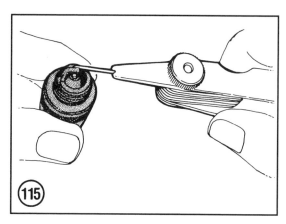

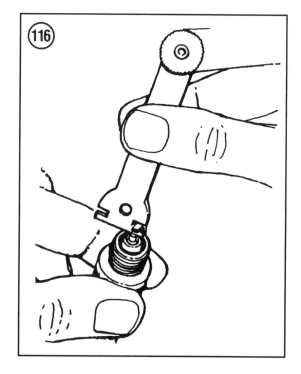

NOTE
If a spark plug is difficult to install, the cylinder head threads may be dirty or slightly damaged. To clean the threads, apply grease to the threads of a spark plug tap and screw it carefully into the cylinder head. Turn the tap slowly until it is completely installed. If the tap cannot be installed, the threads are severely damaged and must be repaired.

5. Tighten the spark plugs an additional 1/2 turn after the gasket has made contact with the head. If you are reinstalling old, regapped plugs and are reusing the old gasket, only tighten an additional 1/4 turn.

CAUTION
Do not over tighten. Besides making the plug difficult to remove, the excessive torque will squash the gasket and destroy its sealing ability.

6. Install the spark plug leads; make sure the leads are on tight.

Reading Spark Plugs

Much information about engine and spark plug performance can be determined by careful examination of the spark plugs. This information is only valid after performing the following steps.

1. Ride the bike a short distance at full throttle in any gear.

2. Move the engine stop switch (**Figure 117**) to the OFF position before closing the throttle and simultaneously pull in the clutch or shift to NEUTRAL; coast and brake to a stop.

3. Remove one spark plug at a time and examine it. Compare it to **Figure 118**. If the insulator is white or burned, the plug is too hot and should be replaced with a colder one.

A too-cold plug will have sooty or oily deposits ranging in color from dark brown to black. Replace with a hotter plug and check for too-rich carburetion or evidence of oil blowby at the piston rings.

If the plug has a light tan or gray colored deposit and no abnormal gap wear or electrode erosion is evident, the plug and the engine are running properly.

If the plug exhibits a black insulator tip, a damp and oily film over the firing end and a carbon layer over the entire nose, it is oil fouled. An oil fouled plug can be cleaned, but it is better to replace it.

4. Repeat for the other park plug. Replace as a pair if either spark plug is bad.

Carburetor Idle Speed Adjustment

Prior to making this adjustment, the air filter elements must be clean and the engine must have adequate compression. See *Compression Test* in this chapter. Otherwise this procedure cannot be done properly.

1. Start the engine and let reach normal operating temperature. Make sure the choke knob is in the open position, pushed in all the way (**Figure 119**).

2. Connect a portable tachometer following the manufacturer's instructions.

3. On the rear carburetor, turn the idle adjust knob (**Figure 120**) in or out to adjust idle speed.

4. The correct idle speed is listed in **Table 6**.

5. Open and close the throttle a couple of times; check for variations in idle speed. Readjust if necessary.

WARNING
*With the engine running at idle speed, move the handlebar from side to side. If the idle speed increases during this movement, the throttle cable may need adjusting or it may be incorrectly routed through the frame. Correct this problem immediately. Do **not** ride the bike in this unsafe condition.*

Carburetor Idle Mixture

The idle mixture (pilot screw) is preset at the factory and *is not to be reset*. Do not adjust the pilot screw unless the carburetors have been overhauled. If so, refer to Chapter Seven for service procedures.

Carburetor Cable Synchronization

Synchronizing the carburetor cables makes sure that one cylinder doesn't try to run faster than the other, cutting power and gas mileage. The only accurate way to synchronize the carburetors is to use a set of vacuum gauges that measure the intake vacuum of both cylinders at the same time.

Refer to **Figure 121** for this procedure.

SPARK PLUG CONDITION

NORMAL

- Identified by light tan or gray deposits on the firing tip.
- Can be cleaned.

GAP BRIDGED

- Identified by deposit buildup closing gap between electrodes.
- Caused by oil or carbon fouling. If deposits are not excessive, the plug can be cleaned.

OIL FOULED

- Identified by wet black deposits on the insulator shell bore and electrodes.
- Caused by excessive oil entering combustion chamber through worn rings and pistons, excessive clearance between valve guides and stems or worn or loose bearings. Can be cleaned. If engine is not repaired, use a hotter plug.

CARBON FOULED

- Identified by black, dry fluffy carbon deposits on insulator tips, exposed shell surfaces and electrodes.
- Caused by too cold a plug, weak ignition, dirty air cleaner, too rich a fuel mixture or excessive idling. Can be cleaned.

LEAD FOULED

- Identified by dark gray, black, yellow or tan deposits or a fused glazed coating on the insulator tip.
- Caused by highly leaded gasoline. Can be cleaned.

WORN

- Identified by severely eroded or worn electrodes.
- Caused by normal wear. Should be replaced.

FUSED SPOT DEPOSIT

- Identified by melted or spotty deposits resembling bubbles or blisters.
- Caused by sudden acceleration. Can be cleaned.

OVERHEATING

- Identified by a white or light gray insulator with small black or gray brown spots and with bluish-burnt appearance of electrodes.
- Caused by engine overheating, wrong type of fuel, loose spark plugs, too hot a plug or incorrect ignition timing. Replace the plug.

PREIGNITION

- Identified by melted electrodes and possibly blistered insulator. Metallic deposits on insulator indicate engine damage.
- Caused by wrong type of fuel, incorrect ignition timing or advance, too hot a plug, burned valves or engine overheating. Replace the plug.

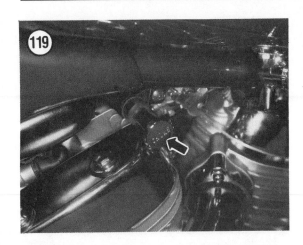

3

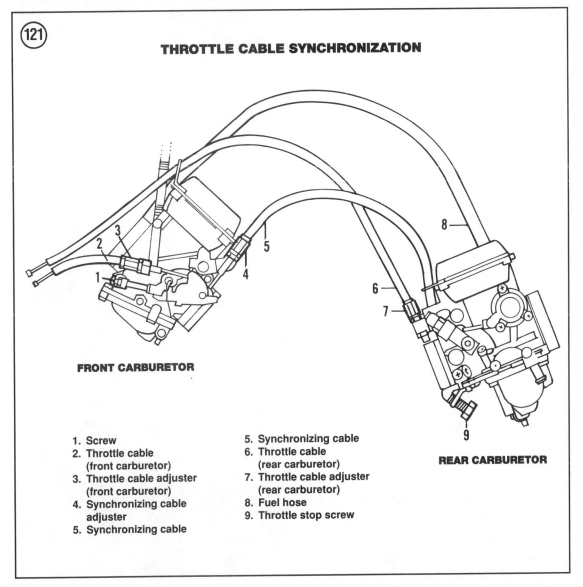

THROTTLE CABLE SYNCHRONIZATION

FRONT CARBURETOR

REAR CARBURETOR

1. Screw
2. Throttle cable
   (front carburetor)
3. Throttle cable adjuster
   (front carburetor)
4. Synchronizing cable
   adjuster
5. Synchronizing cable

5. Synchronizing cable
6. Throttle cable
   (rear carburetor)
7. Throttle cable adjuster
   (rear carburetor)
8. Fuel hose
9. Throttle stop screw

These 2 separate procedures relate to the synchronization of the carburetors after the synchronizing cable (5) has been removed or is incorrectly adjusted-adjusted or when the front throttle cable (2) and/or rear throttle cable (6) have been replaced.

NOTE
Prior to synchronizing the carburetors, the air filters must be clean and the valve clearance properly adjusted.

Synchronizing cable balancing

1. Warm the engine to normal operating temperature.
2. Check and if necessary, adjust the idle speed as described in this chapter. Shut off the engine.
3. Remove the fuel tank as described under *Fuel Tank Removal/Installation* in Chapter Seven.
4. Install an auxiliary fuel tank onto the motorcycle and attach its fuel hose the hose leading to the fuel pump.

NOTE
Carburetor synchronization ***cannot*** *be performed with the stock fuel tank in place because of the lack of room required to install the gauges and make adjustments. An auxiliary fuel tank is required to supply fuel to the carburetors during this procedure.*

NOTE
A fuel tank from small displacement motorcycle, ATV or a lawn mower makes an excellent auxiliary fuel tank. Make sure the tank is mounted securely and positioned so that connecting fuel hose is not kinked or obstructed.

WARNING
When supplying fuel by temporary means, make sure the auxiliary fuel tank is secure and that all fuel lines are tight—no leaks.

5. Remove both vacuum port screws. Refer to **Figure 122** for the front carburetor and **Figure 123** for the rear carburetor.

NOTE
Figure 123 *is shown with the carburetors removed from the engine for clarity.*

Do not remove the carburetors to remove these screws.

6. Connect the vacuum lines from the carb-synch tool to the carburetor vacuum ports, following the manufacturer's instructions. Be sure to route the vacuum lines to the correct cylinder. Balance the carb-synch tool at 1,000 rpm prior to starting this test following the manufacturer's instructions.

7. Start the engine and set the idle speed to 1,000 rpm.

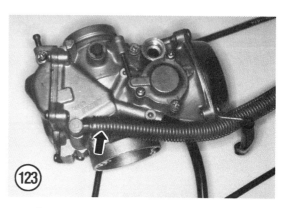

8. Check the gauge readings. If the difference in gauge readings is 10 mm Hg (0.4 in. Hg) or less between the 2 cylinders, the carburetors are considered synchronized.

9. If the carburetors are not synchronized, proceed as follows:

  a. With the engine at idle speed of 1,000 rpm, loosen the locknut and turn the synchronizing cable adjuster (4, **Figure 121**) and the throttle stop screw (9, **Figure 121**) to synchronize the front-to-rear carburetors.

NOTE
To gain the utmost in performance and efficiency from the engine, adjust the carburetors so that the gauge readings are as close to each other as possible.

  b. After the carburetors are balanced, tighten the locknut on the synchronizing cable adjuster.

  c. Reset the idle speed as listed in **Table 6** and shut off the engine.

10. Disconnect the carb-synch tool vacuum lines from the carburetors.

NOTE
Make sure the vacuum port screws are tight to prevent a vacuum leak.

11. Install the vacuum port screws. Refer to **Figure 122** for the front carburetor and **Figure 123** for the rear carburetor.

12. Disconnect the auxiliary fuel tank and install the standard fuel tank.

Throttle cable balancing

1. Perform Steps 1-5 of *Synchronizing Cable Balancing* in the pervious procedure.

2. Remove the bolts securing the fuel tank mounting bracket (**Figure 124**) and remove the bracket.

3. Remove the screw (**Figure 125**) securing the throttle cable joint to the air filter housing and remove the joint from the clip on the air filter housing.

4. Separate the throttle cable joint (**Figure 126**).

5. At the carburetors, loosen locknut on the front carburetor throttle cable (3, **Figure 121**) and the locknut on the rear carburetor throttle cable (7, **Figure 121**).

6. At the carburetors, turn the throttle cable adjuster (3, **Figure 121**) on the front carburetor and the throttle cable adjuster (7, **Figure 121**) on the rear carburetor until the throttle cable ends protrude from the throttle cable joint (**Figure 127**) the exact same amount.

7. Tighten both throttle cable locknuts securely and reconnect the throttle cable joint.

8. Install the throttle cable joint into the clip on the air filter housing and install the screw. Tighten the screw securely.

9. Install the fuel tank mounting bracket and bolts. Tighten the bolts securely.

10. Connect the vacuum lines from the carb-synch tool to the vacuum ports, following the manufacturer's instructions. Be sure to route the vacuum lines to the correct cylinder. Balance the carb-synch tool at 2,000 rpm prior to starting this test following the manufacturer's instructions.

11. Start the engine and increase the engine speed to 2,000 rpm.

12. Check the gauge readings. If the difference in gauge readings is 10 mm Hg (0.4 in. Hg) or less between the 2 cylinders, the carburetors are considered synchronized.

13. If the carburetors are not synchronized, proceed as follows:

a. With the engine running at of 2,000 rpm, loosen the locknut and turn the front carburetor throttle cable adjuster (3, **Figure 121**) to synchronize the front-to-rear carburetors.

NOTE
To gain the utmost in performance and efficiency from the engine, adjust the carburetors so that the gauge readings are as close to each other as possible.

b. After the carburetors are balanced, tighten the locknut on the front carburetor throttle cable adjuster.

c. Reset the idle speed as listed in **Table 5** and shut off the engine.

14. Disconnect the carb-synch tool vacuum lines from the carburetors.

NOTE
Make sure the vacuum port screws are tight to prevent a vacuum leak.

15. Install the vacuum port screws. Refer to **Figure 122** for the front carburetor and **Figure 123** for the rear carburetor.

16. Disconnect the auxiliary fuel tank and install the standard fuel tank.

Table 1 MAINTENANCE SCHEDULE*

Prior to each ride	Inspect tires and rims and check inflation pressure
	Check steering for smooth operation with no excessive play or restrictions
	Check brake operation and for fluid leakage
	Check fuel supply. Make sure there is enough fuel for the intended ride
	Check for fuel leakage
	Check for coolant leakage
	Check all lights for proper operation
	Check engine oil level
	Check final drive oil level
	Check for smooth throttle operation
	Check gearshift pedal operation
	Check clutch operation and for fluid leakage
Initial 600 miles (1,000 km)	Replace engine oil and filter
	Replace final drive oil
	Inspect entire brake system
	Check all hoses–fuel, vacuum, brake, coolant
	Check tightness of all fasteners
	Inspect steering head bearings
Every 4,000 miles (6,4000 km)	Clean and inspect spark plugs
	Inspect valve clearance; adjust if necessary
	Check idle speed; adjust if necessary
	Inspect and clean air filter elements

(continued)

Table 1 MAINTENANCE SCHEDULE* (continued)

Every 4,000 miles (6,4000 km) (continued)	Check electrolyte level in battery, check specific gravity Check fuel, vapor and vacuum hoses Check brake fluid level in front brake master cylinder Check clutch hydraulic hose assembly for leakage Check all brake system components Inspect the brake pads and shoes for wear Inspect the side stand operation
Every 7,500 miles (12,000 km)	Replace both spark plugs Change engine oil and filter Replace both air filter elements Check idle speed; adjust if necessary Inspect fuel lines for damage or leakage Check throttle operation Check choke operation Check coolant level in radiator; top off if necessary Inspect cooling system for leaks Inspect evaporation emission control system (models so equipped) Check brake pad wear in the front caliper assembly Check brake shoe wear indicator on rear brake panel Inspect brake hose for leakage Check brake light switch operation (front and rear) Check headlight aim Inspect entire clutch operating system Check fluid level in clutch master cylinder Inspect the side stand operation Check all suspension components for wear or damage Check tightness of all fasteners Inspect wheels and tires for wear or damage Inspect steering head bearings
Every 2 years	Drain and replace hydraulic brake fluid Drain and replace hydraulic clutch fluid Drain and replace coolant
Every 4 years	Replace the brake hose Replace the clutch hose assembly Replace all coolant hoses Replace fuel lines Replace evaporative emission lines (models so equipped)

* This Suzuki factory maintenance schedule should be considered as a guide to general maintenance and lubrication intervals. Harder than normal use and exposure to mud, water, sand, high humidity, etc. will naturally dictate more frequent attention to most maintenance items.

Table 2 TIRE INFLATION PRESSURE (COLD)*

	Tire pressure			
	Front		**Rear**	
Load	psi	kPa	psi	kPa
Solo riding	28	200	32	225
Dual riding	32	225	36	250

* Tire inflation pressure for factory equipped tires. Aftermarket tires may require different inflation pressure.

Table 3 BATTERY STATE OF CHARGE

Specific gravity	State of charge
1.110-1.130	Discharged
1.140-1.160	Almost discharged
1.170-1.190	One-quarter charged
1.200-1.220	One-half charged
1.230-1.250	Three-quarters charged
1.260-1.280	Fully charged

Table 4 RECOMMENDED LUBRICANTS AND FLUIDS

Fuel	Regular unleaded
U.S. and Canada	87 [(R + M)/2 method] or 91 octane or higher
U.K. and all others	85-95 octane
Engine oil	SAE 10W-40 API grade SE or SF
Capacity	
Change	2.4 ml (2.5 U.S. qt./2.1 Imp. qt.)
Change and filter	2.8 ml (3.0 U.S. qt./2.5 Imp. qt.)
At overhaul	3.3 ml (3.5 U.S. qt./2.9 Imp. qt.)
Coolant	Ethylene glycol
Capacity at change	1.7 ml (1.8 U.S. qt./1.5 Imp. qt.)
Final drive oil	SAE 90 hypoid gear oil with
	GL-5 under API classification
Capacity at change	2-2.2 ml (6.8-7.0 U.S. qt./7.4-7.7 Imp. qt.)
Brake fluid	DOT 4
Clutch hydraulic fluid	DOT 3 or DOT 4
Battery refilling	Distilled water
Fork oil	SAE 10W
Capacity per leg	
1985-1986	3.37 ml (11.4 U.S. oz./11.9 Imp. oz.)
1987	3.55 ml (12.0 U.S. oz./12.5 Imp. oz.)
1988-on	4.13 ml (14.0 U.S. oz./14.5 Imp. oz.)
Oil level each leg	
1985-1986	144 mm (5.67 in.)
1987	117.4 mm (4.62 in.).
1988-on	124.3 mm (4.89 in.)
Cables and pivot points	Cable lube or SAE 10W/30 motor oil

Table 5 MAINTENANCE AND TUNE UP TIGHTENING TORQUES

Item	N·m	ft.-lb.
Oil drain plug	18-23	13-16.5
Valve adjuster locknut	13-16	9.5-11.5
Cylinder head side cover bolts		
(side opposite spark plug)	21-25	15-18

Table 6 TUNE-UP SPECIFICATIONS

Valve clearance	
Intake and exhaust	0.08-0.13 mm (0.003-0.005 in.)
Spark plug type	
1985-1988	NGK DP8EA-9, ND X24EP-U9
1989-on	NGK DPR8EA-9, ND X24EPR-U9
Spark plug gap	0.8-0.9 mm (0.03-0.04 in.)
Idle speed	1,000 ±100 rpm

4

ENGINE

The engine is a V-twin liquid-cooled, 4-stroke design. The cylinders are offset and set at a 45° angle; the cylinders fire on alternate crankshaft rotations. Each cylinder is equipped with a single camshaft and 4 valves. The crankshaft is supported by 2 main bearings in a vertically split crankcase.

Both engine and transmission share a common case and the same wet sump oil supply. The clutch is a wet-type located inside the right crankcase cover. Refer to Chapter Five for clutch and Chapter Six for transmission service procedures.

This chapter provides complete procedures and information for removal, inspection, service and reassembly of the engine.

Table 1 provides complete specifications for the engine and **Table 2** lists all of the engine torque specifications. **Tables 1-5** are located at the end of this chapter.

Before beginning work, re-read Chapter One in the front section of this book. You will do a better job with this information fresh in your mind.

ENGINE PRINCIPLES

Figure 1 explains how the engine works. This will be helpful when troubleshooting or repairing the engine.

SERVICING ENGINE IN FRAME

The following components can be serviced while the engine is mounted in the frame (the bike's frame is a great holding fixture for breaking loose stubborn bolts and nuts):

a. External gearshift mechanism.

b. Clutch.

① **4-STROKE PRINCIPLES**

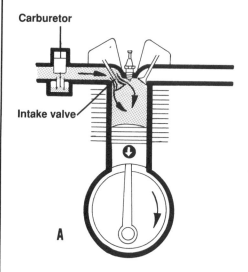

Carburetor

Intake valve

A

As the piston travels downward, the exhaust valve is closed and the intake valve opens, allowing the new air-fuel mixture from the carburetor to be drawn into the cylinder. When the piston reaches the bottom of its travel (BDC), the intake valve closes and remains closed for the next 1 1/2 revolutions of the crankshaft.

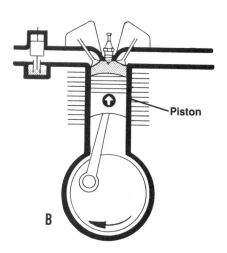

Piston

B

While the crankshaft continues to rotate, the piston moves upward, compressing the air-fuel mixture.

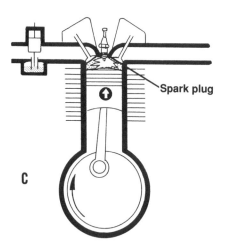

Spark plug

C

As the piston almost reaches the top of its travel, the spark plug fires, igniting the compressed air-fuel mixture. The piston continues to top dead center (TDC) and is pushed downward by the expanding gases.

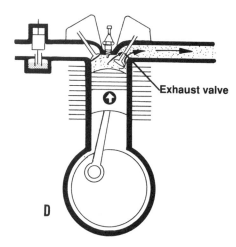

Exhaust valve

D

When the piston almost reaches BDC, the exhaust valve opens and remains open until the piston is near TDC. The upward travel of the piston forces the exhaust gases out of the cylinder. After the piston has reached TDC, the exhaust valve closes and the cycle starts all over again.

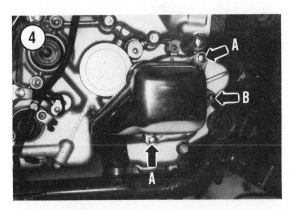

c. Carburetors.

d. Starter motor and gears.

e. Alternator and electrical systems.

f. Oil pump.

ENGINE

Removal/Installation

1. Drain the engine oil and cooling system as described in Chapter Three.

2. Remove both seats, the frame side covers and frame head side covers as described in Chapter Thirteen.

3. Remove the fuel tank as described in Chapter Seven.

4. Remove the carburetor assembly as described in Chapter Seven.

5. Remove the radiator and radiator fan shroud as described in Chapter Nine.

6. Remove the exhaust system as described in Chapter Seven.

7. Remove the battery and battery case as described in Chapter Eight.

8. Remove the bolts securing the secondary drive gear cover (**Figure 2**) and remove the cover.

9. Loosen the clamping band (A, **Figure 3**) securing the rubber boot to the engine and move the rubber boot away from the engine and onto the swing arm.

10. Remove the screw securing the swing arm trim panel (B, **Figure 3**) and remove the panel.

11. Remove the bolts (A, **Figure 4**) and acorn nut (B, **Figure 4**) securing the water pump trim cover and remove the cover.

12. Loosen the clamping screw on the water pump inlet hose clamps. Move the clamps back onto the hose and off of the neck of the fitting on the frame rail and water pump connector. Remove the hose (**Figure 5**) from both fittings.

13. Remove the clutch slave cylinder as described in Chapter Five.

14. Disconnect the spark plug lead (**Figure 6**) from each spark plug. Move the lead out of the way.

15. Disconnect the following electrical wires from the engine:

a. Starter motor.

b. Alternator stator and the pulse generator.

c. Neutral switch.

d. Starter relay.

e. Sidestand check switch.

f. Ground.

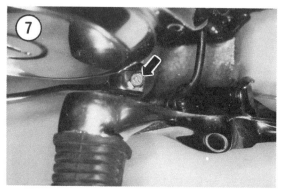

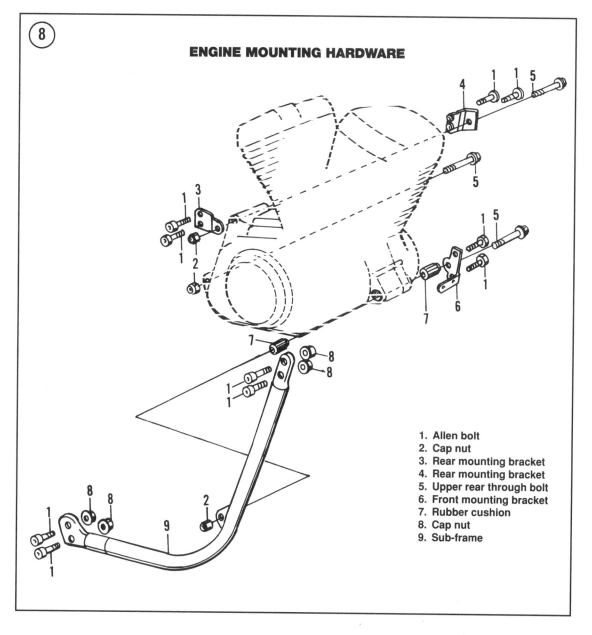

ENGINE MOUNTING HARDWARE

1. Allen bolt
2. Cap nut
3. Rear mounting bracket
4. Rear mounting bracket
5. Upper rear through bolt
6. Front mounting bracket
7. Rubber cushion
8. Cap nut
9. Sub-frame

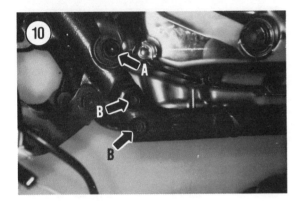

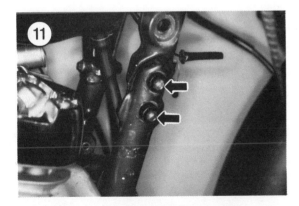

16. Disconnect the crankcase breather hose from the rear cylinder head.

17. Remove the bolt (**Figure 7**) securing the gearshift lever and remove the lever. Reinstall the bolt in the lever to avoid misplacing it.

18. Remove the footpeg assembly as described in Chapter Thirteen.

19. Place wood block(s) and a small hydraulic jack under the engine to support it securely.

20. Take a final look all over the engine to make sure everything has been disconnected.

4

CAUTION
The following steps require the aid of a helper to safely remove the engine assembly from the frame.

21. Make sure the hydraulic jack is still in place and supporting the engine securely.

22. Loosen, but do not remove, all engine mounting bolts and nuts (**Figure 8**).

23. Remove the rear upper through bolt (**Figure 9**), washer and nut.

24. Remove the rear lower through bolt (A, **Figure 10**), washer and nut.

25. Remove the front upper Allen bolts (**Figure 11**) and nuts and the lower Allen bolts (B, **Figure 10**) and nuts securing the sub-frame to the frame.

26. On the right-hand side, remove the nut (**Figure 12**) from the front through bolt.

27. Remove the sub-frame (**Figure 13**) from the engine and frame.

28. On the left-hand side, remove the front through bolt (**Figure 14**) from the engine and frame mounting bracket.

29. Once again, check that everything has been disconnected from the engine.

30. Slowly move the engine forward to disengage the engine output shaft from the drive shaft universal joint. If necessary, use a screwdriver and disengage the drive shaft's universal joint from the output shaft.

31. Slightly lower the engine on the jack and continue to move the engine forward and toward the right-hand side to clear the remaining frame members.

32. Take the engine to a workbench for further disassembly.

33. Install by reversing these removal steps, noting the following:

    a. Apply a light coat of molybdenum disulfide grease to the splines of the output shaft and the universal joint prior to engaging these 2 parts.

    b. Tighten the engine mounting bolts to the torque specifications in **Table 2**.

    c. Fill the engine with the recommended type and quantity of oil as described in Chapter Three.

    d. Refill the cooling system as described in Chapter Three.

    e. Start the engine and check for leaks.

FRONT CYLINDER HEAD COVER AND CAMSHAFT

Front Cylinder
Removal

1. Remove the engine from the frame as described in this chapter.

2. Remove the bolts securing the cylinder head side covers (**Figure 15**) and remove both side covers.

3. On the spark plug side of the cylinder head, remove the insulator (**Figure 16**).

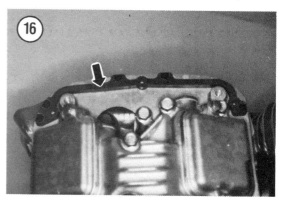

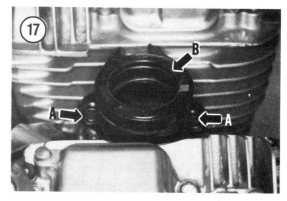

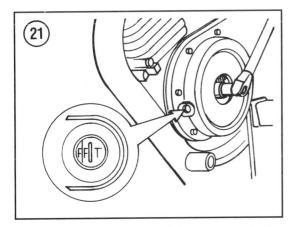

4. Remove the bolts (A, **Figure 17**) securing the intake pipe (B, **Figure 17**) and remove it from the front cylinder.

5. Mark the valve adjuster covers with an "F" and "R" so they will be reinstalled on the correct location.

6. Remove the valve adjuster covers (**Figure 18**).

7. Remove the bolts (A, **Figure 19**) securing the coolant inlet fitting (B, **Figure 19**) and remove the fitting and O-ring seal.

8. Remove the spark plugs from both cylinder heads. This will make it easier to rotate the engine.

NOTE
A cylinder at TDC will have free play in ***both*** *sets of intake and exhaust valve rocker arms indicating that both the intake and exhaust valves are closed.*

CAUTION
The next steps will position the front cylinder at top dead center (TDC) on the compression stroke. This is necessary to avoid damage to the camshaft, rocker arms and related parts.

9. Remove the alternator bolt hole cover on the alternator cover.

10. Use a 17 mm socket and wrench on the alternator rotor bolt (**Figure 20**). Rotate the engine *clockwise*, as viewed from the left-hand side, until the front cylinder is at top dead center (TDC) on the compression stroke. Align the "F/F T" mark with the center of the inspection hole in the alternator rotor (**Figure 21**).

11. With the "F/F T" mark aligned with the center of the inspection hole in the alternator rotor, jiggle both rocker arms and make sure *both* have free play. If one of the rocker arms (either intake or exhaust) is still under tension, rotate the engine an additional 360° until both rocker arms have free play.

12. Again check that the "F/F T" mark is still aligned with the center of the inspection hole in the alternator rotor (**Figure 21**).

13. Using a crisscross pattern, loosen then remove the bolts (**Figure 22**) securing the cylinder head cover.

14. Loosen the cylinder head cover by tapping around the perimeter with a rubber or soft faced mallet. If necessary, *gently* pry the cover loose with a broad-tipped screwdriver.

15. Remove the front cylinder head cover.

16. Straighten the tab on the camshaft sprocket bolt lockwasher and remove the exposed bolt.

CAUTION
If the rear camshaft has been removed, pull up on the camshaft chain and keep it taut, make certain that the camshaft chain is properly meshed onto the crankshaft timing sprocket then rotate the crankshaft. If this step is not followed, the chain may become kinked and cause damage to the crankcases, the camshaft chain and the timing sprocket on the crankshaft.

17. Use a 17 mm socket and wrench on the alternator rotor bolt (**Figure 20**). Rotate the engine *clockwise*, as viewed from the left-hand side, until the other sprocket bolt is visible.

18. Straighten the tab on the other camshaft sprocket bolt lockwasher and remove the exposed bolt and the lockwasher.

19. Disengage the camshaft drive chain from the camshaft sprocket and remove the camshaft.

20. Tie a piece of wire to the camshaft chain and tie it to an external portion of the engine or insert a long drift or long socket extension through the camshaft drive chain (**Figure 23**) to prevent the camshaft chain from falling down into the crankcase.

CAUTION
If the crankshaft must be rotated with the camshaft removed, pull up on the camshaft chain and keep it taut, make certain that the camshaft chain is properly meshed onto the crankshaft timing sprocket then rotate the crankshaft. If this step is not followed, the chain may become kinked and cause damage to the crankcases, the camshaft chain and the timing sprocket on the crankshaft.

21. Inspect the camshaft as described in this chapter.

22. Inspect the cylinder head cover as described in this chapter.

Front Cylinder
Installation

CAUTION
*If the engine has been completely disassembled, first install the rear cylinder camshaft and cylinder head cover then install the front. If only the front cylinder camshaft was removed, the **rear cylinder** must be at TDC on the compression*

stroke prior to installing the front camshaft. This is necessary for correct camshaft timing of both cylinders.

NOTE
*During this procedure, reference is made to the timing marks "R/F T" for the **rear cylinder**. This is correct, since proper camshaft timing is based on the rear cylinder being at TDC on the compression stroke for camshaft installation on both the front and rear cylinders.*

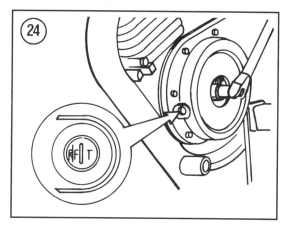

1. Check the timing mark for the *rear cylinder*. Make sure the "R/F T" mark is still aligned with the center of the inspection hole in the alternator rotor (**Figure 24**). If the timing mark is still aligned, proceed to Step 2, if the alignment is *not* correct, proceed as follows:

   a. Pull up on the front camshaft chain and keep it taut, make certain that the camshaft chain is properly meshed onto the crankshaft timing sprocket then rotate the crankshaft in Step b.

   b. Use a 17 mm socket and wrench on the alternator rotor bolt (**Figure 20**). Rotate the engine *clockwise*, as viewed from the left-hand side,

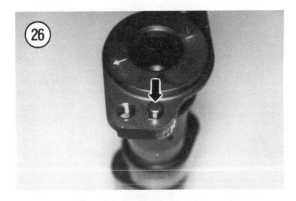

until the rear cylinder is at top dead center (TDC) on the compression stroke. Align the "R/F T" mark with the center of the inspection hole in the alternator rotor (**Figure 24**).

   c. With the "R/F T" mark aligned with the center of the inspection hole in the alternator rotor, jiggle both rocker arms and make sure *both* have free play. If one of rocker arms (either intake or exhaust) is still under tension, rotate the engine an additional 360° until both rocker arms have free play.

   d. Again check that the "R/F T" mark is still aligned with the center of the inspection hole in the alternator rotor (**Figure 24**).

2. Apply a light coat of molybdenum disulfide grease to the camshaft bearing surfaces in the cylinder head.

3. If both camshafts are removed, be sure to install the correct camshaft in the correct cylinder head. The camshafts are marked with a "F" (front cylinder) or "R" (rear cylinder) (**Figure 25**) on the sprocket mounting boss.

4. Apply a *light* coat of cold grease to the locating pin and install it (**Figure 26**) into the end of the camshaft.

5. Install the *front camshaft* into the cylinder head and loop it through the camshaft drive chain. Position the camshaft with the locating pin midway between the 9 and 10 o'clock position (**Figure 27**).

NOTE
When installing the sprocket onto the camshaft be careful not to knock the locating pin out of the camshaft. If the pin works loose it will probably fall down into the crankcase. If this happens the crankcase must be disassembled to retrieve it.

6. Engage the camshaft sprocket with the drive chain and install the sprocket onto the camshaft.

7. Check that the camshaft is still positioned correctly with the locating pin midway between the 9 and 10 o'clock position (A, **Figure 28**) and the timing marks on the end of the camshaft are aligned with the top surface of the cylinder head (B, **Figure 28**).

8. After the sprocket has been installed, make sure the "R/F T" mark is still aligned with the center of the inspection hole in the alternator rotor (**Figure 24**). If necessary, realign the camshaft and sprocket in Steps 5-7.

NOTE
When installing the lockwasher onto the camshaft sprocket, positioned it so it

will cover the locating pin in the end of the camshaft after both sprocket bolts are installed.

9. Install a *new* lockwasher (A, **Figure 29**) and camshaft sprocket bolt (B, **Figure 29**) in the exposed hole. Tighten the bolt only finger tight at this time.

10. Use a 17 mm socket and wrench on the alternator rotor bolt (**Figure 20**). Rotate the engine *clockwise*, as viewed from the left-hand side, until the other sprocket bolt hole is exposed.

> *CAUTION*
> *Apply red Loctite (No. 271) to the sprocket bolt threads prior to installation.*

11. Install the other camshaft sprocket bolt (**Figure 30**) in the exposed hole.

12. Hold down the end of camshaft opposite the camshaft sprocket and tighten the sprocket bolt to the torque specification listed in **Table 2**. Bend up the tab of the lockwasher against the bolt head (**Figure 31**).

13. Use a 17 mm socket and wrench on the alternator rotor bolt (**Figure 20**). Rotate the engine *clockwise*, as viewed from the left-hand side, until the bolt installed in Step 9 is exposed. Remove this bolt and apply red Loctite (No. 271) to the threads prior to installation.

14. Reinstall the camshaft sprocket bolt. Hold down the end of camshaft opposite the camshaft sprocket and tighten the sprocket bolt to the torque specification listed in **Table 2**. Bend up the tab of the lockwasher against the bolt head (**Figure 32**).

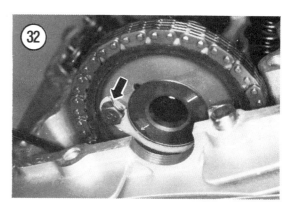

15. Make sure the camshaft shoulder is properly indexed into the groove in the cylinder head (**Figure 33**).

16. Apply a light coat of molybdenum disulfide grease to the bearing surfaces and lobes of the camshaft (**Figure 34**).

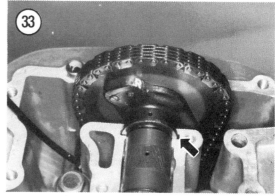

17. Apply a light coat of molybdenum disulfide grease to the camshaft bearing surfaces in the cylinder head cover.

18. Apply a sealant to the edge surfaces of the camshaft end plug and install the plug (**Figure 35**) into the cylinder head. Make sure it is properly seated.

CAUTION
After the modified tie wrap is removed, inspect the end of it to make sure all of it came out and that none of it broke off in the tensioner.

4

19. If the cylinder head and cylinder were removed, *carefully* pull the long modified tie wrap (**Figure 36**) out of the camshaft drive chain tensioner.

20. Clean the sealing surface of both the cylinder head and cover as follows:
   a. Remove the old gaskets and clean off all gasket sealer residue from the cylinder head and cover.
   b. Clean the surface with aerosol electrical contact cleaner and wipe dry with a lint-free cloth.
   c. Apply a coat of ThreeBond No. 1207, or equivalent, to sealing surface of the cylinder head cover. Do *not* apply sealant to the rounded surfaces of the camshaft bearing journal surfaces.

21. Install a new O-ring seal (**Figure 37**) in the cylinder head cover.

22. If removed, install both locating dowels (**Figure 38**) into the cylinder head.

23. Install the cylinder head cover onto the camshaft and the cylinder head. Push it down until it bottoms out. Make sure the camshaft end plug is properly seated between the cylinder head and cover (**Figure 39**).

24. Tighten the bolts (**Figure 22**) in a crisscross pattern, starting with the center bolts (surrounding the camshaft) and working outward. Tighten in 2-3 stages to the torque specification listed in **Table 2**.

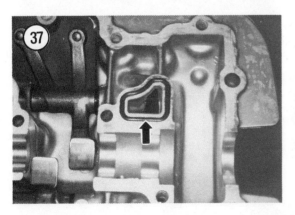

25. Install a new O-ring seal (**Figure 40**) in the coolant inlet fitting. Install the fitting and the bolts (A, **Figure 19**). Tighten the bolts to the same torque specification as the cylinder head bolts.

26. Check the valve clearance at this time and readjust if necessary. Do it at this time since it is much easier to perform valve adjustment with the engine out of the frame. Refer to Chapter Three for the adjustment procedure.

27. Install new O-ring seals (**Figure 41**) in the valve adjuster covers (**Figure 18**) and install the covers and bolts. Tighten the bolts securely.

28. Make sure the O-ring seal (**Figure 42**) is in place in the intake pipe and install it (B, **Figure 17**) onto the cylinder head. Tighten the bolts (A, **Figure 17**) securely.

29. On the spark plug side of the cylinder head, install the insulator (**Figure 16**).

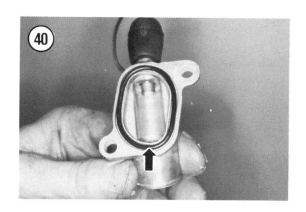

> *NOTE*
> *The cylinder head side cover bolts on the side opposite the spark plug, are also cylinder head cover mounting bolts and must be tightened to the correct torque specification listed in **Table 2**.*

30. Install both cylinder head side covers (**Figure 15**) and bolts. Tighten the bolts, on the side opposite the spark plug, to the torque specification listed in **Table 2**. Tighten the bolts on the other side securely.

REAR CYLINDER HEAD COVER AND CAMSHAFT

Rear Cylinder Removal

1. Remove the engine from the frame as described in this chapter.

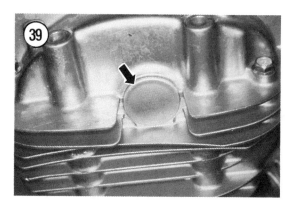

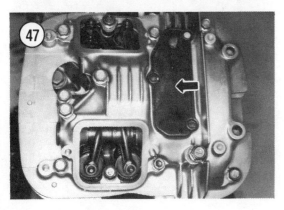

2. Remove the bolts securing the cylinder head side covers (**Figure 43**) and remove both side covers.

3. On the spark plug side of the cylinder head, remove the insulator (**Figure 44**).

4. Mark the valve adjuster covers with an "F" and "R" so they will be reinstalled on the correct location.

5. Remove the valve adjuster covers (**Figure 45**).

6. Remove the bolts securing the crankcase breather cover (**Figure 46**) and remove the cover and gasket (A, **Figure 47**).

7. If not already removed, remove the spark plug from both cylinders. This will make it easier to rotate the engine.

NOTE
A cylinder at TDC will have free play in ***both*** *the both sets of intake and exhaust valve rocker arms indicating that both the intake and exhaust valves are closed.*

CAUTION
The next steps will position the front cylinder at top dead center (TDC) on the compression stroke. This is necessary to avoid damage to the camshaft and related parts.

8. Remove the alternator bolt hole cover on the alternator cover.

9. Use a 17 mm socket and wrench on the alternator rotor bolt (**Figure 48**). Rotate the engine *clockwise*, as viewed from the left-hand side, until the rear cylinder is at top dead center (TDC) on the compression stroke.

Align the "R/F T" mark with the center of the inspection hole in the alternator rotor (**Figure 49**).

10. With the "R/F T" mark aligned with the center of the inspection hole in the alternator rotor, jiggle both rocker arms and make sure *both* have free play. If one of the rocker arms (either intake or exhaust) is still under tension, rotate the engine an additional 360° until both rocker arms have free play.

11. Again check that the "R/F T" mark is still aligned with the center of the inspection hole in the alternator rotor (**Figure 49**).

12. Using a crisscross pattern, loosen then remove the bolts (**Figure 50**) securing the cylinder head cover.

13. Loosen the cylinder head cover by tapping around the perimeter with a rubber or soft faced mallet. If necessary, *gently* pry the cover loose with a broad-tipped screwdriver.

14. Remove the rear cylinder head cover.

15. Straighten the tab on the camshaft sprocket bolt lockwasher and remove the exposed bolt.

CAUTION
If the front camshaft has been removed, pull up on the camshaft chain and keep it taut, make certain that the camshaft chain is properly meshed onto the crankshaft timing sprocket then rotate the crankshaft. If this step is not followed, the chain may become kinked and cause damage to the crankcases, the camshaft chain and the timing sprocket on the crankshaft.

16. Use a 17 mm socket and wrench on the alternator rotor bolt (**Figure 48**). Rotate the engine *clockwise*, as viewed from the left-hand side, until the other sprocket bolt is visible.

17. Straighten the tab on the other camshaft sprocket bolt lockwasher and remove the exposed bolt and the lockwasher.

18. Disengage the camshaft drive chain from the camshaft sprocket and remove the camshaft.

19. Tie a piece of wire to the camshaft chain and tie it to an external portion of the engine or insert a long drift or long socket extension through the camshaft drive chain (**Figure 23**) to prevent the camshaft chain from falling down into the crankcase.

CAUTION
If the crankshaft must be rotated with the camshaft removed, pull up on the

camshaft chain and keep it taut, make certain that the camshaft chain is properly meshed onto the crankshaft timing sprocket then rotate the crankshaft. If this step is not followed, the chain may become kinked and cause damage to the crankcases, the camshaft chain and the timing sprocket on the crankshaft.

20. Inspect the camshaft as described in this chapter.

21. Inspect the cylinder head cover as described in this chapter.

Rear Cylinder
Installation

1. Check the timing mark for the *rear cylinder*. Make sure the "R/F T" mark is still aligned with the center of the inspection hole in the alternator rotor (**Figure 49**). If the timing mark is still aligned,

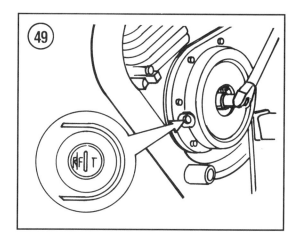

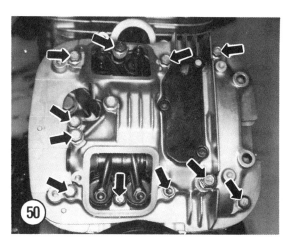

proceed to Step 2, if the alignment is *not* correct, proceed as follows:

CAUTION
If the front camshaft has been removed, have an assistant pull up on the front camshaft chain and keep it taut, make certain that the camshaft chain is properly meshed onto the crankshaft timing sprocket then rotate the crankshaft. If this step is not followed, the chain may become kinked and cause damage to the

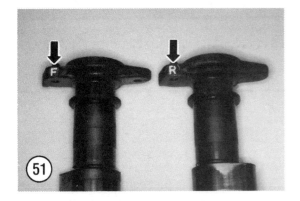

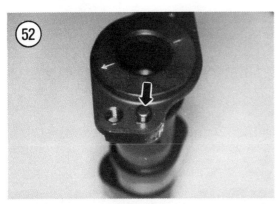

crankcases, the camshaft chain and the timing sprocket on the crankshaft.

a. Pull up on the front camshaft chain and keep it taut, make certain that the camshaft chain is properly meshed onto the crankshaft timing sprocket then rotate the crankshaft in Step b.

b. Use a 17 mm socket and wrench on the alternator rotor bolt (**Figure 48**). Rotate the engine *clockwise*, as viewed from the left-hand side, until the rear cylinder is at top dead center (TDC) on the compression stroke. Align the "R/F T" mark with the center of the inspection hole in the alternator rotor (**Figure 49**).

c. With the "R/F T" mark aligned with the center of the inspection hole in the alternator rotor, jiggle both rocker arms and make sure *both* have free play. If one of rocker arms (either intake or exhaust) is still under tension, rotate the engine an additional 360° until both rocker arms have free play.

d. Again check that the "R/F T" mark is still aligned with the center of the inspection hole in the alternator rotor (**Figure 49**).

2. Apply a light coat of molybdenum disulfide grease to the camshaft bearing surfaces in the cylinder head.

3. If both camshafts are removed, be sure to install the correct camshaft in the correct cylinder head. The camshafts are marked with a "F" (front cylinder) or "R" (rear cylinder) (**Figure 51**) on the sprocket mounting boss.

4. Apply a *light* coat of cold grease to the locating pin and install it (**Figure 52**) into the end of the camshaft.

5. Install the *rear camshaft* into the cylinder head and loop it through the camshaft drive chain (**Figure 53**). Position the camshaft with the locating pin at the 1 o'clock position.

NOTE
When installing the sprocket onto the camshaft be careful not to knock the locating pin out of the camshaft. If the pin works loose it will probably fall down into the crankcase. If this happens the crankcase must be disassembled to retrieve it.

6. Engage the camshaft sprocket with the drive chain and install the sprocket onto the camshaft.

7. Check that the camshaft is still positioned correctly with the locating pin at the 1 o'clock position (A, **Figure 54**) and the timing marks on the end of the camshaft are aligned with the top surface of the cylinder head (B, **Figure 54**).

8. After the sprocket has been installed, make sure the "R/F T" mark is still aligned with the center of the inspection hole in the alternator rotor (**Figure 49**). Realign if necessary, the camshaft and sprocket in Steps 5-7.

NOTE
When installing the lockwasher onto the camshaft sprocket, positioned it so it will cover the locating pin in the end of the camshaft after both sprocket bolts are installed.

9. Install a *new* lockwasher (A, **Figure 55**) and camshaft sprocket bolt (B, **Figure 55**) in the exposed hole. Tighten the bolt only finger tight at this time.

10. Use a 17 mm socket and wrench on the alternator rotor bolt (**Figure 48**). Rotate the engine *clockwise*, as viewed from the left-hand side, until the other sprocket bolt hole is exposed.

CAUTION
Apply red Loctite (No. 271) to the sprocket bolt threads prior to installation.

11. Install the other camshaft sprocket bolt in the exposed hole.

12. Hold down the end of camshaft opposite the camshaft sprocket and tighten the sprocket bolt to the torque specification listed in **Table 2**. Bend up the tab of the lockwasher against the bolt head.

13. Use a 17 mm socket and wrench on the alternator rotor bolt (**Figure 48**). Rotate the engine *clockwise*, as viewed from the left-hand side, until the bolt installed in Step 9 is exposed. Remove this bolt and apply red Loctite (No. 271) to the threads prior to installation.

14. Reinstall the camshaft sprocket bolt. Hold down the end of camshaft opposite the camshaft sprocket and tighten the sprocket bolt to the torque specification listed in **Table 2**. Bend up the tab of the lockwasher against the bolt head (**Figure 56**).

15. Make sure the camshaft shoulder is properly indexed into the groove in the cylinder head (**Figure 57**).

16. Apply a light coat of molybdenum disulfide grease to the bearing surfaces and lobes of the camshaft (**Figure 58**).

17. Apply a light coat of molybdenum disulfide grease to the camshaft bearing surfaces in the cylinder head cover.

18. Apply a sealant to the edge surfaces of the camshaft end plug and install the plug (A, **Figure 59**) into the cylinder head. Make sure it is properly seated.

CAUTION
After the modified tie wrap is removed, inspect the end of it to make sure all of it came out and that none of it broke off in the tensioner.

19. If the cylinder head and cylinder were removed, *carefully* pull the long modified tie wrap out of the camshaft drive chain tensioner.

20. Clean the sealing surface of both the cylinder head and cover as follows:

    a. Remove the old gaskets and clean off all gasket sealer residue from the cylinder head and cover.

    b. Clean the surface with aerosol electrical contact cleaner and wipe dry with a lint-free cloth.

    c. Apply a coat of ThreeBond No. 1207, or equivalent, to sealing surface of the cylinder head cover. Do *not* apply sealant to the rounded surfaces of the camshaft bearing journal surfaces.

21. If removed, install both locating dowels into the cylinder head. Refer to B, **Figure 59** and **Figure 60**.

CAUTION
*During cylinder head cover installation, make sure the small bar (**Figure 61**) over the rocker arm does not fall out.*

22. Install the cylinder head cover onto the camshaft and the cylinder head. Push it down until it bottoms out. Make sure the camshaft end plug (A, **Figure 59**) is properly seated between the cylinder head and cover.

23. Tighten the bolts (**Figure 50**) in a crisscross pattern, starting with the center bolts (surrounding the camshaft) and working outward. Tighten in 2-3 stages to the torque specification listed in **Table 2**.

24. Check the valve clearance at this time and readjust if necessary. Do it at this time since it is much easier to perform valve adjustment with the engine out of the frame. Refer to Chapter Three for the adjustment procedure.

25. Install the breather cover gasket (**Figure 47**) and the breather cover (**Figure 46**). Tighten the bolts to the same torque specification as the cylinder head cover bolts.

26. Install new O-ring seals (**Figure 41**) in the valve adjuster covers (**Figure 45**) and install the covers and bolts. Tighten the bolts securely.

27. On the spark plug side of the cylinder head, install the insulator (**Figure 44**).

NOTE
The cylinder head side cover bolts on the side opposite the spark plug, are also cylinder head cover mounting bolts a:d must be tightened to the correct torque specification listed in ***Table 2***.

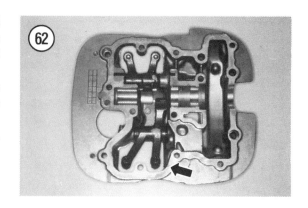

28. Install both cylinder head side covers (**Figure 43**) and bolts. Tighten the bolts, on the side opposite the spark plug, to the torque specification listed in **Table 2**. Tighten the bolts on the other side securely.

Cylinder Head Cover Inspection (Front and Rear Cylinders)

1. Remove all traces of gasket material from the cylinder head cover gasket surfaces (**Figure 62**).

2. After the cylinder head cover has been thoroughly cleaned, place the cover on an inspection surface like a piece of plate glass and check for any warpage at several points with a flat feeler gauge.

3. Measure the warp by inserting a flat feeler gauge between the cylinder head cover gasket surface and the plate glass. There should be no warpage. Replace the cylinder head cover if the gasket surface is warped to or beyond the service limit listed in **Table 1**.

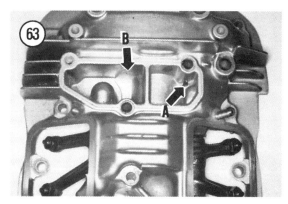

4. On the rear cylinder head cover, perform the following:

    a. Make sure the small opening (A, **Figure 63**) in the breather area is clear. Clean out if necessary with a piece of wire and blow out with compressed air. Also make sure the large opening (B, **Figure 63**) is clear.

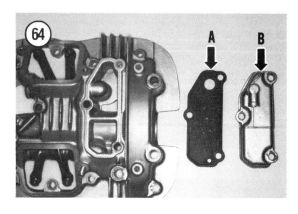

    b. Inspect the gasket (A, **Figure 64**) for damage or deterioration; replace if necessary.

    c. Inspect the breather cover (B, **Figure 64**) for cracks or damage; replace if necessary.

5. Inspect the valve adjustment covers (**Figure 65**) for cracks or damage. Make sure the small bolt hole tabs are not cracked or warped. If these tabs are

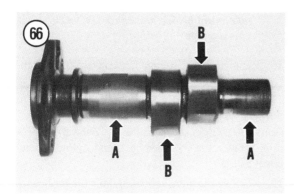

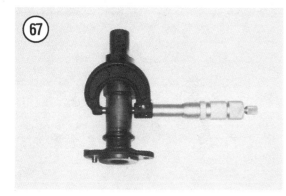

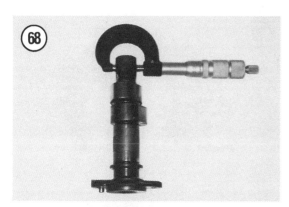

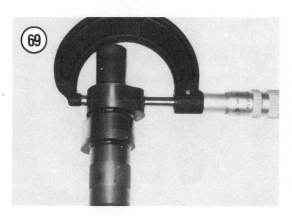

damaged it may result in an oil leak. Replace the cover(s) if necessary.

6. Disassemble and inspect the rocker arms as described in this chapter.

CAMSHAFT

Camshaft Inspection

1. Inspect the camshaft bearing journals (A, **Figure 66**) for wear.

2. Measure both camshaft bearing journals with a micrometer. Refer to **Figure 67** for the center journal and to **Figure 68** for the end journal. Compare to the dimensions given in **Table 3**. If worn to the service limit or less the camshaft must be replaced.

3. Check the camshaft lobes (B, **Figure 66**) for wear. The lobes should show no signs of scoring and the edges should be square. Slight damage may be removed with a silicone carbide oilstone. Use No. 100-120 grit stone initially, then polish with a No. 280-320 grit stone.

4. Even though the camshaft lobe surface appears to be satisfactory, with no visible signs of wear, the camshaft lobes must be measured with a micrometer (**Figure 69**). Compare to the dimensions given in **Table 1**. If worn to the service limit or less the camshaft must be replaced.

5. Place the camshaft on a set of V-blocks and check its runout with a dial indicator. Compare to the dimension given in **Table 1**. If the runout is to the service limit or more the camshaft must be replaced.

6. Make sure the locating pin (**Figure 52**) is installed in the end of the camshaft is a tight fit. If loose, replace the pin.

7. Inspect the camshaft bearing surfaces in the cylinder head (**Figure 70**) and cylinder head cover

(**Figure 71**). They should not be scored or excessively worn. Replace the cylinder head and cylinder head cover as a set, if the bearing surfaces are worn or scored.

8. Inspect the camshaft sprocket teeth (A, **Figure 72**) for wear; replace if necessary.

9. Make sure the camshaft sprocket bolt holes (B, **Figure 72**) and locating pin hole (C, **Figure 72**) are not elongated or damaged. If damaged, replace the camshaft sprocket.

Camshaft Bearing
Clearance Measurement

This procedure requires the use a Plastigage set. The camshaft must be installed into the cylinder head. Before installing the camshaft, wipe all oil residue from the camshaft bearing journals and bearing surfaces in the cylinder head and cylinder head cover.

1. Install the camshaft into the cylinder head with the lobes facing down. Do not attach the drive sprocket to the camshaft.

2. Make sure the locating dowels (**Figure 73**) are in place in the cylinder head.

3. Place a strip of Plastigage material on top of each camshaft center and end bearing journals, parallel to the camshaft.

4. Install the cylinder head cover.

5. Install the bolts securing the cylinder head cover.

6. Tighten the bolts in a crisscross pattern, starting with the center bolts (surrounding the camshaft) and working outward. tighten in 2-3 stages to the torque specification listed in **Table 2**.

> *CAUTION*
> *Do not rotate the camshafts with the Plastigage material in place.*

7. Loosen the cylinder head bolts in 2-3 stages in a crisscross pattern, then remove the bolts.

8. Carefully remove the cylinder head cover.

9. Measure the width of the flattened Plastigage material at the widest point, according to the manufacturer's instructions.

> *CAUTION*
> *Be sure to remove all traces of Plastigage material from the bearing journals in the cylinder head cover. If any material is left in the engine it can plug up an*

oil control orifice and cause severe engine damage.

10. Remove *all* Plastigage material from the camshafts and the bearing caps.

11. If the oil clearance is greater than specified in **Table 1**, and the camshaft bearing journal dimensions were within specification in *Camshaft Inspection*, replace the cylinder head and cylinder head cover as a set.

12. Remove the camshaft from the cylinder head.

ROCKER ARM ASSEMBLIES

Refer to **Figure 74** for this procedure.

Removal

1. Remove the cylinder head cover as described in this chapter.
2. Remove the trim cap (A, **Figure 75**) from the end of each rocker arm shaft.

3. Loosen both rocker arm shafts (B, **Figure 75**).

NOTE
Note that the rocker arms and shafts are different and must be kept separate to avoid the intermixing of parts. Remove one set at a time and place it in a small box and label the rocker arm and shaft either intake or exhaust.

4

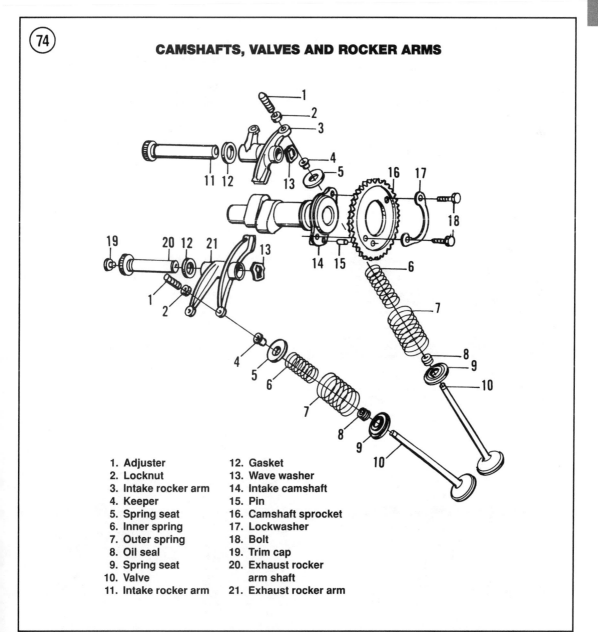

74

CAMSHAFTS, VALVES AND ROCKER ARMS

1. Adjuster	12. Gasket
2. Locknut	13. Wave washer
3. Intake rocker arm	14. Intake camshaft
4. Keeper	15. Pin
5. Spring seat	16. Camshaft sprocket
6. Inner spring	17. Lockwasher
7. Outer spring	18. Bolt
8. Oil seal	19. Trim cap
9. Spring seat	20. Exhaust rocker
10. Valve	arm shaft
11. Intake rocker arm	21. Exhaust rocker arm

4. Withdraw the intake rocker arm shaft and remove the rocker arm and wave washer. Don't lose the gasket from the shaft.

5. Withdraw the exhaust rocker arm shaft and remove the rocker arm and wave washer. Don't lose the gasket from the shaft.

6. Wash all parts in solvent and thoroughly dry with compressed air.

Inspection

1. Inspect the rocker arm pad where it rides on the cam lobe (**Figure 76**) and where the adjusters ride on the valve stems (**Figure 77**). If the pad is scratched or unevenly worn, inspect the camshaft lobe for scoring, chipping or flat spots. Replace the rocker arm if defective as well as the camshaft if it is damaged.

2. Measure the inside diameter of the rocker arm bore (**Figure 78**) and check against the dimensions in **Table 1**. Replace if worn to the service limit or greater.

3. Inspect the rocker arm shaft for signs of wear or scoring. Measure the outside diameter (**Figure 79**)

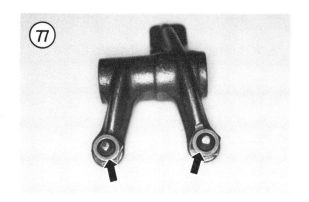

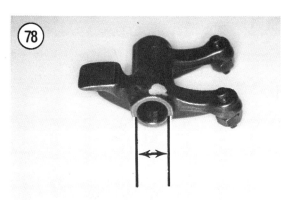

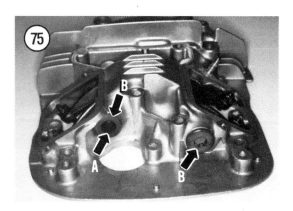

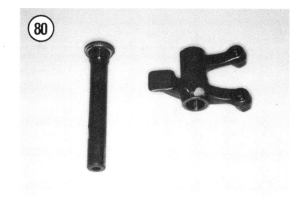

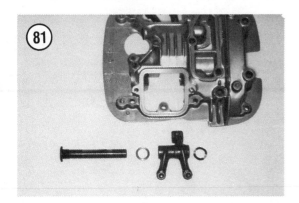

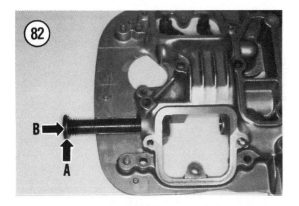

with a micrometer and check against the dimensions in **Table 1**. Replace if worn to the service limit or less.

4. Make sure the oil holes in the rocker arm shaft are clean and clear. If necessary, clean out with a piece of wire and thoroughly clean with solvent. Dry with compressed air.

5. Check the gasket and wave washers for breakage or distortion; replace if necessary.

6. Check the overall condition of the rocker arm and shaft for fractures, wear or damage (**Figure 80**); replace if necessary.

Installation

1. Coat the rocker arm shaft, rocker arm bore and the shaft receptacles in the cylinder head with assembly oil or clean engine oil.

NOTE
The rocker arms and shafts are not identical. Refer to the marks made during removal and be sure to install these parts into the correct location within the cylinder head cover.

2. **Figure 81** shows the correct order of parts as they are to be installed into the cylinder head.

3. Install the gasket (A, **Figure 82**) onto the rocker arm shaft and install the rocker arm shaft (B, **Figure 82**) part way into the cylinder head cover.

4. Position the rocker arm (**Figure 83**) and push the rocker arm shaft through but not past it, allowing room for installation of the wave washer.

5. Install the wave washer (**Figure 84**) then push the rocker arm shaft through the wave washer and into the cylinder head cover until it stops.

6. Make sure all parts are installed correctly as shown in **Figure 85**, then screw the rocker arm into

the cylinder head cover. Tighten the rocker arm shafts (B, **Figure 75**) to the torque specification listed in **Table 2**.

7. Install the trim cap (A, **Figure 75**) into the end of the shaft.

8. Repeat for the other rocker arm assembly.

9. On the intake rocker arm, apply some cold grease to the small bar, then install the small bar (**Figure 61**) into the groove in the cylinder head cover.

CYLINDER HEAD AND CYLINDER

The cylinder head and cylinder are removed from the crankcase as an assembly then separated after removal.

Removal

1. Remove the bolts (A, **Figure 86**) securing the intake pipe and remove it (B, **Figure 86**).

2. Remove the cylinder head covers as described in this chapter.

3. Loosen the screws of the clamping bands (**Figure 87**) on the short coolant hose connecting both cylinder heads. Move the clamps from the fittings of the cylinder heads and back onto the hose.

4. Loosen the screws of the clamping bands on the short coolant hose connecting both cylinders. Move the clamps from the fittings of the cylinders and back onto the hose (**Figure 88**).

5. For removal of the rear cylinder head and cylinder, perform the following:

    a. Loosen the clamping screw (A, **Figure 89**) of water pump on that hose fitting at rear of crankcase. Move the clamp back onto the hose and

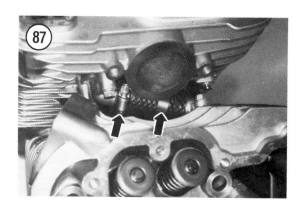

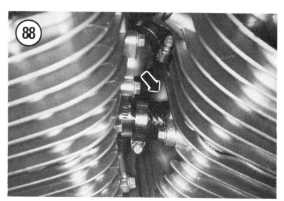

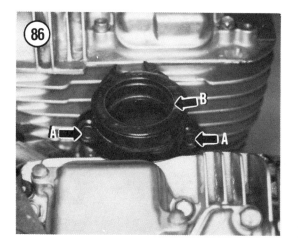

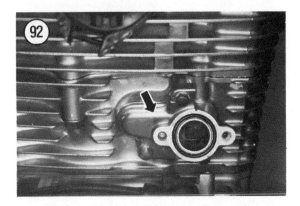

off of the neck of the fitting, then remove the hose (B, **Figure 89**) from the crankcase fitting.

b. Remove the bolts (**Figure 90**) securing the metal coolant inlet pipe to the rear cylinder.

c. Separate the metal coolant pipe from the cylinder.

d. Remove the metal coolant pipe and rubber hose assembly (**Figure 91**) from the engine and frame.

e. Remove the bolts securing the coolant fitting (**Figure 92**) to the base of the cylinder and remove it. Don't lose the O-ring seal on each side of the fitting.

6. Using a crisscross pattern, loosen then remove the bolts (**Figure 93**) securing the cylinder head and cylinder to the crankcase.

CAUTION
Remember the small cooling fins are fragile and may be damaged if tapped or pried too hard. Never use a metal hammer.

7. Loosen the cylinder head and cylinder by tapping around the perimeter base of the cylinder with a rubber or soft faced mallet. If necessary, *gently* pry the cylinder from the crankcase with a broad-tipped screwdriver.

8. Untie the wire, or remove the drift or long socket extension securing the camshaft chain.

9. Carefully lift the cylinder head and cylinder assembly (**Figure 94**), then remove from the piston and the crankcase. Carefully disengage the short coolant hoses from the fittings of the other cylinder and cylinder head. Guide the camshaft chain through the opening in the cylinder head and cylinder and secure it to the exterior of the engine. This will prevent the camshaft chain from falling down into the crankcase.

10. Remove the cylinder base gasket and discard it. Don't lose the locating dowels.

11. If only one cylinder head and cylinder assembly is going to be removed, place a clean shop cloth into the opening in the crankcase opening (**Figure 95**) to prevent the entry of foreign matter.

12. Repeat the procedure for the other cylinder head and cylinder assembly if necessary.

Disassembly

1A. For the front cylinder head and cylinder, remove the bolts (**Figure 96**) at the front and the nut (**Figure 97**) at the rear.

1B. For the rear cylinder head and cylinder, remove the nut at the front and the nut (**Figure 98**) at the rear.

2. Loosen the cylinder head from the cylinder by tapping around the perimeter of the cylinder head with a rubber or soft faced mallet. If necessary, *gently* pry the cylinder head from the cylinder with a broad-tipped screwdriver.

3. Carefully remove the cylinder head (A, **Figure 99**) from the cylinder (B, **Figure 99**).

4. Remove the cylinder head gasket. Don't lose the locating dowels.

5. Remove the camshaft chain guide from the cylinder.

6. Remove the bolts (A, **Figure 100**) securing the camshaft chain tensioner (B, **Figure 100**) and remove the tensioner from the cylinder.

7. Inspect the cylinder head, cylinder and camshaft chain tensioner as described in this chapter.

Assembly

A special tool is required to hold the camshaft chain tensioner spring in the compressed position. The special Suzuki tool, tensioner locking tool (part No. 09918-53810) can be substituted with a homemade tool from a long plastic tie wrap as follows:

    a. Start with a long tie wrap (10-12 in.) (A, **Figure 101**).

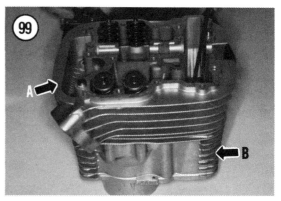

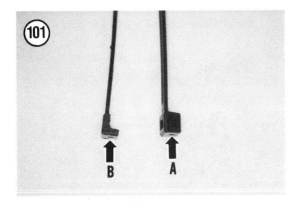

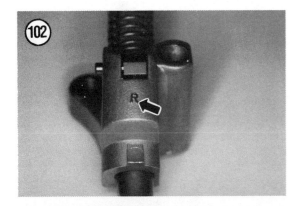

b. Trim the locking end of the tie wrap to achieve an "L" shaped end as shown in B, **Figure 101**.

c. Do not trim away too much of the plastic material as the "L" shaped end must not only hold the ratchet in the compressed position, but it must also be strong enough to not break off and stay in the tensioner when the modified tie wrap is withdrawn later in the procedure.

d. Do *not* shorten the overall length of the tie wrap. It must be this long in order to exit through the top of the cylinder head during assembly so it can be removed later in the installation procedure.

NOTE
The camshaft chain tensioners are unique and must be installed in the correct cylinder. They are marked with a "F" (front) or "R" (rear) **Figure 102**.

1. Install the correct camshaft chain tensioner (B, **Figure 100**) into the cylinder. Install the bolts (A, **Figure 100**) and tighten securely.

NOTE
The camshaft chain tensioner spring must be compressed, and remain compressed, prior to installing the camshaft chain guide.

2. On the camshaft tensioner assembly, release the ratchet with a small screwdriver, push in on the end of the tensioner to compress the spring, then install the "special tie wrap tool" in the ratchet as shown **Figure 103**. This will hold the tensioner in place and keep the spring compressed.

NOTE
The front and rear cylinder head gaskets have a different hole pattern. Be sure to install the correct gasket on the correct cylinder.

NOTE
The camshaft chain guides are unique and must be installed in the correct cylinder. They are marked with an "F" (front) or "R" (rear) as shown in **Figure 104**.

3A. On the front cylinder, perform the following:

a. If removed, install the 2 locating dowels (**Figure 105**) in the cylinder.

b. Install the camshaft chain guide (A, **Figure 106**) into the cylinder. Make sure it is correctly seated in the locator notch at the top of the cylinder (B, **Figure 106**).

c. Install a new cylinder head gasket (**Figure 107**). Make sure all of the gasket holes match the holes in the cylinder (**Figure 108**).

3B. On the rear cylinder, perform the following:

a. Install the camshaft chain guide (A, **Figure 109**) into the cylinder. Make sure it is correctly seated in the locator notch at the top of the cylinder (B, **Figure 109**).

b. If removed, install the 2 locating dowels (A, **Figure 110**) in the cylinder.

c. Install a new cylinder head gasket (B, **Figure 110**). Make sure all of the gasket holes match the holes in the cylinder (**Figure 108**).

CAUTION
The cylinder head and cylinder should fit together without force. If they do not fit together completely, do not attempt to pull them together with the bolts and nuts in the next step. Separate the 2 parts and investigate the cause of the interference. Do not risk damage by trying to force the part together.

4. Carefully install the cylinder head (A, **Figure 99**) onto the cylinder (B, **Figure 99**). Guide the plastic "tie wrap tool" up through the camshaft chain opening in the cylinder head (**Figure 111**). Push the 2 parts together until they bottom out.

5A. On the front cylinder head and cylinder, install the bolts (**Figure 96**) at the front and the nut (**Figure**

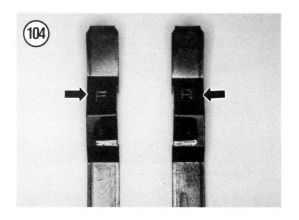
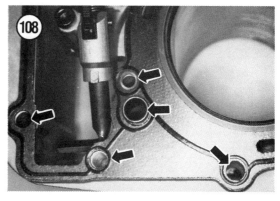

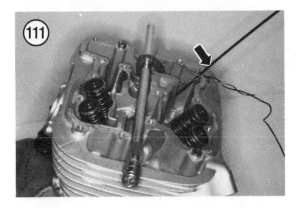

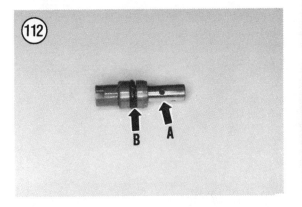

97) at the rear. Tighten the bolts and nut to the torque specification listed in **Table 2**.

5B. On the rear cylinder head and cylinder, install the nut at the front and the nut (**Figure 98**) at the rear. Tighten the nuts to the torque specification listed in **Table 2**.

Installation

1. If used, remove the clean shop cloth from the opening in the crankcase opening.

2. Apply a liberal coat of clean engine oil to the cylinder wall especially at the lower end where the piston will be entering.

3. Also apply clean engine oil to the piston and piston rings. This will make it easier to guide the piston into the cylinder bore.

4. Check that both top surfaces of the crankcase and the bottom surface of the both cylinders are clean prior to installing a new base gasket.

> *NOTE*
> *The front and rear cylinder base gaskets have a slightly different hole pattern. Be sure to install the correct gasket on the correct location on the crankcase.*

5A. On the front cylinder location on the crankcase, perform the following:

    a. If the oil control orifice was removed, make sure the oil hole (A, **Figure 112**) is open and that the O-ring (B, **Figure 112**) is installed. Install the oil control orifice (**Figure 113**) into the crankcase, pushing it down until it bottoms (**Figure 114**).

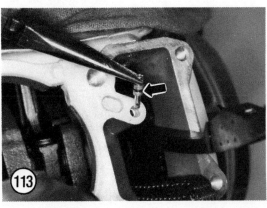

b. If removed, install the locating dowels (A, **Figure 115**).

c. Install a new cylinder base gasket (B, **Figure 115**).

5B. On the rear cylinder location on the crankcase, perform the following:

a. If removed, install the locating dowels (A, **Figure 116**).

b. Install a new cylinder base gasket (B, **Figure 116**).

c. If the oil control orifice was removed, make sure the oil hole (A, **Figure 112**) is open and that O-ring (B, **Figure 112**) is installed. Install the oil control orifice into the crankcase (**Figure 117**), pushing it down until it bottoms (**Figure 118**).

6. Make sure the end gaps of the piston rings are *not* lined up with each other—they must be staggered. Lubricate the piston rings and the inside of the cylinder bore with assembly oil or fresh engine oil.

NOTE
The following step requires the aid of an assistant. The cylinder head and cylinder assembly are long and also quite heavy. Trying to hold onto the cylinder head and cylinder assembly by yourself, while guiding it onto the piston could cause damage to the piston and/or piston rings.

7. Move the cylinder head and cylinder assembly into position on the crankcase.

8. Install the cylinder head and cylinder assembly. Guide the camshaft chain and camshaft tensioner assembly guide into the camshaft chain slot in the cylinder head and cylinder assembly. Make sure the camshaft tensioner guide indexes correctly into the tensioner assembly in the cylinder.

9. Carefully feed the camshaft chain and wire up through the opening in the cylinder head and cylinder and tie it to the exterior of the assembly.

10. Have the assistant start the cylinder down over the piston while you compress each piston ring with your fingers as it enters the cylinder.

11. Slide the cylinder head and cylinder assembly down until it bottoms out on the crankcase.

12. Look down into the camshaft chain cavity and make sure the camshaft chain, camshaft tensioner assembly guide and the chain guide are all posi-

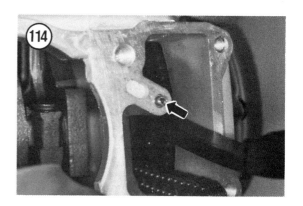

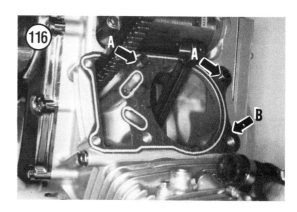

tioned correctly and that the camshaft chain is not binding.

13. Install the bolts (**Figure 93**) securing the cylinder head and cylinder to the crankcase. Using a crisscross pattern, tighten the bolts in 2-3 stages to the torque specification listed in **Table 2**.

14. Both short sections of coolant hose should be replaced at this time, because they are difficult to replace after both cylinder heads and cylinders are installed on the crankcase.

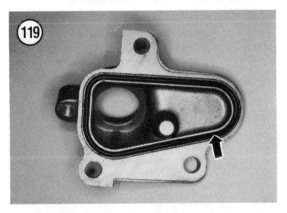

NOTE
Make sure hose clamps are installed onto the short sections of the coolant hoses prior to installing the other cylinder head and cylinder assembly. It would be very difficult to install the clamps onto the hoses once both assemblies are in place on the crankcase.

15. Repeat Steps 6-13 for the other cylinder head and cylinder head assembly. The procedure is the same except the short sections of the coolant hoses must be attached to the fittings on both the cylinder head and cylinder during installation.

16. Apply a light coat of rubber lube, or equivalent, to the inner surface of the coolant hoses, to make installation easier.

17. Once the coolant hoses are installed onto both fittings, move the hose clamps into position and tighten securely. Refer to **Figure 87** for the cylinder heads and **Figure 88** for the cylinders. Do not overtighten as the clamp may cut into the hose.

18. After the rear cylinder head and cylinder have been installed, perform the following:

   a. Inspect the O-ring seals in the coolant fitting for damage, hardness or deterioration. If necessary, install a new O-ring seal into the back (**Figure 119**) and into the front (**Figure 120**) of the coolant fitting.

   b. Apply a light coat of oil to the O-rings.

   c. Install the coolant fitting (**Figure 92**) to the base of the cylinder and install the bolts. Tighten the bolts securely.

   d. Install the metal coolant pipe and rubber hose assembly (**Figure 91**) onto the engine and frame.

   e. Install the hose (B, **Figure 89**) onto the neck of the fitting on the crankcase. Don't tighten the hose clamp at this time.

   f. Install the coolant fitting on the back of the cylinder and install the bolts (**Figure 90**). Tighten the bolts securely.

   g. Tighten the hose clamp screw (A, **Figure 89**) on the hose.

19. Install the cylinder head covers as described in this chapter.

20. Make sure the O-ring (**Figure 121**) is in place in the intake pipe.

21. Install the intake pipe (B, **Figure 86**) and bolts (A, **Figure 86**). Tighten the bolts securely.

Cylinder Head Inspection

1. Remove all traces of gasket material from the cylinder head upper (**Figure 122**) and lower (**Figure 123**) mating surfaces. Do not scratch the gasket surface.

2. *Without removing the valves,* remove all carbon deposits from the combustion chamber (A, **Figure 124**) and valve ports with a wire brush. A blunt screwdriver or chisel may be used if care is taken not to damage the head, valves and spark plug threads.

3. Examine the spark plug threads (B, **Figure 124**) in the cylinder head for damage. If damage is minor or if the threads are dirty or clogged with carbon, use a spark plug thread tap to clean the threads following the manufacturer's instructions. If thread damage is severe, refer further service to a dealer or competent machine shop.

4. After the carbon is removed from the combustion chamber and the valve ports and the spark plug thread hole is repaired, clean the entire head in cleaning solvent. Blow dry with compressed air.

5. Clean away all carbon from the piston crown. Do not remove the carbon ridge at the top of the cylinder bore.

6. Check for cracks in the combustion chamber and exhaust port (A, **Figure 125**). A cracked head must be replaced.

7. Inspect the camshaft bearing area (**Figure 126**) in the cylinder head for damage, wear or burrs. Clean up if damage is minimal; replace cylinder head if necessary.

8. Inspect the cooling fins (B, **Figure 125**) for cracks or damage.

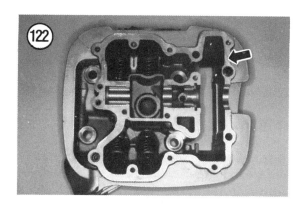

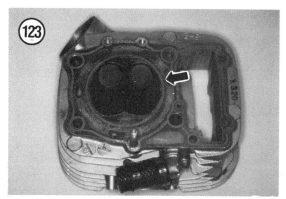

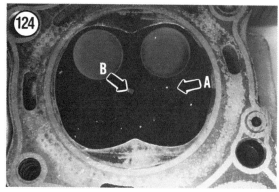

9. Inspect the short hose coolant fitting for signs of leakage. If present, remove the bolts (A, **Figure 127**) securing the fitting and remove it. Install a new O-ring seal and apply fresh engine oil to the O-ring. Reinstall the fitting and tighten the bolts securely.

10. Inspect the short section of coolant hose (B, **Figure 127**) for cracks, hardness or deterioration. Replace if necessary.

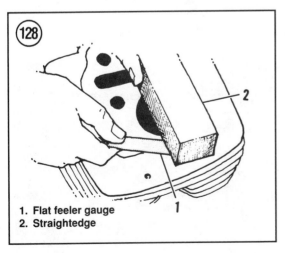

1. Flat feeler gauge
2. Straightedge

11. Inspect the threads of the stud (C, **Figure 127**) for damage. Clean up with an appropriate size metric die if necessary. Make sure the stud it tightly secured into the cylinder head.

12. After the head has been thoroughly cleaned, place a straightedge across the cylinder head/cylinder gasket surface (**Figure 128**) at several points. Measure the warp by inserting a flat feeler gauge between the straightedge and the cylinder head at each location. Maximum allowable warpage is 0.010 in. (0.25 mm). If warpage exceeds this limit, the cylinder head must be replaced.

13. Inspect the valve and valve guides as described in this chapter.

14. Repeat for the other cylinder head.

Cylinder
Inspection

1. Soak old cylinder head gasket material stuck to the cylinder (**Figure 129**) with solvent. Use a broad-tipped *dull* chisel to gently scrape off all gasket residue. Do not gouge the sealing surface as oil, coolant and air leaks will result.

2. Measure the cylinder bore with a cylinder gauge or inside micrometer at the points shown in **Figure 130**.

3. Measure in 2 axes—in line with the piston-pin and at 90° to the pin. If the taper or out-of-round is 0.004 in. (0.10 mm) or greater, the cylinder must be rebored to the next oversize and a new piston and rings installed. Rebore both cylinders even if only one is worn.

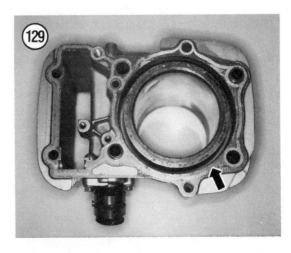

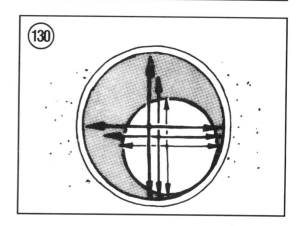

NOTE
The new pistons should be obtained before the cylinders are rebored so that the pistons can be measured. Slight manufacturing tolerances must be taken into account to determine the actual size and working clearance. Piston-to-cylinder wear limit is listed in **Table 1**.

NOTE
The maximum wear limit on the cylinder is listed in **Table 1**. *If the cylinder is worn to this limit, it must be replaced. Never rebore a cylinder if the finished rebore diameter will be this dimension or greater.*

4. If the cylinders are not worn past the service limit, thoroughly check the bore surface (**Figure 131**) for scratches or gouges. If damaged in any way, the bore will require boring and reconditioning.

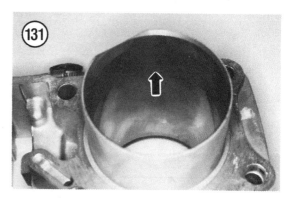

5. If the cylinders require reboring, remove all dowel pins from the cylinders, then take them to a dealer or machine shop for service.
6. After the cylinders have been serviced, perform the following:

CAUTION
A combination of soap and hot water is the only solution that will completely clean cylinder walls. Solvent and kerosene cannot wash fine grit out of cylinder crevices. Any grit left in the cylinders will act as a grinding compound and cause premature wear to the new rings.

a. Wash each cylinder bore in hot soapy water. This is the only way to clean the cylinders of the fine grit material left from the bore and honing procedure.
b. Also wash out any fine grit material from the cooling cores surrounding each cylinder.
c. After washing the cylinder walls, run a clean white cloth through each cylinder wall. It should *not* show any traces of grit or debris. If the rag is the slightest bit dirty, the wall is not thoroughly cleaned and must be rewashed.
d. After the cylinder is cleaned, lubricate the cylinder walls with clean engine oil to prevent the cylinder liners from rusting.

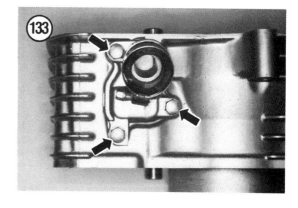

7. Inspect the cooling fins (A, **Figure 132**) for cracks or damage.

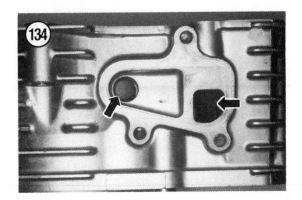

8. Inspect the short hose coolant fitting for signs of leakage. If present, remove the bolts (**Figure 133**) securing the fitting and remove it. Make sure the openings (**Figure 134**) in the cylinder head are open. Install a new O-ring seal and apply fresh engine oil to the O-ring. Reinstall the fitting and tighten the bolts securely.

9. Inspect the short section of coolant hose (B, **Figure 132**) for cracks, hardness or deterioration. Replace if necessary.

10. Repeat for the other cylinder.

4

Camshaft Chain Tensioner and Guide Adjuster Inspection

1. Inspect all parts of the camshaft chain tensioner adjuster for wear or damage (**Figure 135**). Suzuki does not provide any service specifications for the tensioner adjuster.

2. Make sure the ratchet (**Figure 136**) operates correctly.

3. If any part of the tensioner adjuster body or rack is worn or damaged, replace the entire assembly. Replacement parts are not available.

4. Inspect the camshaft chain guides (**Figure 137**) for wear or deterioration. Replace if necessary.

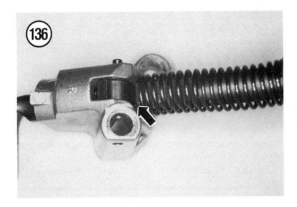

VALVES AND VALVE COMPONENTS

General practice among those who do their own service is to remove the cylinder heads and take them to a machine shop or dealer for inspection and service. Since the cost is relative to the required effort and equipment, this may be the best approach even for the experienced mechanics.

This procedure is included for those who chose to do their own valve service.

Refer to **Figure 138** for this procedure.

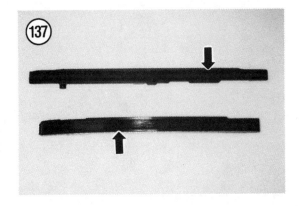

Valve Removal

1. Remove the cylinder head as described in this chapter.

CAUTION
To avoid loss of spring tension, do not compress the springs any more than necessary to remove the keepers.

2. Compress the valve springs with a valve compressor tool (**Figure 139**). Remove the valve keepers (**Figure 140**) and release the compression. Remove the valve compressor tool (**Figure 141**).

3. Remove the valve spring retainer and valve springs.

4. Prior to removing the valve, remove any burrs from the valve stem (**Figure 142**). Otherwise the valve guide will be damaged.

5. Remove the valve.

6. Remove the oil seal and spring seat from the valve guide.

7. Repeat Steps 2-6 for the remainder of valves requiring service.

8. Mark all parts (**Figure 143**) as they are disassembled so that they will be installed in their same locations. The exhaust valves are adjacent to the exhaust port and the intake valves are located next to the intake pipe.

Valve Inspection

1. Clean the valves with a soft wire brush and solvent.

2. Inspect the contact surface of each valve (**Figure 144**) for burning or pitting. Unevenness of the contact surface is an indication that the valve is not serviceable. The valve contact surface can *not* be ground and must be replaced if defective.

3. Inspect each valve stem for wear and roughness and measure the vertical runout of the valve stem as

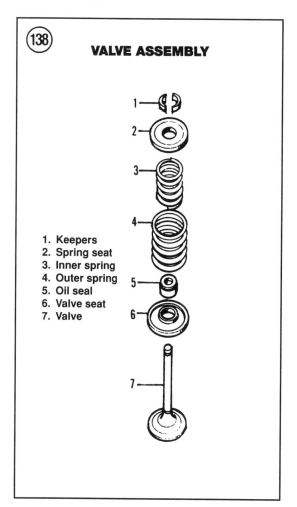

VALVE ASSEMBLY

1. Keepers
2. Spring seat
3. Inner spring
4. Outer spring
5. Oil seal
6. Valve seat
7. Valve

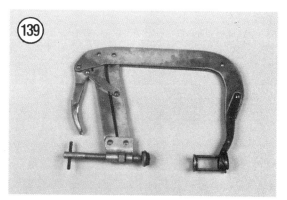

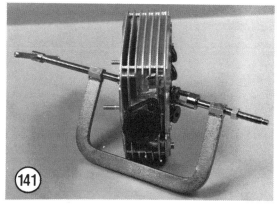

shown in **Figure 145**. The runout should not exceed the service limit listed in **Table 1**.

4. Measure each valve stem for wear (**Figure 146**). If worn to the wear limit listed in **Table 1**, or less the valve must be replaced.

5. Measure each valve seating face for wear (**Figure 147**). If worn to the wear limit listed in **Table 1**, or less the valve must be replaced.

6. Remove all carbon and varnish from each valve guide with a stiff spiral wire brush.

7. Insert each valve in its guide. Hold the valve with the head just slightly off the valve seat and rock it sideways in 2 directions, "X" and "Y," perpendicular to each other as shown in **Figure 148**. If the valve-to-valve guide clearance measured exceeds the limit listed in **Table 1**, measure the valve stem. If the valve stem is worn, replace the valve. If the valve stem is within tolerances, replace the valve guide.

4

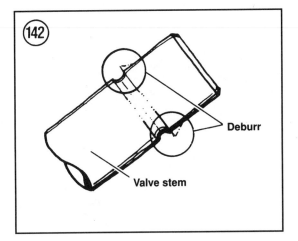

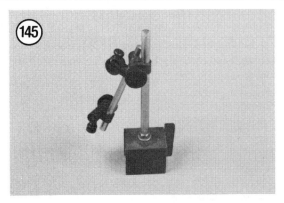

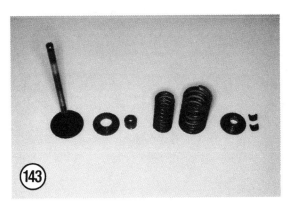

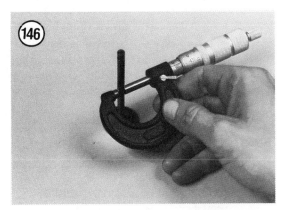

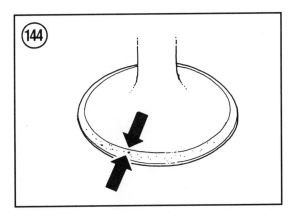

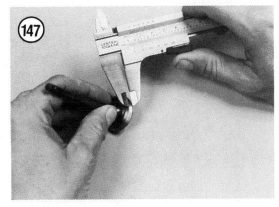

8. Measure each valve spring free length with a vernier caliper (**Figure 149**). All should be within the length specified in **Table 1** with no signs of bends or distortion (**Figure 150**). Replace defective springs in pairs (inner and outer).

9. Check the valve spring retainer and valve keepers. If they are in good condition they may be reused; replace as necessary.

10. Inspect the valve seats (**Figure 151**) in the cylinder head. If worn or burned, they must be reconditioned as described in this chapter.

11. Inspect the valve stem end for pitting and wear. If pitted or worn, the end may be resurfaced providing the finished length (**Figure 152**) is not less than length listed in **Table 1**. Replace the valve(s) if the finished length is less than specified.

Valve Installation

1. Install the valve seat (**Figure 153**). Do not confuse the valve spring retainer (A, **Figure 154**) seat with the spring seat (B, **Figure 154**). The inner diameter is different.

2. Install a new seal on each valve guide (**Figure 155**) and push it down until it bottoms out (**Figure 156**).

3. Coat the valve stems with molybdenum disulfide grease. To avoid damage to the valve stem seal, turn the valve slowly while inserting the valve into the cylinder head (**Figure 157**). Push the valve all the way in (**Figure 158**) until it bottoms.

4. Determine which end of valve springs has closer wound coils (**Figure 159**).

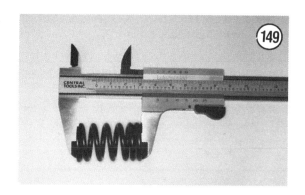

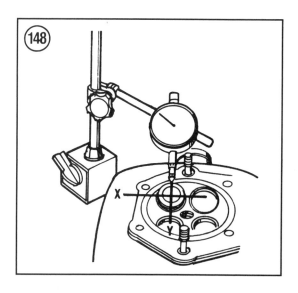

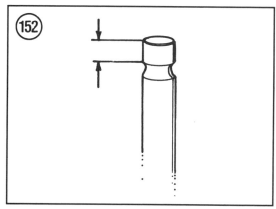

5. Install the inner valve spring (**Figure 160**) and the outer valve spring (**Figure 161**) with the closer wound coils toward the cylinder head.

6. Install the valve spring retainer on top of the valve springs.

CAUTION
To avoid loss of spring tension, do not compress the springs any more than necessary to install the keepers.

4

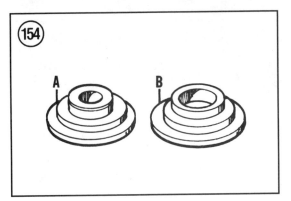

7. Compress the valve springs with a compressor tool (**Figure 141**) and install the valve keepers. Make sure the keepers fit snug into the rounded groove in the valve stem.

8. Remove the compression tool.

9. After all springs have been installed, gently tap the end of the valve stem with a soft aluminum or brass drift and hammer. This will ensure that the keepers are properly seated (**Figure 162**).

> *CAUTION*
> *If the valve stem end has been resurfaced, make sure that the valve stem face (A, **Figure 163**) is above the valve retainers (B, **Figure 163**).*

10. Repeat for all valve assemblies and for the other cylinder head if necessary.

11. Install the cylinder head(s) as described in this chapter.

Valve Guide Replacement

When valve guides are worn so that there is excessive valve stem-to-guide clearance or valve tipping, the guides must be replaced. This job should only be done by a dealer as special tools are required as well as considerable expertise. If the valve guide is replaced; also replace the respective valve.

The following procedure is provided in you choose to perform this task yourself.

> *CAUTION*
> *There **may** be a residual oil or solvent odor left in the oven after heating the cylinder head. If you use a household oven; first check with the person who uses the oven for food preparation to avoid getting into trouble.*

1. If still installed, remove the screws securing the intake pipe onto the cylinder head.

2. If still installed, remove the bolts (**Figure 164**) securing the coolant fitting to the cylinder head and remove the fitting and O-ring seal.

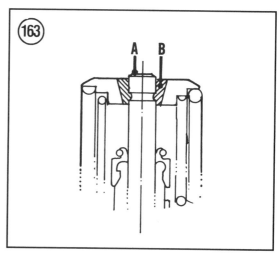

3. The valve guides (**Figure 165**) are installed with a slight interference fit. Place the cylinder head in a heated oven (or on a hot plate). Heat the cylinder head to a temperature between 100-150° C (212-300° F). An easy way to check the proper temperature is to drop tiny drops of water on the cylinder head; if they sizzle and evaporate immediately, the temperature is correct.

CAUTION
Do not heat the cylinder head with a torch (propane or acetylene); never bring a flame into contact with the cylinder head or valve guide. The direct heat will destroy the case hardening of the valve guide and will likely cause warpage of the cylinder head.

4. Remove the cylinder head from the oven and hold onto it with kitchen pot holders, heavy gloves or heavy shop cloths—*it is very hot.*

5. While heating up the cylinder head, place the new valve guides in a freezer (or refrigerator) if possible. Chilling the new guides will slightly reduce their overall diameter while the bores in the hot cylinder

head will be slightly larger due to heat expansion. This size difference will make valve guide installation much easier.

6. Turn the cylinder head upside down on wood blocks. Make sure the cylinder is properly supported on the wood blocks.

7. From the combustion chamber side of the cylinder head, drive out the old valve guide with a hammer and valve guide remover. Use Suzuki special tool, Valve Guide Remover (part No. 09916-44910). Remove the special tool.

8. Remove and discard the valve guide. *Never* reinstall a valve guide that has been removed as it is no longer true nor within tolerances.

9. Insert the valve guide reamer into the valve guide hole in the cylinder head. Use Suzuki special tools, Valve Guide Hole 10.8 mm reamer (A, **Figure 166**), (part No. 09916-34580) and Reamer Handle (B, **Figure 166**), (part No. 09916-34541). Rotate the reamer *clockwise*. Continue to rotate the reamer and work it down through the entire length of the valve guide hole in the cylinder head.

10. While rotating the reamer *clockwise*, withdraw the reamer from the valve guide hole in the cylinder head. Remove the reamer and handle.

CAUTION
Failure to apply fresh engine oil to both the valve guide and the valve guide hole in the cylinder head will result in damage to the cylinder head and/or the new valve guide.

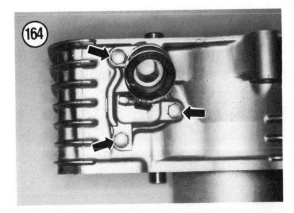

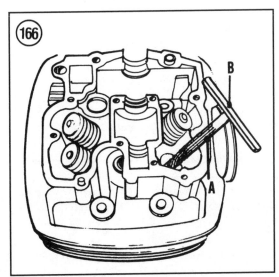

11. Apply fresh engine oil to the new valve guide and the valve guide hole in the cylinder head.

NOTE
The same tool is used for removal and installation of the valve guide. The same valve guide (same part No.) is used for both intake and exhaust valves.

12. From the top side (spring side) of the cylinder head, drive in the new valve guide. Use Suzuki special tools, Valve Guide Attachment (A, **Figure 167**), (part No. 09916-44920) and Valve Guide Remover (B, **Figure 167**), (part No. 09916-44910).

13. After installation, ream the new valve guide as follows:

   a. Use Suzuki special tools, Valve Guide 7mm Reamer (A, **Figure 168**), part No. 09916-34520 and Reamer Handle (B, **Figure 168**), part No. 09916-34541.

   b. Apply cutting oil to both the new valve guide and the valve guide reamer.

CAUTION
Always *rotate the valve guide reamer* ***clockwise****. If the reamer is rotated counterclockwise, damage to a good valve guide will occur.*

   c. Rotate the reamer *clockwise*. Continue to rotate the reamer and work it down through the entire length of the new valve guide. Apply additional cutting oil during this procedure.

   d. Rotate the reamer *clockwise* until the reamer has traveled all the way through the new valve guide.

   e. While rotating the reamer *clockwise*, withdraw the reamer from the valve guide. Remove the reamer.

14. If necessary, repeat Steps 1-13 for any other valve guides.

15. Thoroughly clean the cylinder head and valve guides with solvent to wash out all metal particles. Dry with compressed air.

16. Reface the valve seats as described in this chapter.

17. Install the intake pipe. To prevent a vacuum leak, install a new O-ring seal (**Figure 169**) into the groove in the intake pipe. Install the intake pipes and tighten the screws securely.

18. Install a new O-ring seal (**Figure 170**) into the backside of the coolant fitting and install the fitting

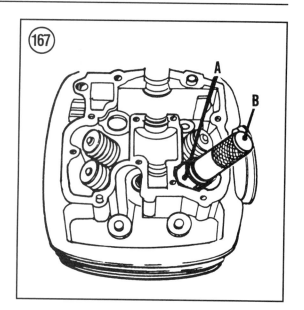

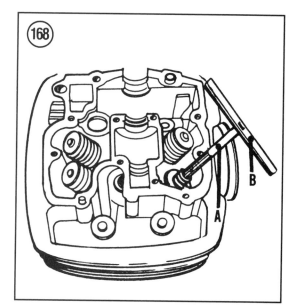

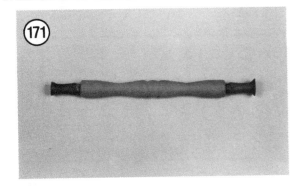

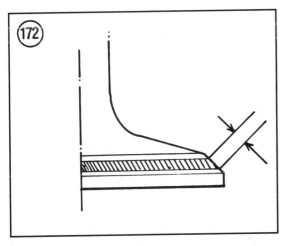

4

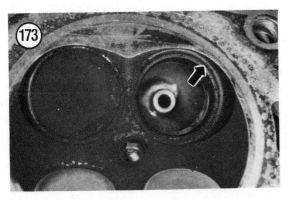

onto the cylinder head. Tighten the bolts (**Figure 164**) securely.

Valve Seat Inspection

1. Remove the valves as described in this chapter.
2. The most accurate method for checking the valve seal is to use Prussian Blue or machinist's dye, available from auto parts stores or machine shops. To check the valve seal with Prussian Blue or machines's dye, perform the following:

    a. Thoroughly clean off all carbon deposits from the valve face with solvent or detergent, then thoroughly dry.

    b. Spread a thin layer of Prussian Blue or machinist's dye evenly on the valve face.

    c. Moisten the end of a suction cup valve tool (**Figure 171**) and attach it to the valve. Insert the valve into the guide.

    d. Using the suction cup tool, tap the valve up and down in the cylinder head. Do *not* rotate the valve or a false indication will result.

    e. Remove the valve and examine the impression left by the Prussian Blue or machinist's dye. If the impression left in the dye (on the valve or in the cylinder head) is not even and continuous and the valve seat width (**Figure 172**) is not within specified tolerance listed in **Table 1**, the cylinder head valve seat must be reconditioned.

3. Closely examine the valve seat (**Figure 173**) in the cylinder head. It should be smooth and even with a polished seating surface.
4. If the valve seat is okay, install the valves as described in this chapter.
5. If the valve seat is not correct, recondition the valve seat as described in this chapter.

Valve Seat Reconditioning

Special valve cutter tools and considerable expertise are required to properly recondition the valve seats in the cylinder heads. You can save considerable money by removing the cylinder heads and taking just the cylinder heads to a dealer or machine shop and have the valve seats ground.

The following procedure is provided in you choose to perform this task yourself.

The Suzuki valve seat cutter and T-handle are available from a Suzuki dealer or from machine shop supply outlets. Follow the manufacturer's instruction in regard to the operating the cutter. You will need the Suzuki Valve Seat Cutter (N-116), a T-handle (N-503), adapter (N-503-1) and the Solid Pilot (N-140-5.5) or equivalent.

The valve seat for both the intake valves and exhaust valves are machined to the same angles. The valve contact surface is cut to 45° angle and the area above the contact surface (closest to the combustion chamber) is cut to a 15° angle (**Figure 174**).

1. Carefully rotate and insert the solid pilot into the valve guide. Make sure the pilot is correctly seated.

2. Use the 45° angle side of the cutter, install the cutter and the T-handle onto the solid pilot.

3. Using the 45° cutter, descale and clean the valve seat with one or two turns.

CAUTION
Measure the valve seat contact area in the cylinder head after each cut to make sure the contact area is correct and to prevent removing too much material. If too much material is removed, the cylinder head must be replaced.

4. If the seat is still pitted or burned, turn the 45° cutter additional turns until the surface is clean. Refer to the previous CAUTION to avoid removing too much material from the cylinder head.

5. Remove the valve cutter, T-handle and solid pilot from the cylinder head.

6. Inspect the valve seat-to-valve face impression as follows:

   a. Spread a thin layer of Prussian Blue or machinist's dye evenly on the valve face.

   b. Moisten the end of a suction cup valve tool (**Figure 171**) and attach it to the valve. Insert the valve into the guide.

   c. Using the suction cup tool, tap the valve up and down in the cylinder head. Do *not* rotate the valve or a false indication will result.

   d. Remove the valve and examine the impression left by the Prussian Blue or machinist's dye.

   e. Measure the valve seat width as shown in **Figure 172**. Refer to **Table 1** for the seat width.

7. If the contact area is too *high* on the valve, or if it is too wide, use the 15° side of the cutter and remove a portion of the top area of the valve seat material to lower and narrow the contact area (**Figure 175**).

8. If the contact area is too *low* on the valve, or too narrow, use the 45° cutter and remove a portion of the lower area of the valve seat material to raise and widen the contact area (**Figure 176**).

9. After the desired valve seat position and width is obtained, use the 45° side of the cutter and T-handle

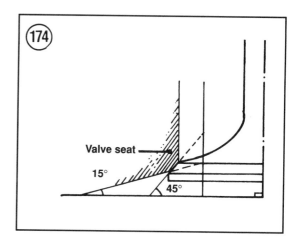
Valve seat
15°
45°

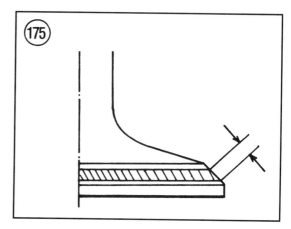

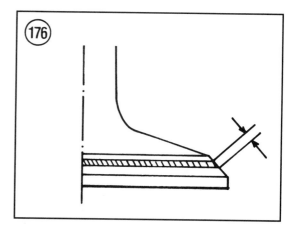

and very lightly clean of any burrs that may have been caused by the previous cuts.

CAUTION
*Do **not** use any valve lapping compound after the final cut has been made.*

10. Check that the finish has a smooth and velvety surface, it should *not* be shiny or highly polished. The final seating will take place when the engine is first run.
11. Repeat Steps 1-10 for all remaining valve seats.
12. Thoroughly clean the cylinder head and all valve components in solvent or detergent and hot water.
13. Install the valve assemblies as described in this chapter and fill the ports with solvent to check for leaks. If any leaks are present, the valve seats must

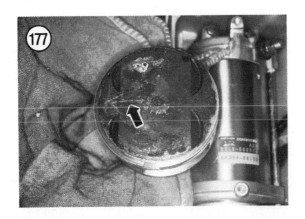

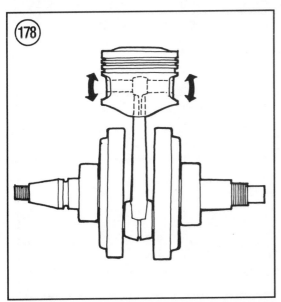

be inspected for foreign matter or burrs that may be preventing a proper seal.
14. If the cylinder head and valve components were cleaned in detergent and hot water, apply a light coat of engine oil to all bare metal steel surfaces to prevent any rust formations.

PISTONS AND PISTON RINGS

Piston
Removal/Installation

1. Remove the cylinder head and cylinder assemblies as described in this chapter.
2. Stuff clean shop cloths into the cylinder bore crankcase opening to prevent objects from falling into the crankcase.
3. Lightly mark the top of the pistons with an "F" (front) or "R" (rear) so they will be installed into the correct cylinder. Also mark an arrow (**Figure 177**) indicating the direction of the piston which is toward the front of the engine.
4. If necessary, remove the piston rings as described in this chapter.
5. Before removing the piston, hold the rod tightly and rock the piston as shown in **Figure 178**. Any rocking motion (do not confuse with the normal sliding motion) indicates wear on the piston pin, piston pin bore or connecting rod small-end bore (more likely a combination of these). Mark the piston and pin so that they will be reassembled into the same set.
6. Remove the clips from each side of the piston pin bore with a small screwdriver, scribe or needlenose pliers (**Figure 179**). Hold your thumb over one edge of the clip when removing it to prevent the clip from springing out.

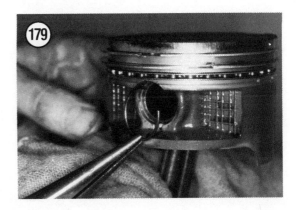

7. Use a proper size wooden dowel or socket extension and push out the piston pin.

CAUTION
Be careful when removing the pin to avoid damaging the connecting rod. If it is necessary to gently tap the pin to remove it, be sure that the piston is properly supported so that lateral shock is not transmitted to the connecting rod lower bearing.

8. If the piston pin is difficult to remove, heat the piston and pin with a butane torch. The pin will probably push right out. Heat the piston to only about 140° F (60° C), i.e., until it is too warm to touch, but not excessively hot. If the pin is still difficult to push out, use a homemade tool as shown in **Figure 180**.

9. Lift the piston from the connecting rod and inspect it as described in this chapter.

10. If the piston is going to be left off for some time, place a piece of foam insulation tube over the end of the rod to protect it.

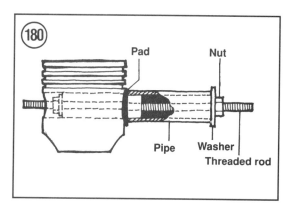

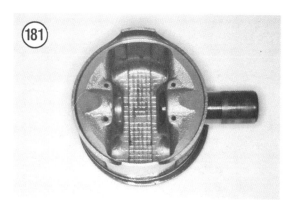

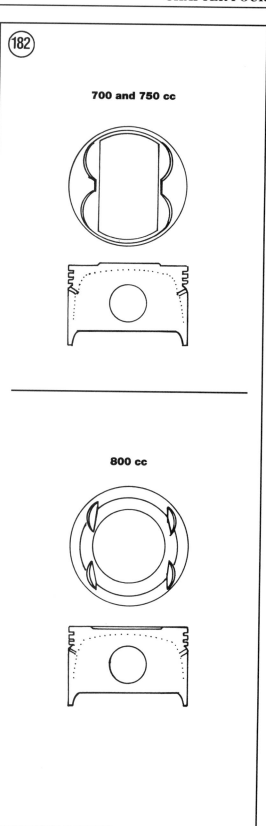

11. Apply molybdenum disulfide grease to the inside surface of the connecting rod piston pin bore.

12. Oil the piston pin with assembly oil or fresh engine oil and install it in the piston until its end extends slightly beyond the inside of the boss (**Figure 181**).

NOTE
*The piston crown design was changed when the engine was increased from 700 and 750 cc to the larger 800 cc as shown in **Figure 182**. If new pistons are going*

to be installed, be sure to install the correct type to avoid any interference.

13. Correctly position the piston-to-connecting rod as follows:

    a. Refer to arrow mark (**Figure 177**) made during disassembly and install the piston with the arrow toward the front of the engine.

    b. If the pistons were not marked, or new pistons are being installed, position the piston with the "triangle" mark on the crown pointing toward the exhaust valve side of the cylinder.

14. Place the piston over the connecting rod.

15. Line up the piston pin with the hole in the connecting rod. Push the piston pin through the connecting rod and into the other side of the piston until it is even with the piston pin clip grooves.

CAUTION
If it is necessary to tap the piston pin into the connecting rod, do so gently with a block of wood or a soft-faced hammer. Make sure you support the piston to prevent the lateral shock from being transmitted to the connecting rod lower bearing.

NOTE
*In the next step, install the clips with the gap away from the cutout in the piston (**Figure 183**).*

16. Install *new* piston pin clips (**Figure 184**) in both ends of the pin boss. Make sure they are seated in the grooves in the piston.

17. Check the installation by rocking the piston back and forth around the pin axis and from side to side along the axis. It should rotate freely back and forth but not from side to side.

18. Install the piston rings as described in this chapter.

19. Repeat Steps 1-18 for the other piston.

Piston Inspection

1. Carefully clean the carbon from the piston crown (**Figure 185**) with a chemical remover or with a soft scraper. Do not remove or damage the carbon ridge around the circumference of the piston above the top ring. If the piston, rings and cylinder are found to be dimensionaly correct and can be reused, removal of the carbon ring from the top of the piston or the

carbon ridge from the top of the cylinder will promote excessive oil consumption.

2. Examine each ring groove for burrs, dented edges and wide wear. Pay particular attention to the top compression ring groove as it usually wears more than the other grooves.

3. If damage or wear indicates piston replacement, select a new piston as described under *Piston Clearance Measurement* in this chapter.

4. Oil the piston pin and install it in the connecting rod. Slowly rotate the piston pin and check for radial and axial play (**Figure 186**). If any play exists, the piston pin should be replaced, providing the rod bore is in good condition.

5. Measure the inside diameter of the piston pin bore (**Figure 187**) with a snap gauge (**Figure 188**) and measure the outside diameter of the piston pin with a micrometer (**Figure 189**). Compare with dimensions given in **Table 1**. Replace the piston and piston pin as a set if either or both are worn.

6. Check the oil control holes (**Figure 190**) in the piston for carbon or oil sludge buildup. Clean the holes with a small diameter drill bit and blow out with compressed air.

7. Check the piston skirt for galling and abrasion which may have been caused by piston seizure. If light galling is present, smooth the affected area with No. 400 emery paper and oil or a fine oilstone. However, if galling is severe or if the piston is deeply scored, replace it.

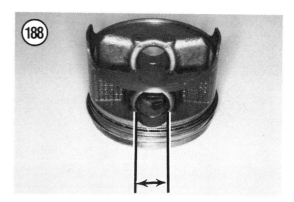

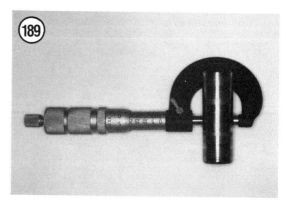

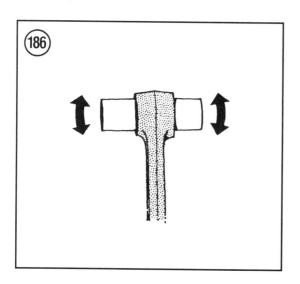

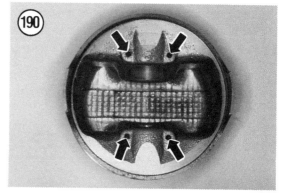

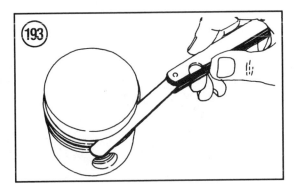

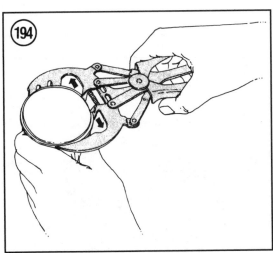

8. If damage or wear indicate piston replacement, select a new piston as described under *Piston Clearance Measurement* in this chapter.

Piston Clearance Measurement

1. Make sure the piston and cylinder walls are clean and dry.
2. Measure the inside diameter of the cylinder bore at a point 1/2 in. (13 mm) from the upper edge with a bore gauge.
3. Measure the outside diameter of the piston across the skirt (**Figure 191**) at right angles to the piston pin. Measure at a distance 0.60 in. (15 mm) up from the bottom of the piston skirt.
4. Subtract the dimension of the piston from the cylinder dimension and compare to the dimension listed in **Table 1**. If clearance is excessive, the piston should be replaced and the cylinder should be re-bored to the next oversize. Purchase the new piston first; measure its diameter and add the specified clearance to determine the proper cylinder bore diameter.

**Piston Ring
Removal/Installation**

> *WARNING*
> *The edges of all piston rings (**Figure 192**) are very sharp. Be careful when handling them to avoid cutting your fingers.*

1. Measure the side clearance of each ring in its groove with a flat feeler gauge (**Figure 193**) and compare to dimensions given in **Table 1**. If the clearance is greater than specified, the rings must be replaced. If the clearance is still excessive with the new rings, the piston must also be replaced.
2. Remove the old rings with a ring expander tool (**Figure 194**) or by spreading the ends with your thumbs just enough to slide the ring up over the piston (**Figure 195**). Repeat for the remaining rings.
3. Carefully remove all carbon buildup from the ring grooves with a broken piston ring (**Figure 196**).
4. Inspect the grooves carefully for burrs, nicks or broken and cracked lands. Recondition or replace the piston if necessary.
5. Check the end gap of each ring. To check the ring, insert the ring, one at a time, into the bottom of the cylinder bore and push it in about 3/4 in. (20 mm)

with the crown of the piston to ensure that the ring is square in the cylinder bore. Measure the gap with a flat feeler gauge (**Figure 197**) and compare to dimensions in **Table 1**. If the gap is greater than specified, the rings should be replaced. When installing new rings, measure their end gap in the same manner as for old ones. If the gap is less than specified, carefully file the ends with a fine-cut file until the gap is correct.

> *NOTE*
> *It is not necessary to measure the oil control ring expander spacer. If the oil control ring rails show wear, all 3 parts of the oil control ring should be replaced as a set.*

6. Roll each ring around its piston groove as shown in **Figure 198** to check for binding. Minor binding is probably caused by groove still dirty or nicked. Small nicks may be cleaned up with a fine-cut file.

> *NOTE*
> *Install the compression rings with their markings facing up.*

7. Install the piston rings—first, the bottom, then the middle, then the top ring—by carefully spreading the ends with your thumbs and slipping the rings over the top of the piston. Remember that the piston rings must be installed with the manufacturer's marks on them toward the top of the piston or there is the possibility of oil pumping past the rings. Install the rings in the order shown in **Figure 199**.

8. Make sure the rings are seated completely in their grooves all the way around the piston and that the

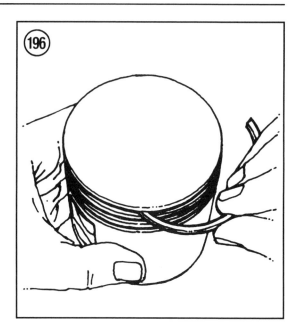

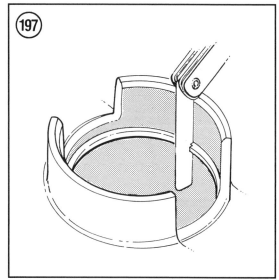

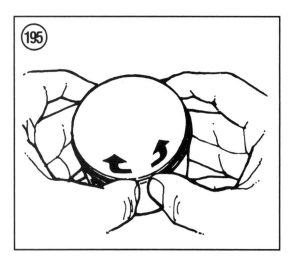

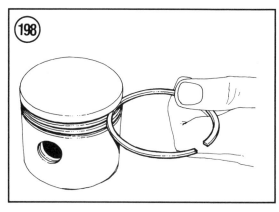

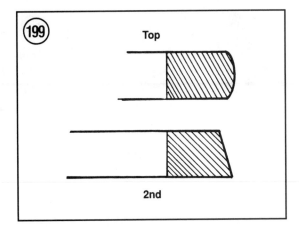

199

Top

2nd

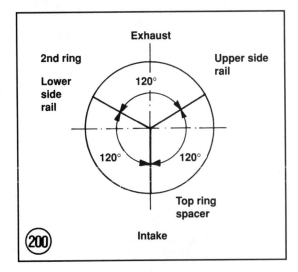

200

Exhaust

2nd ring

Lower side rail

Upper side rail

120°

120°   120°

Top ring spacer

Intake

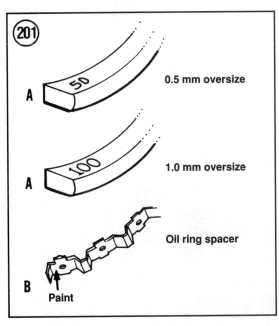

201

50

A

0.5 mm oversize

100

A

1.0 mm oversize

Oil ring spacer

B

Paint

ends are distributed around the piston as shown in **Figure 200**. The important thing is that the ring gaps are not aligned with each other when installed to prevent compression pressure from escaping.

9. If installing oversize compression rings, check the number (A, **Figure 201**) to make sure the correct rings are being installed. The ring numbers should be the same as the piston oversize number.

10. If installing oversize oil rings, check the paint color spot (B, **Figure 201**) to make sure the correct rings are being installed. The paint color spots indicates the following size:

    a. *No color*: standard size.

    b. *Red*: 0.5 mm oversize.

    c. *Yellow*: 1.0 mm oversize.

11. If new rings were installed, measure the side clearance of each ring in its groove with a flat feeler gauge (**Figure 193**) and compare to dimensions given in **Table 1**.

12. After the rings are installed, apply clean engine oil to the rings. Rotate the rings several complete revolutions in their respective grooves. This will assure proper oiling when the engine is first started after and piston service.

OIL PUMP

Removal/Installation

The oil pump can be removed with the engine mounted in the frame; this procedure is shown with the engine removed for clarity.

1. Remove the clutch assembly as described in Chapter Five. During clutch removal, the oil pump driven gear was removed.

2. Remove the bolts (A, **Figure 202**) securing the oil pump to the crankcase and remove the oil pump assembly.

202

A

B

A

A

3. Using needlenose pliers, reach into the crankcase and turn the water pump shaft so the raised tab is vertical (**Figure 203**).

4. Rotate the oil pump drive shaft so the groove (**Figure 204**) will also be vertical when the oil pump is installed into the crankcase.

5. Install the oil pump into the crankcase and align the oil pump drive shaft with the water pump shaft. If necessary, slightly rotate the oil pump shaft (B, **Figure 202**) back and forth to assure correct alignment.

6. Push the oil pump in until it bottoms out.

7. Temporarily install the driven gear. Hold the oil pump in place on the crankcase and rotate the oil pump shaft to make sure it rotates freely with no binding. Remove the driven gear.

8. Install the bolts (A, **Figure 202**) and tighten to the torque specification listed in **Table 2**.

Inspection

There are no replacement parts for the oil pump except for the driven gear and drive chain. Do not try to disassemble the oil pump.

1. Make sure the screw (**Figure 205**) securing the oil pump together is tight.

2. Inspect the oil pump body and cover for cracks (A, **Figure 206**). If worn or damaged, replace the oil pump assembly.

3. Inspect the drive shaft (B, **Figure 206**) for wear or damage. If worn or damaged, replace the oil pump assembly.

4. Inspect the oil pump mounting bosses (**Figure 207**) for fractures or damage. If damaged, replace the oil pump assembly.

5. Inspect the teeth on the driven gear (A, **Figure 208**). Replace the driven gear if the teeth are damaged or any are missing. If the gear is damaged, inspect the drive chain (B, **Figure 208**) as it may also be damaged. Replace the chain if necessary.

PRIMARY DRIVE GEAR

Removal

1. Remove the engine from the frame as described in this chapter.

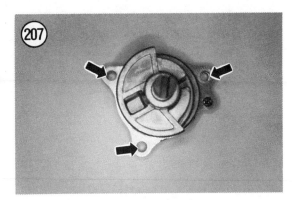

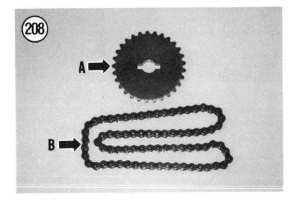

CAUTION
*The primary drive gear bolt has **left-hand** threads. Turn the wrench **clock-wise to loosen** it and **counterclockwise to tighten** it.*

2A. If the clutch assembly is still in place, perform the following:

    a. Stuff shop cloth between the clutch outer housing gear and the primary drive gear (A, **Figure 209**). This will prevent the gear from rotating while loosening the bolt.

    b. Turn the wrench *clockwise* and loosen the primary drive gear bolt (B, **Figure 209**).

2B. If the clutch assembly is removed, perform the following:

    a. If still in place, remove the piston from one of the connecting rods.

    b. Insert a 1/2 in. drive socket extension or round drift through the small end of the connecting rod.

CAUTION
*Use only a **round** extension or drift. Any other shape could cause damage to the connecting rod piston pin hole surface.*

    c. Rotate the crankshaft until the extension or round drift, in the connecting rod, is resting on the top surface of the crankcase.

    d. Turn the wrench *clockwise* and loosen the primary drive gear bolt (A, **Figure 210**).

    e. Remove the socket extension or drift from the connecting rod.

3. If not already removed, remove the clutch assembly as described in Chapter Five.

4. Remove the bolt and the primary drive gear (B, **Figure 210**).

5. Remove the bolt and washer (A, **Figure 211**) securing the rear cylinder camshaft chain tensioner

guide (B, **Figure 211**). Remove the guide and the washer behind it. There is a washer on each side of the tensioner guide. Don't lose the collar in the mounting hole in the tensioner guide.

6. Disengage the rear cylinder camshaft chain (C, **Figure 211**) from the camshaft chain sprocket and remove the chain.

7. Remove the rear cylinder camshaft chain sprocket (**Figure 212**) from the crankshaft.

8. Remove the outer thrust washer (**Figure 213**).

9. Inspect all components as described in this chapter.

Installation

1. Position the outer thrust washer with the beveled side (**Figure 214**) going on first toward the crankshaft surface and install the outer thrust washer.

2. Position the front cylinder camshaft chain sprocket with the alignment mark facing out. This will locate the chain sprocket teeth (**Figure 215**) in toward the crankcase surface.

3. Align the mark (A, **Figure 216**) on the rear cylinder camshaft chain sprocket with the mark (B, **Figure 216**) on the end of the crankshaft and install the sprocket onto the crankshaft (**Figure 212**).

4. Install the rear cylinder camshaft chain (C, **Figure 211**) onto the camshaft chain sprocket and make sure it is properly meshed.

5. Make sure the collar is in place in the tensioner guide mounting hole.

> *CAUTION*
> *The collar must be in place and a washer must be installed on each side of the camshaft chain tensioner guide to allow it to pivot freely on the mounting bolt. If these parts are not installed cor-*

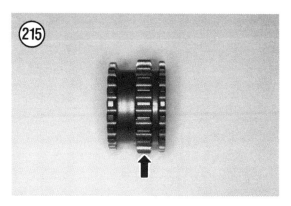

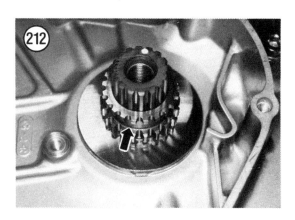

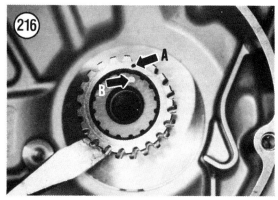

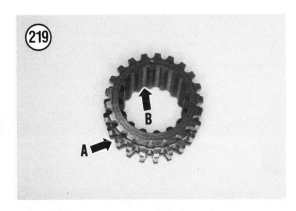

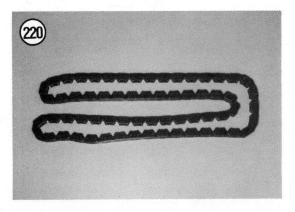

rectly, the guide will be stiff and will not be able to take the slack out of the camshaft chain.

6. Install the rear cylinder camshaft chain tensioner guide (B, **Figure 211**). Place a washer between the tensioner guide and the crankcase surface, then install the bolt and washer (A, **Figure 211**). Tighten the bolt securely.

7. Install the primary drive gear (B, **Figure 210**) and bolt (A, **Figure 210**).

CAUTION
*The primary drive gear bolt has **left-hand** threads. Turn the wrench counterclockwise to tighten it in the following step.*

8. Use the same tool set-up used in Step 2A or 2B of the *Removal* procedure to prevent the crankshaft from rotating while tightening the bolt.

9. Turn the wrench *counterclockwise* and tighten the primary drive gear bolt (A, **Figure 210**) to the torque specification listed in **Table 2**.

10. Install the clutch assembly as described in Chapter Five.

Inspection

NOTE
*If the primary drive gear teeth are damaged, inspect the gear teeth on the clutch outer housing (**Figure 217**) as it may also be damaged and require replacement.*

1. Inspect the primary drive gear (A, **Figure 218**) for chipped or missing teeth, wear or damage. Replace the gear if necessary.

2. Check the inner splines (B, **Figure 218**) for wear or damage, replace the gear if necessary.

3. Inspect the front cylinder camshaft chain sprocket (A, **Figure 219**) for chipped or missing teeth, wear or damage. Replace the sprocket if necessary.

4. Check the inner splines (B, **Figure 219**) for wear or damage, replace the sprocket if necessary.

5. Inspect the front cylinder camshaft chain tensioner guide for deterioration, cracks or damage, replace if necessary.

6. Inspect the camshaft chain (**FIgure 220**) for wear or damage to the links and pins. Replace if necessary.

If the chain is damaged, also inspect the sprocket at each end as they may also be damaged.

7. Measure the camshaft chain for stretching as follows:

    a. Place the chain on a flat surface and pull the chain taut to remove all slack.

    b. Use a vernier caliper and measure the distance between 21 pins (or 20 pitches) as shown in **Figure 221**.

    c. Repeat Steps 7a and 7b several times at various locations around the chain. The chain usually wears and stretches unevenly. It is important to

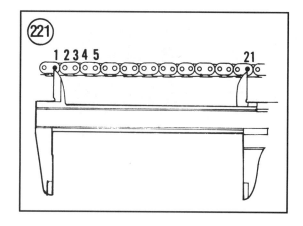

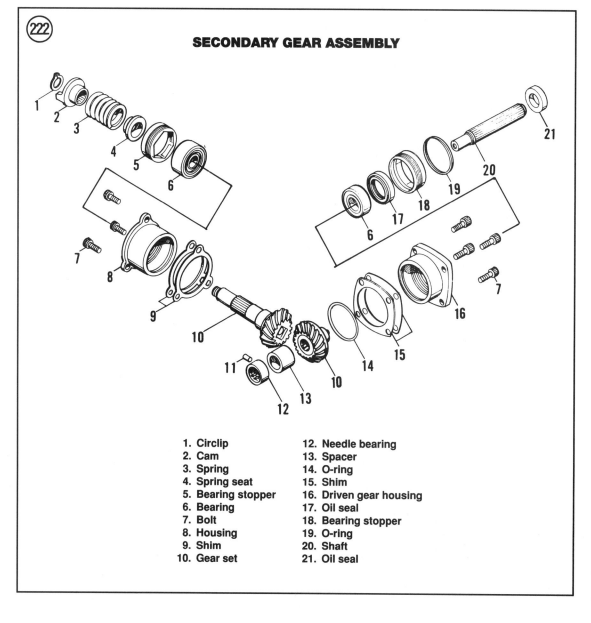

SECONDARY GEAR ASSEMBLY

1. Circlip	12. Needle bearing
2. Cam	13. Spacer
3. Spring	14. O-ring
4. Spring seat	15. Shim
5. Bearing stopper	16. Driven gear housing
6. Bearing	17. Oil seal
7. Bolt	18. Bearing stopper
8. Housing	19. O-ring
9. Shim	20. Shaft
10. Gear set	21. Oil seal
11. Needle bearing	

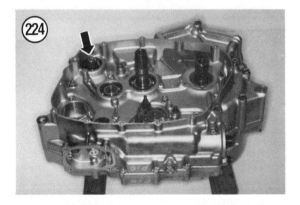

identify and measure the part of the chain that is stretched and worn the most.

d. If the chain has stretched to the service limit of 128.9 mm (5.07 in.) or greater, replace the chain.

SECONDARY GEAR ASSEMBLY

Removal

Refer to **Figure 222** for this procedure.

1. Remove the engine from the frame as described in this chapter.

2. Install the universal joint (**Figure 223**) onto the output shaft of the secondary gear housing. This will keep the internal gears from rotating during nut removal in the following step.

3. Hold onto the universal joint with a large Crescent wrench and loosen the nut (**Figure 224**) securing the secondary gear nut.

4. Remove the nut and washer and the universal joint.

5. Loosen in a crisscross pattern, then remove the secondary gear housing bolts (**Figure 225**).

6. Remove the bolts (**Figure 226**) securing the secondary gear case and remove the case.

7. Remove the secondary bevel gear assembly and bearing (A, **Figure 227**).

8. Separate the crankcase as described in this chapter.

9. Remove the secondary reduction gear (**Figure 228**) from the transmission shaft.

10. Remove the Allen bolts (A, **Figure 229**) securing the secondary bevel drive gear and remove the assembly (B, **Figure 229**) from the crankcase. Also remove the shims located between the assembly and the crankcase mounting surface. Note the number of

shims as the same number must be reinstalled to maintain the correct gear lash between the two bevel gears in the assembly.

11. Inspect the components as described in this chapter.

Installation

1. Apply a light coat of engine oil to the secondary bevel drive gear receptacle in the crankcase.

2. Be sure to install the same number of shims (**Figure 230**) between the assembly and the crankcase mounting surface as noted during removal.

3. Install the secondary bevel drive gear assembly (A, **Figure 231**), then install the secondary reduction gear (B, **Figure 231**) onto the gear assembly to assist in installation.

4. Slowly push the secondary bevel drive gear assembly into the receptacle in the crankcase. Align the mounting bolt holes in the shims and assembly with the holes in the crankcase. After bolt hole alignment is achieved, remove the secondary reduction gear (B, **Figure 231**).

5. Install the Allen bolts (A, **Figure 229**) and tighten to the torque specification listed in **Table 2**.

6. Assemble the crankcase as described in this chapter.

7. Make sure the shaft bearing locating pin (**Figure 232**) is in place in the crankcase.

8. Position the secondary bevel gear assembly bearing (A, **Figure 233**) so it will index properly with the locating pin (B, **Figure 233**) and install the secondary bevel gear assembly and bearing (A, **Fig-**

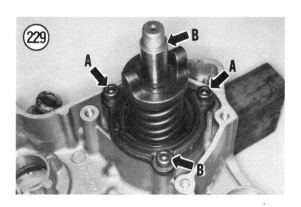

ure 227). Make sure the bearing has seated properly onto the locating pin.

9. If removed, make sure the small O-ring seal is in place, then install the oil control orifice (**Figure 234**). Push it down until it seats completely (**Figure 235**).

10. If removed, install the case locating dowels (B, **Figure 227**) in the crankcase.

NOTE
Use ThreeBond No. 1207, or equivalent gasket sealer. When selecting an equivalent, avoid thick and hard-setting materials.

11. Apply a light coat of gasket sealer to the secondary case sealing surfaces on the crankcase.

12. Correctly position the driven gear housing so the drain hole (**Figure 236**) is facing down.

13. Install the case and bolts (**Figure 226**). Tighten the bolts in 2 stages, initial and final, to the final torque specification listed in **Table 2**.

14. Apply red Loctite (No. 271) to the secondary gear housing bolts prior to installation.

15. Install the secondary gear housing bolts (**Figure 225**) and tighten to the torque specification listed in **Table 2**.

16. Install the universal joint onto the output shaft of the secondary gear housing. This will keep the internal gears from rotating while tightening the nut in the following step.

17. Install the washer and nut (**Figure 224**).

18. Hold onto the universal joint with a large Crescent wrench and tighten the nut securing the secondary gear. Tighten the nut to the torque specification listed in **Table 2**.

NOTE
Make sure the transmission is in neutral.

19. Rotate the universal joint and make sure there is no binding within the secondary gear assembly. If the assembly will not rotate properly, correct the problem at this time. Remove the universal joint.

20. Install the engine into the frame as described in this chapter.

Inspection

Special tools are required to disassemble the driven shaft assembly. Refer this type of work to a Suzuki dealer or competent machine shop.

1. Inspect for chipped or missing teeth on the drive gear (**Figure 237**) and the driven gear (**Figure 238**). If either gear is damaged both the drive and driven gears must be replaced as a set.

2. Inspect the driven gear assembly splines (**Figure 239**) for wear or damage. If damaged, both the drive and driven gears must be replaced as a set. Also check the inner splines of the universal joint as they may also be damaged.

3. Inspect driven gear shaft small roller bearing (**Figure 240**). Make sure it rotates freely with no binding. Replace the bearing if necessary.

4. Inspect the spring (A, **Figure 241**) for wear, cracks or damage and replace if necessary.

5. Install the secondary reduction gear (B, **Figure 241**) onto the drive gear shaft and check for proper engagement. Check the cams (A, **Figure 242**) and ramps (B, **Figure 242**) for wear, cracks or burrs. Replace if necessary.

6. Inspect the secondary reduction gear for chipped or missing teeth (A, **Figure 243**). Inspect the inner and outer bearing surfaces of the bushing (B, **Figure 243**) for wear. Insert the bushing into the gear and

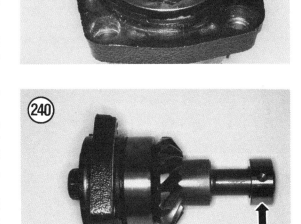

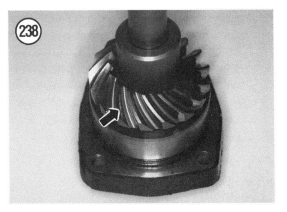

check for looseness or excessive wear. Replace if necessary.

7. Inspect the drive gear assembly shims (**Figure 244**) for wear or damage. Replace if necessary and replace with shims of the exact same thickness. Take the old shims along to ensure an exact matchup as there are 5 different shim thicknesses available from Suzuki.

8. Move the universal joint (**Figure 245**) back and forth and pull in and out on it. Check for looseness or stiffness, replace if necessary.

9. Inspect the universal joint inner splines for wear or damage. Refer to **Figure 246** and **Figure 247**. If the splines are damaged, also check the outer splines on the drive shaft for damage. Replace the universal joint if necessary.

CRANKCASE

Service to the lower end requires that the crankcase assembly be removed from the motorcycle frame and disassembled (split).

Disassembly

1. Remove the engine as described in this chapter.
2. Remove the following exterior assemblies from the crankcase assembly:
   a. Cylinder head and cylinder assemblies: this chapter.
   b. Alternator: Chapter Eight.
   c. Starter clutch assembly: Chapter Eight.
   d. Oil sump and filter: this chapter.
   e. External shift mechanism: Chapter Six.

f. Clutch: Chapter Five

g. Water pump: Chapter Nine.

h. Starter motor: Chapter Eight.

i. Neutral switch: Chapter Eight.

j. Oil pressure switch: Chapter Eight.

3. If still in place, remove the Woodruff key (**Figure 248**) from the crankshaft taper.

4. Remove the bolt and washer (A, **Figure 249**) securing the front cylinder camshaft chain tensioner guide (B, **Figure 249**). Remove the guide and the washer behind it. There is a washer on each side of the tensioner guide. Don't lose the collar in the mounting hole in the tensioner guide.

5. Disengage the front cylinder camshaft chain (C, **Figure 249**) from the camshaft chain sprocket and remove the chain.

6. Shift the transmission into gear.

7. Install the universal joint (**Figure 250**) onto the output shaft of the secondary gear housing. This will keep the transmission shaft and gears from rotating during bolt removal in the following step.

8. Hold onto the universal joint with a large Crescent wrench and loosen the bolt (A, **Figure 251**) securing the transmission main shaft to the crankcase.

9. Remove the bolt and washer (B, **Figure 251**) from the end of the shaft.

10. Remove the secondary gear assembly from the exterior of the crankcase as described in this chapter.

11. Starting with the right-hand side, loosen all bolts 1/2 turn in a crisscross pattern, then remove the bolts. Make sure all bolts are removed. Don't lose the washer (**Figure 252**) under the lower front bolt adjacent to the oil pump mounting area (A, **Figure 253**). This washer must be reinstalled under the

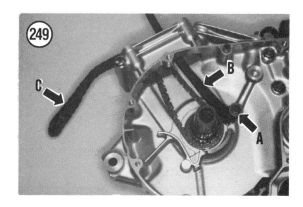

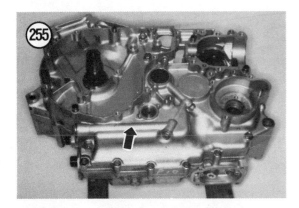

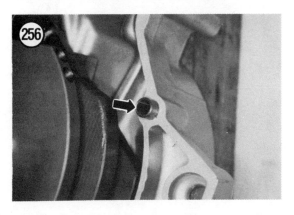

correct bolt during assembly to prevent an oil leak. There is also a washer (**Figure 254**) under the bolt at the top of the crankcase where the 2 cylinders meet (B, **Figure 253**).

12. Turn the crankcase over with the left-hand side facing up.

13. On the left-hand side, loosen all bolts 1/2 turn in a crisscross pattern (**Figure 255**). Remove all bolts. Make sure all bolts are removed.

14. Turn the crankcase back over so the right-hand side is facing up.

4

CAUTION
If it is necessary to pry the crankcase apart, do it very carefully so that you do not mar the gasket surfaces. If you do, the cases will leak and must be replaced as a set. They cannot be repaired.

15. Carefully tap around the perimeter of the crankcase with a plastic mallet (do not use a metal hammer) to help separate the case halves. Separate the case halves by pulling the right-hand crankcase up and off the left-hand case half.

16. After removing the right-hand crankcase half, the transmission and crankshaft assemblies should stay with the left-hand crankcase. Check the right-hand crankcase to make sure no transmission shims are stuck to the bearings. If found, reinstall them immediately in their original positions.

17. Remove the 2 small dowel pins from the left-hand crankcase half. Refer to **Figure 256** and **Figure 257**.

18. Remove the small O-ring (**Figure 258**) from the left-hand crankcase half.

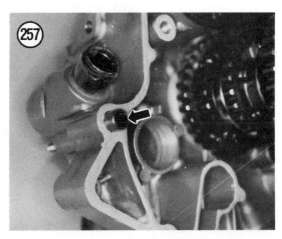

19. Remove the transmission, shift forks and shift drum assemblies from the left-hand crankcase half as described in Chapter Five in this section of the manual.

20. Remove the crankshaft assembly as described in this chapter.

Inspection

The following procedure may include the use of highly specialized and expensive measuring instruments. If such instruments are not readily available, have the measurements performed by a dealer or qualified machine shop.

1. Remove all old gasket residue material from both crankcase mating surfaces.

2. Soak any old gasket material stuck to the surface with solvent. Use a broad-tipped *dull* chisel and gently scrape off all gasket residue. Do not gouge the sealing surfaces as oil and air leaks will result.

3. Remove all oil gallery plugs and sealing washers. Refer to **Figure 259**, **Figure 260** and **Figure 261**.

4. Remove the bolts (A, **Figure 262**) and remove the oil pipe (B, **Figure 262**) and O-rings from the right-hand case half.

5. Remove the oil pressure relief valve (**Figure 263**) from the right-hand crankcase half.

6. Remove the clutch pushrod oil seal (**Figure 264**) from the left-hand crankcase half.

7. Thoroughly clean the inside and outside of both crankcase halves with cleaning solvent. Dry with compressed air. Make sure there is no solvent residue left in either part as it will contaminate the new engine oil.

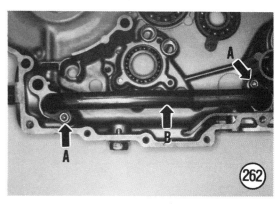

8. Check all bolts and threaded holes for stripping, cross-threading or deposit buildup. Threaded holes should be blown out with compressed air as dirt buildup in the bottom of a hole may prevent the bolt from being torqued properly. Replace damaged bolts and washers.

9. Inspect machined surfaces for burrs, cracks or other damage. Refer to **Figure 265** and **Figure 266**. Repair minor damage with a fine-cut file or oilstone.

10. Make sure that all oil passages throughout both crankcase halves are clean.

11. Apply a light coat of engine oil to the bearing surfaces to prevent any rust formation.

12. Inspect the threads for the oil filter. Clean off with a wire brush if necessary. If the threads are damaged, clean them up with an appropriate size metric thread die.

13. Inspect the crankcase bearings as described in this chapter.

14. Make sure the oil control orifice oil hole (A, **Figure 267**) is clear. Clean out with a piece of wire and compressed air.

15. Inspect the O-ring (B, **Figure 267**) for deterioration or hardness and replace if necessary.

16. Install all items removed during this inspection process.

17. Install new O-ring seals (**Figure 268**) on the oil pipe prior to installation. Tighten the bolts securely.

Crankcase Bearings
Inspection

1. After cleaning the crankcase halves in cleaning solvent and drying with compressed air, lubricate the bearings with engine oil.

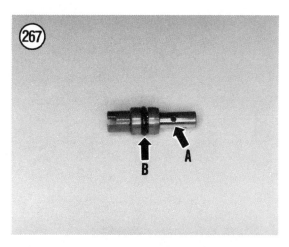

2. With your fingers, rotate the transmission bearing inner races and check for play or roughness. Refer to **Figure 269** and **Figure 270**. Replace the bearing(s) if it is noisy or if it does not spin smoothly.

3. Rotate the shift drum bearing inner race (**Figure 271**) with your finger and check for play or roughness. Replace the bearing if it is noisy or if it does not spin smoothly.

4. Rotate the secondary gear shaft bearing inner race (**Figure 272**) slowly and check for play or roughness. Replace the bearing if it is noisy or does not spin smoothly.

5. Inspect the crankshaft main bearings (**Figure 273**) for wear (bluish tint) or damage. Make sure they are locked in place (**Figure 274**). The bearing inside dimension is measured as described under *Crankshaft Bearing and Oil Clearance Measurement* in this chapter. If the bearings are damaged or worn, have them replaced.

Crankcase Bearings Replacement

Crankshaft main bearings

The crankshaft main bearings are removed and installed from the crankcase halves with a hydraulic press and special tools. After the new bearings are installed, they must be honed.

To avoid damage to a costly set of crankcase halves, this procedure should be entrusted to a Suzuki dealer or machine shop. Improper removal and installation of the bearings could result in costly crankcase damage.

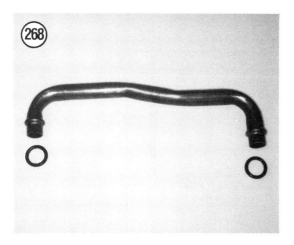

Other than crankshaft main bearings

1. On bearings equipped with retainers, perform the following:

NOTE
The bearing retainer screws had a locking agent applied to the threads during installation and may be difficult to remove. To avoid damage or "rounding" off of the screw head, use the recommended tool in this procedure.

a. Use an impact driver with the appropriate size bit and loosen the screws securing the bearing retainers. Refer to **Figure 275** and **Figure 276**.

b. Remove the screws and retainers.

WARNING
*There **may** be a residual oil or solvent odor left in the oven after heating the crankcase. If you use a household oven, first check with the person who uses the oven for food preparation to avoid getting into trouble.*

c. Heat the crankcase to approximately 205-257° F (95-125° C) in an oven or on a hot plate.

CAUTION
Do not attempt bearing removal by heating the crankcases with a torch as this type of localized heating may warp the cases.

d. Wearing a pair of work gloves for protection, remove the case from the oven and place it on wood blocks for support.

e. Drive out the bearing with a suitable size drift placed on the outside bearing race. A large socket also works well for bearing removal.

2. Perform Steps 1c-1e for the secondary gear shaft bearing and remove the bearing.

3. Special Suzuki tools are required to remove bearings from blind holes (**Figure 269**). Remove these bearings as follows:

a. Install the bearing removers (part No. 09914-79610 and 099923-73210) into the bearing so they grab the backside of the bearing inner race.

b. Attach the slide shaft (part No. 09930-30102) onto the bearing removers.

c. Using a quick in-and-out strokes of the slide shaft, withdraw the bearing from the crankcase.

4. Before installing new bearings, clean the bearing housing and oil passages with solvent. Dry thoroughly with compressed air.

5. Install new crankcase bearings by reversing the removal steps, noting the following:

   a. Installation of the bearings is made easier by first placing the bearings in a freezer for approximately 30 minutes. Then reheat the crankcase half and install the bearing by driving it squarely into position. If the bearing cocks in its bore, remove it and reinstall. It may be necessary to refreeze the bearing and reheat the case half.

   b. Lubricate the bearing races with clean engine oil after installation.

   c. On bearings with retainers, apply red Loctite (No. 271) to the screw threads prior to installation, then install the retainer.

Assembly

1. Prior to installation of all parts, coat all rotating parts with assembly oil or engine oil.

2. Place the left-hand crankcase on wood blocks.

3. Install the crankshaft as described in this chapter. Make sure the connecting rods are positioned correctly within the cylinder openings (**Figure 277**).

4. Install the shift drum, shift forks and transmission assemblies as described in Chapter Five.

5. Install the small O-ring (**Figure 258**) into the left-hand crankcase half. Apply clean engine oil to the O-ring.

6. If removed, install the 2 small dowel pins into the left-hand crankcase half. Refer to **Figure 256** and **Figure 257**.

7. Apply oil to the transmission shafts and crankshaft bearing surfaces.

8. Clean the crankcase mating surfaces of both halves with aerosol electrical contact cleaner.

9. Make sure both crankcase half sealing surfaces are perfectly clean and dry.

NOTE
Use ThreeBond No. 1207, or equivalent gasket sealer. When selecting an equivalent, avoid thick and hard-setting materials.

10. Apply a light coat of gasket sealer to the sealing surfaces of the left-hand half. Make the coating as thin as possible.

11. Align the right-hand crankcase bearings with the left-hand assembly. Join both halves and tap together lightly with a plastic mallet—do not use a metal hammer as it will damage the cases.

NOTE
Due to the spring in the secondary drive gear assembly, the crankcase halves will not come completely together as shown in Figure 278. The gap shown is a normal gap distance, but if the gap is larger than shown, refer to the following CAUTION.

CAUTION
The crankcase halves should fit together without force. If the crankcase halves do not fit together, with the exception of the previously mentioned normal gap, do not attempt to pull them together with the crankcase bolts. Separate the crankcase halves and investi-

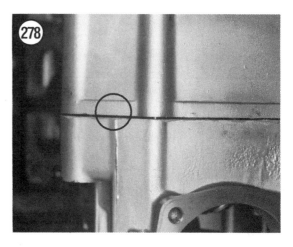

gate the cause of the interference. If the transmission shafts were disassembled, recheck to make sure that a gear is not installed backwards. Do not risk damage by trying to force the cases together.

NOTE
Install all bolts in the crankcase half so that all bolt heads protrude up from the surface of the crankcase the same amount as shown in Figure 279. If they do not, the bolt is installed in the wrong location. Remove the bolt and insert it in the correct hole.

12. Install the bolts in the right-hand crankcase. Tighten in a crisscross pattern in two stages to a final torque listed in **Table 2**.

NOTE
*On the right-hand side, don't forget to install the washer (**Figure 252**) under*

*the lower front bolt adjacent to the oil pump mounting area (A, **Figure 253**). This washer must be reinstalled under the correct bolt during assembly to prevent an oil leak. Also install the washer (**Figure 254**) under the bolt at the top of the crankcase where the 2 cylinders meet (B, **Figure 253**).*

13. Turn the crankcase assembly over and install the bolts in the left-hand crankcase. Tighten in a crisscross pattern in two stages to a final torque listed in **Table 2**.

14. Install the secondary gear assembly onto the exterior of the crankcase as described in this chapter.

15. Shift the transmission into gear.

16. Install the universal joint onto the output shaft of the secondary gear housing. This will keep the transmission shaft and gears from rotating during bolt installation in the following step.

17. Install the washer (A, **Figure 280**) and bolt (B, **Figure 280**) into the end of the transmission mainshaft.

18. Hold onto the universal joint with a large Crescent wrench and tighten the transmission bolt (B, **Figure 280**) to the torque specification listed in **Table 2**.

19. Remove the universal joint.

20. Install, then engage the front cylinder camshaft chain (C, **Figure 249**) onto the camshaft chain sprocket on the crankshaft. Make sure it is properly meshed with the sprocket teeth.

21. Install the front cylinder camshaft chain tensioner guide (B, **Figure 249**). Make sure the collar is in place in the tensioner guide mounting hole. Install a washer on each side of the guide, then install the bolt (A, **Figure 251**) and tighten to the torque specification listed in **Table 2**.

22. If removed, install Woodruff key (**Figure 248**) into the crankshaft taper. Make sure it is centered in the groove.

23. Install the following exterior assemblies onto the crankcase assembly:
   a. Oil pressure switch: Chapter Eight.
   b. Neutral switch: Chapter Eight.
   c. Starter motor: Chapter Eight.
   d. Water pump: Chapter Nine.
   e. Clutch: Chapter Five
   f. External shift mechanism: Chapter Six.
   g. Oil sump and filter: this chapter.
   h. Starter clutch assembly: Chapter Eight.

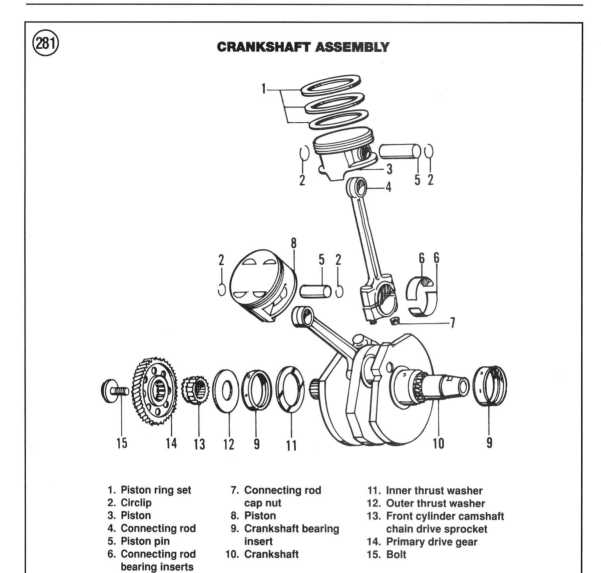

(281)

CRANKSHAFT ASSEMBLY

1. Piston ring set
2. Circlip
3. Piston
4. Connecting rod
5. Piston pin
6. Connecting rod bearing inserts
7. Connecting rod cap nut
8. Piston
9. Crankshaft bearing insert
10. Crankshaft
11. Inner thrust washer
12. Outer thrust washer
13. Front cylinder camshaft chain drive sprocket
14. Primary drive gear
15. Bolt

(282)

(283)

i. Alternator: Chapter Eight.

j. Cylinder head and cylinder assemblies: this chapter.

24. Install the engine as described in this chapter.

CRANKSHAFT AND CONNECTING RODS

Removal/Installation

Refer to **Figure 281** for this procedure.

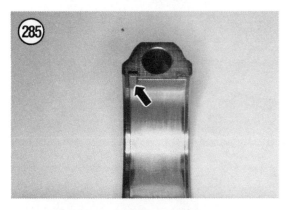

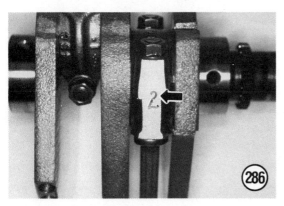

1. Split the crankcase as described in this chapter.

2. Remove the crankshaft assembly (**Figure 282**) from the left-hand crankcase half.

3. Remove the inner thrust washer (**Figure 283**) from the right-hand end of the crankshaft.

4. Remove the connecting rod cap bolt nuts (**Figure 284**) and separate the rods from the crankshaft.

NOTE
The rear cylinder connecting rod is located nearest the tapered end (alternator rotor location) of the crankshaft.

5. Mark each rod and cap as a set. Also mark them with a "F" (front) and "R" (rear) to indicate from what cylinder they were removed.

6. Mark each bearing insert so that it can be reinstalled in its original position, if it is reused.

7. Install the bearing inserts into each connecting rod and cap. Make sure they are locked in place correctly (**Figure 285**).

CAUTION
If the old bearings are reused, be sure they are installed in their exact original positions.

8. Lubricate the bearings and crankpins with molybdenum disulfide grease.

9. Position the connecting rod and cap with the I.D. code number (**Figure 286**) facing toward the *rear* of the engine.

10. Install the caps and tighten the caps nuts evenly, in 2 stages, to the torque specification listed in **Table 2**.

11. Position the inner thrust washer with the oil control grooves facing in toward the crankshaft.

12. Install the inner thrust washer (**Figure 283**) onto the right-hand end of the crankshaft.

NOTE
*When installing the crankshaft, align the front and rear connecting rods with their respective cylinder position (**Figure 277**). Continue to check this alignment until the crankshaft is completely installed.*

13. Position the crankshaft with the tapered end going into the left-hand crankcase and install the crankshaft in the left-hand crankcase (**Figure 282**).

14. Inspect the crankshaft side thrust clearance as described in the following procedure.

15. Assemble the crankcase as described in this chapter.

Crankshaft Side Thrust Clearance

Whenever the crankshaft is removed from the crankcase, the side thrust clearance must be checked. Side thrust clearance is adjusted by replacing the *inner* thrust washer with one of a different thickness.

1. Position the inner thrust washer with the oil control grooves facing in toward the crankshaft.

2. Install the inner thrust washer (**Figure 283**) onto the right-hand end of the crankshaft.

> *NOTE*
> *When installing the crankshaft, align the front and rear connecting rods with their respective cylinder position in the crankcase (**Figure 277**). Continue to check this alignment until the crankshaft is completely installed.*

3. Position the right-hand crankcase half over the splined (right) end of the crankshaft.

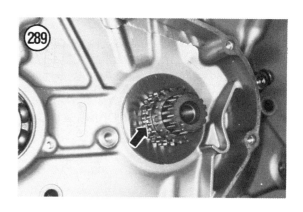

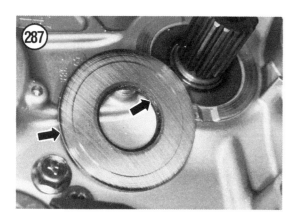

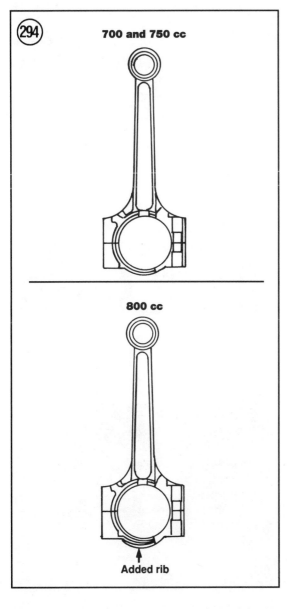

4. Position the outer thrust washer on the outer side of the right-hand crankcase, with the beveled side (**Figure 287**) toward the center of the crankshaft, then install the outer thrust washer (**Figure 288**).

5. Align the mark on the rear cylinder camshaft chain sprocket with the alignment mark on the end of the crankshaft and install the sprocket onto the crankshaft (**Figure 289**). Push it down until it stops against the outer thrust washer.

6. Install the primary drive gear (**Figure 290**) and bolt (**Figure 291**).

7. Have an assistant hold onto the crankshaft and tighten the bolt to the torque specification listed in **Table 2**.

8. Insert a flat feeler gauge (**Figure 292**) between the outer thrust washer and the right-hand crankcase surface. The specified thrust clearance is listed in **Table 1**. If the thrust clearance is incorrect, perform the following:

    a. Reverse Steps 1-7 and remove the crankshaft from the right-hand crankcase half.

    b. Remove and measure the *inner* thrust washer with a Vernier caliper or micrometer (**Figure 293**).

    c. The inner thrust washers are available from a Suzuki dealer in increments of 0.025 mm (0.0010 in.). The thrust washer thickness and part numbers are listed in **Table 3**. Select a new inner thrust washer that will accomplish the specified thrust clearance listed in **Table 1**.

    d. Install the new inner thrust washer and repeat this procedure to make sure the thrust clearance is now within specification.

    e. Remove all components from the right-hand crankcase half, then assemble as described in this chapter.

Connecting Rod Inspection

NOTE
*The connecting rod design was changed when the engine was increased from 700 and 750 cc to the larger 800 cc as shown in **Figure 294**. If new connecting rods are going to be installed, be sure to install the correct type to avoid any interference.*

1. Check each rod and cap for obvious damage such as cracks and burrs.

2. Check the connecting rod small end for wear or scoring.

3. Insert the piston pin into the connecting rod (**Figure 295**) and rotate it. Check for looseness or roughness. Replace the defective part.

4. Measure the inside diameter of the connecting rod small end (**Figure 296**) with an inside micrometer. Compare to the dimension listed in **Table 1**. If the dimension is greater than specified, replace the connecting rod assembly.

5. Take the rods to a machine shop and have them checked for twisting and bending.

6. Examine the bearing inserts (A, **Figure 297**) for wear, scoring or burning. They may be reused if they are in good condition. Before discarding any bearing insert, check the back and note if it is stamped with a number indicating that it is undersize. A previous owner may have fitted the engine with undersize bearings.

7. Inspect the connecting rod threaded studs (B, **Figure 297**) for wear or damaged threads. If damaged, replace the connecting rod and stud.

8. Check bearing clearance as described in this chapter.

Connecting Rod Bearing and Oil Clearance Measurement

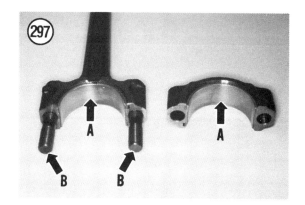

CAUTION
If the old bearings are to be reused, be sure that they are installed in their exact original locations.

1. Wipe bearing inserts and crankpins clean. Install bearing inserts in rod and cap (A, **Figure 297**).

2. Place a piece of Plastigage on one crankpin parallel to the crankshaft.

3. Install rod, cap and nuts, then tighten the nuts to the torque specification listed in **Table 2**.

CAUTION
Do not rotate crankshaft while Plastigage is in place.

4. Remove nuts and the rod cap.

5. Measure width of flattened Plastigage according to the manufacturer's instructions. Measure at both ends of the strip. A difference of 0.001 in. (0.025 mm) or more indicates a tapered crankpin; the crankshaft must be reground or replaced. Use a microme-

ter and measure the crankpin OD (**Figure 298**) to get an exact journal dimension.

6. If the crankpin taper is within tolerance, measure the bearing clearance with the same strip of Plastigage. Correct bearing clearance is specified in **Table 1**. Remove Plastigage strips.

7. If the bearing clearance is greater than specified, use the following steps for new bearing selection.

8. The connecting rods and caps are marked with a code number "1," "2" or "3" (**Figure 299**) indicating the inside diameter of the bore in connecting rod.

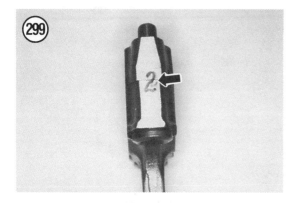

NOTE
On some models, the crankshaft has a mark on each counterbalance while others, both numbers are stamped on 1 counterbalance and look like "L 1 1 R."

9. The crankshaft is marked on the counterbalancer with a "1," "2" or "3" (**Figure 300**) inicating the outside diameter fo the crankpin journal.

10. Select new bearings by cross-referencing the connecting rod journal I.D. code in the vertical column with the crankpin O.D. code number in the horizontal column. Where the columns intersect, the new bearing color is indicated. **Table 4** gives the bearing color and **Table 5** gives bearing color and thickness.

11. After new bearings have been installed, recheck clearance with Plastigage. If the clearance is out of specifications, either the connecting rod or the crankshaft is worn beyond the service limit. Refer the engine to a dealer or qualified specialist.

**Connecting Rod Side
Clearance Measurement**

1. With both connecting rods attached to the crankshaft, insert a flat feeler gauge between the counterweight and the connecting rod big end at the locations shown in **Figure 301**.

2. The specified side clearance is listed in **Table 1**.

3. If the clearance is out of specification, perform the following:

    a. Measure the connecting big end width with a micrometer (**Figure 302**) and compare to the

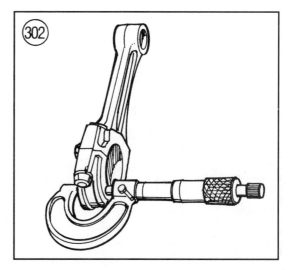

dimension listed in **Table 1**. If the width is less than specified, replace the connecting rod assembly.

  b. Measure the crankpin width with a dial caliper (**Figure 303**) and compare to the dimension listed in **Table 1**.

If the width is greater than specified, replace the crankshaft.

Crankshaft Inspection

1. Clean crankshaft thoroughly with solvent. Clean oil holes with rifle cleaning brushes; flush thoroughly and dry with compressed air. Lightly oil all surfaces immediately to prevent rust.

2. Inspect the connecting rod journals (**Figure 304**) and the main bearing journals (**Figure 305**) for scratches, ridges, scoring, nicks, etc.

3. If the surfaces of all bearing journals are satisfactory, measure the main bearing journals with a micrometer (**Figure 306**) and check for out-of-roundness and taper.

4. Inspect the camshaft chain sprocket (A, **Figure 307**) on the left-hand end. If it is worn or damaged, the crankshaft will have to be replaced.

5. Inspect the taper (B, **Figure 307**) where the alternator rotor is installed on the left-hand end. If it is worn or damaged, the crankshaft will have to be replaced.

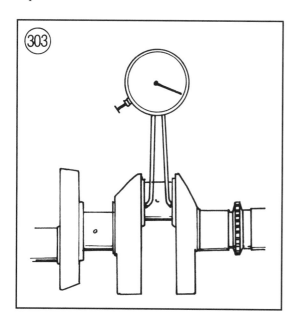

6. Inspect the splines (**Figure 308**) on the right-hand end for wear or damage. Minor damage can be cleaned up with a fine-cut file, but if damage is severe the crankshaft will have to be replaced.

Crankshaft Bearing and Oil Clearance Measurement

1. Wipe bearing inserts in the crankcase and the main bearing journals clean.
2. Use a micrometer and measure the main journal OD (**Figure 306**) at two places. Write these dimensions down.
3. Use a bore gauge and measure the main journal insert ID (**Figure 309**) at two places. Write these dimensions down.
4. To determine oil clearance, subtract the crankshaft OD (Step 2) from the main journal insert ID (Step 3).
5. The oil clearance specification is listed in **Table 1**. If the clearance is out of specifications, either the crankshaft or the bearing insert is worn beyond the service limit.

> *NOTE*
> *The main bearings are removed and installed with a hydraulic press and special tools. After the bearings have been installed, they must be honed to a specific dimension. To avoid damage to a costly set of crankcase halves, this procedure should be entrusted to a Suzuki dealer or machine shop. Improper removal and installation of the bearings could result in severe crankcase damage.*

BREAK-IN

Following cylinder servicing (boring, honing, new rings, etc.) and major lower end work, the engine should be broken-in just as if it were new. The performance and service life of the engine depends greatly on a careful and sensible break-in. For the first 500 miles, no more than one-third throttle should be used and speed should be varied as much as possible within the one-third throttle limit. Prolonged, steady running at one speed, no matter how moderate, is to be avoided, as is hard acceleration.

Following the 500-mile service, increasingly more throttle can be used but full throttle should not be used until the motorcycle has covered at least 1,000 miles and then it should be limited to short bursts until 1,500 miles have been logged.

The mono-grade oils recommended for break-in and normal use provide a superior bedding pattern for rings and cylinders than do multi-grade oils. As a result, piston ring and cylinder bore life are greatly increased. During this period, oil consumption will be higher than normal. It is therefore important to frequently check and correct the oil level. At no time, during break-in or later, should the oil level be allowed to drop below the bottom line on the inspection window; if the oil level is low, the oil will become overheated resulting in insufficient lubrication and increased wear.

500-Mile Service

It is essential that the oil and filter be changed after the first 500 miles. In addition, it is a good idea to change the oil and filter at the completion of break-in (about 1,500 miles) to ensure that all of the particles produced during break-in are removed from the lubrication system. The small added expense may be considered a smart investment that will pay off in increased engine life.

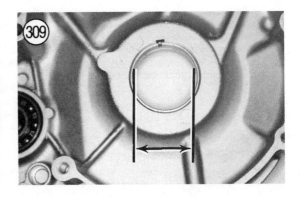

Table 1 ENGINE SPECIFICATIONS

	Specification	Wear limit
General		
Type and number of cylinders	V-2 cylinder, SOHC, liquid cooled	
Bore × stroke		
700 cc	80.0 × 69.6 mm (3.15 × 2.74 in.)	
750 cc	80.0 × 74.4 mm (3.15 × 2.93 in.)	
800 cc	83.0 × 74.4 mm (3.27 × 2.93 in.)	
Displacement		
700 cc	699 cc (43 cu. in.)	
750 cc	747 cc (45.6 cu. in.)	
800 cc	805 cc (49.1 cu. in.)	
Compression pressure	1,300-1,600 kPa (185-228 psi)	
Camshaft (1985-1987)		
Cam lobe height		
1986-1987 (U.S.), 1985 (U.K.)		
Intake	35.925-35.965 mm	35.62 mm
	(1.4144-1.4159 in.)	(1.402 in.)
Exhaust	36.919-36.959 mm	36.61 mm
	(1.4535-1.4551 in.)	(1.441 in.)
1988-on (U.S.), 1986-on (U.K.)		
Intake	35.954-35.994 mm	35.60 mm
	(1.4155-1.4171 in.)	(1.401 in.)
Exhaust	36.919-36.959 mm	36.61 mm
	(1.4535-1.4551 in.)	(1.441 in.)
Journal O.D.		
Center journal	24.959-24.980 mm	—
	(0.9826-0.9835 in.)	—
End journal	19.959-19.980 mm	—
	(0.7858-0.7866 in.)	—
Journal oil clearance		
Intake and exhaust		
Center and end	0.032-0.066 mm	0.150 mm
	(0.0013-0.0026 in.)	(0.0059 in.)
Runout	—	0.10 mm (0.004 in.)
Rocker arm I.D.		
Intake and exhaust	12.000-12.018 mm	—
	(0.4724-0.4731 in.)	
Rocker arm shaft O.D.		
Intake and exhaust	11.966-11.984 mm	—
	(0.4711-0.4718 in.)	
Cylinder head distortion	—	0.05 mm (0.002 in.)
Cylinder head cover distortion	—	0.05 mm (0.002 in.)
Camshaft chain 20-pitch length	—	128.9 mm (5.07 in.)
Valves and valve springs		
Valve stem O.D.		
Intake	5.465-5.480 mm	—
	(0.2126-0.2157 in.)	
Exhaust	5.450-5.465 mm	—
	(0.2146-0.2152 in.)	
Valve guide I.D.		
Intake and exhaust	5.500-5.512 mm	—
	(0.2165-0.2170 in.)	
Valve stem-to-guide clearance		
Intake	0.020-0.047 mm	0.35 mm (0.014 in.)
	(0.0008-0.0019 in.)	
Exhaust	0.035-0.062 mm	0.35 mm (0.014 in.)
	(0.0014-0.0024 in.)	
Valve head tip	—	0.35 mm (0.014 in.)
Valve head thickness	—	0.05 mm (0.002 in.)

(continued)

Table 1 ENGINE SPECIFICATIONS (continued)

	Specification	Wear limit
Valves and valve springs (continued)		
Valve stem end length	—	4.0 mm (0.16 in.)
Valve seat width	0.9-1.1 mm (0.035-0.043 in.)	—
Valve spring free length		
Inner	—	38.3 mm (1.51 in.)
Outer	—	40.1 mm (1.58 in.)
Cylinders		
Bore		
700 & 750 cc	80.000-80.015 mm (3.1496-3.1502 in.)	80.080 mm (3.1527 in.)
800 cc	83.000-83.015 mm (3.2677-3.2683 in.)	83.085 mm (3.2711 in.)
Cylinder/piston clearance		
700 cc	0.050-0.060 mm (0.0020-0.0024 in.	0.120 mm (0.0047 in.)
750 & 800 cc	0.045-0.055 mm (0.0018-0.0022 in.	0.120 mm (0.0047 in.)
Out-of-round	—	0.05 mm (0.002 in.)
Pistons		
700 & 750 cc	79.945-79.960 mm (3.1474-3.1480 in.)	79.880 mm (3.1449 in.)
800 cc	82.950-82.965 mm (3.2657-3.2663 in.)	82.880 mm (3.2630 in.)
Piston pin bore	20.003-20.008 mm (0.7875-0.7877 in.)	20.03 mm (0.7886 in.)
Piston pin outer diameter	19.996-20.000 mm (0.7872-0.7874 in.)	19.988 mm (0.7869 in.)
Piston-to-piston pin clearance	0.002-0.014 mm (0.0001-0.0005 in.)	0.04 mm (0.002 in.)
Piston rings		
Number per piston		
Compression	2	—
Oil control	1	—
Ring end gap		
Top and second	0.20-0.35 mm (0.008-0.016 in.)	0.70 mm (0.028 in.)
Connecting rods		
Piston pin hole I.D.	20.010-20.018 mm (0.7878-0.7881 in.)	20.040 mm (0.7890 in.)
Big end side clearance	0.10-0.20 mm (0.004-0.008 in.)	0.30 mm (0.012 in.)
Big end width	21.95-22.00 mm (0.864-0.866 in.)	—
Big end oil clearance	0.024-0.042 mm (0.0009-0.0017 in.)	0.080 mm (0.003 in.)
Crankshaft		
Crankpin O.D.	40.982-41.000 mm (1.6135-1.6142 in.)	—
Crankpin width	22.10-22.15 mm (0.870-0.872 in.)	—
Main bearing oil clearance	0.020-0.050 mm (0.0008-0.0020 in.)	0.080 mm (0.031in.)
Runout	—	0.05 mm (0.002 in.)

(continued)

4

Table 1 ENGINE SPECIFICATIONS (continued)

	Specification	Wear limit
Crankshaft thrust clearance at primary drive gear		
700 & 750 cc	0.040-0.120 mm (0.0016-0.0047 in.)	—
800 cc	0.050-0.10 mm (0.002-0.004 in.)	—

Table 2 ENGINE TIGHTENING TORQUES

Item	N·m	ft.lb.
Engine mounting bolts and nuts		
Engine mounting bracket	18-28	13-20
Sub-frame Allen bolts and nuts	40-60	29-43.5
Through bolts and nuts	70-80	50.5-63.5
Camshaft sprocket bolts	14-16	10-11.5
Cylinder head cover bolts		
Bolt length 140 mm & 243 mm	21-25	15-18
All other lengths	9-11	6.5-8
Rocker arm shafts	25-30	18-21.5
Cylinder head-to-cylinder nuts	8-12	6-8.5
Cylinder head-to-cylinder bolts	9-11	6.5-8
Cylinder head and cylinder bolts	35-40	25.5-29.0
Oil pump mounting bolts	7-9	5.6.5
Primary drive gear bolt	80-110	58-79.5
Secondary gear bevel gear assembly		
Allen bolts	18-28	13-20
Case bolts		
Initial	12-18	8.5-13
Final	20-24	14.5-17.5
Secondary gear housing bolts	18-28	13-20
Secondary drive gear nut	80-110	58-79.5
Transmission main shaft bolt	60-70	43.5-50.5
Crankcase bolts		
Initial		
6 mm	—	—
8 mm	12-18	8.8-13.0
Final		
6 mm	9-13	6.5-9.5
8 mm	20-24	14.5-17.5
Camshaft chain tensioner guide bolt	8-12	6-8.5
Connecting rod cap nuts		
Initial	22-28	16-20
Final	51-55	37-40

Table 3 CRANKSHAFT SIDE CLEARANCE THRUST WASHER THICKNESS

Part No.	Thrust washer thickness
09060-48001	1.925-1.950 mm (0.0758-0.0768 in.)
09060-48002	1.950-1.975 mm (0.0768-0.0778 in.)
09060-48003	1.975-2.000 mm (0.0778-0.0787 in.)
09060-48004	2.000-2.025 mm (0.0787-0.0797 in.)
09060-48005	2.025-2.050 mm (0.0797-0.0807 in.)
09060-48006	2.050-2.075 mm (0.0807-0.0817 in.)
09060-48007	2.075-2.100 mm (0.0817-0.0827 in.)
09060-48008	2.100-2.125 mm (0.0827-0.0837 in.)
09060-48009	2.125-2.150 mm (0.0837-0.0847 in.)
09060-48010	2.150-2.175 mm (0.0847-0.0857 in.)

Table 4 CONNECTING ROD BEARING SELECTION

	Crankpin journal OD size code		
	1	2	3
Connecting rod ID code number			
Number 1	Green	Black	Brown
Number 2	Black	Brown	Yellow
Number 3	Brown	Yellow	Blue

Table 5 CONNECTING ROD BEARING INSERT COLOR AND THICKNESS

Color	Thickness
Green	1.485-1.488 mm (0.0585-0.0586 in.)
Black	1.488-1.491 mm (0.0586-0.0587 in.)
Brown	1.491-1.494 mm (0.0587-0.0588 in.)
Yellow	1.494-1.497 mm (0.0588-0.0589 in.)
Blue	1.497-1.500 mm (0.0589-0.0590 in.)

4

CHAPTER FIVE

CLUTCH

This chapter provides complete service procedures for the clutch and clutch release mechanism.

The clutch is a wet multi-plate type which operates immersed in the engine oil. It is mounted on the right-hand end of the transmission main shaft. The inner clutch hub is splined to the main shaft and the outer housing can rotate freely on the main shaft. The outer housing is geared to the crankshaft. The clutch pushrod rides within the channel in the transmission main shaft.

The clutch release mechanism is hydraulic and requires no adjustment. The mechanism consists of a clutch master cylinder on the left-hand handlebar, a slave cylinder on the left-hand side of the engine and a pushrod that rides within the channel in the transmission mainshaft.

Specifications for the clutch are listed in **Table 1**. **Tables 1-2** are located at the end of this chapter.

CLUTCH

Removal/Disassembly

The clutch assembly can be removed with the engine in the frame. This procedure is shown with the engine removed and partially disassembled for clarity.

Refer to **Figure 1** for this procedure.

1. Drain the engine oil as described under *Engine Oil and Filter Change* in Chapter Three.

2. Shift the transmission into gear.

5

CLUTCH ASSEMBLY

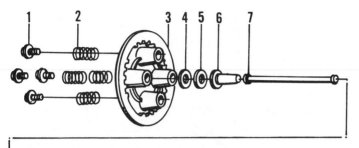

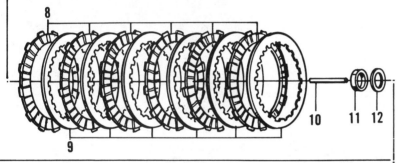

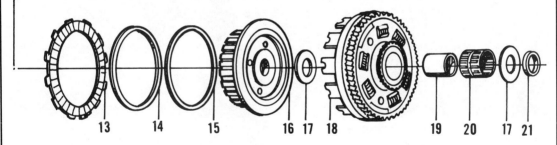

1. Bolt
2. Spring
3. Pressure plate
4. Washer
5. Bearing
6. Lifter guide
7. Lifter rod (right-hand)
8. Friction discs No. 1
9. Clutch plates
10. Lifter rod (left-hand)
11. Clutch nut

12. Washer
13. Friction disc No. 2
14. Judder spring
    (wave washer)
15. Judder spring seat
16. Clutch center
17. Washer
18. Outer housing
19. Collar
20. Needle bearing
21. Spacer

3. Remove the footpeg and rear brake pedal assembly as described under *Footpeg Assembly Removal/Installation* in Chapter Thirteen.

NOTE
*There is a sealing washer under 3 bolts securing the clutch cover (A, **Figure 2**). During assembly these sealing washers must be reinstalled under all 3 bolts to prevent an oil leak.*

4. Remove the bolts securing the clutch cover (B, **Figure 2**). Remove the clutch cover and gasket. Don't lose the locating dowels.

5. Place a shop rag between the primary drive gear and the clutch outer housing (**Figure 3**) to keep the clutch assembly from rotating.

6. Using a crisscross pattern loosen the clutch bolts (**Figure 4**). Remove the shop rag.

7. Remove the bolts and washers.

8. Remove the clutch springs (**Figure 5**) and the pressure plate (**Figure 6**).

9. Remove the friction discs, clutch plates, wave washer and wave washer seat.

10. Remove the thrust washer, bearing and clutch push piece (**Figure 7**).

11. If necessary, remove the clutch pushrod (**Figure 8**) from the transmission shaft.

CAUTION
Do not clamp the "Grabbit" on too tight as it may damage the grooves in the clutch hub.

12. To keep the clutch hub from turning in the next step, attach a special tool such as the "Grabbit" (**Figure 9**) to it.

13. Loosen, then remove the clutch locknut (**Figure 10**) and wave washer (**Figure 11**).

14. Remove the special tool from the clutch center.

15. Remove the clutch hub (**Figure 12**).

16. Remove the thrust washer (**Figure 13**).

17. Remove the circlip (**Figure 14**) securing the oil pump driven gear.

NOTE
If the oil pump is not going to be serviced, place a piece of duct tape over the oil pump shaft locating pin and washer to avoid misplacing them.

5

18. Remove the clutch outer housing, oil pump drive chain and oil pump driven gear as an assembly (**Figure 15**).

19. Remove the needle bearing (**Figure 16**), bushing (**Figure 17**), washer (**Figure 18**) and spacer (**Figure 19**) from the transmission shaft.

20. Inspect all components as described in this chapter.

Inspection

Refer to **Table 1** for clutch specifications.

1. Clean all clutch parts in petroleum-based solvent such as kerosene and thoroughly dry with compressed air.

2. Measure the free length of each clutch spring as shown in **Figure 20**. Compare to the specifications listed in **Table 1**. Replace any springs that have sagged to the service limit or less.

> *NOTE*
> *The thickness of the No. 2 inner narrow friction disc (13, **Figure 1**) is different from all other No. 1 friction discs. Be sure to measure and record its thickness separately.*

3. Measure the thickness of each friction disc at several places around the disc as shown in **Figure 21**. Compare to the specifications listed in **Table 1**. Replace any friction disc that is worn to the service limit or less.

4. Measure the claw width of all claws on each friction disc as shown in **Figure 22**. Compare to the specifications listed in **Table 1**. Replace any friction disc that is worn to the service limit or less.

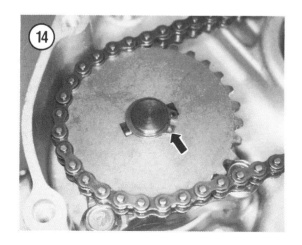

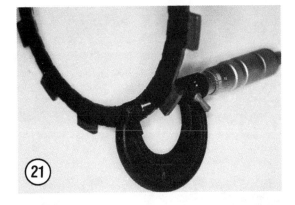

5. Check the clutch plates (**Figure 23**) for surface damage from heat or lack of oil. Replace any plate that is damaged in any way.

6. Check the clutch plates for warpage with a flat feeler gauge on a surface plate such as a piece of plate glass (**Figure 24**). Compare to the specifications listed in **Table 1**. Replace any plate that is warped to the service limit or more.

NOTE
If any of the friction discs, clutch plates or clutch springs require replacement, you should consider replacing all of them as a set to retain maximum clutch performance.

5

7. Inspect the slots (**Figure 25**) in the clutch outer housing for cracks, nicks or galling where they come in contact with the friction disc tabs. If any severe damage is evident, the housing must be replaced.

8. Inspect the driven gear teeth (A, **Figure 26**) and oil pump drive chain sprocket teeth (B, **Figure 26**) on the clutch outer housing for damage. Remove any small nicks with an oilstone. If damage is severe, the clutch outer housing must be replaced.

9. Inspect the damper springs (**Figure 27**). If they are sagged or broken the housing must be replaced.

10. Inspect the outer grooves (**Figure 28**) and studs (**Figure 29**) in the clutch hub. If either show signs of wear or galling the clutch hub should be replaced.

11. Inspect the inner splines (**Figure 30**) in the clutch hub for damage. Remove any small nicks with an oilstone. If damage is severe, the clutch hub must be replaced.

12. Inspect the spring receptacles (**Figure 31**) in the clutch pressure plate for wear or damage. Replace the clutch pressure plate if necessary.

13. Check the inner surface (C, **Figure 26**) of the clutch outer housing, where the needle bearing rides, for signs of wear or damage. Replace the clutch outer housing if necessary.

14. Check the needle bearing (**Figure 32**). Make sure it rotates smoothly with no signs of wear or damage. Replace if necessary.

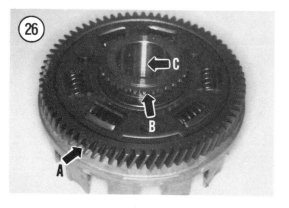

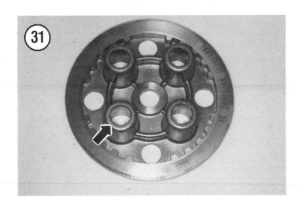

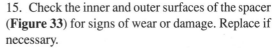

15. Check the inner and outer surfaces of the spacer (**Figure 33**) for signs of wear or damage. Replace if necessary.

16. Install the spacer into the needle bearing and rotate the spacer (**Figure 34**) and check for wear. Replace either/or both parts if necessary.

17. Check the clutch release rack (**Figure 35**) for wear or damage. Replace if necessary.

18. Check the clutch release rack bearing (**Figure 36**). Make sure it rotate smoothly with no signs of wear or damage. Replace if necessary.

19. Install the bearing (**Figure 37**) and washer (**Figure 38**) onto the release rack and rotate them by

5

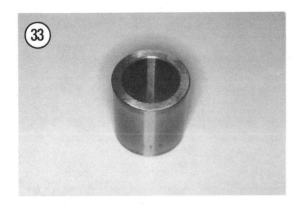

hand. Make sure all parts rotate smoothly. Replace any worn part.

20. Inspect the clutch right-hand push rod and left-hand push rod for bending (**Figure 39**). Roll it on a surface plate or piece of plate glass. Suzuki does not provide service information for this component, but if the rod(s) is bent or deformed in any way it must be replaced. Otherwise it may hang up in the channel within the transmission shaft, causing erratic clutch operation.

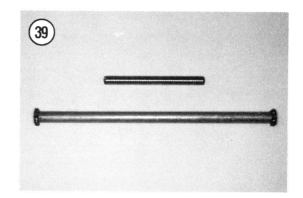

Assembly/Installation

Refer to **Figure 1** for this procedure.

1. Install the spacer (**Figure 19**), the washer (**Figure 18**) and bushing (**Figure 17**) onto the transmission shaft.

2. Apply a good coat of clean engine oil to the needle bearing and install the needle bearing (**Figure 16**).

3. If used, remove the duct tape from the oil pump shaft locating pin and washer. Make sure the locating pin and washer (**Figure 40**) are still in place on the oil pump drive shaft.

4. Position the oil pump driven gear with the shoulder (A, **Figure 41**) facing toward the engine and mesh the drive chain (B, **Figure 41**) onto the gear.

5. Mesh the drive chain onto the sprocket on the backside of the clutch outer housing (C, **Figure 41**).

6. Hold this assembly together and install it onto the transmission shaft as well as the oil pump drive shaft (**Figure 15**). Push the clutch outer housing down until it stops.

7. Make sure the oil pump driven gear is properly meshed with the locating pin (**Figure 42**) on the oil pump drive shaft.

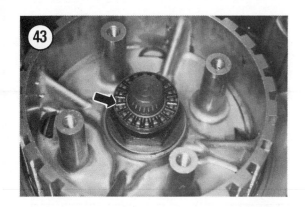

8. Install the circlip (**Figure 14**) securing the oil pump driven gear and make sure it is properly seated.

9. Install the thrust washer (**Figure 13**).

10. Install the clutch hub (**Figure 12**).

11. Position the wave washer with the dished side facing out and install the wave washer (**Figure 11**).

12. Use the same special tool (**Figure 9**) set-up used in Step 12 of *Removal/Disassembly* to hold the clutch hub for the following step.

13. Install the clutch locknut (**Figure 10**) and tighten to the torque specification listed in **Table 2**.

14. Remove the special tool from the clutch hub.

15. If removed, install the clutch pushrod (**Figure 8**) into the transmission shaft.

16. Install the clutch push piece (**Figure 7**).

17. Apply a good coat of clean engine oil to the needle bearing and install the needle bearing (**Figure 43**) and washer (**Figure 44**) onto the clutch push piece.

18. Install the wave washer seat (**Figure 45**) onto the clutch hub.

19. Position the wave washer with the dished side going on first and install the wave washer (**Figure 46**) onto the clutch hub.

NOTE
If new friction discs and clutch plates are being installed, apply new engine oil to all surfaces to avoid having the clutch lock up when used for the first time.

20. Install the No. 2 narrow friction disc (**Figure 47**) onto the clutch hub. Make sure it seats correctly next to the wave washer (**Figure 48**).

21. Install a clutch plate (**Figure 49**) then a friction disc onto the clutch hub. At this point the assembled parts should look like those in **Figure 50**.

22. Continue to install the clutch plates and friction discs, alternating them until all are installed. The last item installed is a friction disc (**Figure 51**).

23. Install the clutch pressure plate (**Figure 6**).

24. Install the springs (**Figure 5**), washers and bolts (**Figure 4**).

25. Place a shop rag between the primary drive gear and the clutch outer housing to keep the clutch assembly from rotating.

26. Using a crisscross pattern tighten the clutch bolts (**Figure 4**) to the torque specification listed in **Table 2**. Remove the shop rag.

27. Make sure the locating dowels (A, **Figure 52**) are in place.

28. Install a new clutch cover gasket (B, **Figure 52**).

NOTE
Be sure to install the gasket under the 3
*bolts (A, **Figure 53**). Refer to **Figure 54**,*
***Figure 55** and **Figure 56**. If not in-*
stalled, an oil leak will result.

29. Install the clutch cover and the bolts (B, **Figure 53**). Tighten the bolts securely.

30. Install the footpeg and rear brake pedal assembly as described under *Footpeg Assembly Removal/Installation* in Chapter Thirteen.

31. Refill the engine oil as described under *Engine Oil and Filter Change* in Chapter Three.

CLUTCH HYDRAULIC SYSTEM

The clutch is actuated by hydraulic fluid pressure and is controlled by the hand lever on the clutch

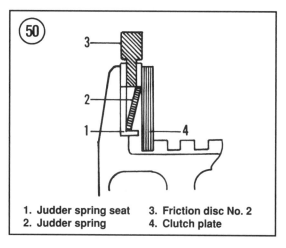

1. Judder spring seat   3. Friction disc No. 2
2. Judder spring   4. Clutch plate

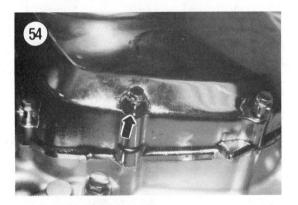

master cylinder located on the left-hand handlebar. As clutch components wear, the fluid level in the reservoir will be lower as it automatically adjusts for wear. There is no routine adjustment necessary nor possible.

When working on the clutch hydraulic system, it is necessary that the work area and all tools be absolutely clean. Any tiny particles or foreign matter and grit in the clutch slave cylinder or the master cylinder can damage the components. Also, sharp tools must not be used inside the slave cylinder or on the piston. If there is any doubt about your ability to correctly and safely carry out major service on the clutch hydraulic components, take the job to a dealer or other qualified specialist.

WARNING
*Throughout the text, reference is made to hydraulic fluid. Hydraulic fluid is the same as DOT 3 or DOT 4 brake fluid. Use only DOT 3 or DOT 4 brake fluid; **do not use other types of fluids** as they are not compatible. Do not intermix silicone based (DOT 5) brake fluid as it can cause clutch component damage leading to clutch system failure.*

MASTER CYLINDER

Removal/Installation

CAUTION
Cover the fuel tank, front fender and instrument cluster with a heavy cloth or plastic tarp to protect them from accidental hydraulic fluid spills. Wash hydraulic fluid from any painted or plated surfaces or plastic parts immediately, as it will destroy the finish. Use soapy water and rinse completely.

1. Remove the screws, washers and lockwashers securing the clutch interlock switch cover (**Figure 57**). Remove the cover and electrical cable from the master cylinder body.
2. If you have a shop syringe, draw all of the hydraulic fluid out of the master cylinder reservoir.
3. Place a shop cloth under the union bolt to catch any spilled hydraulic fluid that will leak out.
4. Unscrew the union bolt (**Figure 58**) securing the clutch hose to the master cylinder. Don't lose the sealing washer on each side of the hose fitting. Tie

the loose end of the hose up to the handlebar and place the loose end in a reclosable bag (**Figure 59**) to prevent the entry of moisture and foreign matter.

5. Remove the rear view mirror (A, **Figure 60**).

6. Remove the caps, clamping bolts and the clamp (B, **Figure 60**) securing the master cylinder to the handlebar and remove the master cylinder.

7. Install by reversing these removal steps while noting the following:

 a. Tighten the upper clamp bolt first, then the lower to the torque specification listed in **Table 2**.

 b. Place a sealing washer on each side of the clutch hose fitting and install the union bolt.

 c. Tighten the union bolt to the torque specification listed in **Table 2**.

 d. Bleed the clutch as described under *Bleeding The System* in this chapter.

Disassembly

Refer to **Figure 61** for this procedure.

1. Remove the master cylinder as described in this chapter.

2. Remove the starter interlock switch plunger (**Figure 62**) from the master cylinder.

3. Remove the screws securing the top cover and remove the top cover and the diaphragm.

4. Pour out any residual hydraulic fluid and discard it. *Never* re-use hydraulic fluid.

5. Remove the bolt and nut (A, **Figure 63**) securing the hand lever and remove the lever (B, **Figure 63**).

6. Remove the push rod (A, **Figure 64**) and rubber boot (B, **Figure 64**) from the area where the hand lever actuates the piston assembly.

7. Using circlip pliers, remove the internal circlip (**Figure 65**) from the body. Remove the washer behind the circlip

8. Remove the piston assembly and the spring.

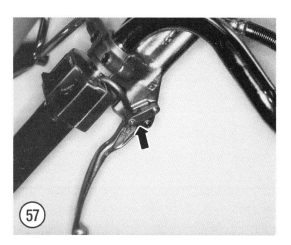

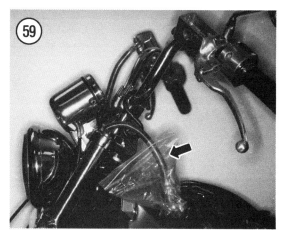

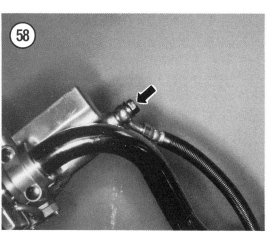

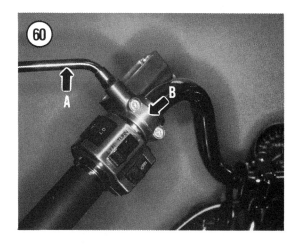

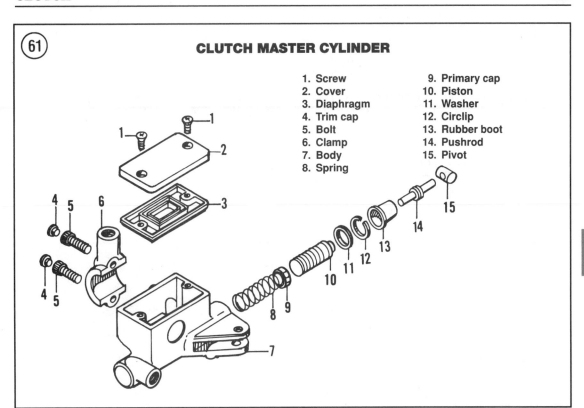

CLUTCH MASTER CYLINDER

1. Screw
2. Cover
3. Diaphragm
4. Trim cap
5. Bolt
6. Clamp
7. Body
8. Spring
9. Primary cap
10. Piston
11. Washer
12. Circlip
13. Rubber boot
14. Pushrod
15. Pivot

5

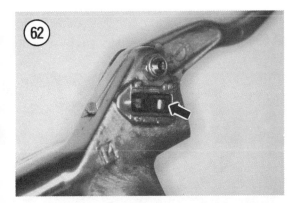

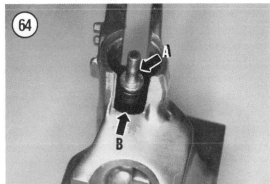

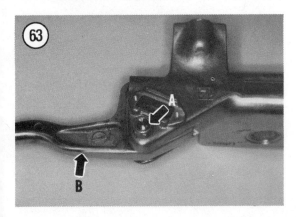

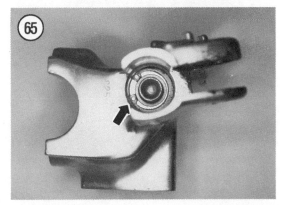

Inspection

1. Clean all parts in denatured alcohol or fresh hydraulic fluid.

2. Inspect the body cylinder bore (**Figure 66**) surface for signs of wear and damage. If less than perfect, replace the master cylinder assembly. The body cannot be replaced separately.

3. Inspect the primary (A, **Figure 67**) and the secondary cup (B, **Figure 67**) for wear.

4. Replace the piston assembly if either the primary or secondary cup and/or spring requires replacement.

5. Inspect the piston contact surfaces (C, **Figure 67**) for signs of wear and damage. If less than perfect, replace the piston assembly.

6. Check the end of the piston (A, **Figure 68**) for wear caused by the push rod. If worn, replace the piston assembly.

7. Check the end of the push rod (B, **Figure 68**) for wear caused by the piston. If worn, replace the push rod.

8. Measure the cylinder bore (**Figure 66**) with a bore gauge. Replace the master cylinder if the inside diameter is worn to the service limit dimension listed in **Table 2** or greater.

9. Measure the outside diameter of the piston with a micrometer (**Figure 69**). Replace the piston assembly if the outside diameter is worn to the service limit dimension listed in **Table 2** or less.

10. Make sure the passage (**Figure 70**) in the bottom of the master cylinder body is clear. Clean out if necessary.

11. Inspect the pivot hole on the hand lever. If worn or elongated the lever must be replaced.

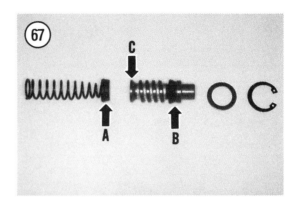

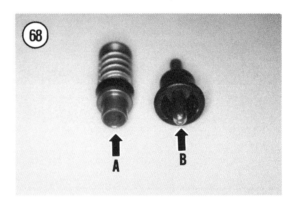

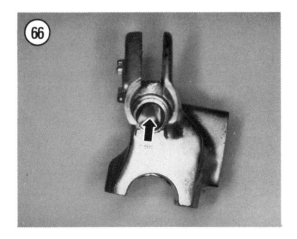

12. Check the top cover and diaphragm (**Figure 71**) for damage and deterioration and replace as necessary.

13. Inspect the threads in the bore for the union bolt. If worn or damaged, clean out with a thread tap or replace the master cylinder assembly.

14. Check the hand lever pivot lugs (**Figure 72**) on the master cylinder body for cracks. If damaged, replace the master cylinder assembly.

Assembly

1. Soak the new cups in fresh hydraulic fluid for at least 15 minutes to make them pliable. Coat the inside of the cylinder bore with fresh hydraulic fluid prior to the assembly of parts.

CAUTION
When installing the piston assembly, do not allow the cups to turn inside out as they will be damaged and allow hydraulic fluid leakage within the cylinder bore.

2. Install the spring and primary cup assembly into the cylinder together. Install the spring with the tapered end (**Figure 73**) facing toward the primary cup.

3. Install the piston assembly into the cylinder (**Figure 74**).

4. Install the washer (**Figure 75**) and the circlip (**Figure 76**). Make sure the circlip is correctly seated in the groove (**Figure 65**).

5. Slide in the rubber boot (B, **Figure 64**) and install the pushrod (A, **Figure 64**).

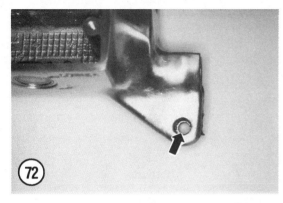

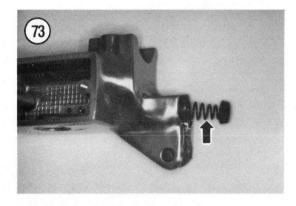

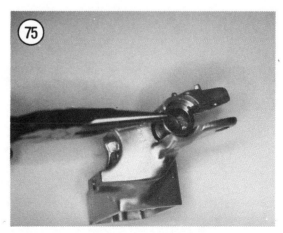

6. Install the diaphragm and top cover. Do not tighten the cover screws at this time as hydraulic fluid will have to be added later when the system is bled.

7. Install the starter interlock switch plunger (**Figure 77**) into the receptacle in the master cylinder body.

8. Install the master cylinder as described in this chapter.

Clutch Hose Assembly
Removal/Installation

There is no factory-recommended replacement interval but it is a good idea to replace the clutch hose assembly every four years or when either flexible section shows signs of cracking or damage.

The clutch hose assembly is made up of flexible hose that is attached to each end of a metal pipe. This assembly cannot be serviced and if any portion is defective the entire hose assembly must be replaced.

CAUTION
Cover the front fender and instrument cluster with a heavy cloth or plastic tarp to protect them from accidental hydraulic fluid spills. Wash hydraulic fluid off any painted or plated surfaces or plastic parts immediately, as it will destroy the finish. Use soapy water and rinse completely.

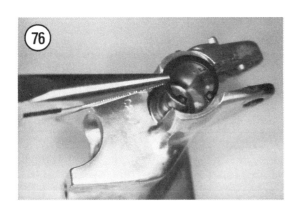

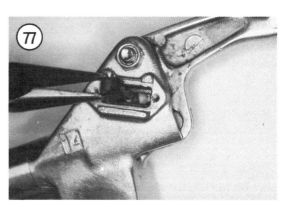

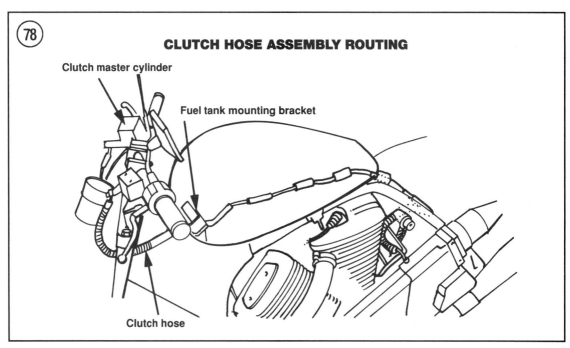

CLUTCH HOSE ASSEMBLY ROUTING

Clutch master cylinder

Fuel tank mounting bracket

Clutch hose

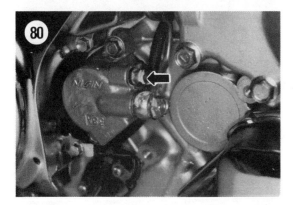

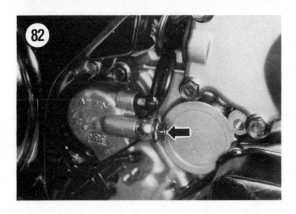

Refer to **Figure 78** for this procedure.

1. Remove the fuel tank as described under *Fuel Tank Removal/Installation* in Chapter Seven.

2. Remove the bolts securing the secondary drive cover (**Figure 79**) and remove the cover.

3. Remove the cap and attach a hose to the bleed valve (**Figure 80**) on the slave cylinder and place the loose end in a container.

4. Open the bleed valve and apply the lever on the clutch master cylinder to pump the hydraulic fluid out of the master cylinder and the clutch hose assembly. Continue to operate the lever until the fluid is pumped out of the hose assembly. Close the bleed valve and remove the hose. Dispose of this hydraulic fluid—never re-use hydraulic fluid.

5. Clean the top of the master cylinder of all dirt and foreign matter.

6. Loosen the screws (**Figure 81**) securing the master cylinder top cover. Pull up and loosen the cover and the diaphragm. This will allow air to enter the reservoir and allow any residual hydraulic fluid to drain out more quickly in the next steps.

7. Place a container under the clutch hose at the slave cylinder.

8. Remove the union bolt and sealing washers (**Figure 82**) securing the clutch hose to the slave cylinder.

9. Remove the clutch hose and let any residual hydraulic fluid drain out into the container. Dispose of this hydraulic fluid—never re-use hydraulic fluid. To prevent the entry of moisture and dirt, tape over the threaded bore in the slave cylinder.

> *WARNING*
> *Dispose of this hydraulic fluid—never re-use hydraulic fluid. Contaminated hydraulic fluid can cause clutch problems.*

10. Place a shop cloth under the union bolt to catch any spilled hydraulic fluid that will leak out.

11. Unscrew the union bolt (**Figure 83**) securing the clutch hose to the master cylinder. Don't lose the sealing washer on each side of the hose fitting.

12. Remove any tie wraps or hose clamps securing the hose assembly to the frame.

> *NOTE*
> *Prior to removing the clutch hose make a drawing of the hose routing through the frame. It is very easy to forget how it was, once it has been removed. Re-*

5

place the hose exactly as it was, avoiding any sharp turns.

13. Pull the clutch hose (**Figure 84**) out from the front fork area and from along the top if the frame.

14. Install a new hose, sealing washers and union bolts in the reverse order of removal, noting the following:

   a. Be sure to install new sealing washers (**Figure 85**) and in the correct positions.
   b. Tighten the fittings and union bolts to the torque specifications listed in **Table 2**.
   c. Bleed the clutch system as described under *Bleeding the System* in this chapter.
   d. Test ride the bike slowly at first to make sure the clutch is operating correctly.

SLAVE   CYLINDER

Removal

> *CAUTION*
> *Cover the fuel tank, front fender and instrument cluster with a heavy cloth or plastic tarp to protect them from accidental hydraulic fluid spills. Wash hydraulic fluid from any painted or plated surfaces or plastic parts immediately, as it will destroy the finish. Use soapy water and rinse completely.*

1. Remove the bolts securing the left-hand chrome cover (**Figure 79**) and remove the cover.

2. Remove the cap and attach a hose to the bleed valve (**Figure 80**) on the slave cylinder, then place the loose end in a container.

3. Open the bleed valve and apply the lever on the clutch master cylinder to pump the hydraulic fluid out of the master cylinder and the clutch hose assembly. Continue to operate the lever until the fluid is pumped out of the hose assembly. Close the bleed valve and remove the hose. Dispose of this hydraulic fluid—never re-use hydraulic fluid.

4. Clean the top of the master cylinder of all dirt and foreign matter.

5. Loosen the screws (**Figure 81**) securing the master cylinder top cover. Pull up and loosen the cover and the diaphragm. This will allow air to enter the reservoir and allow any residual hydraulic fluid to drain out more quickly in the next steps.

6. Place a container under the clutch hose at the slave cylinder.

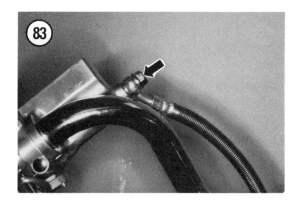

7. Remove the union bolt and sealing washers (**Figure 82**) securing the clutch hose to the slave cylinder.

8. Remove the clutch hose and let any residual hydraulic fluid drain out into the container. Dispose of this hydraulic fluid—never re-use hydraulic fluid. To prevent the entry of moisture and dirt, tape over the threaded bore in the slave cylinder.

> *WARNING*
> *Dispose of this hydraulic fluid— never re-use hydraulic fluid. Contaminated hydraulic fluid can cause clutch problems.*

9. Remove the bolts (**Figure 86**) securing the slave cylinder to the crankcase and remove the slave cylinder assembly.

Disassembly/Inspection/Assembly

Refer to **Figure 87** for this procedure.

1. Remove the spring.

2. Remove the retainer (**Figure 88**) from the top of the piston.

3. Place a shop cloth or piece of soft wood at the end of the slave cylinder against the piston.

4. Place the slave cylinder assembly on the workbench with the piston facing down.

> *WARNING*
> *In the next step, the piston may shoot out of the slave cylinder body like a bullet. Keep your fingers out of the way. Wear shop gloves and apply air pressure gradually. Do **not** use high pressure air or place the air hose nozzle directly against the hydraulic line fitting inlet in the slave cylinder body. Hold the air nozzle away from the inlet allowing some of the air to escape.*

5. Apply the air pressure in short spurts to the hydraulic line fitting inlet and force the piston out. Use a service station air hose if you don't have an air compressor.

6. Remove the piston and seal.

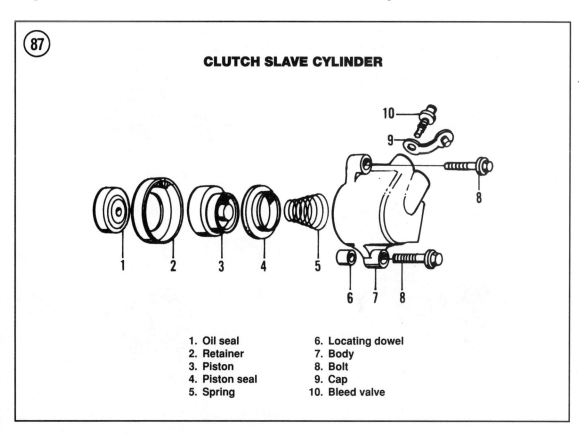

CLUTCH SLAVE CYLINDER

1. Oil seal
2. Retainer
3. Piston
4. Piston seal
5. Spring
6. Locating dowel
7. Body
8. Bolt
9. Cap
10. Bleed valve

CAUTION
In the following step, do not use a sharp tool to remove the piston seal from the piston. Do not damage the piston surface.

7. Use a piece of plastic or wood and carefully remove the piston seal from the piston. Discard the piston seal as it must be replaced.

8. Inspect the slave cylinder body (**Figure 89**) for damage. If damaged, replace the slave cylinder as an assembly. The body cannot be replaced separately.

9. Inspect the hydraulic fluid passageway (**Figure 90**) at base of the piston bore. Make sure it is clean and open. Apply compressed air to the opening and make sure it is clear. Clean out passage, if necessary, with fresh hydraulic fluid.

10. Inspect the cylinder wall (**Figure 91**) for scratches, scoring or other damage. If either rusty or corroded, replace the slave cylinder as an assembly.

11. Measure the cylinder bore with a bore gauge. Replace the slave cylinder if the inside diameter is worn to the service limit dimension listed in **Table 2** or greater.

12. Inspect the piston (**Figure 92**) for scratches, scoring or other damage. If damaged, replace the slave cylinder as an assembly. The piston cannot be replaced separately.

13. Measure the outside diameter of the piston with a micrometer (**Figure 93**). Replace the slave cylinder if the outside diameter is worn to the service limit dimension listed in **Table 2** or less.

14. Inspect the caliper mounting bolt holes on the body. If worn or damaged, replace the slave cylinder assembly.

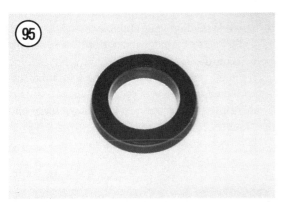

15. Remove the bleed screw (A, **Figure 94**). Make sure it is clean and open. Apply compressed air to the opening and make sure it is clear. Clean out if necessary with fresh hydraulic fluid.

16. Inspect the threads in the bore (B, **Figure 94**) for the union bolt. If worn or damaged, clean out with a metric thread tap or replace the slave cylinder assembly.

17. Inspect the spring for damage or sagging. Replace if necessary. Suzuki does not provide service information for spring free length.

18. If serviceable, clean the slave cylinder with rubbing alcohol and rinse with clean hydraulic fluid.

5

NOTE
Never reuse the old piston seal. Very minor damage or age deterioration can make the seal useless.

19. Coat the new piston seal (**Figure 95**) with fresh hydraulic fluid.

20. Carefully install the new piston seal in the groove in piston (**Figure 96**). Make sure the seal is properly seated in the groove.

21. Coat the piston, cylinder wall and piston seal with fresh hydraulic fluid.

22. Position the spring with the tapered end toward the piston and install the spring into the backside of the piston.

23. Carefully install the piston into the slave cylinder (**Figure 97**). Push the piston in until it bottoms out (**Figure 98**).

24. Install the retainer (**Figure 88**) over the piston.

Installation

1. Make sure the clutch push rod seal (A, **Figure 99**) is in place and is not leaking.
2. Push the clutch push rod (B, **Figure 99**) all the way in until it bottoms out.
3. If removed, install the locating dowels (C, **Figure 99**).
4. Install the slave cylinder assembly onto the crankcase.
5. Install the bolts (**Figure 86**) securing the slave cylinder to the crankcase. Tighten the bolts securely.
6. Install a sealing washer (**Figure 85**) on each side of the hose fitting. Install the union bolt securing the clutch hose to the slave cylinder. Tighten the union bolt to the torque specification listed in **Table 2**.
7. Install the chrome cover and tighten the bolts securely.

BLEEDING THE SYSTEM

This procedure is not necessary unless the clutch feel spongy, there has been a leak in the system, a component has been replaced or the hydraulic fluid has been replaced.

1. Remove the bolts securing the left-hand chrome cover (**Figure 79**) and remove the cover.
2. Remove the dust cap (**Figure 80**) from the bleed valve on the slave cylinder.
3. Connect a piece of clear tubing to the bleed valve on the slave cylinder.
4. Place the other end of the tube into a clean container.
5. Fill the container with enough fresh hydraulic fluid to keep the end submerged.

> *CAUTION*
> *Cover the wheel with a heavy cloth or plastic tarp to protect it from the accidental spilling of hydraulic fluid. Wash any fluid from any plastic, painted or plated surface immediately; as it will destroy the finish. Use soapy water and rinse completely.*

6. Clean the top cover of the master cylinder of all dirt and foreign matter.
7. Remove the screws securing the master cylinder top cover (**Figure 81**). Remove the top cover and diaphragm.

8. Fill the master cylinder almost to the top lip; insert the diaphragm and the cover, or cap, loosely. Leave the cover in place during this procedure to prevent the entry of dirt.

> *WARNING*
> *Use hydraulic fluid from a sealed container marked DOT 3 or DOT 4 only. Do not intermix different brands or types as they may not be compatible. Do not intermix a silicone based (DOT 5) brake fluid as it can cause clutch component damage leading to clutch system failure.*

> *NOTE*
> *During this procedure, it is very important to check the fluid level in the clutch master cylinder reservoir often. If the reservoir runs dry, you'll introduce more air in the system which will require starting over.*

9. If the clutch master cylinder was drained, it must be bled first as follows:

  a. Remove the union bolt and hose from the master cylinder.
  b. Slowly apply the clutch lever several times while holding your thumb over the opening in the master cylinder and perform the following:
  c. With the lever applied, slightly release your thumb pressure. Some of the hydraulic fluid and air bubbles will escape.
  d. Apply thumb pressure and pump lever once more.
  e. Repeat this procedure until you can feel resistance at the lever.

10. Quickly reinstall the hose, sealing washers and the union bolt. Tighten the union bolt.

11. Refill the master cylinder. Pump the lever again and perform the following:

    a. Loosen the union bolt 1/4 turn. Some hydraulic fluid and air bubbles will escape.

    b. Tighten the union bolt and repeat this procedure until no air bubbles escape.

12. Tighten the union bolts to the torque specification listed in **Table 2**.

13. Slowly apply the clutch lever several times as follows:

    a. Pull the lever in and hold it in the applied position.

    b. Open the bleed valve about one-half turn. Allow the lever to travel to its limit.

    c. When this limit is reached, tighten the bleed valve.

14. As the fluid enters the system, the level will drop in the reservoir. Maintain the level to just about the top of the reservoir to prevent air from being drawn into the system.

15. Continue to pump the lever and fill the reservoir until the fluid emerging from the hose is completely free of bubbles.

> *NOTE*
> *Do not allow the reservoir to empty during the bleeding operation or more air will enter the system. If this occurs, the entire procedure must be repeated.*

> *NOTE*
> *If you are having trouble getting all of the bubbles out of the system, refer to the*

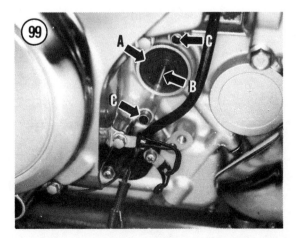

Reverse Flow Bleeding at the end of this section.

16. Hold the lever in, tighten the bleed valve, remove the bleed tube and install the bleed valve dust cap.

17. If necessary, add fluid to correct the level in the reservoir.

18. Install the diaphragm and the cover. Tighten the screws securely.

19. Test the feel of the clutch lever. It should be firm and should offer the same resistance each time it's operated. If it feels spongy, it is likely that there is still air in the system and it must be bled again. When all air has been bled from the system and the fluid level is correct in the reservoir, make sure all fittings and connections are tight, then double-check for leaks.

20. Test ride the bike slowly at first to make sure that the clutch is operating properly.

Reverse Flow Bleeding

This bleeding procedure can be used if you are having a difficult time freeing the system all of bubbles.

Using this procedure, the hydraulic fluid will be forced into the system in a reverse direction. The fluid will enter the slave cylinder, flow through the clutch hose assembly and into the clutch master cylinder reservoir. If the system is already filled with hydraulic fluid, the existing fluid will be flushed out of the top of the master cylinder by the new hydraulic fluid being forced into the slave cylinder. Siphon the fluid from the reservoir, then hold a shop cloth under the clutch master cylinder reservoir to catch any additional fluid that will be forced out.

A special reverse flow tool called the EZE Bleeder is available or a home made tool can be fabricated for this procedure.

To make this home made tool, perform the following:

> *NOTE*
> *The brake fluid container must be plastic—not metal. Use vinyl tubing of the correct inner diameter to ensure a tight fit on the caliper bleed valve.*

    a. Purchase a 12 oz. (345 ml) *plastic* bottle of DOT 3 or DOT 4 brake fluid.

b. Remove the cap, drill an appropriate size hole and adapt a vinyl hose fitting onto the cap.

c. Attach a section of vinyl hose to the hose fitting on the cap and secure it with a hose clamp. This joint must be a tight fit as the plastic brake fluid bottle will be squeezed to force the hydraulic fluid out past this fitting and through the hose.

d. Remove the moisture seal from the plastic bottle of brake fluid and screw the cap and hose assembly onto the bottle.

1. Clean the top cover of the master cylinder of all dirt and foreign matter.

2. Remove the screws securing the master cylinder top cover (**Figure 81**). Remove the top cover and diaphragm.

3. Fill the master cylinder almost to the top lip; insert the diaphragm and the cover, or cap, loosely. Leave the cover in place during this procedure to prevent the entry of dirt.

4. Remove the dust cap (**Figure 80**) from the bleed valve on the slave cylinder.

5. Attach the vinyl hose to the bleed valve on the caliper. Make sure the hose is tight on the bleed valve.

6. Open the bleed valve and squeeze the plastic bottle forcing this hydraulic fluid into the clutch system.

NOTE
If necessary, siphon hydraulic fluid from the reservoir to avoid overflow of fluid.

7. Observe the hydraulic fluid entering the clutch master cylinder reservoir. Continue to apply pressure from the bottle, until the fluid entering the reservoir is free of all air bubbles.

8. Close the bleed valve, then disconnect the hose from the bleed valve.

9. Install the dust cap onto the bleed valve on the slave cylinder.

10. At this time the clutch system should be free of bubbles. Apply the clutch lever and check for proper clutch operation. If the system still feels spongy, perform the typical bleeding procedure in the beginning of this section.

Table 1 CLUTCH SPECIFICATIONS

Item	Standard	Wear limit
Friction disc		
Disc No. 1	2.92-3.08 mm	2.62 mm (0.103 in.)
	(0.115-0.121 in.)	
Disc No. 2	3.45-3.55 mm	3.15 mm (0.124 in.)
	(0.136-0.140 in.)	
Friction disc claw width	15.8-16.0 mm	15.0 mm (0.591 in.)
	(0.622-0.630 in.)	
Clutch plate thickness	1.55-1.65 mm	—
	(0.0628-0.0632 in.)	
Clutch plate warpage	—	0.10 mm (0.004 in.)
Clutch spring free length	—	34.0 mm (1.34 in.)
Clutch master cylinder		
Piston OD	13.957-13.984 mm	—
	(0.5495-0.5506 in.)	
Cylinder bore ID	14.000-14.043 mm	—
	(0.5512-0.5524 in.)	
Clutch slave cylinder		
Piston OD	38.042-38.075 mm	—
	(1.4977-1.4990 in.)	
Cylinder bore ID	38.100-38.162 mm	—
	(1.5000-1.5024 in.)	

5

Table 2 CLUTCH TIGHTENING TORQUES

Item	N•m	ft.-lb.
Clutch locknut	50-70	36-50.5
Clutch spring bolts	11-13	8-9.5
Clutch union bolt	20-25	14.5-18
Clutch master cylinder clamp bolt	5-8	3.5-6.0

CHAPTER SIX

TRANSMISSION AND GEARSHIFT MECHANISMS

This chapter provides complete service procedures for the transmission shaft assemblies and the external and the internal shift mechanism.

Table 1 is located at the end of this chapter.

EXTERNAL GEARSHIFT MECHANISM

The external gearshift mechanism is located on the same side of the crankcase as the clutch assembly. To remove the internal shift mechanism (shift drum and shift forks), it is necessary to remove the engine and split the crankcase as described in Chapter Four.

The gearshift lever is subject to a lot of abuse. If the bike has been in a hard spill, the gearshift lever may have been hit and the gearshift shaft bent. It is very hard to straighten the shaft without subjecting the crankcase halves to abnormal stress where the shaft enters the crankcase. If the shaft is bent enough to prevent it from being withdrawn from the crankcase, there is little recourse but to cut the shaft off with a hacksaw very close to the crankcase. It is much cheaper in the long run to replace the shaft than risk damaging a very expensive crankcase assembly.

Removal

This procedure is shown with the engine removed and partially disassembled for clarity. It is not necessary to remove the engine from the frame for this procedure.

Refer to **Figure 1** for this procedure.

1. Remove the bolt (**Figure 2**) securing the shift lever and remove the lever (**Figure 3**) from the shift shaft.

2. Remove the clutch assembly as described under *Clutch Removal/Installation* in Chapter Five.

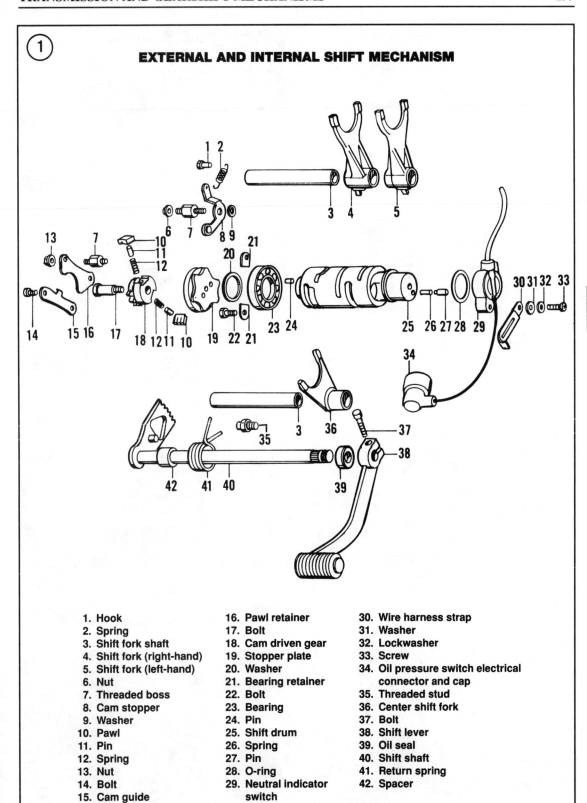

EXTERNAL AND INTERNAL SHIFT MECHANISM

1. Hook
2. Spring
3. Shift fork shaft
4. Shift fork (right-hand)
5. Shift fork (left-hand)
6. Nut
7. Threaded boss
8. Cam stopper
9. Washer
10. Pawl
11. Pin
12. Spring
13. Nut
14. Bolt
15. Cam guide
16. Pawl retainer
17. Bolt
18. Cam driven gear
19. Stopper plate
20. Washer
21. Bearing retainer
22. Bolt
23. Bearing
24. Pin
25. Shift drum
26. Spring
27. Pin
28. O-ring
29. Neutral indicator switch
30. Wire harness strap
31. Washer
32. Lockwasher
33. Screw
34. Oil pressure switch electrical connector and cap
35. Threaded stud
36. Center shift fork
37. Bolt
38. Shift lever
39. Oil seal
40. Shift shaft
41. Return spring
42. Spacer

3. Withdraw the gearshift shaft (**Figure 4**) from the crankcase. See information regarding a *bent gearshift shaft* in the introductory paragraph of this procedure.

4. Remove the bolt (**Figure 5**) securing the cam gear assembly.

5. Remove the nuts (A, **Figure 6**) securing the pawl retainer (B, **Figure 6**) and remove the pawl retainer.

6. Remove the screws securing the cam guide (**Figure 7**) and remove the cam guide.

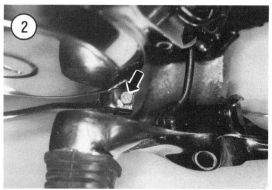

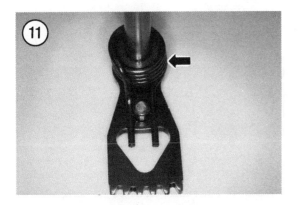

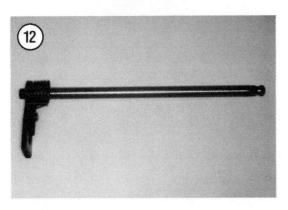

7. Unhook the spring (**Figure 8**) from the stopper arm.

8. Remove the cam gear assembly (**Figure 9**) from the end of the shift drum. Don't lose the pawls, springs and pins in the assembly. Store these small parts in a reclosable plastic bag to avoid misplacing any small parts.

9. Remove the washer (**Figure 10**) from the end of the shift drum.

Inspection

1. Inspect the return spring (**Figure 11**) on the gearshift shaft assembly. If broken or weak it must be replaced.

2. Inspect the gearshift shaft assembly (**Figure 12**) for bending, wear or other damage; replace if necessary.

3. Inspect the gear teeth (**Figure 13**) on the gearshift shaft assembly. If broken or damaged the gearshift shaft must be replaced.

4. Disassemble the cam gear assembly (**Figure 14**) and inspect the pawls, springs and pins for wear or damage. Replace any worn or damaged parts.

6

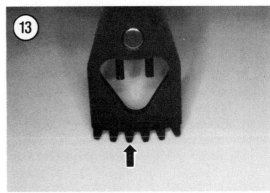

5. Inspect the ramps (**Figure 15**) on the backside of the stopper plate for wear or damage. Replace the stopper plate if necessary.

6. Inspect the cam driven gear receptacle (**Figure 16**) in the stopper plate for wear or damage. Replace the stopper plate if necessary.

7. Inspect the gear teeth (**Figure 17**) on the cam drive gear. If broken or damaged the cam drive gear must be replaced.

8. Assemble the cam gear assembly as follows:

   a. Install the springs into the cam gear body.

   b. Position the pawl pins with the rounded end facing out and install them onto the springs.

   c. Install the pawls onto the pins and into the cam gear body.

   d. The pin grooves in the pawls are offset. When the pawls are installed correctly the wider shoulder (A, **Figure 18**) must face toward the outside.

   e. Hold the pawls in place and place the assembly into an aerosol spray paint can top.

Installation

1. Compress the spring-loaded shift pawls with your fingers. Install the cam gear assembly into the receptacle of the cam driven gear (**Figure 19**).

2. Install the washer (**Figure 10**) into the end of the shift drum.

3. Align the locating holes (A, **Figure 20**) on the backside of the cam gear assembly with the locating pins (B, **Figure 20**) on the end of the shift drum and install the cam gear assembly (**Figure 9**) onto the end of the shift drum.

4. Hook the spring (**Figure 8**) onto the stopper arm.

5. Install the cam guide (**Figure 7**) and screws. Apply a small amount of red Loctite (No. 271) to the

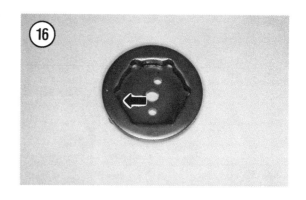

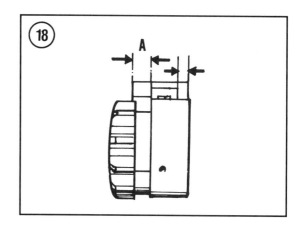

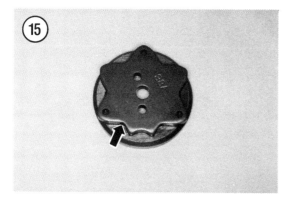

screw threads prior to installation. Tighten the screws securely.

6. Install the pawl retainer (B, **Figure 6**) and the nuts (A, **Figure 6**). Apply a small amount of red Loctite (No. 271) to the threaded studs prior to installing the nuts. Tighten the nuts securely.

7. Install the bolt (**Figure 5**) securing the cam gear assembly. Apply a small amount of red Loctite (No. 271) to the bolt threads prior to installing the bolt. Tighten the bolt securely

8. Apply clean engine oil to the gearshift shaft and install the gearshift shaft (**Figure 21**) into the crankcase. Align the center of the cam gear with the center of the gearshift shaft gear (**Figure 22**), then push the shaft assembly all the way in (**Figure 4**).

9. Install the clutch assembly as described in Chapter Five.

10. Align the split on the gearshift lever joint with the alignment mark on the gearshift lever and install the lever (**Figure 3**) onto the gearshift shaft. Tighten the clamping bolt securely (**Figure 2**).

TRANSMISSION

To gain access to the transmission and internal shift mechanism it is necessary to remove the engine and split the crankcase as described in Chapter Four.

Refer to **Table 1** at the end of the chapter for transmission and gearshift mechanism specifications.

Removal/Installation

1. Remove the engine and split the crankcase as described under *Crankcase Disassembly* in Chapter Four.

2. Remove the reduction gear (**Figure 23**) and bushing from the secondary bevel drive gear assembly.

NOTE
If you are unable to remove the mainshaft assembly from the crankcase, make sure the bolt and washer was removed from the right-hand end of the mainshaft during crankcase disassembly.

3. Remove the countershaft assembly (A, **Figure 24**) and main shaft assembly (B, **Figure 24**) from the left crankcase.

4. Inspect the transmission shaft assemblies as described under *Preliminary Inspection* in this chapter.

6

NOTE
Prior to installation, coat all bearing surfaces with assembly oil.

5. Install the countershaft assembly (**Figure 25**). Push the countershaft in until it bottoms completely.
6. Apply a light coat of multipurpose grease to the backside of the washer to help hold it in place.
7. Hold onto the washer (**Figure 26**) next to the 2nd gear and install the mainshaft assembly (B, **Figure 24**). Properly mesh the gears with the countershaft gears and push it in until it bottoms out completely.
8. Install the reduction gear (**Figure 23**) and bushing onto the secondary bevel drive gear assembly.
9. After both transmission assemblies are installed, perform the following:
    a. Shift both shafts into NEUTRAL. Hold onto the mainshaft and rotate the countershaft. The countershaft should rotate freely. If it does not, shift the gear that is engaged so that both shafts are in NEUTRAL.
    b. Rotate both shaft assemblies by hand. Make sure there is no binding. This is the time to find that something may be installed incorrectly— not after the crankcase is completely assembled.
10. Reassemble the crankcase as described under *Crankcase Assembly* and install the engine as described in Chapter Four.

Preliminary Inspection

After the transmission shaft assemblies have been removed from the crankcase, clean and inspect the assemblies prior to disassembling them. Place the assembled shaft into a large can or plastic bucket and thoroughly clean with a petroleum based solvent such as kerosene and a stiff brush. Dry with compressed air or let it sit on rags to drip dry. Repeat for the other shaft assembly.
1. After they have been cleaned, visually inspect the components of the assemblies for excessive wear. Any burrs, pitting or roughness on the teeth of a gear will cause wear on the mating gear. Minor roughness can be cleaned up with an oilstone but there's little point in attempting to remove deep scars.

NOTE
Defective gears should be replaced. It is a good idea to replace the mating gear

on the other shaft even though it may not show as much wear or damage.

2. Carefully check the engagement dogs. If any is chipped, worn, rounded or missing, the affected gear must be replaced.
3. Rotate the transmission bearings (**Figure 27**) in both crankcase halves by hand. Check for roughness, noise and radial play. Any bearing that is suspect should be replaced as described in this chapter.

4. If the transmission shafts are satisfactory and are not going to be disassembled, apply assembly oil or engine oil to all components and reinstall them in the crankcase as described in this chapter.

NOTE
If disassembling a used, well run-in (high milage) transmission for the first time by yourself, pay particular attention to any additional shims that may have been added by a previous owner. These may have been added to take up

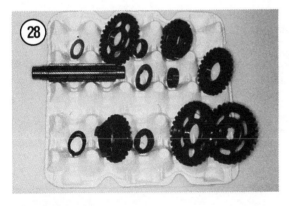

the tolerance of worn components and must be reinstalled in the same position since the shims have developed a wear pattern. If new parts are going to be installed these shims may be eliminated. This is something you will have to determine upon reassembly.

**Transmission
Service Notes**

1. A divided container, such as a restaurant type egg carton can be used to help maintain correct alignment and positioning of the parts. As you remove a part from the shaft set it in one of the depressions in the same position from which it was removed. Refer to **Figure 28** for the mainshaft and **Figure 29** for the countershaft. This is an easy way to remember the correct relationship of all parts.

2. The circlips are a tight fit on the transmission shafts. It is recommended that all circlips be replaced during reassembly.

3. Circlips will turn and fold over making removal and installation difficult. To ease replacement, open the circlips with a pair of circlip pliers while at the same time holding the back of the circlip with a pair of pliers and remove them. Repeat for installation.

**Mainshaft
Disassembly/Inspection**

Refer to **Figure 30** for this procedure.

1. If not cleaned in the *Preliminary Inspection* sequence, place the assembled shaft into a large can or plastic bucket and thoroughly clean with solvent and a stiff brush. Dry with compressed air or let it sit on rags to dry.

2. Slide off the reduction gear.

3. Slide off the 1st gear and 1st gear bushing.

4. Slide off the splined washer and remove the circlip.

5. Slide off the 4th gear.

6. Remove the circlip and slide off the splined washer.

7. Slide off the 3rd gear and 3rd gear bushing.

8. From the other end of the shaft, remove the washer.

9. Slide off the 2nd gear and 2nd gear bushing.

10. Slide off the 5th gear.

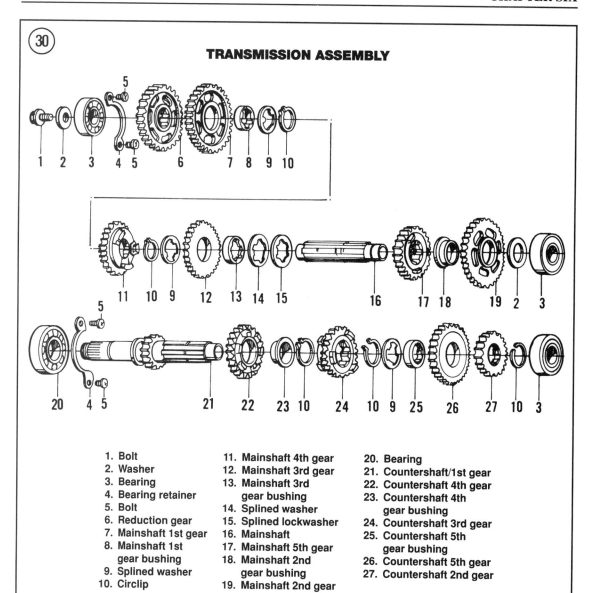

TRANSMISSION ASSEMBLY

30

1. Bolt
2. Washer
3. Bearing
4. Bearing retainer
5. Bolt
6. Reduction gear
7. Mainshaft 1st gear
8. Mainshaft 1st gear bushing
9. Splined washer
10. Circlip
11. Mainshaft 4th gear
12. Mainshaft 3rd gear
13. Mainshaft 3rd gear bushing
14. Splined washer
15. Splined lockwasher
16. Mainshaft
17. Mainshaft 5th gear
18. Mainshaft 2nd gear bushing
19. Mainshaft 2nd gear
20. Bearing
21. Countershaft/1st gear
22. Countershaft 4th gear
23. Countershaft 4th gear bushing
24. Countershaft 3rd gear
25. Countershaft 5th gear bushing
26. Countershaft 5th gear
27. Countershaft 2nd gear

31

32

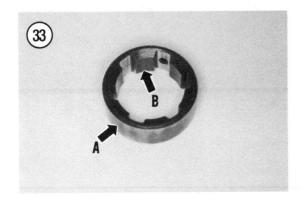

11. Slide off the splined lockwasher.

12. Rotate the splined washer in either direction to disengage the tangs from the grooves on the transmission shaft. Slide off the splined washer.

13. Check each gear for excessive wear, burrs, pitting, or chipped or missing teeth (**Figure 31**). Make sure the lugs (**Figure 32**) on the gears are in good condition.

14. Check each gear bushing (A, **Figure 33**) for excessive wear, pitting or damage. Replace if necessary.

15. Check each gear bushing inner splines (B, **Figure 33**) for excessive wear or damage. Replace if necessary.

16. On gears with bushings, inspect the inner surface of the gear (**Figure 34**) where the bushing rides for wear, pitting or damage.

17. Inspect the splined lockwasher and splined washer for wear, cracks or damage. Replace if necessary.

18. Inspect the circlips and splined washers for bending wear or damage. Replace if necessary.

19. Inspect the shift fork-to-gear clearance as described under *Internal Gearshift Mechanism* in this chapter.

> *NOTE*
> *Defective gears should be replaced. It is a good idea to replace the mating gear on the countershaft even though it may not show as much wear or damage.*

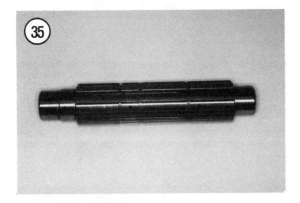

20. Make sure that all gears and bushings slide smoothly on the mainshaft splines.

> *NOTE*
> *It is recommended that all circlips be replaced every time the transmission is disassembled to ensure proper gear alignment. Do not expand a circlip more than necessary to slide it over the shaft.*

21. Inspect the splines and circlip grooves (**Figure 35**) of the mainshaft. If any are damaged, the shaft must be replaced.

Mainshaft Assembly

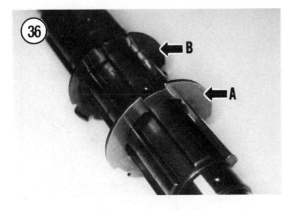

1. Apply a light coat of clean engine oil to all sliding surfaces prior to installing any parts.

2. Slide on the splined washer (A, **Figure 36**). Rotate the splined washer in either direction to engage

the tangs into the transmission shaft first groove on the end of the transmission shaft with the stepped end.

3. Slide on the splined lockwasher (B, **Figure 36**). Push it on until the tangs go into the open areas of the splined washer and lock the washer into place (**Figure 37**). Make sure the splined washer and splined lockwasher are installed in the correct shaft groove as shown in **Figure 38**.

4. Position the 5th gear with the shift fork groove going on first and install the 5th gear (**Figure 39**).

5. Position the 2nd gear bushing with the shoulder side going on first and slide on the bushing (**Figure 40**).

6. Position the 2nd gear with the shoulder side (**Figure 41**) going on first and slide on the 2nd gear (**Figure 42**).

7. Apply a light coat of multipurpose grease to the backside of the washer to hold it in place. Install the washer (**Figure 43**).

8. Turn the mainshaft around.

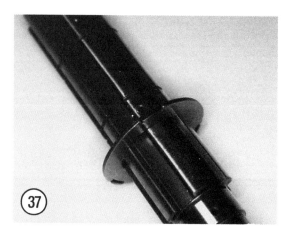

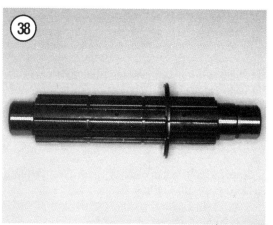

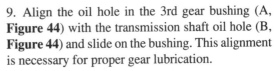

9. Align the oil hole in the 3rd gear bushing (A, **Figure 44**) with the transmission shaft oil hole (B, **Figure 44**) and slide on the bushing. This alignment is necessary for proper gear lubrication.

10. Slide on the 3rd gear (**Figure 45**).

11. Slide on the splined washer and install the circlip (**Figure 46**). Make sure the circlip is seated correctly in the mainshaft groove (**Figure 47**).

12. Position the 4th gear with the shift fork groove going on first and install the 4th gear (**Figure 48**).

13. Install the circlip (A, **Figure 49**) and slide on the splined washer (B, **Figure 49**).

14. Align the oil hole in the 1st gear bushing (A, **Figure 50**) with the transmission shaft oil hole (B, **Figure 50**) and slide on the bushing. This alignment is necessary for proper gear lubrication.

15. Position the 1st gear with the shoulder side (**Figure 51**) going on first and slide on the 1st gear (**Figure 52**).

16. Position the reduction gear with the wide shoulder side (**Figure 53**) going on first and slide on the 1st gear (**Figure 54**). If installed correctly, the splined portion of the reduction gear should be flush with the end of the mainshaft splines (**Figure 55**).

17. Refer to **Figure 56** for correct placement of all gears. Make sure all circlips are correctly seated in the mainshaft grooves.

18. Make sure each gear engages the adjoining gear properly, where applicable.

Countershaft
Disassembly/Inspection

Refer to **Figure 30** for this procedure.

1. If not cleaned in the *Preliminary Inspection* sequence, place the assembled shaft into a large can or plastic bucket and thoroughly clean with solvent and a stiff brush. Dry with compressed air or let it sit on rags to dry.

2. Remove the circlip and slide off the 2nd gear.

3. Slide off the 5th gear and the 5th gear bushing.

4. Slide off the splined washer and remove the circlip.

5. Slide off the 3rd gear.

6. Remove the circlip.

7. Slide off the 4th gear and 4th gear bushing.

8. Check each gear for excessive wear, burrs, pitting, chipped teeth or missing teeth (**Figure 31**).

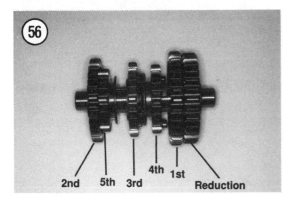

2nd   5th   3rd   4th   1st   Reduction

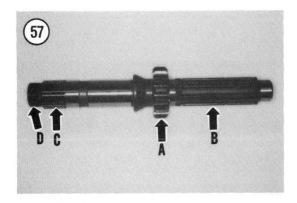

D   C   A   B

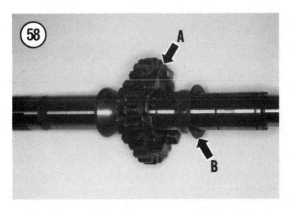

A

B

Make sure the lugs (**Figure 32**) on the gears are in good condition.

9. Check each gear bushing (A, **Figure 33**) for excessive wear, pitting or damage.

10. Inspect the inner splines of the bushing (B, **Figure 33**) for wear or damage. Replace if necessary.

11. On gears with bushings, inspect the inner surface of the gear (**Figure 34**) where the bushing rides for wear, pitting or damage.

12. Inspect the circlips and splined washers for bending wear or damage. Replace if necessary.

13. Inspect the splined washer for wear, cracks or damage. Replace if necessary.

14. Inspect the shift fork-to-gear clearance as described under *Internal Gearshift Mechanism* in this chapter.

NOTE
Defective gears should be replaced. It is a good idea to replace the mating gear on the mainshaft even though it may not show as much wear or damage.

NOTE
The 1st gear (A, Figure 57) is part of the countershaft. If the gear is defective, the countershaft must be replaced.

15. Make sure that all gears slide smoothly on the countershaft splines.

NOTE
It is recommended that all circlips be replaced every time the transmission is disassembled to ensure proper gear alignment. Do not expand a circlip more than necessary to slide it over the shaft.

16. Inspect the splines (B, **Figure 57**) and circlip grooves of the countershaft. If any are damaged, the shaft must be replaced.

17. Inspect the clutch hub splines (C, **Figure 57**) and clutch nut threads (D, **Figure 57**) of the countershaft. If any splines any are damaged, the shaft must be replaced. If the threads have burrs or have minor damage, clean with a proper size metric thread die.

Countershaft Assembly

1. Apply a light coat of clean engine oil to all sliding surfaces prior to installing any parts.

2. Slide on the 4th gear (A, **Figure 58**).

3. Position the 4th gear bushing with the flange side gong on last. Slide on the 5th gear bushing (B, **Figure 58**) and push it all the way into the 5th gear.

4. Install the circlip (**Figure 59**). Make sure the circlip is correctly seated in the countershaft groove.

5. Position the 3rd gear with the shift dog side going on last and slide the 3rd gear on (**Figure 60**).

6. Install the circlip (A, **Figure 61**) and slide on the splined washer (B, **Figure 61**).

7. Align the oil hole in the 5th gear bushing (A, **Figure 62**) with the transmission shaft oil hole (B, **Figure 62**) and slide on the bushing. This alignment is necessary for proper gear lubrication.

8. Position the 5th gear with the shift dog side going on first and slide the 5th gear on (**Figure 63**).

9. Slide on the 2nd gear (**Figure 64**) and install the circlip. Make sure the circlip (**Figure 65**) is correctly seated in the countershaft groove.

10. Refer to **Figure 66** for correct placement of all gears. Make sure all circlips are correctly seated in the countershaft grooves.

11. After both transmission shafts have been assembled, mesh the 2 assemblies together in the correct position (**Figure 67**). Check that gear engages properly to the adjoining gear properly, where applicable. This is your last check prior to installing the shaft assemblies into the crankcase; make sure they are correctly assembled.

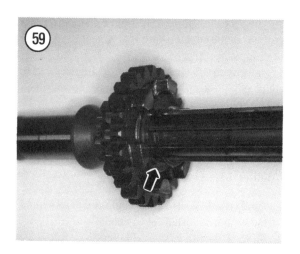

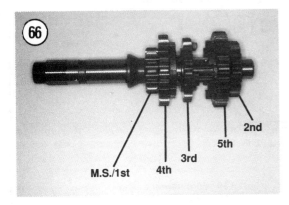

M.S./1st   4th   3rd   5th   2nd

INTERNAL GEARSHIFT MECHANISM

Removal/Disassembly

Refer to **Figure 68** for this procedure.

1. Remove the engine as described under *Crankcase Disassembly* in Chapter Four.

NOTE
Note the location of the electrical wire strap (A, Figure 69). It must be reinstalled in the same location during installation.

2. Remove the screws securing the neutral switch (B, **Figure 69**) and remove the neutral switch assembly.
3. Remove the O-ring seal (**Figure 70**) from the receptacle in the crankcase.
4. Remove the switch contact plunger (**Figure 71**) and spring from the end of the gearshift drum.
5. Remove the external gearshift mechanism as described in this chapter.
6. Split the crankcase as described under *Crankcase Disassembly* in Chapter Four.
7. Mark shift forks with a "R," "C" and "L" (right, center and left) so they will be reinstalled in the correct position.
8. Hold onto the shift forks and withdraw both shift fork shafts (**Figure 72**) one at a time.
9. Swing the shift forks away from the shift drum.
10. Remove the shift drum (**Figure 73**).
11. Remove all 3 shift forks (**Figure 74**).
12. Thoroughly clean all parts in solvent and dry with compressed air.

Inspection

1. Inspect each shift fork for signs of wear or cracking. Check for any arc-shaped wear or burned marks on the fingers of the shift forks (**Figure 75**). This indicates that the shift fork has come in contact with the gear. The fork fingers have become excessively worn and the fork must be replaced.
2. Check the bore of each shift fork (A, **Figure 76**) and the shift fork shaft (B, **Figure 76**) for burrs, wear or pitting. Replace any worn parts.
3. Install each shift fork onto the shaft (**Figure 77**) and make sure it moves freely on the shaft with no binding.

6

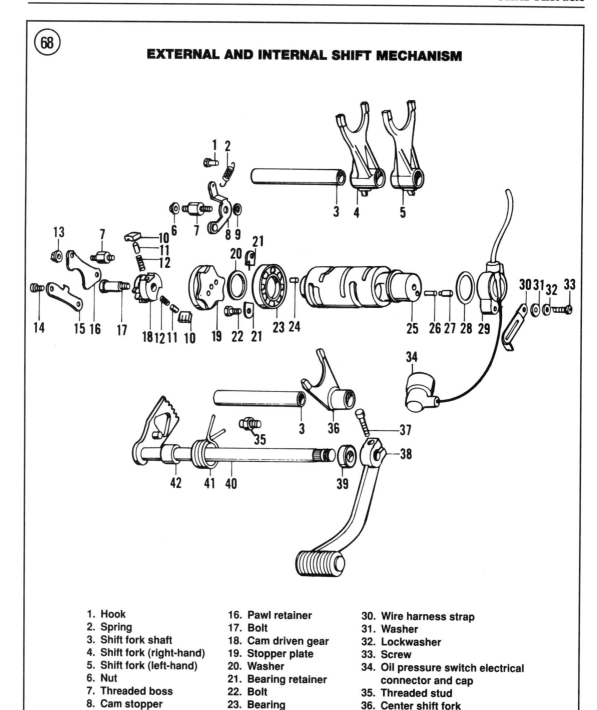

EXTERNAL AND INTERNAL SHIFT MECHANISM

1. Hook
2. Spring
3. Shift fork shaft
4. Shift fork (right-hand)
5. Shift fork (left-hand)
6. Nut
7. Threaded boss
8. Cam stopper
9. Washer
10. Pawl
11. Pin
12. Spring
13. Nut
14. Bolt
15. Cam guide
16. Pawl retainer
17. Bolt
18. Cam driven gear
19. Stopper plate
20. Washer
21. Bearing retainer
22. Bolt
23. Bearing
24. Pin
25. Shift drum
26. Spring
27. Pin
28. O-ring
29. Neutral indicator switch
30. Wire harness strap
31. Washer
32. Lockwasher
33. Screw
34. Oil pressure switch electrical connector and cap
35. Threaded stud
36. Center shift fork
37. Bolt
38. Shift lever
39. Oil seal
40. Shift shaft
41. Return spring
42. Spacer

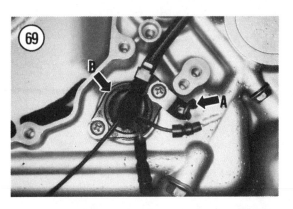

6

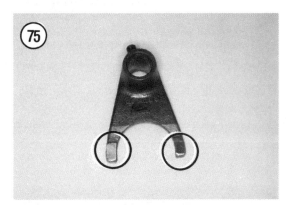

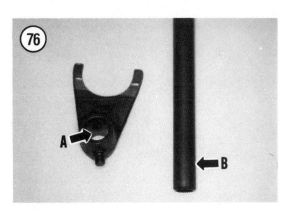

4. Check the cam follower pins (**Figure 78**) on each shift fork that rides in the shift drum for wear or damage. Replace the shift fork(s) as necessary.

5. Roll the shift fork shaft on a flat surface such as a piece of plate glass and check for any bends. If the shaft is bent, it must be replaced.

6. Check the grooves in the shift drum (**Figure 79**) for wear or roughness. If any of the groove profiles have excessive wear or damage, replace the shift drum.

7. Inspect the cam gear locating pins and threaded hole (**Figure 80**) in the end of the shift drum for wear or damage. Replace the shift drum if necessary.

8. Check the neutral switch contact plunger and spring for wear or damage. If the spring has sagged, replace it.

9. Check the shift drum bearings (**Figure 81**). Make sure they operate smoothly with no signs of wear or damage. If damaged, replace as described under *Crankcase Bearings Removal/Installation* in Chapter Four.

> *CAUTION*
> *It is recommended that marginally worn shift forks be replaced. Worn forks can cause the transmission to slip out of gear, leading to more serious and expensive damage.*

10. Inspect the shift fork-to-gear clearance as follows:

    a. Install each shift fork into its respective gear. Use a flat feeler gauge and measure the clearance between the fork and the gear as shown in

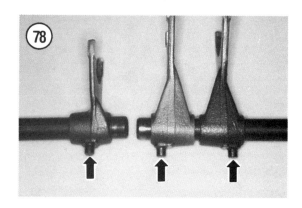

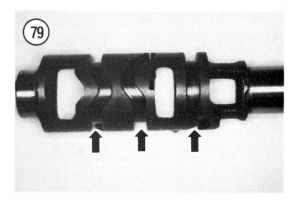

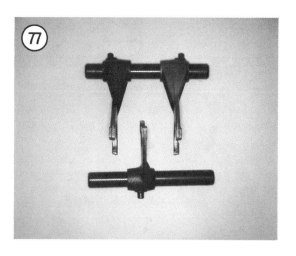

Figure 82. Compare to the specifications listed in **Table 1**.

b. If the clearance is greater than specified in **Table 1**, measure the width of the gearshift fork fingers with a micrometer (**Figure 83**). Replace the shift fork(s) worn to the service limit listed in **Table 1**.

c. If the shift fork finger width is within tolerance, measure the shift fork groove width in the gears. Compare to the specifications listed in **Table 1**. Replace the gear(s) if the groove is worn to the service limit or more.

Assembly/Installation

1. Apply a light coat of oil to the shift fork shafts, the inside bores of the shift forks, the shift drum bearing surfaces and to the bearings in the crankcase prior to installing any parts.

2. Install all 3 shift forks (**Figure 84**) into their respective gears. Refer to marks made in Step 7 of *Removal/Disassembly*.

3. Swing the shift forks out to allow room for the installation of the shift drum.

NOTE
After installing the shift drum, make sure it rotates smoothly with no binding.

4. Install the shift drum (**Figure 73**) and push it down until it stops.

5. Swing the shift forks into place in the shift drum. Make sure the guide pin on each fork is indexed into its respective groove in the shift drum.

6. Install the shift shaft all the way through the "L" and "R" shift forks. Push it down until it bottoms out in the crankcase.

7. Install the other shift shaft all the way through the "C" shift fork. Push it down until it bottoms out in the crankcase.

8. Make sure the shift fork guide pins are correctly meshed with the grooves in the shift drum (**Figure 85**).

9. Assemble the crankcase as described in Chapter Four.

10. Install the external gearshift mechanism as described in this chapter.

11. Install the switch contact spring and plunger (**Figure 86**) into the end of the gearshift drum. Make sure they are completely seated (**Figure 71**).

12. Apply a light coat of oil to the O-ring and install the O-ring seal (**Figure 70**) into the receptacle in the crankcase. Make sure it is seated correctly.

13. Install the neutral switch (B, **Figure 69**), the electrical wire strap (A, **Figure 69**) and screws. Tighten the screws securely.

14. Install the engine as described in Chapter Four.

Table 1 TRANSMISSION AND GEARSHIFT SPECIFICATIONS

Item	Specifications	Wear limit
Shift fork-to-groove		
in gear clearance	0.1-0.3 mm	0.5 mm (0.02 in.)
	0.004-0.012 in.)	
Shift fork groove width in gear		
4th and 5th gear	5.50-5.60 mm	—
	(0.217-0.220 in.)	
3rd gear	4.50-4.60 mm	—
	(0.117-0.181 in.)	
Shift fork finger thickness		
4th and 5th gear (right and left)	5.30-5.40 mm	—
	(0.209-0.213 in.)	
3rd gear (center)	4.30-4.40 mm	—
	(0.169-0.173 in.)	
Transmission gear ratios		
1st gear	2.090 (34:11)	
2nd gear	1.631 (31:19)	
3rd gear	1.227 (27:22)	
4th gear	1.000 (25:25)	
5th gear	0.851 (23:27)	
Primary reduction ratio	1.690 (71:42)	
Secondary reduction ratio	1.133 (30:30 × 17:15)	
Final reduction ratio	3.090 (34:11)	

CHAPTER SEVEN

FUEL, EMISSION CONTROL AND EXHAUST SYSTEMS

The fuel system consists of the fuel tank, the shutoff valve, fuel pump, 2 carburetors and a separate air filter assembly for each carburetor. The exhaust system consists of 2 exhaust pipes and 2 mufflers.

The emission controls consist of crankcase emission system and on California models the Evaporative Emission Control System.

This chapter includes service procedures for all parts of the fuel system and exhaust system. Air filter service is covered in Chapter Three.

Carburetor specifications are covered in **Table 1** located at the end of this chapter.

> *NOTE*
> *Where differences occur relating to the United Kingdom (U.K.) models they are identified. If there is no (U.K.) designation relating to a procedure, photo or illustration it is identical to the United States (U.S.) models.*

CARBURETOR OPERATION

For proper operation, a gasoline engine must be supplied with fuel and air mixed in proper proportions by weight. A mixture in which there is an excess of fuel is said to be rich. A lean mixture is one which contains insufficient fuel. A properly adjusted carburetor supplies the proper mixture to the engine under all operating conditions.

Each carburetor consists of several major systems. A float and float valve mechanism maintains a constant fuel level in the float bowl. The pilot system supplies fuel at low speeds. The main fuel system supplies fuel at medium and high speeds. A starter (choke) system supplies the very rich mixture needed to start a cold engine.

CARBURETOR SERVICE

Major carburetor service (removal and cleaning) should be performed if the engine performs poorly, hesitates and there is little or no response to mixture adjustment is observed. Alterations in jet size, throttle slide cutaway, and changes in jet needle position, etc., should be attempted only if you're experienced in this type of "tuning" work; a bad guess could result in costly engine damage or, at least, poor performance. If, after servicing the carburetor and making the adjustments described in this chapter, the bike does not perform correctly (and assuming that other factors affecting performance are correct, such as ignition component condition, etc.), the bike should be checked by a dealer or a qualified performance tuning specialist.

CARBURETOR ASSEMBLY

Removal/Installation

Remove the 2 carburetors and the throttle cable assembly that is attached to both carburetors as an assembled unit.

1. Remove the seat(s) as described under *Seat Removal/Installation* in Chapter Thirteen.

2. Remove the fuel tank as described in this chapter.

3. Disconnect the battery negative lead as described in Chapter Three.

4. Remove the screws securing both the right- and left-hand frame head side covers (**Figure 1**). Remove both side covers.

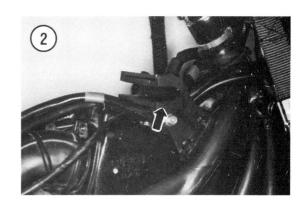

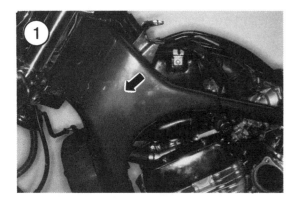

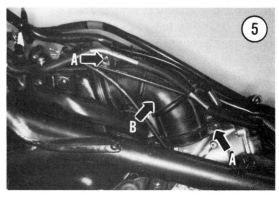

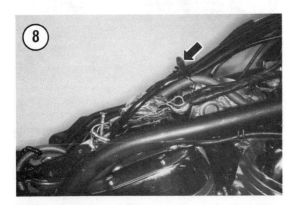

5. Remove the bolts securing the fuel tank mounting bracket (**Figure 2**) and remove the bracket.

6. Remove the screw (**Figure 3**) securing the throttle cable joint to the air filter housing and remove the joint from the clip on the air filter housing.

7. Separate the throttle cable joint and disconnect the 2 carburetor throttle cables (**Figure 4**) from the plastic fitting of the throttle grip throttle cable, then move the throttle grip throttle cable out of the way.

8. Loosen the clamping band screws (A, **Figure 5**) at each end of the front air filter inlet pipe. Slide the clamping bands onto the inlet pipe and remove the inlet pipe (B, **Figure 5**).

9. Remove the screw (A, **Figure 6**) securing the choke knob assembly to the frame, then move the choke knob assembly (B, **Figure 6**) out of the way. Do not try to disconnect the choke cable from the carburetor at this time.

10. Loosen the screws on the clamping bands securing carburetors to the intake tubes (**Figure 7**). Slide the clamping bands away from the carburetors.

11. Remove the clamp (**Figure 8**) securing the throttle cables and hoses together. Separate the cables and hoses.

12. Unhook the clamps and move the carburetor breather hose (A, **Figure 9**) from the inlet pipe.

13. Loosen the clamping band screws (B, **Figure 9**) at each end of the rear air filter inlet pipe. Slide the clamping bands onto the inlet pipe and remove the inlet pipe (C, **Figure 9**).

14. On California models, disconnect the evaporation hose from each carburetor.

15. On the rear carburetor, open the hose clamps and move the hose (**Figure 10**) out of the way.

16. Move the rear carburetor assembly partially up and out of the frame area, then perform the following:

7

a. Unscrew and disconnect the choke cable (**Figure 11**) from the rear carburetor. Move the cable out of the way.

b. Loosen the locknuts on the throttle cable at the rear carburetor. Remove the throttle cable from the bracket (A, **Figure 12**) on the carburetor and disconnect the cable end (B, **Figure 12**) from the throttle wheel.

17. Carefully remove the carburetor assembly and attached cables. Make sure all cables and hoses necessary for carburetor removal, are disconnected. Take the assembly to a workbench for disassembly and cleaning.

18. Install by reversing these removal steps, noting the following:

a. Make sure the carburetors are fully seated in the rubber holders attached to the cylinder head. You should feel a solid "bottoming out" when they are correctly seated.

b. Make sure the screws on the clamping bands are tight to avoid a vacuum loss and possible valve damage due to a lean fuel mixture.

c. Adjust the throttle cable as described under *Throttle Cable Adjustment* in Chapter Three.

CARBURETOR SERVICE

Carburetor disassembly and assembly is separated into three different procedures. The piston valve assembly and coasting valve are basically the same on both the front and rear carburetor and is covered in one procedure. The components in the float chamber area, floats and jets, vary considerably between the front and rear carburetors and are covered separately to avoid confusion.

Piston Valve Assembly and Coasting Valve

Refer to the following illustrations for this procedure:

a. **Figure 13**: front carburetor.

b. **Figure 14**: rear carburetor.

It is recommended to disassemble only one carburetor at a time to prevent accidental interchange of parts.

Disassembly

1. Remove the screws (A, **Figure 15**) securing the top cover and remove the cover (B, **Figure 15**). Note

the location of any hose clamps, that must be reinstalled in the same location.

2. Remove the spring and the piston valve/diaphragm from the carburetor.

3. Loosen the screws (**Figure 16**) securing the jet needle stopper plate.

4. Use needlenose pliers and remove the stopper plate from the piston valve (**Figure 17**).

5. Turn the assembly over and remove the jet needle and spring.

6. Remove the screws securing the coasting valve cover and remove the cover (**Figure 18**).

7. Remove the spring (**Figure 19**) and the diaphragm (A, **Figure 20**) from the carburetor.

Assembly

1. Install the coasting valve diaphragm (A, **Figure 20**) onto the carburetor. Align the hole in the diaphragm with the hole in the carburetor body (B, **Figure 20**).

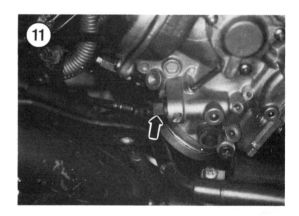

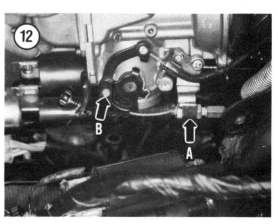

(13) **FRONT CARBURETOR ASSEMBLY**

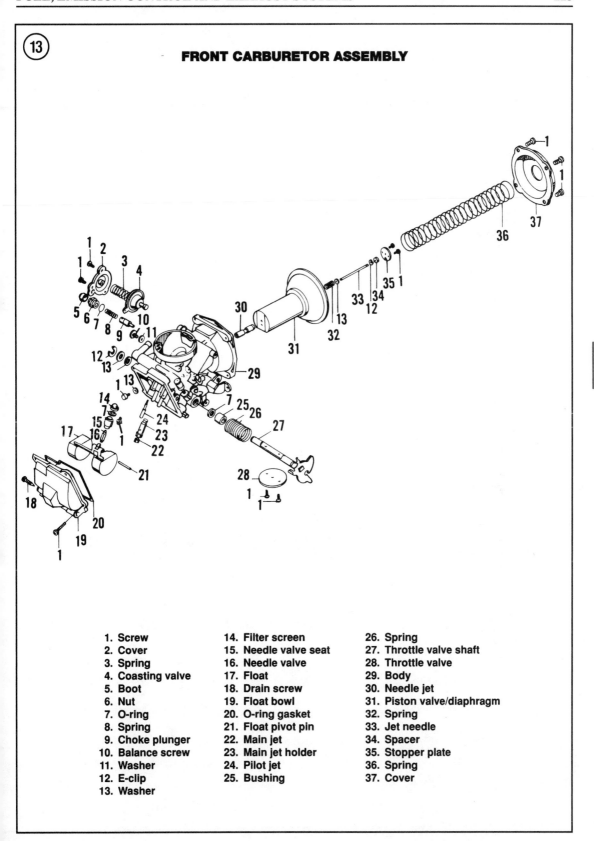

7

1. Screw	14. Filter screen	26. Spring
2. Cover	15. Needle valve seat	27. Throttle valve shaft
3. Spring	16. Needle valve	28. Throttle valve
4. Coasting valve	17. Float	29. Body
5. Boot	18. Drain screw	30. Needle jet
6. Nut	19. Float bowl	31. Piston valve/diaphragm
7. O-ring	20. O-ring gasket	32. Spring
8. Spring	21. Float pivot pin	33. Jet needle
9. Choke plunger	22. Main jet	34. Spacer
10. Balance screw	23. Main jet holder	35. Stopper plate
11. Washer	24. Pilot jet	36. Spring
12. E-clip	25. Bushing	37. Cover
13. Washer		

(14)

REAR CARBURETOR ASSEMBLY

1. Screw
2. Clip
3. Cover
4. Spring
5. Screw
6. Stopper plate
7. Spacer
8. Jet needle
9. Washer
10. Spring
11. Piston valve/diaphragm
12. Needle jet
13. Boot
14. Nut
15. O-ring
16. Spring
17. Choke plunger
18. Pilot screw
19. Spring
20. O-ring
21. Washer
22. Throttle valve shaft
23. Throttle stop screw
24. Throttle valve
25. Pilot jet
26. Balance screw
27. Needle valve
    stopper screw
28. Main jet
29. Drain screw
30. Float bowl
31. Gasket
32. Float pivot pin
33. Float
34. Needle valve assembly
35. Filter screen
36. Cover
37. Spring
38. Coasting valve
39. Body

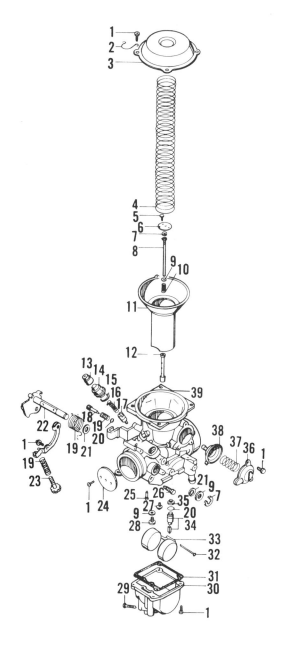

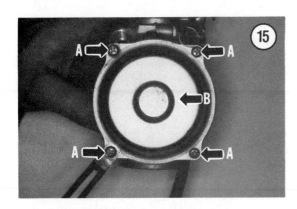

2. Install the spring (**Figure 19**) onto the diaphragm.

3. Install the coasting valve cover (**Figure 18**) and screws. Tighten the screws securely.

4. Install the spring (**Figure 21**) into the piston valve.

5. Install the jet needle (**Figure 22**) through the spring and into the hole in the bottom of the piston valve.

6. Use needlenose pliers and install the stopper plate and screws into the piston valve (**Figure 17**).

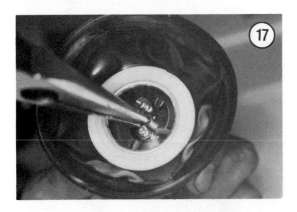

7

Align the screw holes and tighten the screws securely.

7. Install the piston valve/diaphragm into the carburetor (**Figure 23**). Be sure to align the tab hole in the diaphragm with the hole in the carburetor body (**Figure 24**).

8. Insert your finger into the carburetor venturi and hold the piston valve up so the diaphragm is in the raised position. This will lessen the chances of it getting pinched when the top cover is installed.

9. Install the spring (A, **Figure 25**) into the piston valve and install the top cover (B, **Figure 25**). Make sure the diaphragm tab hole is still aligned with the hole in the body.

10. Push the cover down while guiding the jet needle into the needle jet (**Figure 26**). Push the cover all the way down and install the screws and any hose clamps in the correct location.

11. Tighten the screws (A, **Figure 15**) securely.

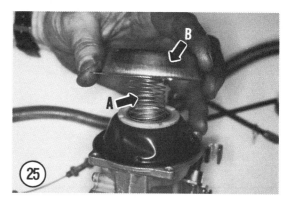

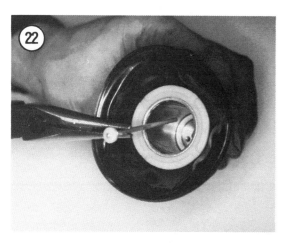

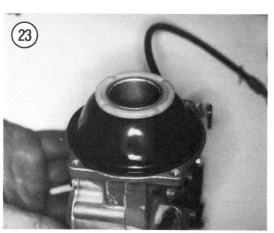

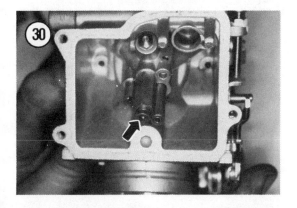

Front Carburetor
Float Chamber and Carburetor Body
Disassembly

Refer to **Figure 13** for this procedure.

1. Remove the screws (**Figure 27**) securing the float bowl and remove the float bowl and O-ring seal.

2. Push the float pin (A, **Figure 28**) out of the mounting boss and remove it.

3. Remove the float (B, **Figure 28**) and needle valve assembly.

4. Remove the screw (A, **Figure 29**) securing the needle valve seat and filter assembly. Remove the needle valve seat and filter assembly (B, **Figure 29**).

5. Unscrew the main jet (**Figure 30**) and the main jet holder (**Figure 31**).

6. Unscrew the pilot jet (**Figure 32**).

7. Remove the needle jet (**Figure 33**).

8. Remove the O-ring seal (**Figure 34**) from the float bowl.

7

9. Remove the drain screw (**Figure 35**) from the float bowl.

> *NOTE*
> *Further disassembly is neither necessary nor recommended. If throttle shaft, choke shaft or butterfly (**Figure 36**) is damaged, take the carburetor body to a dealer for replacement.*

10. Clean and inspect all parts as described under *Cleaning and Inspection* in this chapter.

Front Carburetor
Float Chamber and Carburetor Body
Assembly

Refer to **Figure 13** for this procedure.

1. Install the drain screw (**Figure 35**) into the float bowl and tighten securely.

2. Install the needle jet and carefully push it in until it seats (**Figure 37**).

3. Install the pilot jet (**Figure 32**) and tighten securely.

4. Install the main jet holder (**Figure 31**) and tighten securely.

5. Install the main jet (**Figure 30**) and tighten securely.

6. Make sure the O-ring seal is on needle valve and install the needle valve seat and filter assembly (B, **Figure 29**). Push the assembly down until it is completely seated.

7. Install the screw (A, **Figure 29**) securing the needle valve seat and filter assembly and tighten securely.

8. Install the needle valve assembly (**Figure 38**) onto the float tang and install the float (B, **Figure 28**).

9. Install the float pin (A, **Figure 28**) through the mounting boss, float and other mounting boss. Push the pin in until it is completely seated. Move the float up and down to make sure it moves freely.

10. Check the float height and adjust if necessary as described in this chapter.

11. Make sure the float bowl seal is correctly seated in the float bowl groove (**Figure 34**).

12. Install the float bowl and screws (**Figure 27**) and tighten securely.

13. After the carburetor have been disassembled the idle speed should be adjusted and the carburetors synchronized as described in this chapter.

Rear Carburetor
Float Chamber and Carburetor Body
Disassembly

Refer to **Figure 39** for this procedure.

1. Remove the screws (**Figure 40**) securing the float bowl and remove the float bowl and gasket.

2. Unscrew the main jet (**Figure 41**).

3. To remove the needle jet (A, **Figure 42**); turn the carburetor body on it side and tap on the other side

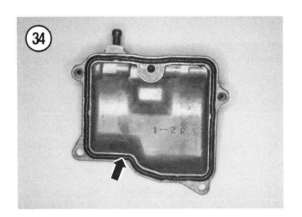

of the carburetor body. Once the needle jet is loose, withdraw it through the piston valve portion of the carburetor body with needle nose pliers (**Figure 43**).

4. Unscrew the pilot jet (**Figure 44**).

5. Push the float pin out of the mounting boss and remove it.

6. Remove the float and needle valve assembly (A, **Figure 45**).

7. Remove the screw (B, **Figure 45**) securing the needle valve seat and filter assembly.

8. Remove the gasket (**Figure 46**) from the float bowl.

9. Remove the drain screw (**Figure 47**) from the float bowl.

NOTE
*Further disassembly is neither necessary nor recommended. If throttle or choke shafts or butterfly (**Figure 36**) is*

damaged, take the carburetor body to a dealer for replacement.

10. Clean and inspect all parts as described under *Cleaning and Inspection* in this chapter.

Rear Carburetor
Float Chamber and Carburetor Body
Assembly

Refer to **Figure 39** for this procedure.

1. Install the drain screw (**Figure 47**) into the float bowl and tighten securely.

2. Make sure the O-ring seal is on needle valve and install the needle valve seat and filter assembly. Push the assembly down until it is completely seated.

3. Install the screw (B, **Figure 45**) securing the needle valve seat and filter assembly and tighten securely.

4. Install the needle valve assembly onto the float tang and install the float (A, **Figure 45**).

5. Install the float pin through the mounting boss, float and other mounting boss. Push the pin in until it is completely seated. Move the float up and down to make sure it moves freely.

6. Check the float height and adjust if necessary as described in this chapter.

7. Install the pilot jet (**Figure 48**) and tighten securely.

CAUTION
In the next step, make sure that the flat portion on the needle jet is correctly aligned with the protrusion in the main jet stantion. If alignment is not correct, you will be unable to screw the main jet into the needle jet.

8. Position the needle jet so the flat portion (A, **Figure 49**) aligns with the protrusion (B, **Figure 49**) in the main jet stantion of the carburetor body.

9. Using needle nose pliers, install the needle jet in through the piston valve portion of the carburetor body (**Figure 43**).

10. Observe the float bowl end of the needle jet to make sure alignment is still correct, then carefully push the needle jet in until it bottoms out (B, **Figure 42**).

11. Install the main jet (**Figure 50**) and tighten securely (**Figure 41**).

7

REAR CARBURETOR ASSEMBLY

1. Screw
2. Clip
3. Cover
4. Spring
5. Screw
6. Stopper plate
7. Spacer
8. Jet needle
9. Washer
10. Spring
11. Piston valve/diaphragm
12. Needle jet
13. Gasket
14. Nut
15. O-ring
16. Spring
17. Choke plunger
18. Pilot screw
19. Spring
20. O-ring
21. Washer
22. Throttle valve shaft
23. Throttle stop screw
24. Throttle valve
25. Pilot jet
26. Balance screw
27. Needle valve
    stopper screw
28. Main jet
29. Drain screw
30. Float bowl
31. Gasket
32. Float pivot pin
33. Float
34. Needle valve assembly
35. Filter screen
36. Cover
37. Spring
38. Coasting valve
39. Body

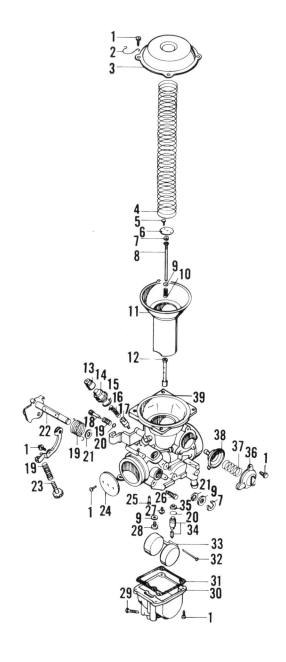

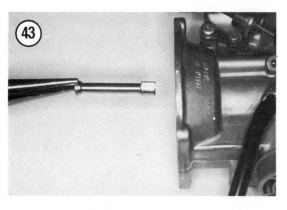

7

12. Install the gasket (**Figure 46**) into the float bowl. Make sure it seats completely.

13. Install the float bowl and screws (**Figure 40**). Tighten the screws securely.

14. After the carburetors have been disassembled the idle speed should be adjusted and the carburetors synchronized as described in this chapter.

Cleaning and Inspection (Both Front and Rear Carburetors)

> *NOTE*
> *Figures accompaning these procedures show components for both the front and rear carburetor assemblies.*

1. Thoroughly clean and dry all parts. Suzuki does not recommend the use of a caustic carburetor cleaning solvent. Instead, clean carburetor parts in a petroleum based solvent. Then rinse in clean water.

2. Allow the carburetor to dry thoroughly before assembly and blow dry with compressed air. Blow out the jets and needle jet holder with compressed air.

3. Inspect all O-ring seals. O-ring seals (**Figure 51**) tend to become hardened after prolonged use and heat and therefore lose their ability to seal properly.

> *CAUTION*
> *If compressed air is not available, allow the parts to air dry or use a clean lint-free cloth. Do **not** use a paper towel to dry carburetor parts, as small paper particles may plug openings in the carburetor body or jets.*

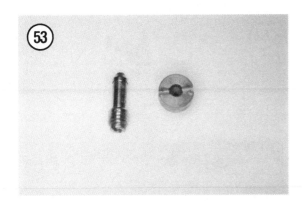

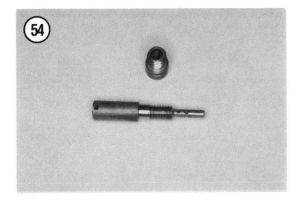

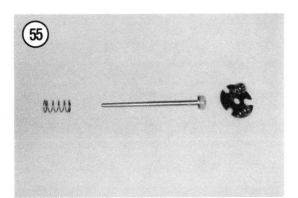

CAUTION
*Do **not** use a piece of wire to clean openings or jets, because minor gouges can alter flow rate and upset the fuel/air mixture.*

4. Make sure the holes in the needle jet (**Figure 52**) are clear. Clean out if they are plugged in any way. Replace the needle jet if you cannot unplug the holes.

5. Make sure the holes in the main jet and pilot screw are clear. Refer to **Figure 53** and **Figure 54**. Clean out if they are plugged in any way. Replace the main jet or pilot screw if you cannot unplug the holes.

6. Examine the jet needle parts (**Figure 55**) of the piston valve/diaphragm assembly for wear or damage. Make sure the diaphragm (A, **Figure 56**) is not torn or cracked. Replace any damaged or worn parts.

7. Inspect the piston valve (B, **Figure 56**) portion of the piston valve/diaphragm assembly for wear or damage. Replace the assembly if necessary.

8. Clean and inspect the filter screen (**Figure 57**) of the needle valve. Replace if any area is broken or starting to deteriorate.

9. Inspect the float (**Figure 58**) for deterioration or damage. If the float is suspected of leakage, place it

7

in a container of non-caustic solution and push it down. If the float sinks or if bubbles appear (indicating a leak); replace the float assembly.

10. Make sure all openings (**Figure 59**) in the carburetor body are clear. Clean out if they are plugged in any way.

11. Inspect the choke plunger (A, **Figure 60**) and spring (B, **Figure 60**) for wear or damage. Replace if necessary.

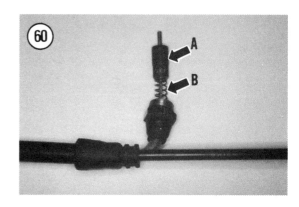

Carburetor Separation

The carburetors can be removed, disassembled, cleaned, assembled and reinstalled without disconnecting any of the cables or lines from either carburetor. If necessary, they can be separated, but first tag each cable and connector prior to removal for ease of re-assembly.

Refer to **Figure 61** for the identification of the cables and fuel and vent lines:

   a. A: Synchronizing cable.
   b. B: No. 2 throttle cable (front carburetor).
   c. C: No. 1 Throttle cable (rear carburetor).
   d. D: Fuel line.
   e. E: Vent lines.

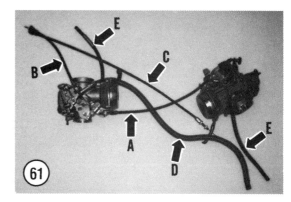

1. To disconnect the carburetor synchronizing cable, perform the following:

   a. At the front carburetor, loosen the locknut (A, **Figure 62**) and disconnect the cable end from the throttle wheel (B, **Figure 62**).
   b. Disconnect the cable from the bracket on the front carburetor (C, **Figure 62**).
   c. At the rear carburetor, disconnect the cable end from the throttle wheel (A, **Figure 63**) and disconnect the cable from the bracket on the carburetor (B, **Figure 63**).
   d. Remove the cable.

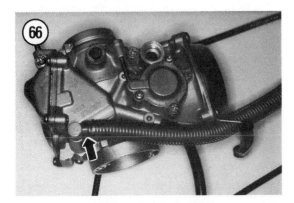

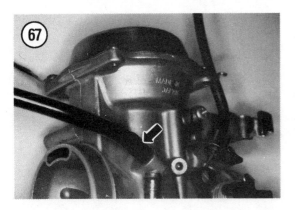

2. To disconnect the No. 2 throttle cable, perform the following:

   a. Loosen the locknut (A, **Figure 64**) and disconnect the cable end from the throttle wheel (B, **Figure 64**).

   b. Remove the No. 2 throttle cable (C, **Figure 64**) along with the No. 1 throttle cable (D, **Figure 64**) that was disconnected during carburetor removal.

   c. Remove the throttle cable assembly.

3. To remove the choke cable, perform the following:

   a. Unscrew the nut (A, **Figure 65**) securing the choke cable to the front carburetor.

   b. Remove the choke cable assembly (B, **Figure 65**) from the front carburetor.

4. If necessary, remove the fuel line (**Figure 66**) from the fitting on the front carburetor.

5. If necessary, remove the vent line (**Figure 67**) from the fitting on the front carburetor.

6. Install all vent lines, the fuel line, choke and throttle cable assemblies by reversing these removal steps. Synchronize the carburetors as described in Chapter Three.

CARBURETOR ADJUSTMENTS

Float Adjustment

   The carburetor assembly has to be removed and partially disassembled for this adjustment.

1. Remove the carburetor assembly as described in this chapter.

2A. On the front carburetor, remove the screws (**Figure 68**) securing the float bowl and remove the float bowl and O-ring seal.

2B. On the rear carburetor, remove the screws (**Figure 69**) securing the float bowl and remove the float bowl and gasket.

3. Hold the carburetor assembly with the carburetor inclined until the float arm is just touching the float needle—not pushing it down. Use a float level gauge, vernier caliper or small ruler and measure the distance from the carburetor body to the bottom surface of the float body. Refer to **Figure 70** for the front carburetor and **Figure 71** for the rear carburetor. The correct height is listed in **Table 1**.

4. Adjust by carefully bending the tang (**Figure 72**) on the float arm. If the float level is too high, the result will be a rich fuel/air mixture. If it is too low, the mixture will be too lean.

5. Reassemble and install the carburetors.

Rejetting The Carburetors

Do not try to solve a poor running engine problem by rejetting the carburetors if all of the following conditions hold true:

a. The engine has held a good tune in the past with the standard jetting.

b. The engine has not been modified.

c. The motorcycle is being operated in the same geographical region under the same general climatic conditions as in the past.

d. The motorcycle was and is being ridden at average highway speeds.

If those conditions all hold true, the chances are that the problem is due to a malfunction in the carburetor or in another component that needs to be repaired. Changing carburetor jet size probably won't solve the problem. Rejetting the carburetors may be necessary if any of the following conditions hold true:

a. Non-standard type of air filter elements are being used.

b. A non-standard exhaust system is installed on the motorcycle.

c. Any of the top end components in the engine (pistons, camshafts, valves, compression ratio, etc.) have been modified.

d. The motorcycle is in use at considerably higher or lower altitudes or in a considerably hotter or colder climate than in the past.

e. The motorcycle is being operated at considerably higher speeds than before and changing to colder spark plugs does not solve the problem.

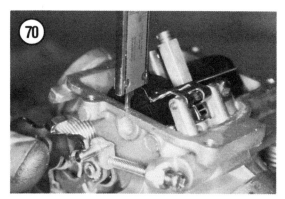

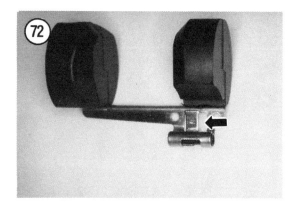

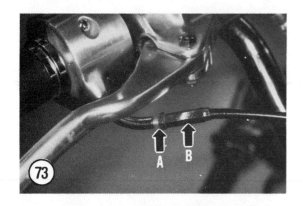

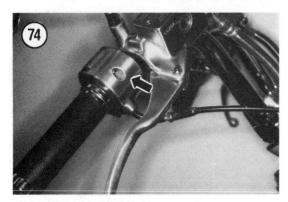

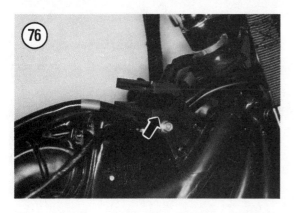

f. Someone has previously changed the carburetor jetting.

g. The motorcycle has never held a satisfactory engine tune.

If it is necessary to re-jet the carburetors, check with a dealer or motorcycle performance tuner for recommendations as to the size of jets to install for your specific situation.

If you do change the jets do so only one size at a time. After rejetting, test ride the bike and perform a spark plug test; refer to *Reading Spark Plugs* in Chapter Three.

THROTTLE CABLE REPLACEMENT

This procedure describes the replacement of the throttle cable from the throttle grip to the throttle cable connector at the carburetor assembly. Replacement of the throttle cables attached to both carburetors is covered under *Carburetor Separation* in this chapter.

1. Remove the seat(s) as described under *Seat Removal/Installation* in Chapter Thirteen.

2. Remove the fuel tank as described in this chapter.

3. Disconnect the battery negative lead as described in Chapter Three.

4. Loosen the throttle cable locknut (A, **Figure 73**) at the throttle grip. Turn the adjuster (B, **Figure 73**) to achieve the maximum amount of slack in the throttle cable.

5. Remove the screws securing the right-hand switch assembly (**Figure 74**) together and separate the switch halves.

6. Disengage the throttle cable from the throttle grip.

7. Remove the throttle cable (**Figure 75**) from the upper half of the right-hand switch assembly.

8. Remove the bolts securing the fuel tank mounting bracket (**Figure 76**) and remove the bracket.

9. Remove the screw (**Figure 77**) securing the throttle cable joint to the air filter housing and remove the joint from the clip on the air filter housing.

10. Separate the throttle cable joint (**Figure 78**) and disconnect the 2 carburetor throttle cables (**Figure 79**) from the plastic fitting on the throttle grip throttle cable.

NOTE
The piece of string attached in the next step will be used to pull the new throttle

cable back through the frame so it will be routed in exactly the same position as the old one was.

11. Tie a piece of heavy string or cord (approximately 3 ft. [1 m long]) to the throttle cable joint end of the throttle cable. Wrap this end with masking or duct tape. Tie the other end of the string to the frame in the adjacent area.

12. At the throttle grip end of the cable, carefully pull the cable (and attached string) out through the frame. Make sure the attached string follows the same path as the cable through the frame.

13. Remove the tape and untie the string from the old cable.

14. Lubricate the new cable as described under *Control Cable* in Chapter Three.

15. Tie the string to the new throttle cable and wrap it with tape.

16. Carefully pull the string back through the frame routing the new cable through the same path as the old cable.

17. Remove the tape and untie the string from the cable and the frame.

18. Connect the 2 carburetor throttle cables (**Figure 79**) onto the plastic fitting on the throttle grip throttle cable.

19. Connect the throttle cable joint and make sure both halves are securely attached together (**Figure 78**).

20. Install the throttle cable joint into the clip on the air filter housing and install the screw (**Figure 77**) securing the throttle cable joint. Tighten the screw securely.

21. Install the fuel tank mounting bracket (**Figure 76**) and bolts. Tighten the bolts securely.

22. Insert the throttle cable into the upper half of the right-hand switch assembly (**Figure 75**).

23. Engage the throttle cable with the receptacle of the throttle grip.

24. Install the upper half and install the screws securing the right-hand switch assembly (**Figure 74**) together.

25. Connect the battery negative lead as described in Chapter Three.

26. Install the fuel tank as described in this chapter.

27. Install the seat(s) as described in Chapter Thirteen.

28. Adjust the throttle cable as described under *Throttle Cable Adjustment* Chapter Three.

29. Synchronize the throttle cables as described under *Carburetor Synchronization* in Chapter Three.

30. Test ride the bike slowly at first and make sure the throttle is operating correctly.

FUEL TANK

Removal/Installation

Refer to **Figure 80** for this procedure.

1. Remove the rider's seat as described under *Seat Removal/Installation* in Chapter Thirteen.

2. Disconnect the battery negative lead as described in Chapter Three.

3. Turn the fuel shutoff valve (**Figure 81**) to the OFF position.

4. Disconnect the fuel line (**Figure 82**) from the fuel valve. Plug the end of the line with a golf tee to prevent the entry of foreign matter and prevent any loss of any residual fuel in the line.

5. Remove the bolt and washer (**FIgure 83**) securing the rear of the fuel tank.

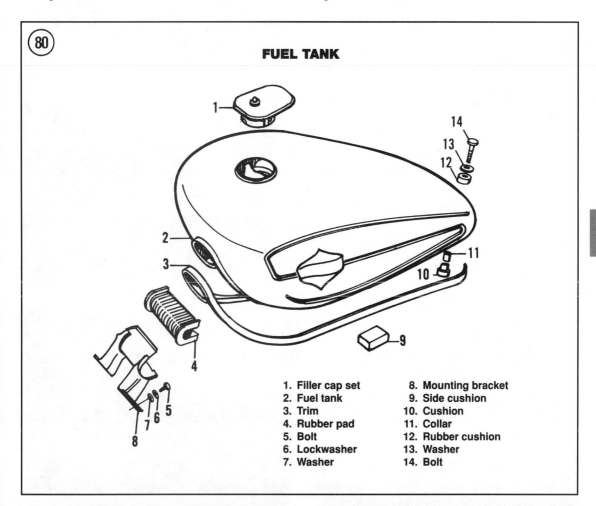

FUEL TANK

1. Filler cap set
2. Fuel tank
3. Trim
4. Rubber pad
5. Bolt
6. Lockwasher
7. Washer
8. Mounting bracket
9. Side cushion
10. Cushion
11. Collar
12. Rubber cushion
13. Washer
14. Bolt

7

6. Pull the fuel tank partially up at the rear.

7. On California models, disconnect the evaporative emission system vent line from the fuel tank.

8. Lift up and pull the tank (**Figure 84**) to the rear to remove the fuel tank from the frame.

9. Inspect the rubber cushion (**Figure 85**) in the front mounting bracket where the fuel tank attaches to the frame. Replace the cushion if it is damaged or starting to deteriorate.

10. Inspect the mounting bracket (A, **Figure 86**) for cracks or damage. If necessary, remove the bolts (B, **Figure 86**) on each side and remove the bracket.

11. Install by reversing these removal steps, noting the following:

    a. Make sure the rubber cushion (**Figure 85**) is in place in the mounting bracket.

    b. Make sure the fuel line (**Figure 82**) is secure on the fuel valve.

    c. Start the engine and check for fuel leaks.

FUEL SHUTOFF VALVE AND FILTER

Removal/Installation

Refer to **Figure 87** for this procedure.

> *WARNING*
> *Some fuel may spill in the following procedure. Work in a well-ventilated area at least 50 feet from any sparks or flames, including gas appliance pilot lights. Do not allow anyone to smoke in the area. Keep a BC rated fire extinguisher handy.*

1. Remove the fuel tank as described in this chapter.

2. Place a blanket or several towels on the work bench to protect the surface of the fuel tank.

3. Turn the fuel tank on its side (**Figure 88**) with the fuel shutoff valve side up.

4. Remove the bolts and washers (A, **Figure 89**) securing the shutoff valve to the fuel tank and remove the valve (B, **Figure 89**).

5. After removing the valve, insert the corner of a lint-free cloth into the opening in the tank to prevent the entry of foreign matter or tape it closed.

6. Inspect the shutoff valve mounting O-ring; replace if necessary.

7. Clean the filter portion of the valve with a medium soft toothbrush and blow out with compressed

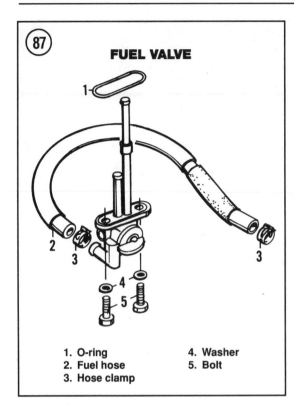

FUEL VALVE

1. O-ring
2. Fuel hose
3. Hose clamp
4. Washer
5. Bolt

air. Replace the filter if it is broken in any area or starting to deteriorate.

8. Install by reversing the removal steps. Pour a small amount of gasoline in the tank after installing the valve and check for leaks. If a leak is present, solve the problem immediately—do not reinstall the fuel tank with a leaking valve.

FUEL PUMP

The electromagnetic fuel pump is located on the left-hand side of the bike below one of the ignition coils. Fuel pump testing procedures are located in Chapter Eight.

Removal/Installation

> *WARNING*
> *Some fuel may spill in the following procedure. Work in a well-ventilated area at least 50 feet from any sparks or flames, including gas appliance pilot lights. Do not allow anyone to smoke in the area. Keep a BC rated fire extinguisher handy.*

1. Remove the rider's seat as described under *Seat Removal/Installation* in Chapter Thirteen.

2. Disconnect the battery negative lead as described in Chapter Three.

3. Turn the fuel shutoff valve (**Figure 81**) to the OFF position.

4. Remove the bolt securing the frame left-hand side cover (**Figure 90**) and remove the cover.

5. Disconnect both fuel lines (A, **Figure 91**) from the base of the fuel pump. Plug the end of the lines with golf tees to prevent the entry of foreign matter and prevent loss of residual fuel in the lines.

6. Loosen the clamping bolt and nut (B, **Figure 91**) on the mounting bracket.

7. Pull the fuel pump (C, **Figure 91**) down and out of the mounting bracket and disconnect the 2-pin electrical connector on 1986 models or 4-pin electrical connector on 1987-on models.

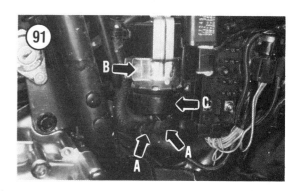

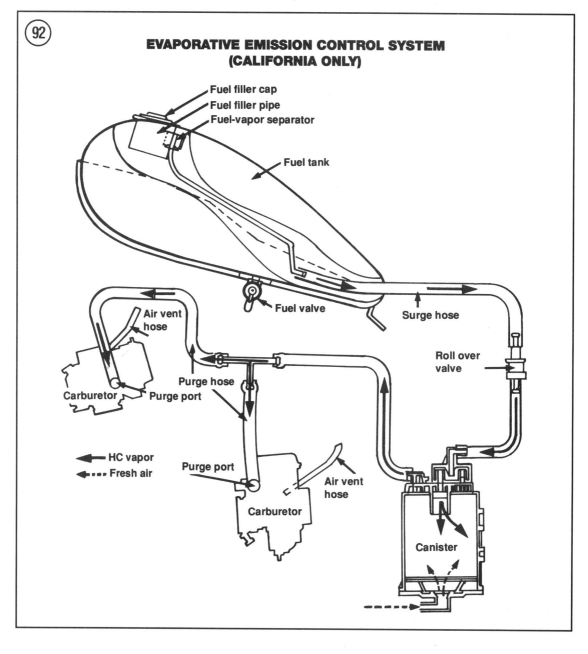

EVAPORATIVE EMISSION CONTROL SYSTEM
(CALIFORNIA ONLY)

8. Install by reversing these removal steps, noting the following:

   a. Make sure the electrical connector is free of corrosion and is tight.

   b. Prior to installing the frame side cover, reconnect the battery negative lead and start the engine to check for a fuel leak. If a leak is present, solve the problem immediately.

CRANKCASE BREATHER SYSTEM (U.S. ONLY)

To comply with air pollution standards, all models are equipped with a closed crankcase breather system. The system routes the engine combustion gases into the air filter air boxes where they are burned in the engine.

Inspection/Cleaning

Make sure that all hose clamps are tight. Check hoses for deterioration and replace if necessary.

Open the end of each drain tube attached to each air filter air case and drain out all residue. This cleaning procedure should be done more frequently if a considerable amount of riding is done at full throttle or in the rain.

EVAPORATIVE EMISSION CONTROL SYSTEM (CALIFORNIA MODELS ONLY)

To comply with the California Air Resources Board, an evaporative emission control system is installed on all models sold in California.

Fuel vapor from the fuel tank is routed into a charcoal canister. This vapor is stored when the engine is not running. When the engine is running these vapors are drawn through a purge control valve and into the carburetors to be burned. **Figure 92** is a basic schematic layout of the system. **Figure 93** and **Figure 94** show the hose routing and components of the system.

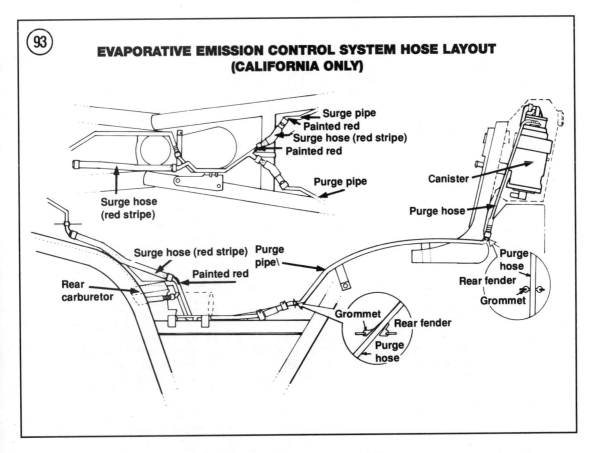

93

EVAPORATIVE EMISSION CONTROL SYSTEM HOSE LAYOUT (CALIFORNIA ONLY)

Surge pipe
Painted red
Surge hose (red stripe)
Painted red
Purge pipe
Canister
Surge hose (red stripe)
Purge hose
Surge hose (red stripe)
Purge pipe\
Painted red
Rear carburetor
Grommet
Rear fender
Purge hose
Purge hose
Rear fender
Grommet

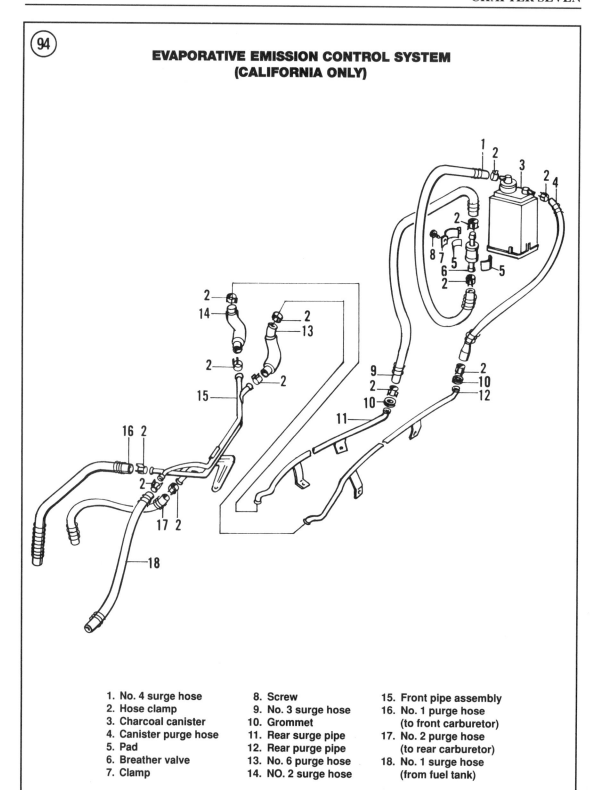

**EVAPORATIVE EMISSION CONTROL SYSTEM
(CALIFORNIA ONLY)**

1. No. 4 surge hose
2. Hose clamp
3. Charcoal canister
4. Canister purge hose
5. Pad
6. Breather valve
7. Clamp
8. Screw
9. No. 3 surge hose
10. Grommet
11. Rear surge pipe
12. Rear purge pipe
13. No. 6 purge hose
14. NO. 2 surge hose
15. Front pipe assembly
16. No. 1 purge hose
    (to front carburetor)
17. No. 2 purge hose
    (to rear carburetor)
18. No. 1 surge hose
    (from fuel tank)

Make sure all hose clamps are tight. Check all hoses for deterioration and replace as necessary.

Prior to removing the hoses from any of the parts of this system, mark each hose and fitting with a piece of masking tape to identify where the hose goes. There are so many vacuum hoses on these models it can be very confusing where each one is supposed to be attached.

The charcoal canister is located behind the pillion seat back rest.

Purge Control Valve and Charcoal Canister Removal/Installation

1. Carefully pry the pillion seat back rest off the tool box cover.
2. Insert the ignition key in the tool box cover (**Figure 95**) and remove the cover.
3. Remove the screws and nuts securing the charcoal canister cover and remove the cover.

NOTE
Prior to removing the hoses from the purge control valve and the charcoal canister, mark each hose and fitting with a piece of masking tape to identify where each hose goes.

4. Unhook the rubber strap and remove the charcoal canister from the mounting bracket. Remove the canister from the bracket and disconnect the hoses from it.
5. Disconnect the hoses from the control valve.

6. Remove the screws securing the control valve to the right-hand side of the canister mounting bracket and remove control valve.
7. Install by reversing these removal steps, noting the following:
   a. Be sure to attach the hoses to the correct fitting of the charcoal canister and the purge control valve.
   b. Make sure the hoses are not kinked, twisted or in contact with any sharp surfaces.

EXHAUST SYSTEM

The exhaust system is a vital performance component and frequently, because of its design, it is a vulnerable piece of equipment. Check the exhaust system for deep dents and fractures and repair or replace them immediately. Check the muffler frame mounting flanges for fractures and loose bolts. Check the cylinder head mounting flanges for tightness. A loose exhaust pipe connection can rob the engine of power.

Removal/Installation

Refer to **Figure 96** for the following procedure.
1. Loosen the clamping bolt where both mufflers attach at the common connector just forward of the rear wheel.
2. Loosen the clamping bolts where the exhaust pipes connect to the mufflers. Refer to **Figure 97** for the right-hand side or **Figure 98** for the left-hand side.
3. Remove the bolt, washer and nut (**Figure 99**) securing the muffler to the frame mounting bracket.
4. Disengage the muffler from the common connector of the other muffler, then remove the muffler.
5. Repeat Step 3 for the other muffler, then remove that muffler.
6. On the front cylinder, perform the following:
   a. Remove the bolts (A, **Figure 100**) securing the exhaust pipe clamp (B, **Figure 100**) to the cylinder head.
   b. Pull the exhaust pipe off the cylinder head and remove it from the engine and frame.
7. On the rear cylinder, perform the following:
   a. Remove the bolts (A, **Figure 101**) securing the exhaust pipe clamp (B, **Figure 101**) to the cylinder head.
   b. Pull the exhaust pipe off the cylinder head and remove it from the engine and frame.

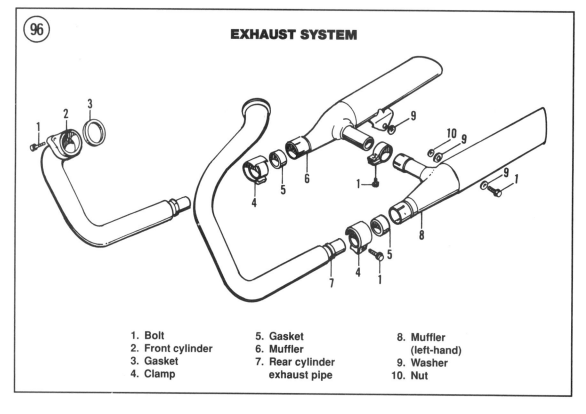

EXHAUST SYSTEM

1. Bolt
2. Front cylinder
3. Gasket
4. Clamp
5. Gasket
6. Muffler
7. Rear cylinder
   exhaust pipe
8. Muffler
   (left-hand)
9. Washer
10. Nut

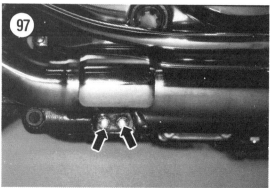

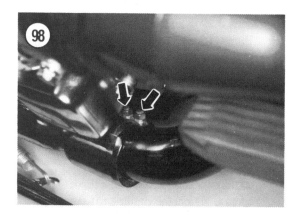

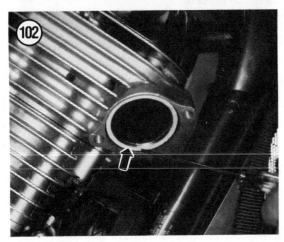

8. Inspect the gaskets at all joints; replace as necessary.

9. Be sure to install a new gasket in each exhaust port. Refer to **Figure 102** for the front cylinder or **Figure 103** for the rear cylinder.

10. Attach the exhaust pipes to the engine.

11. Install the exhaust pipe cylinder head bolts, but tighten only finger-tight until the rest of the exhaust system is installed.

12. Install both mufflers and mounting bolts, washers and nuts; do not tighten at this time. Make sure the exhaust pipes are correctly seated in the exhaust ports.

13. Tighten the exhaust pipe cylinder head bolts first to minimize exhaust leaks at the cylinder head. Tighten the bolts securely.

14. Tighten the rest of the exhaust system bolts securely.

15. After installation is complete, start the engine and make sure there are no exhaust leaks.

7

Table 1 CARBURETOR SPECIFICATIONS

1986-1991 U.S. & Canadian Models		
	Rear cylinder	**Front cylinder**
Carburetor type	Mikuni BS34SS	Mikuni BDS34SS
Model No. (U.S.)		
1986	38A00	38A00
1987-1991		
California	38A70	38A70
49-state	38A40	38A40
Model No. (Canada)		
1986	38A20	38A20
1987-1991	38A80	38A80
Venturi diameter	34.0 mm	34.0 mm
	(1.34 in.)	(1.34 in.)
Needle clip position	fixed	fixed
Main jet No.	132.5	132.5
Main air jet	0.7 mm	0.7 mm
	(continued)	

Table 1 CARBURETOR SPECIFICATIONS (continued)

	Rear cylinder	Front cylinder
1986-1991 U.S. & Canadian Models (continued)		
Jet needle		
U.S.	5D23	5D21
Canada	5D22	5D22
Throttle valve	110	110
Pilot jet	40	32.5
Starter jet	40	37.5
Needle jet		
U.S.	P-1	P-0
Canada	P4	P-3
Pilot screw	pre-set	pre-set
Pilot air jet	pre-set	pre-set
Float level	26.7-28.7 mm	10.5-12.5 mm
	(1.05-1.13 in.)	(0.41-0.49 in.)
1992-on U.S. and Canadian Models		
Carburetor type	Mikuni BS36SS	Mikuni BDS36SS
Model No. (U.S.)		
California	38E5	38E5
49-state	38E1	38E1
Model No. (Canada)	38E4	38E4
Venturi diameter	36.0 mm	36.0 mm
	(1.41 in.)	(1.41 in.)
Needle clip position	fixed	fixed
Main jet No.	132.5	127.5
Main air jet	1.6 mm	1.6 mm
Jet needle	5D35	5D47
Throttle valve	125	110
Pilot jet	45	40
Starter jet	25	22.5
Needle jet	P-7	P-2
Pilot screw	pre-set	pre-set
Pilot air jet	pre-set	pre-set
Float level	26.7-28.7 mm	10.1-11.1 mm
	(1.05-1.13 in.)	(0.32-0.40 in.)
1985-1991 U.K. Models		
Carburetor type	Mikuni BS34SS	Mikuni BDS34SS
Model No.		
1985	38A20	38A20
1986	38A80	38A80
1987-1991	38A90	38A90
Venturi diameter	34.0 mm	34.0 mm
	(1.34 in.)	(1.34 in.)
Needle clip position	fixed	fixed
Main jet No.	132.5	132.5
Main air jet	0.7 mm	0.07 mm
Jet needle	5D22	5D22
Throttle valve	110	110
Pilot jet	40	32.5
Starter jet	40	37.5
Needle jet	P-4	P-3
Pilot screw	pre-set	pre-set
Pilot air jet	pre-set	pre-set
Float level	26.7-28.7 mm	10.5-12.5 mm
	(1.05-1.13 in.)	(0.41-0.49 in.)

(continued)

Table 1 CARBURETOR SPECIFICATIONS (continued)

	1992-on U.K. Models Rear cylinder	Front cylinder
Carburetor type	Mikuni BS36SS	Mikuni BDS36SS
Model No.	38E0	38E0
Venturi diameter	36.0 mm	
	36.0 mm	(1.41 in.)(1.41 in.)
Needle clip position	fixed	fixed
Main jet No.	107.5	95
Main air jet	1.8 mm	1.8 mm
Jet needle	5F109	5F109
Throttle valve	115	115
Pilot jet	42.5	40
Starter jet	25	22.5
Needle jet	P-3	P-4
Pilot screw	pre-set	pre-set
Pilot air jet	pre-set	pre-set
Float level	26.7-28.7 mm	10.1-11.1 mm
	(1.05-1.13 in.)	(0.32-0.40 in.)

7

ELECTRICAL SYSTEM

This chapter contains operating principles, service procedures and test procedures for all electrical and ignition components. Information regarding the battery and spark plugs are covered in Chapter Three.

The electrical system includes the following systems:

  a. Charging system.
  b. Ignition system.
  c. Starting system.
  d. Lighting system.
  e. Directional signal system.
  f. Switches.
  g. Various electrical components.

Tables 1-5 are located at the end of this chapter.

NOTE
Where differences occur relating to the United Kingdom (U.K.) models they are identified. If there is no (U.K.) designation relating to a procedure, photo or illustration it is identical to the United States (U.S.) models.

NOTE
Most motorcycle dealers and parts suppliers will not accept the return of any electrical part. When testing electrical components, three general requirements to make are: (1) that you follow the test procedures as described in this chapter; (2) that your test equipment is

*working properly; and (3) that you are familiar with the test equipment and its operation. If a test result shows that a component is defective, have a Suzuki dealer **retest** the component to verify your test results prior to purchasing the new part.*

ELECTRICAL CONNECTORS

The Suzuki Interceptor is equipped with many electrical components, connectors and wires. Corrosion-causing moisture can enter these electrical connectors and cause poor electrical connections leading to component failure. Troubleshooting an electrical circuit with one or more corroded electrical connectors can be time-consuming and frustrating.

When reconnecting electrical connectors, pack them in a dielectric grease compound. Dielectric grease is especially formulated for sealing and waterproofing electrical connectors and will not interfere with the current flow through the electrical connectors. Use only this compound or an equivalent designed for this specific purpose. Do *not* use a substitute that may interfere with the current flow within the electrical connector. Do *not* use silicone sealant.

After cleaning both the male and female connectors, make sure they are thoroughly dry. Pack one of the connector halves with dielectric grease compound before joining the 2 connector halves. On multi-pin connectors, pack the male side and on single-wire connectors, pack the female side. Use a good-size glob so that it will squish out when the two halves are pushed together. For best results, the

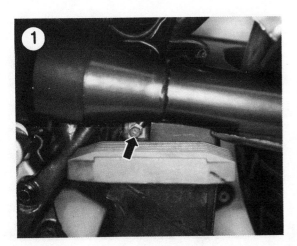

compound should fill the entire inner area of the connector. On multi-pin connectors, also pack the backside of both the male and female side with the compound to prevent moisture from entering the backside of the connector. After the connector is fully packed, wipe the exterior of all excessive compound.

Get into the practice of cleaning and sealing all electrical connectors every time they are unplugged. This may prevent a breakdown on the road and also save you time when troubleshooting a circuit.

Always make sure all ground connections are free of corrosion and are tight at various locations on the bike.

BATTERY NEGATIVE TERMINAL

Some of the component replacement procedures and some of the test procedures in this chapter require disconnecting the battery negative (–) lead as a safety precaution.

1. Remove the bolt and disconnect the battery negative (**Figure 1**) lead.

2. Reach into the battery case and move the negative lead out of the way so it will not accidentally make contact with the battery negative terminal.

3. Connect the battery negative lead to the terminal and tighten the bolt securely.

CHARGING SYSTEM

The charging system consists of the battery, alternator and a solid-state voltage regulator/rectifier (**Figure 2**).

Alternating current generated by the alternator is rectified to direct current. The voltage regulator maintains constant voltage to the battery and electrical loads (lights, ignition, etc.) regardless engine speed and load.

A malfunction in the charging system generally causes the battery to remain undercharged. To prevent damage to the alternator and the regulator/rectifier when testing and repairing the charging system, note the following precautions:

1. Always disconnect the negative battery cable, as described in this chapter, before removing a component from the charging system.

8

2. When it is necessary to charge the battery, remove the battery from the motorcycle and recharge it as described in Chapter Three.

3. Inspect the physical condition of the battery. Look for bulges or cracks in the case, leaking electrolyte or corrosion build-up.

4. Check the wiring in the charging system for signs of chafing, deterioration or other damage.

5. Check the wiring for corroded or loose connections. Clean, tighten or reconnect as required.

Leakage Test

Perform this test prior to performing the output test to determine if some electrical component is remaining on and draining the battery.

NOTE
Due to the location of the battery and its leads it is necessary to remove the battery from the motorcycle to perform this test.

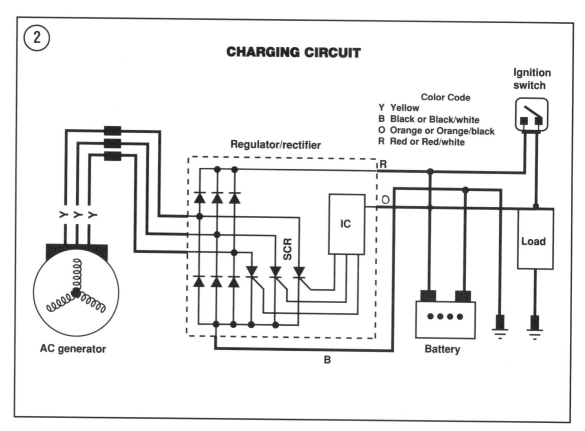

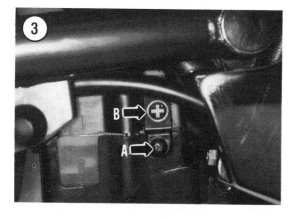

1. Remove the battery as described under *Battery Removal/Installation* in Chapter Three.

2. Turn the ignition switch OFF.

NOTE
Make sure there is a good electrical connection at both ends of the jumper wire. Otherwise the test results may be faulty.

3. Connect a jumper wire from the battery positive (+) lead and the battery positive (+) terminal.

4. Connect an ammeter between the battery negative (−) lead and the negative (−) terminal of the battery.

5. The ammeter should read less than 0.1 mA. If the amperage is greater, this indicates there is a voltage drain in the system that will discharge the battery.

6. Install the battery as described in Chapter Three.

Charging System Output Test

Whenever a charging system trouble is suspected, make sure the battery is fully charged and in good condition before going any further. Clean and test the battery as described in Chapter Three. Make sure all electrical connectors are tight and free of corrosion.

NOTE
This procedure requires the use of an assistant due to the location of the battery. Have an assistant attach the positive test lead on the left-hand side of the

bike while you work on the right-hand side along with the meter while having access to the throttle grip. This will lessen the possibility of getting burned on one of the ***HOT*** *mufflers.*

1. Start the engine and let it reach normal operating temperature. Shut off the engine.

2. Connect a portable tachometer following the manufacturer's instructions.

3. Remove the screw (A, **Figure 3**) securing the battery positive (+) cable terminal protector, remove the protector (B, **Figure 3**).

4. Restart the engine and let it idle.

WARNING
The exhaust system is ***HOT***. *Protect your hands while connecting the test leads to the battery terminals.*

5. Have the assistant connect a 0-20 DC voltmeter positive test lead to the positive (+) test lead to the battery positive terminal (**Figure 4**) on the left-hand side of the bike.

6. Attach the voltmeter negative (−) test lead to the negative terminal (**Figure 1**) on the left-hand side of the bike (**Figure 5**).

7. Increase engine speed to 5,000 rpm. The voltage reading should be between 14-15 V. If the voltage is less than 14 V or greater than 15 V, inspect the alternator no-load performance and voltage regulator as described in this chapter. The voltage regulator/rectifier are separate from the alternator and either component can replaced individually if faulty

8. If the charging voltage is too high; the voltage regulator/rectifier is probably at fault.

9. After the test is completed; shut off the engine and disconnect the voltmeter and portable tachometer.

10. Install the battery positive (+) cable terminal protector (B, **Figure 3**) and tighten the screw securely.

Charging System No-load Test

1. Remove the rider's seat and the frame side covers (A, **Figure 6**) as described in Chapter Thirteen.

2. Start the engine and let it reach normal operating temperature. Shut off the engine.

3. Connect a portable tachometer following the manufacturer's instructions.

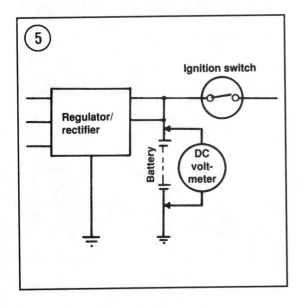

4. Locate the alternator's 3 individual electrical connectors containing yellow wires (B, **Figure 6**) and disconnect all 3 wire connectors.

5. Restart the engine and let it idle.

NOTE
In Step 7 connect the voltmeter test leads to the alternator side of the electrical connectors disconnected in Step 4.

6. Increase engine speed to 5,000 rpm.

7. Connect a 0-150 V (AC) voltmeter between two of the yellow wire connectors as shown in **Figure 7**. Voltage should be above 65V (AC). Move one of the voltmeter probes to the other (3rd) yellow wire connector and check voltage again. Voltage should again be above 65V (AC).

8. If any test indicates less than specified voltage, the alternator is faulty and must be replaced.

9. Shut off the engine.

10. After completing the test, disconnect the voltmeter and portable tachometer.

11. Reconnect the alternator's 3 individual yellow wire electrical connectors going to the voltage regulator/rectifier. Make sure connectors are corrosion free and tight.

12. Install the frame side covers and the rider's seat and as described in Chapter Thirteen.

VOLTAGE REGULATOR/RECTIFIER

Testing

Suzuki specifies the use of a specific multi-meter for accurate testing of the regulator/rectifier unit. The specified meter is the Suzuki Pocket Tester (part No. 09900-25002). Because of the different resistance value characteristics of the semiconductors used in this meter, the use of another meter may give you a different reading. This meter can be purchased through a Suzuki dealer or you can remove the regulator/rectifier unit and have the dealer test it for you.

1. Remove the rider's seat and the frame side covers (A, **Figure 6**) as described in Chapter Thirteen.

2. Disconnect the regulator/rectifier unit 6-pin electrical connector containing 5 wires. On 1985-1991 models the wire colors are; 2 red, 1 orange and 2 black/white. On 1992-on models the wire colors are; 2 red/white, 1 orange/black and 2 black/white.

3. Locate the 3 individual electrical connectors containing yellow wires (B, **Figure 6**) and disconnect all 3 wire connectors.

4. Set the pocket tester to the × 1k ohms scale.

5A. On 1985-1991 models, refer to **Figure 8** for test connections and values.

5B. On 1992-on models, refer to **Figure 9** for test connections and values.

6. If any of the meter readings differ from the stated values, first check the condition of the battery in the multimeter; an old battery can cause inaccurate readings. If the readings are still incorrect with a new battery, replace the regulator/rectifier unit as described in this chapter.

7. If the voltage regulator/rectifier check out okay, install the frame side covers and the rider's seat and as described in Chapter Thirteen.

Voltage Regulator/Rectifier Removal/Installation

1. Remove the rider's seat and the frame side covers (A, **Figure 6**) as described in Chapter Thirteen.

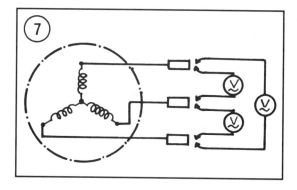

2. Disconnect the battery negative (–) lead (A, **Figure 10**) as described in this chapter.

3. Disconnect the regulator/rectifier unit 6-pin electrical connector containing 5 wires. On 1985-1991 models the wire colors are; 2 red, 1 orange and 2 black/white. On 1992-on models the wire colors are; 2 red/white, 1 orange/black and 2 black/white. Also disconnect the 3 individual yellow wire electrical connectors.

4. Remove the bolts located under the voltage regulator/rectifier (B, **Figure 10**) which attach regulator/rectifier to the frame.

5. Carefully pull the electrical wiring harness out through the frame, noting its path and remove the voltage regulator/rectifier assembly from the frame.

6. Install by reversing these removal steps, noting the following:

   a. Tighten the mounting bolts securely.

   b. Make sure all electrical connections are tight and free of corrosion.

   c. Connect the battery negative (–) lead.

ALTERNATOR

The alternator is a form of electrical generator in which a magnetized field called a rotor revolves around a set of stationary coils called a stator assembly. As the rotor revolves, alternating current is induced in the stator coils. The current is then rectified to direct current and is used to operate the electrical systems on the motorcycle and to keep the battery charged. The rotor is permanently magnetized.

Rotor Testing

The rotor is permanently magnetized and cannot be tested except by replacing it with a known good one. The rotor can lose magnetism from old age or a sharp hit. If defective, the rotor must be replaced; it cannot be re-magnetized.

(8) **VOLTAGE REGULATOR/RECTIFIER TESTING (1985-1991)**

Unit: kΩ

(–) Probe of tester to:	(+) Probe of tester to:			
		R	O	B/W	Y
R			∞	∞	∞
O		Approx. 80		Approx. 35	Approx. 50
B/W		Approx. 8.5	Approx. 5.2		Approx. 3
Y		Approx. 3	∞	∞	

(9) **VOLTAGE REGULATOR/RECTIFIER TESTING (1992-ON)**

Unit: kΩ

(–) Probe of tester to:	(+) Probe of tester to:			
		R/W	O/B	B/W	Y
R/W			∞	∞	∞
O/B		Approx. 80		Approx. 35	Approx. 50
B/W		Approx. 8.5	Approx. 5.2		Approx. 3
Y		Approx. 3	∞	∞	

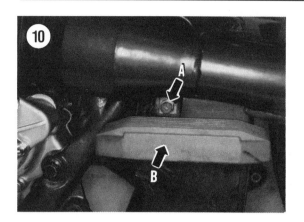

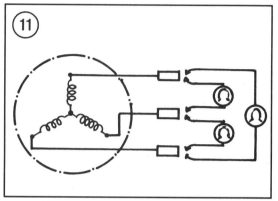

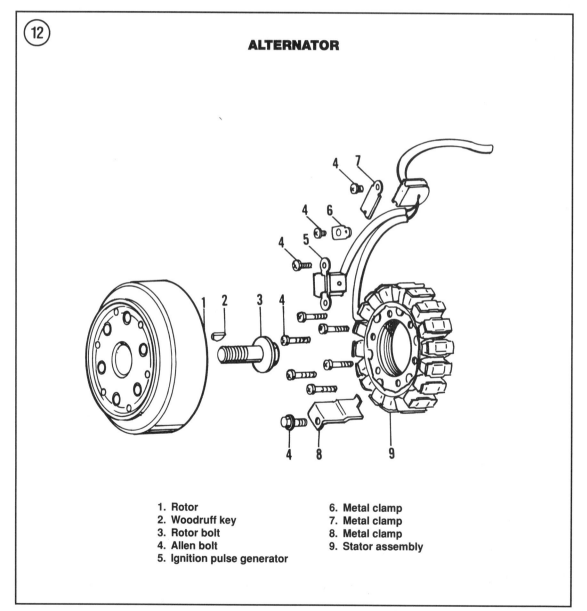

ALTERNATOR

1. Rotor
2. Woodruff key
3. Rotor bolt
4. Allen bolt
5. Ignition pulse generator
6. Metal clamp
7. Metal clamp
8. Metal clamp
9. Stator assembly

Stator Testing

1. Remove the rider's seat and the frame side covers (A, **Figure 6**) as described in Chapter Thirteen.

2. Start the engine and let it reach normal operating temperature. Shut off the engine.

3. Locate the alternator's 3 individual electrical connectors containing yellow wires (B, **Figure 6**) and disconnect all 3 wire connectors.

4. Connect an ohmmeter set at R × 1 (to check continuity) between two of the yellow terminals on the alternator stator side of the connector (**Figure 11**). Move one of the probes to the third yellow terminal.

5. Replace the stator assembly if any yellow terminal indicates no continuity (infinite resistance) to the other two yellow terminals. This would indicate an open in the stator coil winding.

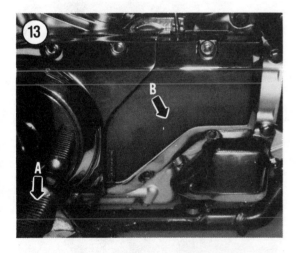

6. Use an ohmmeter set at R × 1 to check continuity between ground and each yellow terminal on the alternator stator side of the connector.

7. Replace the stator assembly if any yellow terminal shows continuity (indicated resistance) to ground. This would indicate an short within the stator coil winding.

NOTE
Prior to replacing the stator assembly, check the electrical wires to and within the electrical connector for any opens or poor connections.

8. If the stator assembly fails either of these tests, it must be replaced as described in this chapter.

Stator Assembly Removal/Installation

The stator assembly and the ignition pulse generator(s) are attached to the back side of the alternator cover.

Refer to **Figure 12** for this procedure.

NOTE
Some of the photos in this procedure are shown with the engine removed from the frame and partially disassembled for clarity. It is not necessary to remove the engine to perform this procedure.

1. Remove the rider's seat and the frame side covers (A, **Figure 6**) as described in Chapter Thirteen.
2. Remove the front footpeg assembly (A, **Figure 13**) as described under *Front Footpeg Assembly Removal/Installation* in Chapter Thirteen.
3. Remove the bolts securing the secondary drive cover (B, **Figure 13**) and remove the cover.
4. Locate the alternator's 3 individual electrical connectors containing yellow wires (B, **Figure 6**) and disconnect all 3 wire connectors.
5. Remove the starter motor as described in this chapter. The alternator stator electrical harness is routed under the starter motor and cover.
6. Remove the bolts securing the alternator cover (**Figure 14**) and remove the cover and gasket. Note the following:
    a. Carefully pull the electrical wiring harness out through the bottom of the starter motor cavity in the crankcase and through the opening in the side of the crankcase (**Figure 15**).

b. Don't lose the locating dowels.

c. Note the location of the gasket under the upper rear bolt on the cover. This gasket must be reinstalled in the same location during installation of the cover.

d. Note the location of the wiring harness clamps (**Figure 16**) under the cover bolts.

7. Place several shop cloths on the workbench to protect the chrome finish of the alternator cover. Turn the alternator cover upside down on these cloths.

8. Remove the screws and small metal clamps (A, **Figure 17**) securing the stator assembly wiring harness to the alternator cover. Note the location of each of these metal clamps because they must all be reinstalled in the same location.

NOTE
The 1985-1987 models are equipped with 2 ignition signal generators. On 1988-on models there is only one signal generator.

9. Remove the other screw(s) securing the ignition signal generator(s), (B, **Figure 17**) to the alternator cover.

10. Remove the bolts securing the stator assembly (C, **Figure 17**) to the cover. Carefully pull the rubber grommet (D, **Figure 17**) loose from the cover and remove the stator and ignition signal generator assembly from the cover.

NOTE
The stator assembly and the ignition signal generator(s) are removed as an assembly, but they are 2 separate parts and can be replaced individually. The 2 separate wiring harnesses are covered by a single insulating tube as they exit the cover. This insulating tube can be removed and the individual parts replaced. Carefully wrap the 2 wiring harnesses with a quality electrical tape after replacing one of the parts.

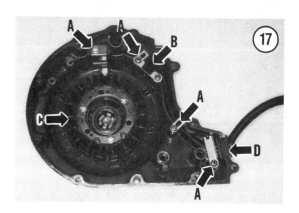

11. Install by reversing these removal steps, noting the following:

a. Tighten the bolts securing the alternator stator assembly securely.

b. All small metal clamps (A, **Figure 17**) securing the stator assembly and ignition signal generator(s) wiring harness to the cover must be reinstalled and must be installed in the correct

location. These clamps secure the wiring harness to the cover and away from the spinning rotor. If these wires come in contact with the rotor they will be damaged.

c. Install the gasket (A, **Figure 18**) under the upper rear bolt on the cover. Failure to install this gasket will result in and oil leak.

d. Make sure the rubber grommet (B, **Figure 18**) is installed correctly in the cover and seats tightly up against the surface of the crankcase.

e. Make sure the electrical connectors are free of corrosion and are tight.

f. Install the locating dowels (A, **Figure 19**) and a new gasket (B, **Figure 19**).

g. Be sure to install the wiring harness clamps (**Figure 16**) under the cover bolts in the correct location.

Rotor
Removal/Installation

Refer to **Figure 12** for this procedure.

NOTE
This procedure are shown with the engine removed from the frame and partially disassembled for clarity. It is not necessary to remove the engine to perform this procedure.

1. Remove the alternator stator assembly as described in this chapter.

2. Remove the starter idler gear No. 2 and its shaft (**Figure 20**).

3. Withdraw the No. 1 idler gear shaft (A, **Figure 21**) then remove the No. 1 idler gear (B, **Figure 21**).

4A. If the engine is still in the frame; shift the transmission into gear and have an assistant apply the rear brake. This will prevent the alternator rotor from turning in the next step.

4B. If the engine has been removed; place an open-end wrench onto the hex fitting (A, **Figure 22**) on the rotor to prevent the alternator rotor from turning in the next step.

NOTE
*In Step 5, do not remove the rotor bolt. Break it loose, then loosen it several turns and leave it in place (A, **Figure 23**). The bolt must remain installed because it is used in conjunction with the rotor remover tool in Step 6.*

5. Loosen, but do not remove, the alternator rotor bolt (B, **Figure 22**). Loosen it several turns and leave it in place.

> *CAUTION*
> *Don't try to remove the rotor without a puller; any attempt to do so will ultimately lead to some form of damage to the engine and/or rotor. Many aftermarket pullers are available from motorcycle dealers or mail order houses. The cost of one of these pullers is low and it makes an excellent addition to any mechanic's tool box. If you can't buy or borrow one, have the dealer remove the rotor.*

6. Install the rotor removal tool, Suzuki special tool (part No. 09930-30720) onto the threads of the rotor (B, **Figure 23**).
7. Hold the rotor remover tool (A, **Figure 24**) with a 36 mm open-end wrench and turn the center bolt (B, **Figure 24**). Turn the center bolt until the rotor disengages from the crankshaft taper.

> *NOTE*
> *If the rotor is difficult to remove, strike the end of the puller (not the rotor as it will be damaged) firmly with a hammer. This will usually break it loose.*

> *CAUTION*
> *If normal rotor removal attempts fail, do not force the puller as the threads may be stripped from the rotor causing expensive damage. Take the bike to a dealer and have the rotor removed.*

8. Unscrew and remove the rotor puller from the rotor.
9. Unscrew the bolt from the crankshaft and remove it from the rotor.
10. Reach behind the rotor and hold onto the starter clutch gear and remove the rotor and the starter clutch as an assembly from the crankshaft.
11. It is not necessary to remove the starter clutch from the back side of the rotor. If inspection is necessary, refer to *Starter Gears* in this chapter.
12. Inspect the inside of the rotor (**Figure 25**) for small bolts, washers or other metal "trash" that may have been picked up by the magnets. These small metal bits can cause severe damage to the alternator stator assembly.

13. Inspect the rotor keyway (**Figure 26**) for wear or damage. If damage is severe, replace the rotor.

14. Install by reversing these removal steps, noting the following:

　a. Use an aerosol electrical contact cleaner and clean all oil residue from the crankshaft taper

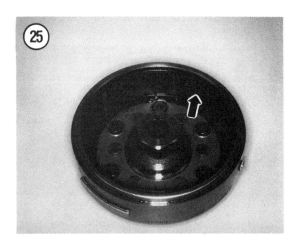

where the rotor slides onto it and the matching tapered surface in the rotor. This is to assure a good tight fit of the rotor onto the crankshaft.

b. If removed, install and center the Woodruff key (**Figure 27**) in the crankshaft slot.

c. Apply red Loctite (No. 271) to the rotor bolt threads prior to installation.

d. Tighten the rotor bolt (A, **Figure 23**) to the torque specification listed in **Table 1**.

TRANSISTORIZED IGNITION SYSTEM

The Intruder is equipped with a solid-state, transistorized ignition system that uses no breaker points. The ignition circuit is shown **Figure 28**.

The signal generator consists of a raised tab on the alternator rotor and signal generator(s), attached to the alternator cover next to the alternator stator coil assembly.

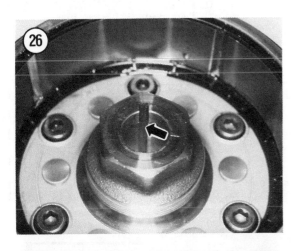

As the alternator rotor is turned by the crankshaft the raised tab passes the pickup coil(s) and a signal is sent to the ignition unit. This signal turns the ignitor unit transistor alternately ON and OFF. As the transistor is turned ON and OFF, the current passing through the primary windings of the ignition coil, is also turned ON and OFF. Thus it induces the secondary current in the ignition coil secondary windings to fire the spark plugs.

Transistorized Ignition System Precautions

Certain measures must be taken to protect the ignition system. Instantaneous damage to the semiconductors in the system will occur if the following precautions are not observed.

1. Never disconnect any of the electrical connections while the engine is running.

2. Keep all connections between the various units clean and tight. Be sure that the wiring connectors are pushed together firmly to help keep out moisture. Also pack the connectors with dielectric compound as described at the beginning of this chapter.

3. Do not substitute another type of ignition coil.

Troubleshooting

Problems with the transistorized ignition system fall into one of the following categories. See **Table 2**.

a. Weak spark.

b. No spark.

Ignition Signal Generator Testing

NOTE
The 1985-1987 models are equipped with 2 ignition signal generators. On 1988-on models there is only one signal generator.

1. Remove the seat and the frame side covers (A, **Figure 6**) as described in Chapter Thirteen.

2A. On 1985-1987 models, disconnect the 4-pin electrical connector containing 4 signal generator wires (1 green, 1 blue, 1 black and 1 yellow wire) from the ignitor unit (**Figure 29**).

2B. On 1988-on models, disconnect the signal generators 2-pin electrical connector (1 green and 1 blue wire) from the ignitor unit.

8

IGNITION CIRCUIT

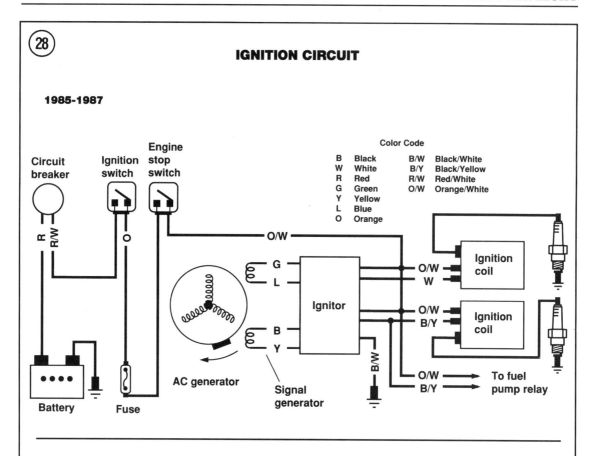

1985-1987

Circuit breaker

Ignition switch

Engine stop switch

Color Code

B	Black	B/W	Black/White
W	White	B/Y	Black/Yellow
R	Red	R/W	Red/White
G	Green	O/W	Orange/White
Y	Yellow		
L	Blue		
O	Orange		

R   R/W

O/W

G

L

Ignitor

O/W
W

Ignition coil

O/W
B/Y

Ignition coil

B/W

O/W → To fuel
B/Y → pump relay

Battery   Fuse   AC generator   Signal generator

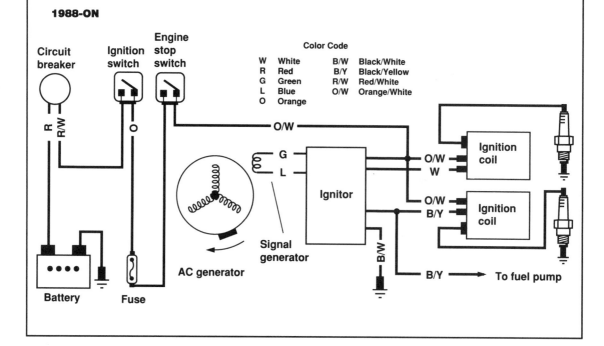

1988-ON

Circuit breaker

Ignition switch

Engine stop switch

Color Code

W	White	B/W	Black/White
R	Red	B/Y	Black/Yellow
G	Green	R/W	Red/White
L	Blue	O/W	Orange/White
O	Orange		

R   R/W

O/W

G

L

Ignitor

O/W
W

Ignition coil

O/W
B/Y

Ignition coil

B/W

Signal generator

AC generator

B/Y → To fuel pump

Battery   Fuse

3. Use an ohmmeter set at R × 1000 and check the resistance between the following wires in the signal generator side of the electrical connector.

    a. 1985-1987 models: between the green and blue terminals and between the black and yellow terminals.

    b. 1988-on models: between the green and blue terminals.

The specified resistance is listed in **Table 3**.

4. If the resistance shown is less than specified or there is no indicated resistance (infinite resistance) between the 2 wires, the signal generator has an open or short and must be replaced as described in this chapter.

5. If the signal generator(s) checks out okay, reconnect the electrical connector. Make sure the electrical connector is free of corrosion and is tight.

6. Install the frame covers and the rider's seat.

Ignition Signal Generator
Removal/Installation

The alternator stator assembly and the ignition signal generator(s) are removed as an assembly, but they are 2 separate parts and can be replaced individually. The 2 separate wiring harnesses are covered by a single insulating tube as they exit the alternator cover.

1. Remove the alternator stator as described in this chapter.

2. Remove the covering from the electrical harnesses and separate the 2 harnesses.

3. Replace the ignition signal generator(s).

4. Carefully wrap the 2 wiring harnesses with a quality electrical tape after replacing one of the parts.

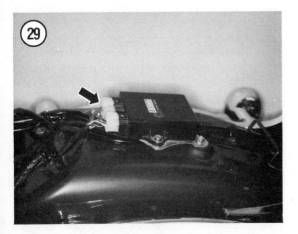

5. Install the alternator stator as described in this chapter.

Ignition Coil
Testing

The ignition coil is a form of transformer which develops the high voltage required to jump the spark plug gap. The only maintenance required is that of keeping the electrical connections clean and tight and occasionally checking to see that the coils are mounted securely.

If the condition of the coil(s) is doubtful, there are several checks which may be made.

> *NOTE*
> *The spark plug must ground against a piece of bare metal on the engine or frame. If necessary, carefully scrape away some of the engine paint.*

First as a quick check of coil condition, disconnect the high voltage lead from the spark plug. Remove one of the spark plugs from one of the cylinder heads as described under *Spark Plugs* in Chapter Three. Connect a new or known good spark plug to the high voltage lead and place the spark plug base on a good ground like the engine cylinder head. Position the spark plug so you can see the electrodes.

> *WARNING*
> *If it is necessary to hold the high voltage lead, do so with an insulated pair of pliers. The high voltage generated by the signal generator could produce serious or fatal shocks.*

Turn the engine over with the starter. If a fat blue spark occurs the coil is in good condition; if not proceed as follows. Make sure that you are using a known good spark plug for this test. If the spark plug used is defective the test results will be incorrect.

Reinstall the spark plug in the cylinder head and connect the high voltage lead.

> *NOTE*
> *In order to get accurate resistance measurements the coil must be warm (minimum temperature is 20° C [68° F]). If necessary, start the engine and let it warm up to normal operating temperature. If the engine will not start,*

8

warm the ignition coils with a portable hair dryer.

1. Remove the rider's seat as described in Chapter Thirteen.

2. Disconnect the battery negative lead as described in this chapter.

3. Remove the fuel tank as described under *Fuel Tank Removal/Installation* in Chapter Seven.

4. Disconnect all ignition coil wires (including the spark plug leads from the spark plugs) before testing.

NOTE
In Step 5 and Step 6, the resistance specification is not as important as the fact that there is continuity between the terminals. If the ignition coil windings are in good condition the resistance values will be near those specified.

5. Use an ohmmeter set at R × 1 and measure the primary coil resistance between the positive (+) and the negative (−) terminals on the top of the ignition coil (**Figure 30**). The specified resistance value is listed in **Table 3**.

6. Use an ohmmeter set at R × 1,000 measure the secondary coil resistance between the spark plug lead and one of the primary coil terminals (**Figure 30**). The specified resistance value is listed in **Table 3**.

7. Repeat Step 5 and Step 6 for the other ignition coil.

8. If the coil resistance does not meet (or come close to) either of these specifications, the coil must be replaced. If the coil exhibits visible damage, it should be replaced as described in this chapter.

9. Reconnect all ignition coil wires to the ignition coil.

10. Install the fuel tank as described in Chapter Seven.

11. Install the rider's seat as described in Chapter Thirteen.

Ignition Coil Removal/Installation

1. Remove the rider's seat as described in Chapter Thirteen.

2. Disconnect the battery negative lead as described in this chapter.

3. Remove the fuel tank as described under *Fuel Tank Removal/Installation* in Chapter Seven.

4. Disconnect the primary leads (A, **Figure 31**) from the ignition coil.

5. Disconnect the high voltage lead (B, **Figure 31**) from the spark plug.

6. Remove the bolts (C, **Figure 31**) securing the ignition coil to the frame and remove the coil.

7. If necessary, repeat Steps 4-6 for the other ignition coil.

8. Install by reversing these removal steps. Make sure all electrical connections are free of corrosion and are tight.

Ignitor Unit Testing

Complete testing of the ignitor unit requires a special Suzuki electronic test tool (Ignitor Checker) and should be tested by a Suzuki dealer as these tools are expensive. If the ignition signal generator(s) and the ignition coils are working correctly, then this simple test can be run to confirm that the ignitor unit is working properly.

The dealer will either test the ignitor unit with the special tool or perform a "remove and replace" test to see if the ignitor unit is faulty. The "remove and replace" test is expensive if you purchase a new ignitor unit and it does *not* solve your particular ignition system problem. Remember, you *cannot* return the ignitor unit for refund. Most motorcycle dealers will *not* accept returns on any electrical component since they could be damaged internally even though they look okay externally.

Make sure all connections between the various components are clean and tight. Be sure that the wiring connectors are pushed together firmly and

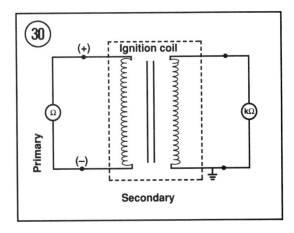

packed with a dielectric compound to help keep out moisture.

1. Remove the rider's seat and the frame side covers as described in Chapter Thirteen.

2. Test the ignition signal generator and both ignition coils as described in this chapter prior to performing this test. If any one of these units is faulty, this test will not provide any usable test results.

3. Test the ignitor unit's ability to produce a spark. Perform the following:

  a. Disconnect the high voltage lead from one of the spark plugs. Remove the spark plug from the cylinder head as described under *Spark Plugs* in Chapter Three.

NOTE
The spark plug must ground against a piece of bare metal on the engine or frame. If necessary, carefully scrape away some of the engine paint.

  b. Connect a new or known good spark plug to the high voltage lead and place the spark plug base on a good ground like the engine cylinder head cover. Position the spark plug so you can see the electrodes.

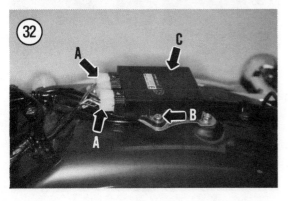

WARNING
If it is necessary to hold the high voltage lead, do so with an insulated pair of pliers. The high voltage generated by the ignitor unit could produce serious or fatal shocks.

  c. Turn the engine over rapidly with the starter and check for a spark. If there is a fat blue spark, the ignitor unit is working properly.

  d. If a weak spark or no spark is obtained and the signal generator and ignition coils are okay, have the ignitor unit tested by a Suzuki dealer.

  e. Reinstall the spark plug and connect the high voltage lead onto the spark plug.

4. If all of the ignition components are okay, then check the following:

  a. Check for an open or short in the wire harness between each component in the system.

  b. Again, make sure all connections between the various components are clean and tight. Be sure that the wiring connectors are pushed together firmly to help keep out moisture.

Ignitor Unit
Replacement

1. Remove the rider's seat and the frame side covers as described in Chapter Thirteen.

2. Disconnect the battery negative lead as described in this chapter.

3. Disconnect the electrical connectors (A, **Figure 32**) from the ignitor unit.

4. Remove the screw and washer (B, **Figure 32**) on each side securing the ignitor unit. Remove the ignitor unit (C, **Figure 32**) from the mounting bracket on top of the rear fender.

5. Install a new ignitor unit onto the mounting bracket and tighten the screws securely.

6. Attach both electrical wire connectors to it. Make sure both electrical connectors are free of corrosion and are tight.

7. Connect the battery negative lead.

8. Install the frame side covers and rider's seat.

STARTER SYSTEM

The starter system includes an ignition switch, a starter switch, clutch interlock switch, sidestand in-

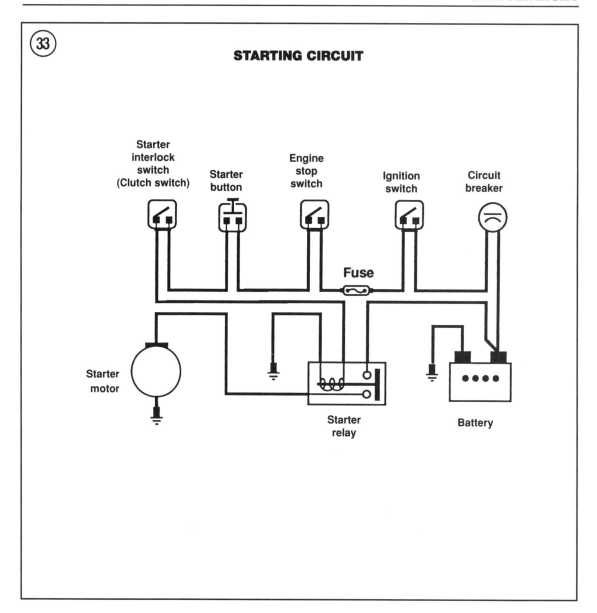

(33)

STARTING CIRCUIT

Starter interlock switch (Clutch switch)

Starter button

Engine stop switch

Ignition switch

Circuit breaker

Fuse

Starter motor

Starter relay

Battery

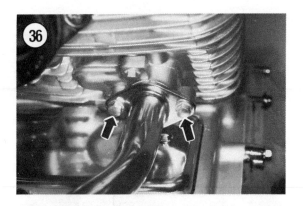

terlock switch (1987-on models), starter relay, battery and starter motor as shown in **Figure 33**. Each component of this system is covered separately in this chapter except for the battery that is covered in Chapter Three.

ELECTRIC STARTER

Removal/Installation

1. Drain the cooling system as described under *Coolant Change* in Chapter Three.

2. Disconnect the battery negative (–) lead as described in this chapter.

3. Remove the battery case (A, **Figure 34**) as described under *Battery Case Removal/Installation* in this chapter.

NOTE
Some of the following photographs are shown with the engine removed from the frame and partially disassembled for clarity. The starter motor can be removed with the engine in the frame.

4. At the fitting at the back of the crankcase, loosen the clamping screw (**Figure 35**) on the water pump outlet hose. Move the clamp back onto the hose and off of the neck of the fitting, then remove the hose (B, **Figure 34**) from the crankcase fitting.

5. Remove the bolts (**Figure 36**) securing the metal coolant inlet pipe to the rear cylinder.

6. Remove the metal coolant pipe (C, **Figure 34**) away from the cylinder.

7. Remove the metal coolant pipe and rubber hose assembly from the engine and frame.

8. Remove the screws securing the starter motor cover and remove the cover (**Figure 37**).

9. Slide back the rubber boot (**Figure 38**) on the electrical cable connector.

10. Remove the nut and disconnect the starter electrical motor cable (A, **Figure 39**) from the starter motor.

NOTE
*Only 1 of the starter motor mounting bolts (B, **Figure 39**) is visible in the figure. Be sure to remove both bolts.*

11. Remove the 2 bolts (B, **Figure 39**) securing the starter motor to the crankcase.

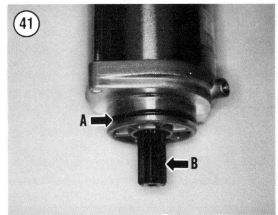

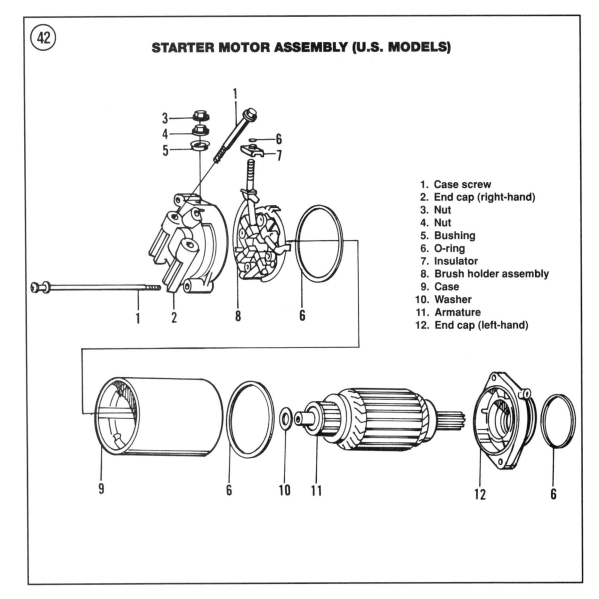

STARTER MOTOR ASSEMBLY (U.S. MODELS)

1. Case screw
2. End cap (right-hand)
3. Nut
4. Nut
5. Bushing
6. O-ring
7. Insulator
8. Brush holder assembly
9. Case
10. Washer
11. Armature
12. End cap (left-hand)

12. Partially lift up and pull the starter motor toward the right-hand side to disengage it from the idler gears. Remove the starter motor (C, **Figure 39**) from the top of the crankcase.

13. Install by reversing these removal steps, noting the following:

a. When installing the water pump outlet hose onto the rear cylinder, install a new O-ring seal (**Figure 40**) into the receptacle in the cylinder and apply a light coat of clean engine oil to the O-ring.

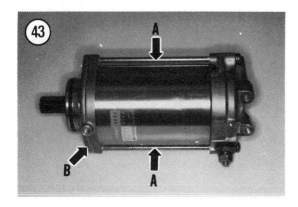

b. Install all components removed.

c. Refill the cooling system with the recommended type and quantity of coolant. Refer to *Coolant Change* in Chapter Three.

d. Start the engine and check for leaks.

Preliminary Inspection

The overhaul of a starter motor is best left to an expert. This procedure shows how to detect a defective starter.

Inspect the O-ring seal (A, **Figure 41**). O-ring seals tend to harden after prolonged use and heat and therefore lose their ability to seal properly. Replace as necessary.

Inspect the gear (B, **Figure 41**) for chipped or missing teeth. If damaged, the starter assembly must be replaced.

Disassembly
(U.S. Models)

Refer to **Figure 42** for this procedure.

1. Remove the case screws and washers (A, **Figure 43**), then separate the left-hand end cap (B, **Figure 43**) from the case.

2. Withdraw the case from armature coil assembly and right-hand case.

3. Remove the both nuts, bushing and insulator (A, **Figure 44**) securing the brush holder assembly to the right-hand end cap.

4. Withdraw the threaded stud of the brush holder from the right-hand end cap and remove the end cap (B, **Figure 44**). The insulator and O-ring seal will usually stay on the threaded stud.

5. Remove the washer (A, **Figure 45**) from the end of the armature.

6. Carefully pull the brush holder assembly (B, **Figure 45**) from the armature.

CAUTION
Do not immerse the wire windings in the case or the armature coil in solvent as the insulation may be damaged. Wipe the windings with a cloth lightly moistened with solvent and thoroughly dry.

7. Clean all grease, dirt and carbon from all components.

8. Inspect the starter motor components as described in this chapter.

Assembly
(U.S. Models)

1. If removed, install the O-ring seal into both the right-hand (**Figure 46**) and left-hand (**Figure 47**) end caps.

2. Push all 4 brushes into their holders and carefully install the brush holder assembly (B, **Figure 45**) onto the armature. Push it down until it stops.

3. Install the washer (A, **Figure 45**) onto the end of the armature.

4. The locating tab (A, **Figure 48**) on the brush holder must align with the raised boss (B, **Figure 48**) on the case during installation (**Figure 49**).

5. Make sure the O-ring and insulator (C, **Figure 48**) are still in place on the threaded stud of the brush holder.

6. Install the threaded stud of the brush holder into the right-hand end cap (B, **Figure 44**).

7. Install the bushing and nuts (A, **Figure 44**) securing the brush holder assembly to the right-hand end cap. Tighten the first nut securely, then install the other nut only finger-tight.

8. Install the case onto the armature coil assembly and right-hand end cap.

9. Correctly align the case screw holes in both end caps and push the caps onto the case until they bottom out.

10. Apply a small amount of blue Loctite (No. 242) to the case bolt threads prior to installation.

11. Install the case screws and washers (A, **Figure 43**) and tighten securely.

Disassembly
(U.K. Models)

Refer to **Figure 50** for this procedure.

1. Remove the case screws and washers, then separate the right-hand and left-hand end caps from the case.

2. Remove the negative (–) brush holder (**Figure 51**) from the case.

3. Withdraw the armature coil assembly (**Figure 52**) from the case.

NOTE
Before removing the nuts and washers, write down their description and order. They must be reinstalled in the same order to insulate this set of brushes from the case.

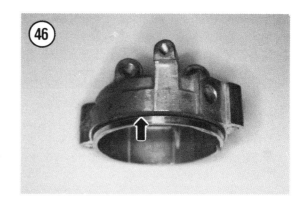

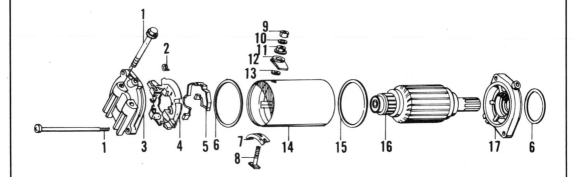

STARTER MOTOR ASSEMBLY
(U.K. MODELS)

1. Case screw
2. Brush spring
3. End cap
   (right-hand)
4. Brush holder
   assembly (negative)
5. Brush holder
   assembly (positive)
6. O-ring
7. Inner bushing
8. Bolt

9. Nut
10. Lockwasher
11. Nut
12. Outer bushing/
    flange
13. Gasket
14. Case
15. O-ring
16. Armature
17. End cap
    (left-hand)

8

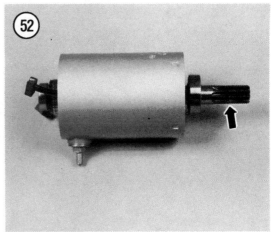

4. Remove the flange nut, outer bushing (**Figure 53**) and O-ring (**Figure 54**) securing the brush positive and negative brush sets.

5. Remove the bolt (**Figure 55**) and the inner bushing (**Figure 56**).

6. Remove the positive (+) brush holder (**Figure 57**) from the end of the case.

CAUTION
Do not immerse the wire windings in the case or the armature coil in solvent as the insulation may be damaged. Wipe the windings with a cloth lightly moistened with solvent and thoroughly dry.

7. Clean all grease, dirt and carbon from all components.

8. Inspect the starter motor components as described in this chapter.

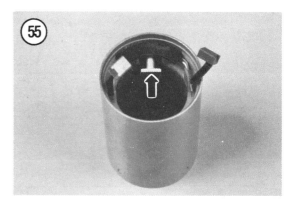

Assembly
(U.K. Models)

1. Install the positive (+) brush holder (**Figure 57**).

2. Install the inner bushing (**Figure 56**).

3. Install the bolt (**Figure 55**) and install the O-ring (**Figure 54**).

4. Install the outer bushing and flange nut (**Figure 53**) securing the brush assembly to the case.

5. Insert the armature coil assembly (**Figure 52**) into the left-hand end of the case.

6. Release the springs from the brushes (**Figure 58**) in the negative (–) brush holder.

7. Move the positive (+) brushes out so the negative (–) brush holder can be installed over them. Carefully align the positive brush wires with the notches in the negative brush holder.

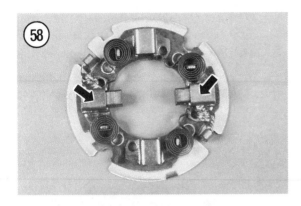

8. Install the negative (–) brush holder into the end of the case. Align the notch in the holder with the locating tab (**Figure 59**) in the case.

9. Install the positive (+) brushes into their receptacles in the negative brush holder.

10. Rotate the end of the spring *counterclockwise* and index the spring end into the backside of the brush. Repeat for all 4 brushes.

11. Inspect the O-ring seal (**Figure 60**) in the right-hand end cap; replace if necessary.

12. Install the right-hand end cap.

13. Inspect the O-ring seal (**Figure 61**) in the left-hand end cap; replace if necessary.

14. Align the raised tab on the negative (–) brush holder with the locating notch (**Figure 62**) in the right-hand end cap and install the end cap.

15. Align the raised marks on the right hand end cap with the notch on the left-hand end cap (**Figure 63**).

16. Apply a small amount of blue Loctite No. 242 to the case screw threads prior to installation. Install the case screws and washers, then tighten securely.

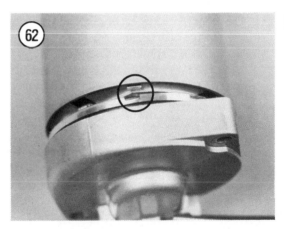

Inspection
(All Models)

1. Measure the length of each brush (**Figure 64**) with a vernier caliper. If the length is 9.0 mm (0.35 in.) or less for any one of the brushes, the brush sets must be replaced. The brushes cannot be replaced individually.

2. Inspect the commutator. Refer to A, **Figure 65** for U.S. models or A, **Figure 66** for U.K. models. The mica should be just below the surface of the copper bars. On a worn commutator the mica and copper bars may be worn to the same level (**Figure 67**). If necessary, have the commutator serviced by a dealer or electrical repair shop.

3. Inspect the commutator copper bars (**Figure 68**) for discoloration. If a pair of bars are discolored, grounded armature coils are indicated.

4. Use an ohmmeter and perform the following:
   a. Check for continuity between the commutator bars (**Figure 69**); there should be continuity (indicated resistance) between any two of the bars.
   b. Check for continuity between the commutator bars and the shaft (**Figure 70**); there should be *no* continuity (infinite resistance).
   c. If the unit fails either of these tests, the starter assembly must be replaced. The armature cannot be replaced individually.

5. Use an ohmmeter and perform the following:
   a. Check for continuity between the starter cable terminal and the starter case; there should be continuity (indicated resistance).
   b. Check for continuity between the starter cable terminal and the brush wire terminal; there should be *no* continuity (infinite resistance).

c. If the unit fails either of these tests, the starter assembly must be replaced. The case/field coil assembly cannot be replaced individually.

6A. On U.S. models, inspect the bearing (B, **Figure 65**) for the armature coil assembly. It must rotate freely with no signs of wear. If the bearing is worn,

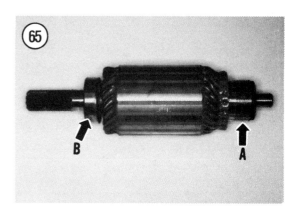

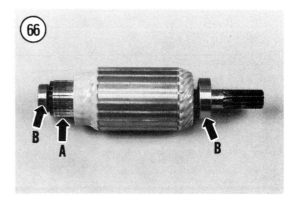

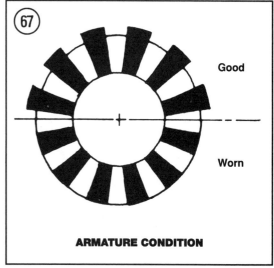

ARMATURE CONDITION

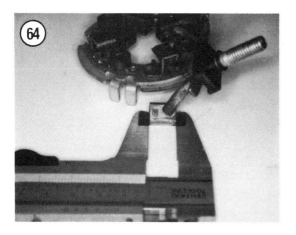

replace the armature coil assembly. The bearings cannot be replaced individually.

6B. On U.K. models, inspect the bearings (B, **Figure 66**) at each end of the armature coil assembly. It must rotate freely with no signs of wear. If the bearing is worn, replace the armature coil assembly. The bearings cannot be replaced individually.

7. Inspect the oil seal (**Figure 71**) in the left-hand end cap for wear, damage or deterioration. The oil seal cannot be replaced. If damaged, replace the left-hand end cap.

8. Inspect the right-hand end cap for wear or damage, replace if necessary.

9. On U.S. models, inspect the right-hand end cap bushing (**Figure 72**) for wear or damage, replace the end cap if necessary.

10. Inspect the case assembly for wear or damage. Make sure the field coils (**Figure 73**) are bonded securely in place. If damaged or any field coils are loose, replace the case assembly.

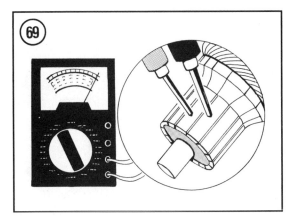

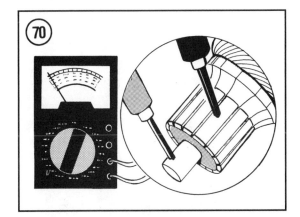

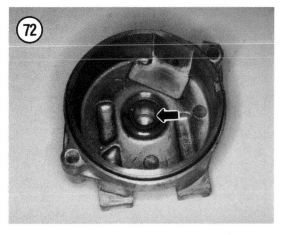

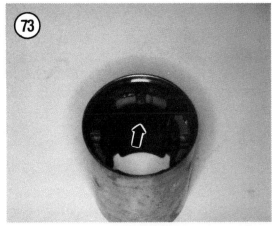

8

11. On U.S. models, inspect the brush holder assembly (**Figure 74**) for wear or damage, if damaged; replace the assembly.

12. On U.K. models, perform the following:

a. Inspect the positive (+) brush holder and brush springs (**Figure 75**) assembly for wear or damage; replace any damaged parts.

b. Inspect the negative (−) brush holder and brush springs (**Figure 76**) assembly for wear or damage. The springs are the only replacement parts available for this assembly.

STARTER CLUTCH AND GEARS

The starter gears can be removed with the engine in the frame. This procedure is shown with the engine removed for clarity.

Refer to **Figure 77** for this procedure.

Removal

1. Remove the alternator stator assembly as described in this chapter.

2. Remove the starter idler gear No. 2 and its shaft (**Figure 78**).

3. Withdraw the No. 1 idler gear shaft (A, **Figure 79**) then remove the No. 1 idler gear (B, **Figure 79**).

4. Remove the alternator rotor assembly as described in this chapter.

NOTE
The starter driven gear may come off with the alternator rotor in Step 4 or stay on the crankshaft.

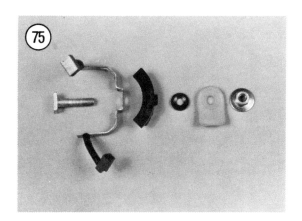

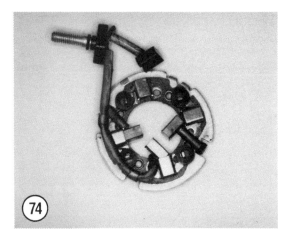

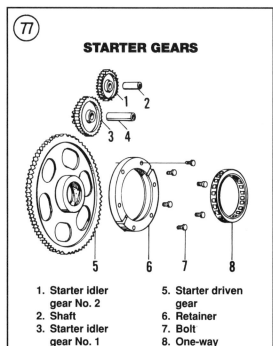

STARTER GEARS

1. Starter idler gear No. 2
2. Shaft
3. Starter idler gear No. 1
4. Shaft
5. Starter driven gear
6. Retainer
7. Bolt
8. One-way clutch

5. If still installed on the crankshaft, remove the starter driven gear from the crankshaft.

6. If removed, install the starter driven gear into the backside of the alternator rotor.

7. Try to rotate the starter driven gear (**Figure 80**). It should rotate freely in one direction and be locked up in the other direction.

8. If the starter driven gear will rotate in both directions or is locked up in both directions, replace the starter clutch as described in this chapter.

Inspection

1. Inspect the starter idler gears (**Figure 81**) for wear or damage. Replace if necessary. Insert the shaft into its respective gear and rotate the gear. Suzuki does not provide specifications for the shafts nor the inside diameter of the gears. If there is a noticeable amount of play, replace the gear(s) and shaft(s) as a set.

2. Inspect the starter driven gear (**Figure 82**) for wear, chipped or missing teeth. Replace if necessary.

3. Inspect the starter driven gear inner bushing (**Figure 83**) where it rides on the crankshaft and the outer

8

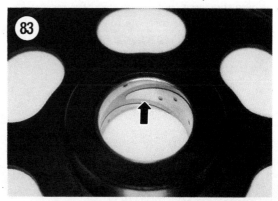

surface (**Figure 84**) where it engages the one-way clutch. If either surface is damaged, replace the gear.

4. Inspect the rollers (**Figure 85**) of the one-way clutch for burrs, wear or damage. Replace if necessary.

Installation

1. If removed, install the starter driven gear into the backside of the alternator rotor (**Figure 80**).

2. Install the starter driven gear and alternator rotor assembly onto the crankshaft. Tighten the rotor bolt as described in this chapter.

3. Install the No. 1 idler gear (B, **Figure 79**) then install the No. 1 idler gear shaft (A, **Figure 79**).

4. Install the starter idler gear No. 2 and its shaft (**Figure 78**).

5. Install the alternator stator assembly as described in this chapter.

Starter Clutch Replacement

1. If still installed, remove the starter driven gear from the backside of the alternator rotor (**Figure 80**).

2. Hold onto the center of the rotor with a 36 mm offset wrench.

3. Remove the 6mm Allen bolts (**Figure 86**) securing the starter clutch assembly to the backside of the rotor.

4. Separate the starter clutch one-way clutch and retainer from backside of the rotor.

5. Install a new one-way clutch with the flange side going on first.

6. Install the retainer, align the bolt holes and turn the assembly over.

7. Apply red Loctite (No. 271) to the 6mm Allen bolt threads prior to installation.

8. Use the same tool set-up used for removal to hold the alternator rotor stationary while tightening the bolts. Tighten the Allen bolts in a crisscross pattern to the torque specification listed in **Table 1**.

STARTER RELAY

Testing

1. Remove the rider's seat and frame left-hand side cover (**Figure 87**) as described in Chapter Thirteen.

CAUTION
*When disconnecting the starter electrical wire from the starter solenoid, do **not** touch the other electrical terminal of the starter relay—this would result in a short.*

2. Disconnect the electrical wire (A, **Figure 88**) going from the starter relay to the starter. Leave the other electrical wire connected to the relay.

3. Shift the transmission into NEUTRAL.

4. Turn the ignition switch ON.

5. Pull in on the clutch lever until it bottoms out.

6. Press the START button.

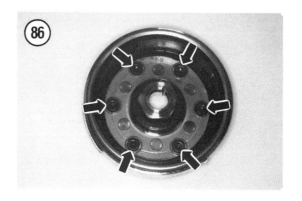

7. Have an assistant connect an ohmmeter between the positive and negative terminals (B, **Figure 88**) on top of the relay and check for continuity. If there is continuity (low resistance) the relay is okay. If there is no continuity (infinite resistance), the relay may be faulty, proceed to Step 8.

8. Disconnect the battery (+) wire and the ground (–) wire from the large terminals on the relay.

9. Disconnect the relay coil wire 2-pin electrical connector containing 2 wires (1 yellow/green, 1 black/white) from the harness.

10. Connect an ohmmeter to the terminals in the relay side of the 2-pin electrical connector and check the resistance. The specified resistance is 2-6 ohms. If the resistance is not within specified range, the relay coil is faulty and the relay must be replaced.

11. If the relay checks out okay, install all electrical wires to the relay and to the large terminals tighten the nuts securely. Make sure the electrical connec-

tors are on tight and that the rubber boot is properly installed to keep out moisture.

12. Install the side cover and seat.

Removal/Installation

1. Remove the rider's seat and frame left-hand side cover (**Figure 87**) as described in Chapter Thirteen.

2. Slide off the rubber protective boots and disconnect the large electrical wires from the top terminals of the relay (B, **Figure 88**).

3. Disconnect the relay coil wire 2-pin electrical connector containing 2 wires (1 yellow/green, 1 black/white) from the harness.

4. Remove the bolt and nut securing the relay to the frame and remove the relay and coil wiring and connector from the frame.

5. Replace by reversing these removal steps, noting the following:

    a. Install all electrical wires to the solenoid and on the large terminals tighten the nuts securely.

    b. Make sure the electrical connectors are on tight and that the rubber boot is properly installed to keep out moisture.

LIGHTING SYSTEM

The lighting system consists of a headlight, taillight/brakelight, directional lights, indicator lights and a speedometer illumination light. **Table 4** lists replacement bulbs for these components.

Always use the correct wattage bulb as indicated in this section. The use of a larger wattage bulb will give a dim light and a smaller wattage bulb will burn out prematurely.

Headlight Bulb and Lens Replacement

Refer to **Figure 89** for this procedure.

1. Remove the screw (**Figure 90**), on each side, at the bottom of the headlight case.

2. Pull out on the bottom of the headlight trim ring and disengage it from the headlight case. Remove the trim ring and headlight lens unit assembly from the case.

3. Disconnect the electrical connector (**Figure 91**) from the backside of the bulb.

4. Remove the rubber cover (**Figure 92**) from the back of the headlight lens unit.

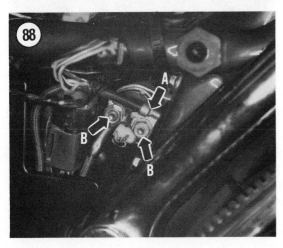

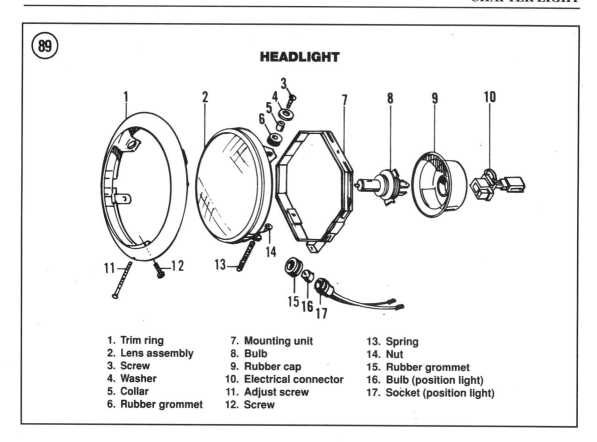

HEADLIGHT

1. Trim ring
2. Lens assembly
3. Screw
4. Washer
5. Collar
6. Rubber grommet
7. Mounting unit
8. Bulb
9. Rubber cap
10. Electrical connector
11. Adjust screw
12. Screw
13. Spring
14. Nut
15. Rubber grommet
16. Bulb (position light)
17. Socket (position light)

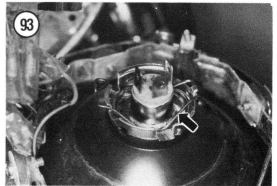

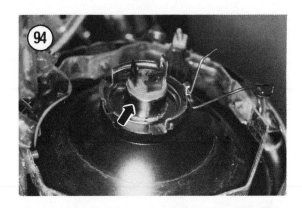

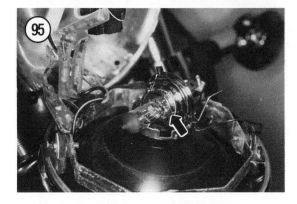

CAUTION
Carefully read all instructions shipped with the replacement quartz bulb. Do not touch the bulb glass with your fingers because any traces of skin oil on the quartz halogen bulb will drastically reduce bulb life. Clean any traces of oil from the bulb with a cloth moistened in alcohol or lacquer thinner.

5. Unhook the clip (**Figure 93**) and remove the light bulb (**Figure 94**). Replace with a new bulb (**Figure 95**).

6. To remove the headlight lens unit, perform the following:

    a. Remove the adjustment screws (**Figure 96**).

    b. Remove the screws, washers and spacers (**Figure 97**) securing the lens unit to the mounting ring and remove the mounting ring and trim ring from the lens unit.

7. Install by reversing these removal steps, noting the following.

    a. Install the rubber cover with the "TOP" arrow (A, **Figure 98**) facing upward.

    b. Make sure the electrical connector (B, **Figure 98**) is on tight and that the rubber cover is properly installed to keep out moisture.

    c. Adjust the headlight as described in this chapter.

8

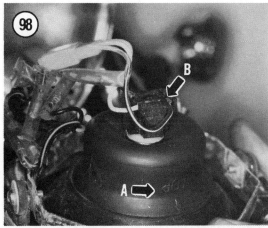

Front Position Light
Bulb Replacement
(U.K.Models)

1. Reach up under the headlight case and remove the socket/bulb and electrical connector from the headlight case.
2. Remove the bulb from the socket.
3. Replace the bulb and install the socket assembly.

Headlight Case
Removal/Installation

1. Remove the headlight bulb and lens assembly from the headlight case as described in this chapter.
2. Disconnect the electrical wire connectors (A, **Figure 99**) within the headlight case and withdraw the wires from the case (B, **Figure 99**).
3. Remove the nuts (**Figure 100**) securing the headlight case to the lower fork bridge and remove the case assembly.
4. Install by reversing these removal steps.
5. Adjust the headlight as described in this chapter.

Headlight Adjustment

Adjust the headlight horizontally and vertically according to Department of Motor Vehicle regulations in your area.

Turn the screws on the bottom of the trim ring, until the aim is correct. To adjust the headlight horizontally, turn the left-hand adjust screw (A, **Figure 101**). To adjust the headlight vertically turn the right-hand adjust screw (B, **Figure 101**).

Taillight/Brakelight
Bulb Replacement

Refer to **Figure 102** for this procedure.
1. Remove the screws (**Figure 103**) securing the lens and remove the lens and gasket.
2. Wash out the inside and outside of the lens with a mild detergent and wipe dry.
3. Inspect the lens gasket and replace it if damaged or deteriorated.
4. Push in and turn the bulb (A, **Figure 104**) counterclockwise and remove the bulb.
5. Carefully wipe off the reflector surface (B, **Figure 104**) behind the bulb with a soft cloth.

6. Replace the bulb (A, **Figure 104**) and install the lens and gasket; do not over-tighten the screws as the lens may crack.

License Plate Light
Bulb Replacement

Refer to **Figure 102** for this procedure.
1. Working behind the license plate assembly, remove the nuts and lockwashers securing the light assembly.

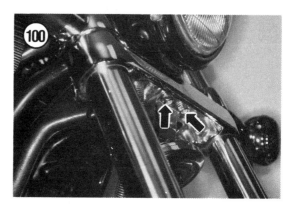

TAILLIGHT/BRAKELIGHT AND LICENSE PLATE LIGHT

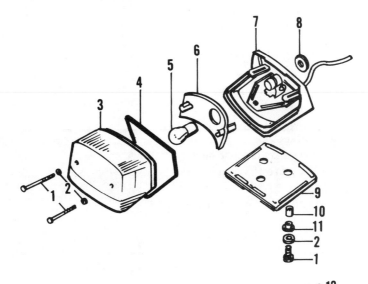

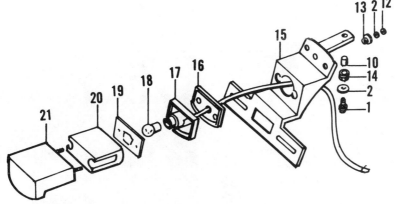

1. Screw	11. Collar
2. Washer	12. Nut
3. Lens (tail/	13. Collar
brakelight)	14. Rubber bushing
4. Gasket	15. Bracket
5. Bulb	16. Plate
6. Reflector	17. Housing
7. Base	18. Bulb
8. Nut	19. Gasket
9. Rubber cushion	20. Lens
10. Collar	21. Cover

8

2. Remove the cover (**Figure 105**) and the lens (**Figure 106**) from the housing on the license plate bracket. Don't lose the mounting hole collars in the bracket.

3. Wash out the inside and outside of the lens with a mild detergent and wipe dry.

4. Inspect the lens gasket (**Figure 107**) and replace it if damaged or deteriorated.

5. Push in and turn the bulb (A, **Figure 108**) counterclockwise and remove the bulb.

6. If necessary, remove the housing and plate (B, **Figure 108**) from the bracket.

7. If removed, install the housing and plate (B, **Figure 108**) onto the bracket.

8. If removed, install the gasket onto the housing.

9. Replace the bulb (A, **Figure 108**) and install the lens and cover.

10. Make sure mounting hole collars are in place in the bracket.

11. Install the lockwashers and nuts securing the assembly. Tighten the nuts securely.

Directional Signal Light
Bulb Replacement

1. Remove the screws (**Figure 109**) securing the lens and remove the lens.

2. Push in and turn the bulb (A, **Figure 110**) counterclockwise and remove the bulb.

3. Wash out the inside and outside of the lens with a mild detergent and wipe dry.

4. Carefully wipe off the reflector surface (B, **Figure 110**) behind the bulb with a soft cloth.

5. Replace the bulb (A, **Figure 110**) and install the lens and gasket; do not over-tighten the screws as the lens may crack.

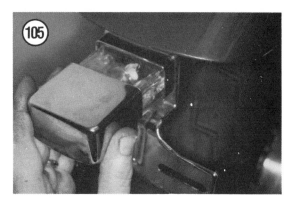

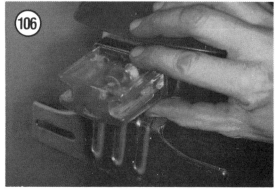

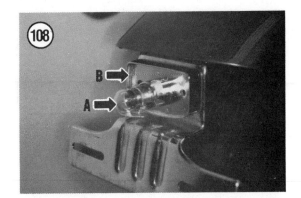

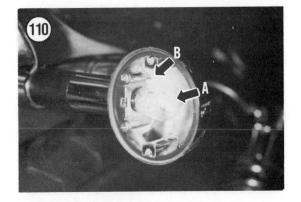

Speedometer Illumination Light Indicator Light Replacement

1. Remove the screws and washers (A, **Figure 111**) securing the speedometer assembly in the case.

2. Carefully pull the speedometer housing (B, **Figure 111**) up and out of the case.

3. Carefully pull the defective lamp holder/electrical wire assembly from the backside of the speedometer housing.

4. Pull the bulb straight out of the holder and replace the defective bulb.

NOTE
If a new bulb will not work, check the wire connections for loose or broken wires. Also check the bulb socket for corrosion. Replace as necessary.

5. Push the lamp socket/electrical wire assembly back into the housing. Make sure it is completely seated to prevent the entry of water and moisture.

6. Make sure the gasket (C, **Figure 111**) is in place and install the speedometer housing (B, **Figure 111**) into the case.

7. Install the screws and washers (A, **Figure 111**) securing the speedometer assembly in the case.

SWITCHES

Switches can be tested for continuity with an ohmmeter (see Chapter One) or a test light at the switch connector plug by operating the switch in each of its operating positions and comparing results with the switch operation. For example, **Figure 112** shows a continuity diagram for the ignition switch. It shows which terminals should

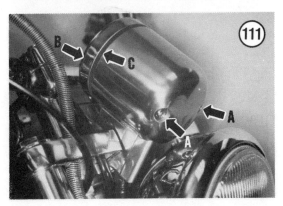

Color / Position	Red/white	Orange	Gray	Brown
Off				
On	●——————●		●——————●	
Park	●———			———●

IGNITION SWITCH

show continuity when the ignition switch is in a given position.

When the ignition switch is in the PARK position, there should be continuity between terminals red/white and brown. This is indicated by the line on the continuity diagram. An ohmmeter connected between these 2 terminals should indicate little or no resistance and a test lamp should light. When the ignition switch is OFF, there should be no continuity between any of the terminals.

Testing

If the switch or button doesn't perform properly, replace it. Refer to the following figures when testing the switches:

- a. Ignition switch: **Figure 112**.
- b. Engine stop switch and start switch: **Figure 113**.
- c. Sidestand switch: **Figure 114**.
- d. Clutch switch: **Figure 115**.
- e. Headlight switch (U.K.): **Figure 116**.
- f. Front brake switch: **Figure 117**.
- g. Rear brake switch: **Figure 118**.

CLUTCH SWITCH

Position \ Color	Yellow/green	Yellow/green
On (Squeeze lever)	●———————●	
Off		

HEADLIGHT SWITCH (U.K.)

Position \ Color	Yellow/white	Orange/red	Orange/black	Gray
On	●———●		●———●	
S			●———●	
Off				

ENGINE STOP AND START SWITCH

Position \ Color	Orange/white (Red tube)	Orange/white	Yellow/green
Off			
Run	●———●		
Start (Push)		●———●	

FRONT BRAKE SWITCH

Position \ Color	Orange	White/blue
On (Squeeze lever)	●———————●	
Off		

SIDESTAND CHECK SWITCH

Position \ Color	Green/white	Brown/white
On (Down position)	●———————●	
Off (Upright position)		

REAR BRAKE SWITCH

Position \ Color	Orange	White/blue
On (Depress pedal)	●———————●	
Off		

119

DIMMER SWITCH

Position \ Color	White	Yellow	Orange/ red
Hi		●———●	
Lo	●———●		

120

DIRECTIONAL SIGNAL SWITCH

Position \ Color	Blue	Light blue	Light green
Right		●————————●	
Off			
Left	●———●		

121

NEUTRAL INDICATOR SWITCH

Position \ Color	Black	Ground
Neutral	●————————●	
The others		

122

HORN SWITCH

Position \ Color	Green	Blue/ white
On (Push)	●————————●	
Off		

h. Dimmer switch: **Figure 119**.

i. Directional signal switch: **Figure 120**.

j. Neutral indicator switch: **Figure 121**.

k. Horn switch: **Figure 122**.

When testing switches, note the following:

a. First check the fuses as described under *Fuses* in this chapter.

b. Check the battery as described under *Battery* in Chapter Three; charge the battery to the correct state of charge, if required.

c. Disconnect the negative (–) cable from the battery, as described in this chapter, if the switch connectors are not disconnected in the circuit.

CAUTION
Do not attempt to start the engine with the battery negative (–) cable disconnected or you may damage the wiring harness.

d. When separating 2 electrical connectors, depress the retaining clip and pull on the electrical connector housings and *not* the wires.

NOTE
Electrical connectors can be serviced by disconnecting them and cleaning with electrical contact cleaner. Multiple pin connectors should be packed with a dielectric compound (available at most automotive and motorcycle supply stores).

e. After locating a defective circuit, check the electrical connectors to make sure they are clean and properly connected. Make sure there are no bent metal pins on the male side of the connector (**Figure 123**). Check all wires going into a electrical connector housing to make

123

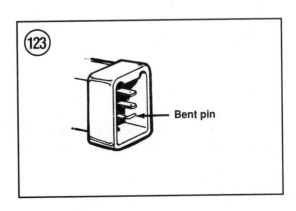

Bent pin

sure each wire is properly positioned and that the wire end is not loose (**Figure 124**).

f. To properly connect electrical connectors, push them together until they click and are locked into place (**Figure 125**).

g. When replacing handlebar switch assemblies, on models with electrical wiring external of the handlebar, make sure the wiring is routed correctly so that it is not crimped when the handlebar is turned from side to side. Also secure the wiring to the handlebar with the plastic tie wraps.

NOTE
*On some models, the switch electrical wires run through the interior of the handlebar. The wiring enters a opening in the handlebar adjacent to the switch (**Figure 126**) and exits at the base of the handlebar by the speedometer. On these models, if the electrical wiring cannot be disconnected at the switch assembly, the electrical wiring must be pulled through the handlebar during removal and again during installation.*

Ignition Switch
Removal/Installation

1. Remove the rider's seat and frame left-hand side cover (A, **Figure 127**) as described in Chapter Thirteen.

2. Disconnect the battery negative (–) lead as described in this chapter.

3. Follow the wiring harness from the ignition switch to the wiring harness.

4. Disconnect the ignition switch 4-pin electrical connector containing 4 wires (1 red/white, 1 orange, 1 gray and 1 brown).

5. Remove the mounting screw and washer (B, **Figure 127**) securing the ignition switch to the frame on the left-hand side.

6. Remove the switch assembly (C, **Figure 127**) from the frame.

7. Install the new ignition switch onto the frame and tighten the screw securely.

8. Reconnect the 4-pin electrical connector. Make sure the electrical connector is free of corrosion and is tight.

9. Connect the battery negative (–) lead as described in this chapter.

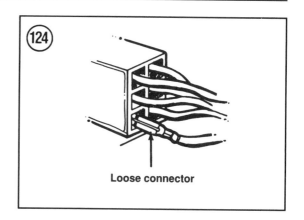
Loose connector

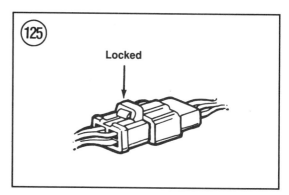
Locked

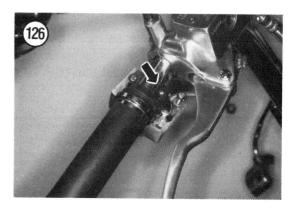

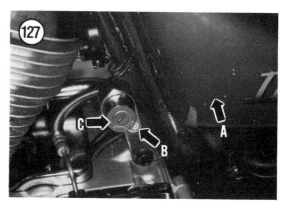

10. Install the side cover and seat.

Right-hand Combination Switch and on 1985-1987, Front Brake Light Switch (Engine Start and Stop Switch and on U.K. Models the Headlight Switch) Removal/Installation

The right-hand combination switch assembly contains both the engine start, engine stop switch and on U.K. models the Headlight Switch. If any

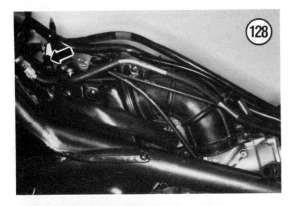

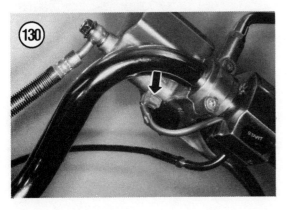

portion of the switch is faulty the entire switch assembly must be replaced.

1. Remove the seat as described under *Seat Removal/Installation* in Chapter Thirteen.

2. Disconnect the battery negative (–) lead as described in this chapter.

3. Remove the fuel tank as described under *Fuel Tank Removal/Installation* in Chapter Seven.

NOTE
The location of the electrical connectors, and the color of the wiring, vary with the different type of handlebars, different years and with the country the bike is sold in. Therefore the exact location of the connector(s) is not shown in this procedure.

4. Follow the right-hand switch electrical wiring either on the exterior of the handlebar or where the internal wiring exits at the base of the handlebar by the speedometer. Follow these wires to the area along the top of the frame rails. The electrical connectors are located either by the front air filter case (**Figure 128**) or by the rear air filter case (**Figure 129**).

5. Locate and disconnect the electrical connector(s).

6A. On 1985-1987 models, remove the screws and disassemble the front brake light switch. The electrical connector is part of the switch assembly and will be removed along with the rest of the wiring harness.

6B. On 1988-on models, disconnect the electrical connector (**Figure 130**) from the front brake light switch. This wire goes from the start switch to the front brake light switch.

7. Remove the electrical wire harness from any clips on the frame and carefully pull the harness out from the frame.

8. Remove the screws securing the right-hand combination switch together and remove the switch assembly (**Figure 131**).

9. Install a new switch and tighten the screws securely. Do not over-tighten the screws or the plastic switch housing may crack.

10. Reconnect the electrical connector(s)

11. Make sure the electrical connector(s) are free of corrosion and are tight. Install a tie wrap to hold the electrical wires to the front of the frame. The wires

8

must be retained in this manner to allow room for the fuel tank.

12. Connect the battery negative (–) lead as described in this chapter.

13. Install the fuel tank as described in Chapter Seven.

14. Install the seat as described in Chapter Thirteen.

Left-hand Combination Switch and Starter Interlock Switch
(Headlight Dimmer Switch, Directional Signal Switch, Horn Switch and on U.K. Models the Passing Switch)
Removal/Installation

The left-hand combination switch assembly contains both the headlight dimmer switch, turn signal switch, horn switch and on U.K. models the Passing Switch. If any portion of the switch is faulty the entire switch assembly must be replaced.

1. Remove the seat as described under *Seat Removal/Installation* in Chapter Thirteen.

2. Disconnect the battery negative (–) lead as described in this chapter.

3. Remove the fuel tank as described under *Fuel Tank Removal/Installation* in Chapter Seven.

> *NOTE*
> *The location of the electrical connectors, and the color of the wiring, vary with the different types of handlebars, different years and with the country the bike is sold in. Therefore the exact location of the connector(s) is not shown in this procedure.*

4. Follow the left-hand switch electrical wiring either on the exterior of the handlebar or where the internal wiring exits at the base of the handlebar by the speedometer. Follow these wires to the area along the top of the frame rails. The electrical connectors are located either by the front air filter case (**Figure 128**) or by the rear air filter case (**Figure 129**).

5. Locate and disconnect the electrical connector(s).

6. Remove the screws and disassemble the starter interlock switch (A, **Figure 132**) on the clutch lever. The electrical connector is part of the switch assembly and will be removed along with the rest of the wiring harness.

7. Remove the electrical wire harness from any clips on the frame and carefully pull the harness out from the frame.

8. Remove the screws securing the left-hand combination switch together and remove the switch assembly (B, **Figure 132**).

9. Install a new switch and tighten the screws securely. Do not over-tighten the screws or the plastic switch housing may crack.

10. Reconnect the electrical connector(s)

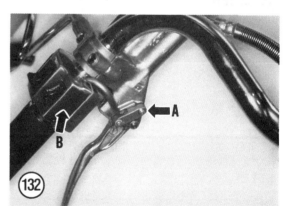

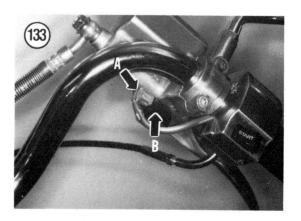

11. Make sure the electrical connector(s) are free of corrosion and are tight. Install a tie wrap to hold the electrical wires to the front of the frame. The wires must be retained in this manner to allow room for the fuel tank.

12. Connect the battery negative (−) lead as described in this chapter.

13. Install the fuel tank as described in Chapter Seven.

14. Install the seat as described in Chapter Thirteen.

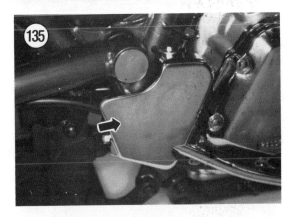

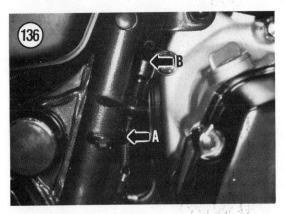

Front Brake Light Switch
(1988-on Models)
Removal/Installation

NOTE
The front brake light switch on 1985-1987 models is removed along with the right-hand combination switch assembly as previously described.

1. Disconnect the electrical connector (A, **Figure 133**) from the switch.

2. Remove the screws securing the front brake light switch to the front brake lever housing and remove the switch assembly (B, **Figure 133**).

3. Install a new switch and tighten the screws securely.

4. Reconnect the 2 individual electrical connectors.

5. Make sure the electrical connectors are free of corrosion and are tight.

Rear Brake Light Switch
Removal/Installation

1. Remove the rider's seat and frame right-hand side cover (**Figure 134**) as described in Chapter Thirteen.

2. Remove the trim panel (**Figure 135**) at the rear of the rear brake pedal.

3. Disconnect the return spring (A, **Figure 136**) from the switch.

4. Remove the switch (B, **Figure 136**) from the frame mounting bracket.

5. Remove any tie wraps securing the wiring to the frame.

6. Follow the 2 electrical wires (1 white/black, 1 orange/green) from the switch to where it connects to the harness.

7. Locate and disconnect the individual electrical connectors.

8. Remove the switch and electrical wires from the frame.

9. Install by reversing these removal steps, noting the following:
   a. Make sure the electrical connectors are free of corrosion and are tight.
   b. Adjust the switch as described in this chapter.

Rear Brake Light Switch Adjustment

1. Turn the ignition switch to the ON position.

2. Depress the brake pedal. The brake light should come on just as the brake begins to work.

3. To make the brake light come on earlier, hold the brake light switch body and turn the adjusting nut *clockwise* as viewed from the top. Turn the adjusting nut (**Figure 137**) *counterclockwise* to delay the light from coming on.

> *NOTE*
> *Some rider's prefer the brake light to come on a little early. This way, they can tap the pedal without braking to warn drivers who are following too closely.*

Neutral Switch
Removal/Installation

The neutral switch is located on the left-hand side of the bike next to the clutch slave cylinder (**Figure 138**).

1. Remove the bolts securing the secondary drive cover (**Figure 139**) and remove the cover.

2. Disconnect the sidestand check switch electrical connectors (**Figure 140**) from the neutral switch electrical harness.

3. Disconnect the electrical connector (**Figure 141**) from the oil pressure switch.

4. Remove the starter motor as described in this chapter. The neutral switch electrical harness is routed under the starter motor and cover.

5. Remove any tie-wraps securing the electrical harness to the frame.

6. From the neutral switch, follow the electrical harness to the electrical connector in the upper portion of the frame and disconnect the electrical connector.

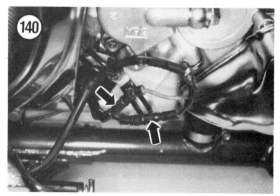

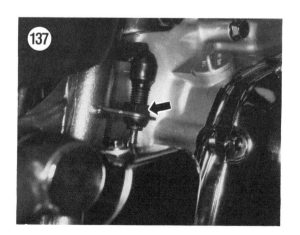

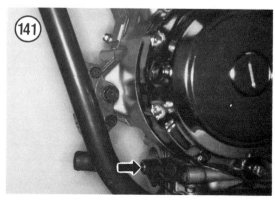

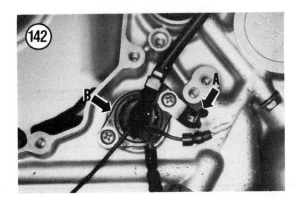

NOTE
Steps 7-9 are shown with the engine removed from the frame and partially disassembled for clarity. It is not necessary to remove the engine from the frame for this procedure.

NOTE
*Note the location of the electrical wire strap (A, **Figure 142**). It must be reinstalled in the same location during installation.*

7. Remove the screws securing the neutral switch (B, **Figure 142**) and separate the neutral switch assembly from the crankcase.

8. Remove the O-ring seal (**Figure 143**) from the receptacle in the crankcase.

9. To avoid the loss of small parts, remove the switch contact plunger (**Figure 144**) and spring from the end of the gearshift drum.

10. Carefully remove the electrical harness from the frame noting its path through the frame. The harness for the new switch must follow the same path.

11. Install the switch contact spring and plunger (**Figure 145**) into the end of the gearshift drum. Make sure they are completely seated (**Figure 144**).

12. Apply a light coat of oil to the O-ring and install the O-ring seal (**Figure 143**) into the receptacle in the crankcase. Make sure it is seated correctly.

13. Install the neutral switch (B, **Figure 142**), the electrical wire strap (A, **Figure 142**) and screws. Tighten the screws securely.

14. Continue the installation by reversing these removal steps, noting the following:

a. Be sure to reconnect the electrical connectors to the oil pressure switch and the sidestand check switch.

b. Make sure all electrical connectors are free of corrosion and are tight.

c. Secure the electrical harness under the wire strap as shown in **Figure 138**.

d. Attach any tie-wraps securing the electrical wire to the frame.

Sidestand Check Switch
Removal/Installation

1. Place the bike on the sidestand.

2. Remove the bolts securing the secondary drive cover (**Figure 139**) and remove the cover.

8

3. Disconnect the sidestand check switch electrical connectors (**Figure 140**) from the neutral switch electrical harness.

NOTE
The sidestand check switch is attached to the front footpeg bracket assembly.

4. Unhook the wire wrap (A, **Figure 146**) securing the wiring harness to the footpeg assembly.

5A. Using an off-set Phillips screwdriver, loosen then remove the screws securing the switch (B, **Figure 146**) to the footpeg assembly and remove the switch.

5B. If you don't have an off-set Phillips screwdriver, perform the following:

  a. Remove the clips (A, **Figure 147**) from the bolts securing the front footpeg assembly (B, **Figure 147**) to the frame.

  b. Remove the bolts and lower the footpeg assembly.

  c. Remove the screws (**Figure 148**) securing the switch to the footpeg assembly and remove the switch.

6. Install by reversing these removal steps, noting the following:

  a. If the front footpeg assembly was removed, tighten the bolts to the torque specification listed in **Table 1** and install the clips (A, **Figure 147**) on the 2 outboard bolts on each side.

  b. Make sure all electrical connectors are free of corrosion and are tight.

  c. Secure the electrical harness under the wire strap as shown in **Figure 138**.

Oil Pressure Switch
Removal/Installation

1. Drain the engine oil as described under *Engine Oil and Oil Filter Change* in Chapter Three.

NOTE
In the following steps, the engine is shown removed from the frame and partially disassembled for clarity. It is not necessary to remove the engine nor disassemble it for this procedure.

2. Pull the rubber boot (A, **Figure 149**) off the switch.

3. Disconnect the oil pressure sending switch wire (B, **Figure 149**).

4. Unscrew the oil pressure switch (C, **Figure 149**) from the crankcase.

5. Apply a light coat of gasket sealer to the switch threads prior to installation. Install the switch and tighten securely.

6. Connect the oil pressure sending switch wire and tighten the screw securely.

7. Move the rubber boot back into place on the switch. Make sure it is installed correctly to protect the switch from moisture and corrosion.

8. Refill the engine with the specified type and quantity engine oil.

ELECTRICAL COMPONENTS

This section contains information on electrical components other than switches. Some of the test procedures covered in this section instruct taking a meter reading within the electrical connector while

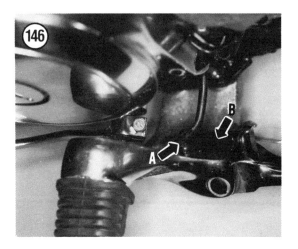

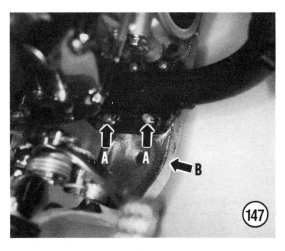

it is still attached to a specific part. Under these conditions make sure that the meter test lead has penetrated the connector and is touching the bare metal wire *not* the insulation on the wire. If the test lead does not touch the bare metal wire the readings will be false and may lead to the unnecessary purchase of an expensive electrical part that cannot be returned for a refund. Most dealers and parts houses will not accept any returns on electrical parts.

If you are having trouble with some of these components, perform some quick preliminary checks and they may save you a lot of time.

   a. Disconnect each electrical connector and check that there are no bent metal pins on the male side of the electrical connector. A bent pin will not connect to its mating receptacle in the female end of the connector causing an open circuit.

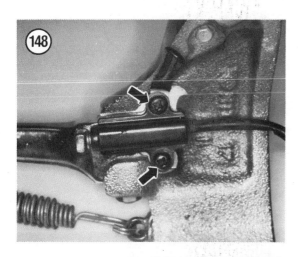

   b. Check each female end of the connector. Make sure that the metal connector on the end of each wire is pushed in all the way into the plastic connector. If not, carefully push them in with a narrow bladed screwdriver.

   c. Check all electrical wires where they enter the individual metal connector in both the male and female plastic connector.

   d. After all is checked out, push the connectors together and make sure they are fully engaged and locked together.

Battery Case
Removal/Installation

Refer to **Figure 150** for this procedure.
1. Remove the battery as described under *Battery* in Chapter Three.
2. Remove the trim panel (**Figure 135**) at the rear of the rear brake pedal.
3. On the left-hand side of the bike, remove the bolts securing the voltage regulator/rectifier (A, **Figure 151**) and tie it up out of the way.
4. Remove the bottom bolt (B, **Figure 151**) from each side that secures the battery case to the frame.
5. Remove the top bolt (**Figure 152**) from each side that secures the battery case to the frame.
6. Lower the battery case down and out of the frame.
7. If the battery case is corroded by electrolyte spillage, thoroughly clean with baking soda and water and rinse thoroughly. Then clean with solvent and dry completely. Repaint any areas of bare metal.
8. Install by reversing these removal steps.

Speedometer and
Indicator Lamp Housing
Removal/Installation

Refer to **Figure 153** for this procedure.
1. Remove the fuel tank as described under *Fuel Tank Removal/Installation* in Chapter Seven.
2. Disconnect the battery negative lead as described in Chapter Three.
3. Remove the screws securing both the right- and left-hand frame head side covers (**Figure 154**). Remove both side covers.
4. Remove the bolts securing the fuel tank mounting bracket (**Figure 155**) and remove the bracket.
5. Remove the headlight case (A, **Figure 156**) as described in this chapter. Move it out of the way.

8

BATTERY CASE

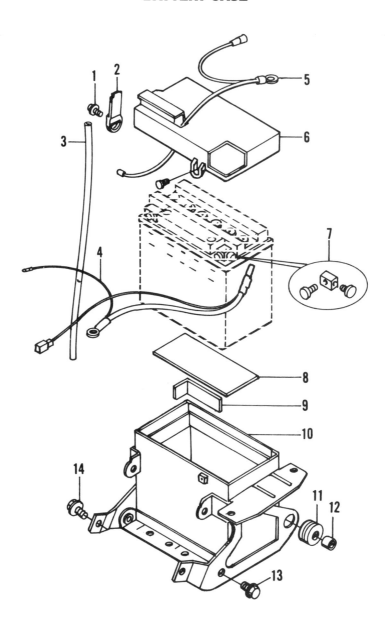

1. Screw
2. Positive terminal cover
3. Vent tube
4. Negative (–) cable
5. Positive (+) cable
6. Cover
7. Cable connector
8. Cushion
9. Cushion
10. Case
11. Rubber grommet
12. Collar
13. Bolt
14. Bolt

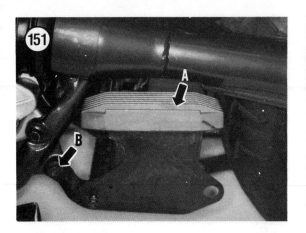

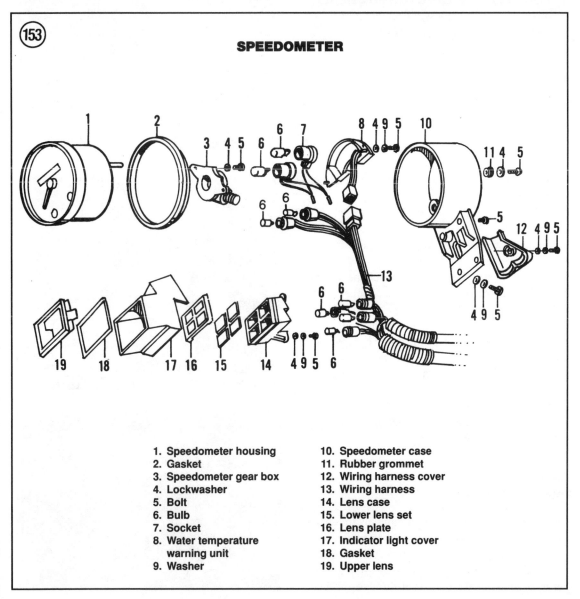

SPEEDOMETER

1. Speedometer housing
2. Gasket
3. Speedometer gear box
4. Lockwasher
5. Bolt
6. Bulb
7. Socket
8. Water temperature warning unit
9. Washer
10. Speedometer case
11. Rubber grommet
12. Wiring harness cover
13. Wiring harness
14. Lens case
15. Lower lens set
16. Lens plate
17. Indicator light cover
18. Gasket
19. Upper lens

8

6. Unscrew the speedometer drive cable (B, **Figure 156**) from the left-hand side of the speedometer case.

7. Remove the screws and washers securing the wiring harness cover (C, **Figure 156**) from the base of the case.

8. Follow both electrical wiring harnesses back through the top of the frame and disconnect the multi-pin and individual electrical connectors.

9. Carefully pull the wiring harnesses out through the steering head area.

10. Remove the screws and washers securing the headlight and indicator lamp assembly to the base of the upper fork bridge.

11. Remove the speedometer and indicator lamp assembly and wiring harnesses from the frame.

12. Install by reversing these removal steps.

13. Make sure the electrical connectors are free of corrosion and are tight.

Fuel Pump
Resistance Check

1. Remove the rider's seat as described under *Seat Removal/Installation* in Chapter Thirteen.

2. Disconnect the battery negative lead as described in Chapter Three.

3. Turn the fuel shutoff valve (**Figure 157**) to the OFF position.

4. Remove the bolt securing the frame left-hand side cover and remove the cover.

5. Disconnect the 2-pin electrical connector on 1985-1986 models or 4-pin electrical connector on 1987-on models.

6. Connect an ohmmeter between both terminals of the fuel pump electrical connector. The specified resistance is 1-2 ohms. If the resistance shown is infinity or lower than specified; replace the fuel pump.

7. Install by reversing these removal steps.

8. Make sure the electrical connector is free of corrosion and is tight.

Fuel Pump
Fuel Pump Flow Test

The electromagnetic fuel pump pumps fuel from the fuel tank to the carburetors. When the ignition switch is turned ON the electromagnet is energized, pulling the armature and the diaphragm up. This causes a vacuum and pulls fuel through the inlet

check valve. As the armature reaches the limit of its upward travel, the contact points are opened in the switch and the circuit is broken. The electromagnet is pushed down by the return spring which in turn pushes the fuel through the outlet check valve and to the carburetor assembly. This continuing up and down movement moves or pumps the fuel from the fuel tank into the carburetors.

Figure 158 is a schematic of the fuel pump circuit.

1. Remove the fuel pump as described under *Fuel Pump Removal/Installation* in Chapter Seven.

> *WARNING*
> *Perform this test with **kerosene**. Do **not** use gasoline due to the extreme fire hazard.*

> *NOTE*
> *The fuel pump should pump over 600 ml (1.27 U.S. pints) of fuel in 1 minute. Have sufficient kerosene in the container and use a graduated beaker large enough to contain this amount of fuel. If you have a smaller graduated beaker, run the test for only 30 seconds and multiply the amount of fuel delivered by 2 to achieve the same results.*

2. Connect a short section of fuel line to the fuel pump fitting that goes to the carburetors. Place the loose end of the fuel line into a graduated beaker.

3. Connect another piece of hose to the fuel pump fitting that goes to the fuel tank. Place the loose end of the fuel line into the container of kerosene.

4. Connect jumper wires from a 12V battery to the fuel pump electrical connector as follows:

   a. Connect the battery positive (+) lead to the black/brown terminal.

   b. Connect the battery negative (–) lead to the black/white terminal.

5. Allow the fuel to run out of the fuel line (into the graduated beaker) for 1 minute.

6. Disconnect the battery from the fuel pump.

7. The fuel pump specified flow capacity for one minute is over 600 ml (1.27 U.S. pints) of fuel in 1 minute.

8. If the fuel pump does not flow to the specified capacity, install a new pump.

9. Disconnect the fuel hoses from the fuel pump and drain out any residual kerosene from the fuel pump. Any kerosene remaining within the fuel pump will not harm the carburetor nor the engine.

10. Install by reversing these removal steps.

11. Make sure the electrical connector is free of corrosion and is tight.

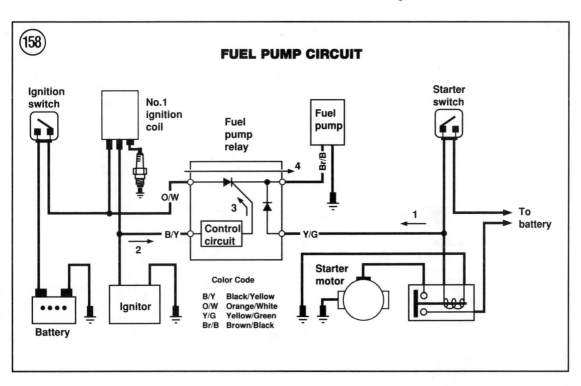

FUEL PUMP CIRCUIT

Fan Motor Thermo Switch
Removal/Testing/Installation

The fan motor thermo switch controls the radiator fan according to engine coolant temperature. This switch is attached to the upper rear side of the radiator next to the inlet hose.

Figure 159 is a schematic of the fan motor thermo switch circuit.

> *NOTE*
> *If the cooling fan is not operating cor-*
> *rectly, make sure that the cooling fan*
> *fuse has not blown prior to starting this*
> *test. Also clean off any rust or corrosion*
> *from the electrical terminals on the*
> *thermostatic switch.*

1. Remove the screws securing the radiator cover (**Figure 160**) and remove the cover.

2. Disconnect the fan motor thermo switch black electrical connector (**Figure 161**).

3. Place a jumper wire between the fan motor thermo switch black electrical connector and a good ground.

4. Turn the ignition switch ON, the cooling fan should start running.

5. If the fan does not run, either the fan or the wiring to the fan is faulty.

6. If the fan now runs, the fan motor thermo switch may be defective; test the fan motor thermo switch as follows.

> *NOTE*
> *The fan motor thermo switch is located*
> *in such a cramped work area that it is*
> *easier to first remove the radiator, then*
> *remove the switch from the radiator.*

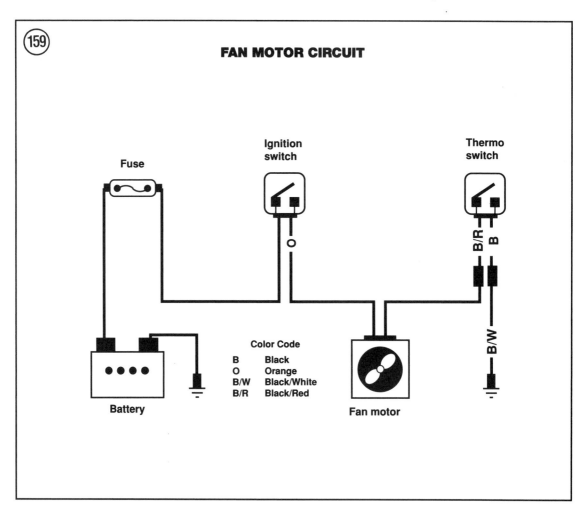

(159)

FAN MOTOR CIRCUIT

Fuse

Ignition switch

Thermo switch

B/R   B

B/W

Color Code

B   Black
O   Orange
B/W   Black/White
B/R   Black/Red

Battery

Fan motor

7. Remove the radiator as described under *Radiator Removal/Installation* in Chapter Nine.

8. Pull back the rubber boot (A, **Figure 162**) and disconnect the electrical connector from the fan motor thermo switch.

9. Unscrew the fan motor thermo switch (B, **Figure 162**) and O-ring from the radiator.

10. Attach ohmmeter leads to the electrical connectors of the fan motor thermo switch. At room tem-

perature there should be no continuity (infinite resistance).

11. Suspend the fan motor thermo switch in a small pan of 50:50 mixture of distilled water and antifreeze. The fan motor thermo switch must be positioned so that all of it's threads are submerged in the coolant.

12. Place a thermometer in the pan of coolant (use a cooking or candy thermometer that is rated for temperatures higher than the test temperature). Do not let the switch or the thermometer touch the pan as it will give a false readings.

> WARNING
> *Wear safety glasses or goggles and gloves during this test. Protect yourself accordingly as the coolant is heated to a high temperature.*

13. Heat the coolant slowly until the temperature reaches 110° C (230° F).

14. Maintain this temperature for at least 3 minutes before taking a reading. A sudden change in temperature will cause a different ohmmeter reading. After this 3 minute interval is completed, check the ohmmeter; there should be continuity (low resistance).

15. Turn the heat off and keep the ohmmeter test leads attached. When the coolant reaches 104° C (219° F), check the ohmmeter; there should be no continuity (infinite resistance).

16. If the switch fails either of these tests the switch must be replaced. If the fan motor thermo switch tests okay, it can be reinstalled.

17. Allow switch to cool and remove it from the small pan.

18. Make sure the O-ring seal in place on the fan motor thermo switch.

19. Apply a light coat of silicone based sealant to the threads of the fan motor thermo switch and install the switch in the radiator.

20. Tighten the fan motor thermo switch to the torque specification listed in **Table 1**.

21. Install the radiator as described in Chapter Seven.

22. Refill the cooling system with the recommended type and quantity of coolant. Refer to Chapter Three.

23. Attach the electrical wires to the fan motor thermo switch. Make sure the connections are tight and free from oil and corrosion.

24. Install the radiator cover.

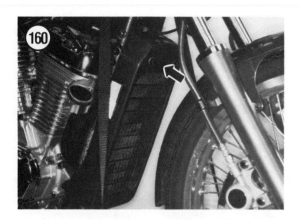

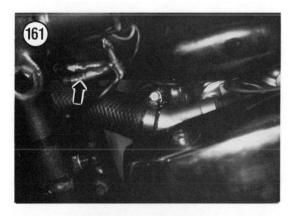

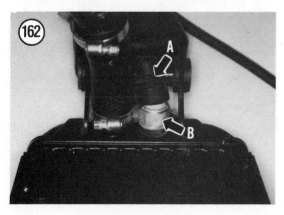

Thermo Sensor
Removal/Testing/Installation

The coolant thermo sensor is attached to the thermostat housing and controls the temperature gauge on the instrument cluster.

1. Remove the fuel tank as described under *Fuel Tank Removal/Installation* in Chapter Seven.

2. Partially drain the cooling system as described under *Coolant Change* in Chapter Three. Drain just enough coolant to lower the coolant level in the radiator to below the radiator upper hose. This will reduce the amount of coolant lost while removing the sensor.

3. Remove the bolts securing the cylinder head trim cover (A, **Figure 163**) on the left-hand side.

4. Pull the rubber boot and the electrical connector (B, **Figure 163**) from the end of the thermo sensor.

> *NOTE*
> *Figure 164 is shown with the engine removed from the frame for clarity.*

5. Unscrew the thermo sensor from the coolant inlet fitting (**Figure 164**) of the front cylinder head.

> *WARNING*
> *Wear safety glasses or goggles and gloves during this test. Protect yourself accordingly as the coolant is heated to a very high temperature and can result in severe burns if not handled properly.*

6. Suspend the thermo sensor in a small pan of 50:50 mixture of distilled water and coolant. The sensor must be positioned so that all of it's threads are submerged in the coolant.

7. Place a thermometer in the pan of coolant (use a cooking or candy thermometer that is rated for temperatures higher than the test temperature). Do not let the thermo sensor or the thermometer touch the pan as it will give a false readings.

8. Heat the coolant slowly and check the resistance readings as shown in **Figure 165**.

9. If the sensor readings do not correspond to those listed in **Table 5** during any of the temperature ranges the sensor must be replaced.

10. Apply a light coat of a silicone based sealant to the threads of the thermo sensor and install the sensor in the thermostat housing. Tighten the thermo sensor to the torque specification listed in **Table 1**.

11. Connect the electrical connector and rubber boot onto the thermo sensor. Make sure the connection is tight and free from corrosion.

12. Refill the cooling system as described under *Coolant Change* in Chapter Three.

13. Install the cylinder head trim cover (A, **Figure 163**) on the left-hand side and tighten the bolts securely.

14. Install the fuel tank as described in Chapter Seven.

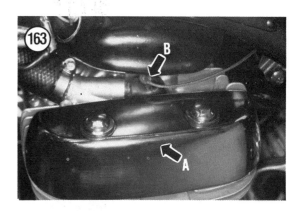

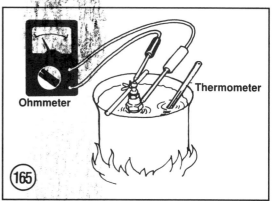

Sidestand Check Switch
(1987-on Models)

The sidestand check switch system is provided on 1987 and later models. This system prevents the engine from being started with the sidestand down and the transmission in gear. A special circuit between the battery and ignition coil consists of a relay, neutral indicator lamp, diode and switches decides whether the ignition circuit can be completed to allow starting of the engine.

Figure 166 is a schematic of the sidestand check switch circuit.

The ignition circuit is completed under the 2 following different situations:

a. The transmission in NEUTRAL and the sidestand DOWN.

b. The transmission in GEAR and the sidestand UP.

Diode testing

1. Remove the seat as described under *Seat Removal/Installation* in Chapter Thirteen.

2. Locate the diode on top of the frame rail adjacent to the rear air filter case.

3. Disconnect the 3-pin electrical connector containing 3 wires (1 blue/white, 1 blue, 1 green) from the diode.

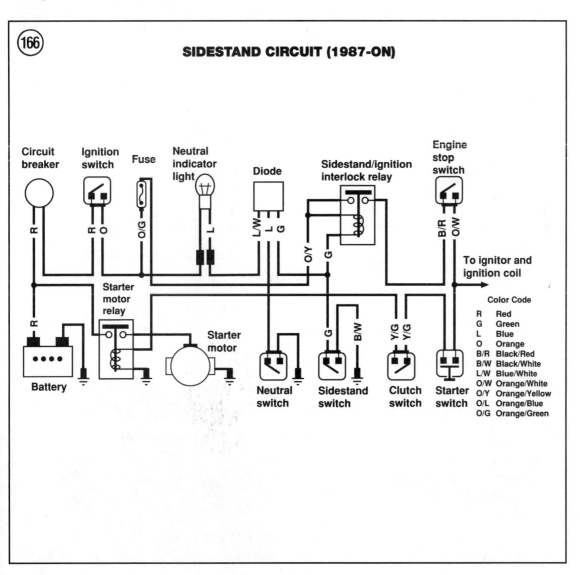

4. Use an ohmmeter and check for continuity between one of the end terminals on the diode and the center terminal. There should be continuity (low resistance) in one direction and no continuity (infinite resistance) with the test leads reversed.

5. Repeat Step 4 with the other end terminal and the center terminal.

6. If the diode fails either of these tests, the diode is defective and must be replaced.

7. Attach the electrical connector to the diode and make sure the electrical connector is free of corrosion and is tight.

Switch testing

1. Remove the seat as described under *Seat Removal/Installation* in Chapter Thirteen.

2. Disconnect the sidestand check switch electrical connector.

3. Use an ohmmeter and check for continuity between the 2 terminals (1 green, 1 black/white) on the switch side of the connector as follows:

    a. With the sidestand DOWN, there should be no continuity (infinite resistance).

    b. With the sidestand UP, there should be continuity (low resistance).

4. Either replace the switch as described in this chapter or reconnect the electrical connector to the switch. Make sure the electrical connector is free of corrosion and is tight.

5. Install the seat as described in Chapter Thirteen.

Relay testing

1. Remove the seat as described under *Seat Removal/Installation* in Chapter Thirteen.

2. Disconnect the electrical connector and remove the relay from the mounting bracket under the seat (**Figure 167**).

3. Refer to **Figure 168** and perform the following:

    a. Connect an ohmmeter between terminals No. 1 and No. 2. There should be no continuity (infinite resistance).

    b. Connect a 12 volt battery positive (+) cable to the No. 3 terminal and the battery negative (–) cable to the No. 4 terminal.

    c. With battery voltage applied to the No. 3 and No. 4 terminals; reconnect an ohmmeter between terminals No. 1 and No. 2. This time

there should be continuity (indicated resistance).

4. If the relay fails either one of these tests it is defective and must be replaced.

5. Reinstall the relay into the mounting bracket under the seat.

6. Reconnect the electrical connector to the relay. Make sure the electrical connector is free of corrosion and is tight.

7. Install the fuel tank as described in Chapter Seven.

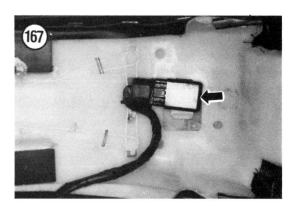

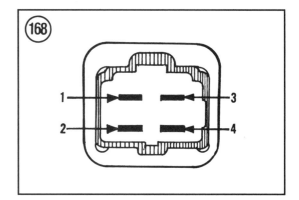

8. Install the seat as described in Chapter Thirteen.

Horn Testing

1. Disconnect horn wires from harness.
2. Connect a 12 volt battery to the horn.
3. If the horn is good it will sound. If not, replace it.

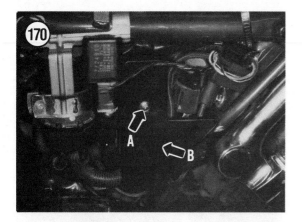

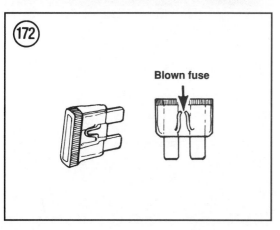

Blown fuse

Horn
Removal/Installation

1. Disconnect the electrical connectors from the horn.
2. Remove the bolts, washers and nuts securing the horn (**Figure 169**) to the steering stem. Remove the horn.
3. Install by reversing these removal steps. Make sure the electrical connectors are free of corrosion and are tight.

FUSES

The fuse panel is located under the frame left-hand side cover.

Whenever the fuse blows, find out the reason for the failure before replacing the fuse. Usually, the trouble is a short circuit in the wiring. This may be caused by worn-through insulation or a disconnected wire shorted to ground.

> *CAUTION*
> *Never substitute metal foil or wire for a fuse. Never use a higher amperage fuse than specified. An overload could result in a fire and complete loss of the bike.*

> *CAUTION*
> *When replacing a fuse, make sure the ignition switch is in the OFF position. This will lessen the chance of a short circuit.*

Fuse Replacement

1. Remove the rider's seat as described under *Seat Removal/Installation* in Chapter Thirteen.
2. Remove the frame left-hand side cover.
3. Remove the screw (A, **Figure 170**) attaching the fuse panel cover and remove the cover (B, **Figure 170**).
4. Remove the fuse (**Figure 171**) with your fingers and inspect it. If the fuse is blown there will be a break in the element (**Figure 172**). Inside the cover is a spare fuse (**Figure 173**).
5. Install the new fuse and push it all the way down until it seats completely, then install the cover and screw. Tighten the screw securely but don't overtighten it as the cover may fracture.
6. Install the seat.

8

Fuse Panel
Removal/Installation

1. Remove the rider's seat as described under *Seat Removal/Installation* in Chapter Thirteen.
2. Remove the frame left-hand side cover.
3. Remove the directional signal relay (A, **Figure 174**) from the mounting bracket on the frame.
4. Disconnect the electrical connector (B, **Figure 174**) from the base of the fuse panel.
5. Remove the screw securing the fuse panel (C, **Figure 174**) to the frame and remove it.
6. Install by reversing these removal steps.
7. Make sure the electrical connector is free of corrosion and is tight.

CIRCUIT BREAKER

The wiring harness is protected by a circuit breaker. The circuit breaker protects the electrical system when the main circuit load exceeds the rated amperage. When an overload occurs, the red button pops out on the breaker face panel and the circuit is open. The circuit will remain open until the problem is solved and the breaker is re-set.

The circuit breaker is located just behind the fuse panel (**Figure 175**).

To reset, wait approximately 10 minutes for the circuit breaker to cool down, then push the red button in. If the red button pops out again—the problem still exists in the electrical system and must be corrected.

WIRING DIAGRAMS

Wiring diagrams for all models are located at the end of this book.

Table 1 ELECTRICAL SYSTEM TIGHTENING TORQUES

Item	N•m	ft.-lb.
Alternator rotor bolt	140-160	101.5-115.5
Starter clutch retainer		
6 mm Allen bolts	23-28	16.5-20.0
Front footpeg assembly bolts	15-25	11-18
Fan motor thermo switch	10-15	7-11.0
Thermo sensor	12-15	8.5-11.0

Table 2 IGNITION TROUBLESHOOTING

Symptoms	Probable cause
Weak spark	Poor connections in circuit (clean and retighten all connections)
	High voltage leak (replace defective wire)
	Defective ignition coil (replace coil)
No spark	Broken wire (replace wire)
	Defective ignition coil (replace coil)
	Defective signal generator (replace signal generator assembly)
	Defective ignitor unit (replace ignitor unit)
	Faulty engine stop switch (replace switch)

Table 3 ELECTRICAL SYSTEM SPECIFICATIONS

Regulator/rectifier	Transistorized, non-adjustable
Regulated voltage	14-15 V at 5,000 rpm
Alternator no-load voltage	More than 65 V at 5,000 rpm
Battery	
Type designation	YB16B-A
Capacity	12V/16 amphour
Starter motor	
Brush length limit	9 mm (0.35 in.)
Commutator under cut limit	0.2 mm (0.008 in.)
Starter relay resistance	2-6 ohms
Ignition signal generator	
resistance	50-200 ohms
Ignition coil resistance	
Primary resistance	2-6 ohms
Secondary resistance	10,000-25,000 ohms
Stator coil resistance	
1985-1989	0.2-0.5 ohms
1990-on	0.1-1.0 ohms

8

Table 4 REPLACEMENT BULBS

U.S. and Canadian Models	
Item	Voltage/wattage
Headlight (high/low beam)	12V 60/55W
Taillight/brakelight	
1986-1987	12V 8/23W
1988-on	12V 5/21W
(continued)	

Table 4 REPLACEMENT BULBS (continued)

U.S. and Canadian Models (continued)	
Item	**Voltage/wattage**
Directional signal	
1986-1987	
Front	12V 8/23W
Rear	12V 23W
1988-on	
Front	12V 5/21W
Rear	12V 21W
License plate light	12V 8W
High beam indicator light	12V 1.7 W
Instrument and all other	
indicator lights	12V 3W
Other than U.S. and Canadian Models	
Item*	**Voltage/wattage**
Headlight (high/low beam)	12V 60/55W
Parking light	
E-02, E-24	12V 3.4W
E-15, E-16, E-18, E-22	12V 4W
Taillight/brakelight	
E-02, E-15, E-16, E-18, E-22	12V 5/21W
E-24	12V 8/23W
License plate light	
E-02, E-15, E-16, E-18, E-22	12V 5W
E-24	12V 8W
Directional signal	
E-02, E-15, E-16, E-18, E-22	12V 21W
E-24	12V 23W
Speedometer light	12V 21W
High beam indicator light	12V 1.7W
All other indicator lights	12V 3W

* E-02= England, E-15= Finland, E-16 Norway, E-18= Switzerland, E-22= West Germany, E-24= Austria

Table 5 TEMPERATURE GAUGE THERMO SENSOR READINGS

Temperature	Resistance (ohms)
50° C (122° F)	156
80° C (176° F)	53
100° C (212° F)	28

CHAPTER NINE

LIQUID COOLING SYSTEM

The pressurized liquid cooling system consists of a radiator, water pump, thermostat, coolant reserve tank and a electric cooling fan.

CAUTION
*Drain and flush the cooling system at least every 2 years. Refer to **Coolant Change** in Chapter Three. Refill with a mixture of ethylene glycol antifreeze (formulated for aluminum engines) and purified water. Do not reuse the old coolant as it deteriorates with use. **Do not** operate the cooling system with only purified water (even in climates where antifreeze protection is not required). This is important because the engine is all aluminum; it will not rust but it will oxidize internally and have to be replaced. Refer to **Coolant Change** in Chapter Three.*

This chapter describes the repair and replacement of the cooling system components. **Table 1** lists all of the cooling system specifications. **Table 1** is located at the end of this chapter. For routine maintenance and pressure testing of the system, refer to Chapter Three.

The cooling system must be cool prior to removing any component of the system.

WARNING
*Do **not** remove the radiator fill cap (**Figure 1**) when the engine is HOT. The coolant is very hot and is under pressure. Severe scalding could result if the escaping coolant comes in contact with your skin.*

HOSES AND HOSE CLAMPS

The small diameter coolant hoses are very stiff and are sometimes difficult to install onto the metal fittings of the various cooling system parts. Prior to installing the hoses, apply a small amount of Armor All or rubber lube to the inside surface of these hoses and they will slide on much easier.

Different type of hose clamps are used on the various hoses. Either the clamping screw type that is released with a screwdriver or the clamping band type where the ends must be pinched open with a pair of gas pliers. These clamps are used at specific locations due to space limitations around a specific part. Be sure to reinstall the correct type of clamp at the correct location.

COOLING SYSTEM CHECK

Two checks should be made before disassembly if a cooling system fault is suspected.

1. Run the engine until it reaches operating temperature. While the engine is running a pressure surge should be felt when the water pump outlet hose (**Figure 2**), is squeezed.

2. If a substantial coolant loss is noted, one of the head gaskets may be blown. In extreme cases sufficient coolant will leak into a cylinder(s) when the bike is left standing for several hours so the engine cannot be turned over with the starter. White smoke (steam) might also be observed at the muffler(s) when the engine is running. Coolant may also find its way into the oil supply. Check the dipstick; if it looks like green chocolate malt (milky or foamy) there is coolant in the oil system. If so, correct the cooling system immediately.

> *CAUTION*
> *After the cooling system problems are corrected, drain and thoroughly flush the engine oil system to eliminate all coolant residue. Refill with fresh engine oil; refer to Chapter Three. Recheck the condition of the oil and drain and refill if necessary.*

PRESSURE CHECK

If the cooling system requires repeated refilling, there is probably a leak somewhere in the system. Perform *Cooling System Inspection* in Chapter Three.

RADIATOR

Removal/Installation

Refer to **Figure 3** for this procedure.

1. Drain the cooling system as described under *Coolant Change* in Chapter Three.

2. Remove the seat as described in Chapter Thirteen.

3. Disconnect the battery negative lead as described under *Battery* in Chapter Three.

4. Remove the fuel tank as described under *Fuel Tank Removal/Installation* in Chapter Seven.

5. Remove the screws securing both the right- and left-hand frame head side covers. Remove both side covers.

6. Remove the screws securing the radiator cover (**Figure 4**) and remove the cover.

7. Loosen the radiator upper mounting bolt (**Figure 5**) and nut.

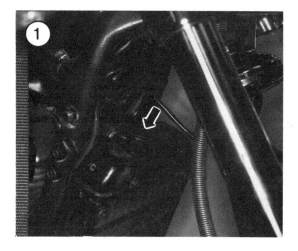

③
RADIATOR AND FAN ASSEMBLY

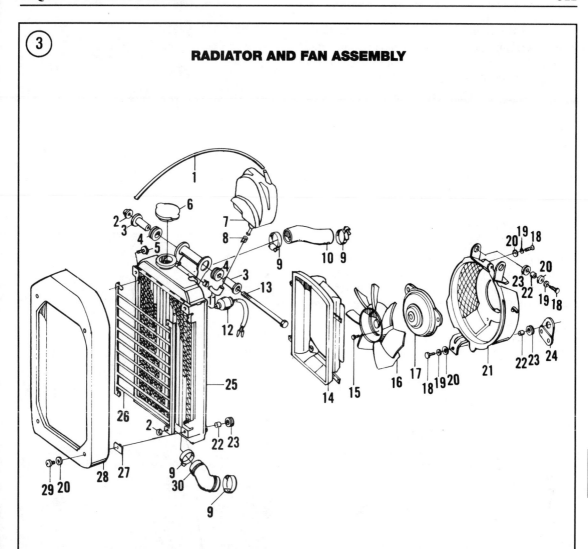

1. Overflow hose
2. Nut
3. Spacer
4. Rubber grommet
5. Bolt
6. Radiator cap
7. Coolant reserve cap
8. Hose clamp
9. Hose clamp
10. Radiator upper hose
11. Hose
12. Cooling fan switch
13. Bolt
14. Fan duct
15. Bolt
16. Fan blade
17. Fan motor
18. Bolt
19. Lockwasher
20. Washer
21. Fan shroud
22. Collar
23. Rubber grommet
24. Bracket
25. Radiator
26. Grille
27. Special nut
28. Radiator cap cover
29. Screw
30. Radiator lower hose

9

8. Loosen the clamping screw on the upper hose clamp (A, **Figure 6**). Move the clamp back onto the hose and off the neck of the front cylinder head fitting . Leave the hose attached to the radiator.

9. Loosen the clamping screw on the upper hose clamp (A, **Figure 7**). Move the clamp back onto the hose and off of the neck of the fitting on the frame rail. Leave the hose attached to the radiator.

10. Disconnect the fan motor thermo switch individual electrical connector (B, **Figure 6**).

11. Remove the bolt (B, **Figure 7**) securing the radiator at the bottom.

12. Remove the radiator upper mounting bolt (**Figure 5**) and nut loosened in Step 7.

13. Carefully pull the radiator and reserve tank (C, **Figure 6**) slightly forward and down. Remove the radiator and reserve tank assembly from the frame.

14. Install by reversing these removal steps, noting the following:

  a. Replace both radiator hoses if either is starting to deteriorate or is damaged.

  b. Make sure the fan motor thermo switch electrical connections are free of corrosion and are tight.

  c. Make sure the collar (A, **Figure 8**) is in place on each side of the radiator upper mount.

  d. Refill the cooling system with the recommended type and quantity of coolant as described in Chapter Three.

Inspection

1. If not already removed, remove the screws securing the grille (**Figure 9**) and remove the grille from the front of the radiator.

2. If compressed air is available, use short spurts of air directed to the *backside* of the radiator and blow out dirt and bugs.

3. Flush off the exterior of the radiator (A, **Figure 10**) with a garden hose on low pressure. Spray both the front and the back to remove all road dirt and bugs. Carefully use a whisk broom or stiff paint brush to remove any stubborn dirt.

> *CAUTION*
> *Do not press too hard or the cooling fins and tubes may be damaged causing a leak. Do not use a wire brush.*

4. Carefully straighten out any bent cooling fins with a broad tipped screwdriver or putty knife.

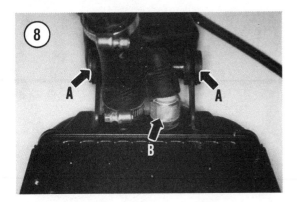

5. Check for cracks or leakage (usually a moss-green colored residue) at the filler neck, the inlet and outlet hose fittings (B, **Figure 10**) and the upper and lower tank seams (C, **Figure 10**).

6. Inspect the upper and lower (**Figure 11**) mounting brackets. Check for cracks or fractures and repair if necessary.

7. If the condition of the radiator is doubtful, have it checked as described under *Pressure Check* in Chapter Three. The radiator can be pressure checked while removed or installed on the bike.

8. To prevent oxidation to the radiator, touch up any area where the black paint is worn off. Use a good quality spray paint and apply several *light* coats of paint. Do not apply heavy coats as this will cut down on the cooling efficiency of the radiator.

9. If necessary, unscrew the thermostatic switch (B, **Figure 8**) from the radiator. Apply a silicone based sealant to the threads of the switch and install the switch in the radiator and tighten securely.

COOLING FAN, SHROUD AND FAN DUCT

Removal/Installation

Refer to **Figure 3** for this procedure.

1. Remove the radiator as described in this chapter.

2. Disconnect the thermostatic switch individual electrical connectors (B, **Figure 6**).

3. Remove the lower bolt, lockwasher and washer (**Figure 12**) securing the fan, fan shroud and fan duct assembly.

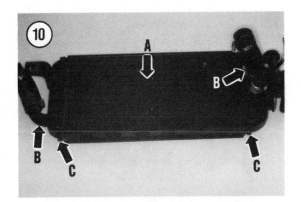

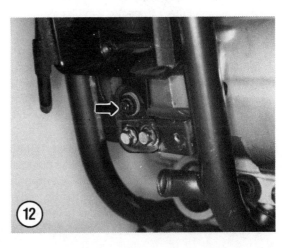

4. Remove the upper bolt, lockwasher and washer (A, **Figure 13**) securing the fan, fan shroud and fan duct assembly to each side.

5. Remove the assembly from the frame (B, **Figure 13**).

6. To remove the fan duct, remove the screws (A, **Figure 14**) securing the fan duct to the fan and fan shroud assembly. Remove the fan duct (A, **Figure 15**).

7. To remove the fan motor and fan, remove the screws (B, **Figure 14**) securing the assembly to the fan shroud and remove the assembly.

8. To remove the fan blade from the motor, remove the screws securing the fan blade (B, **Figure 15**). Remove the fan blade from the motor.

9. Install by reversing these removal steps, noting the following:

   a. Apply blue Loctite (No. 242) to the threads on the fan motor mounting screws. Install the screws and tighten securely.

   b. Refill the cooling system with the recommended type and quantity of coolant as described in Chapter Three.

THERMOSTAT AND HOUSING

Thermostat
Removal/Installation

The thermostat is located on the side of the water pump on the left-hand side of the engine just forward of the swing arm left-hand pivot point.

1. Drain the cooling system as described under *Coolant Change* in Chapter Three.

2. Remove the bolts (A, **Figure 16**) and acorn nut (B, **Figure 16**) securing the water pump trim cover and remove the cover.

3. Loosen the clamping screw on the water pump inlet hose clamps. Move the clamps back onto the hose and off of the neck of the fitting on the frame rail and water pump connector. Remove the hose (A, **Figure 17**) from both fittings.

4. Remove the screws securing the water pump connector (B, **Figure 17**) and remove the connector from the water pump cover. The thermostat may stay with the connector or with the water pump cover; remove the thermostat (**Figure 18**) from either part.

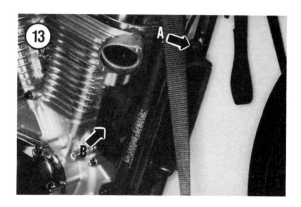

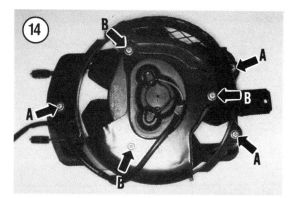

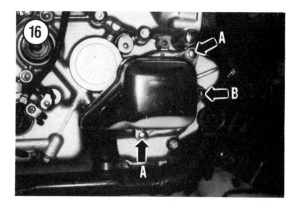

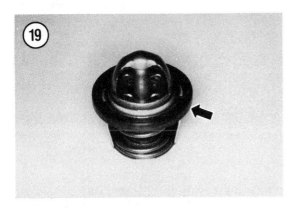

5. Clean the mating surfaces of both the water pump cover and the water pump connector of all dirt and any old coolant residue.

6. If reusing the same thermostat, inspect it as follows:

    a. Inspect the perimeter rubber seal (**Figure 19**) for damage or deterioration. Replace the thermostat if this area is damaged to prevent a coolant leak.

    b. Make sure the return spring (**Figure 20**) is operating correctly and has not sagged. Replace the thermostat if necessary.

7. Install the thermostat into the connector (**Figure 18**). Push it in until it seats completely. Make sure the rubber sealing surface of the thermostat is not damaged during installation.

8. Install the water pump connector (B, **Figure 17**) onto the water pump cover and install the screws. Tighten the screws securely in a crisscross pattern.

9. Replace the water pump inlet hose hoses if it is starting to deteriorate or is damaged.

10. Install the water pump inlet hose onto both fittings and tighten the clamping screw on the water pump inlet hose clamps.

11. Install the water pump trim cover, bolts (A, **Figure 16**) and acorn nut (B, **Figure 16**) and tighten securely.

12. Refill the cooling system with the recommended type and quantity of coolant as described in Chapter Three.

Thermostat Testing

Test the thermostat to ensure proper operation. The thermostat should be replaced if it remains open at normal room temperature or stays closed after the specified temperature has been reached during the test procedure.

1. Place the thermostat on a small piece of wood in a pan of water (**Figure 21**).

2. Place a thermometer in the pan of water (use a cooking or candy thermometer that is rated higher than the test temperature).

3. Gradually heat the water and continue to gently stir the water until it reaches 73.5-76.5° C (164.3-169.7° F). At this temperature the thermostat valve should start to open.

4. Continue to heat the water until the temperature reaches 90° C (194° F) and beyond. At this tempera-

ture, the thermostat valve should have opened to the maximum of 6.0 mm (0.24 in.).

> *NOTE*
> *Valve operation is sometimes sluggish;*
> *it usually takes 3-5 minutes for the valve*
> *to operate properly.*

5. If the valve fails to open in Step 3 or to the dimension listed in Step 4, the thermostat should be replaced (it cannot be serviced). Be sure to replace it with one of the correct temperature rating.

WATER PUMP

Removal

Refer to **Figure 22** for this procedure.

1. Drain the cooling system as described under *Coolant Change* in Chapter Three.

2. Remove the bolts (A, **Figure 16**) and acorn nut (B, **Figure 16**) securing the water pump trim cover and remove the trim cover.

3. Loosen the clamping screw on the water pump inlet hose clamps. Move the clamps back onto the hose and off of the neck of the fitting on the frame rail and water pump connector. Remove the hose (A, **Figure 17**) from both fittings.

> *NOTE*
> *The remaining steps are shown with*
> *the engine removed from the frame for*
> *clarity. It is not necessary to remove*
> *the engine for water pump removal*
> *and installation.*

4. Remove the remaining bolt (A, **Figure 23**) securing the water pump cover. Slide the cover off the threaded stud in the crankcase and remove the water pump cover (B, **Figure 23**) from the crankcase.

5. Rotate the impeller (**Figure 24**) until the holes in the impeller align with the Phillips screws securing the water pump assembly to the crankcase.

6. Remove the Phillips screws (**Figure 25**) securing the water pump assembly to the crankcase.

7. Withdraw the water pump and gasket from the crankcase.

8. If necessary, remove the bolts (A, **Figure 26**) securing the connector (B, **Figure 26**) to the water pump cover and remove the connector and thermostat.

Inspection

1. Inspect the water pump assembly for wear or damage. Rotate the impeller (A, **Figure 27**) and shaft to make sure the bearing (**Figure 28**) is not worn or damaged. If the bearing is damaged, replace the bearing.

2. Check the impeller blades for cracks or damage; replace the impeller if necessary.

3. Remove the O-ring seal (B, **Figure 27**) from the housing. This seal must be replaced each time the water pump is removed to prevent an oil leak. Install a new O-ring seal.

4. Remove the O-ring seal from the pump cover. This seal must be replaced each time the water pump is removed to prevent an coolant leak. Install a new O-ring seal.

Disassembly/Assembly

The water pump can be disassembled for replacement of the bearing, oil seal, mechanical seal and impeller. If only one or two of these parts is faulty;

WATER PUMP

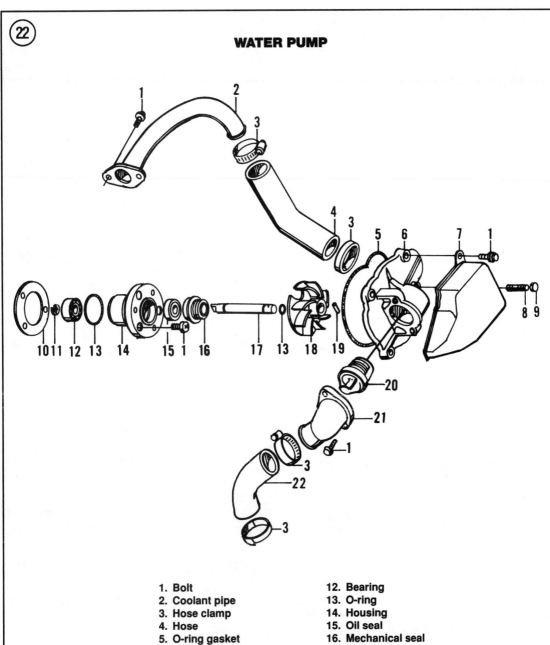

1. Bolt
2. Coolant pipe
3. Hose clamp
4. Hose
5. O-ring gasket
6. Water pump cover
7. Water pump trim cover
8. Threaded stud
9. Cap nut
10. Gasket
11. E-ring
12. Bearing
13. O-ring
14. Housing
15. Oil seal
16. Mechanical seal
17. Shaft
18. Impeller
19. Pin
20. Thermostat
21. Connector
22. Hose

9

replace them. If the condition of the water pump is doubtful and most of these parts require replacement it is suggested the water pump assembly be replaced with a new one.

Refer to **Figure 22** for this procedure.

> *CAUTION*
> *Do not try to remove the bearing from the housing without the Suzuki special tools. If substitute tools are used, the housing may be damaged and must be replaced.*

> *NOTE*
> ***Figure 29*** *is shown with the water pump removed from the crankcase, turned over, then set back into the crankcase to hold the assembly upside down in order to remove the E-clip.*

1. Remove the E-clip (**Figure 29**) securing the shaft into the water pump housing.

2. Carefully withdraw the impeller and shaft out of the housing and mechanical seal (**Figure 30**).

3. If necessary, remove the impeller and pin from the shaft.

4. If the mechanical seal is removed, also remove the oil seal in the housing behind it.

5. To remove the bearing, perform the following:

    a. Install the Suzuki special tool, bearing remover (part No. 09921-20200), into the backside of the housing.

    b. Attach the Suzuki special tool, sliding shaft (part No. 09930-30102), onto the bearing remover.

    c. Using the weight on the slide shaft, withdraw the bearing from the housing.

6. To remove the oil seal, use the same tool set-up and same procedure used for bearing removal.

7. To replace the mechanical seal, perform the following:

    a. Turn the housing over with the backside facing up and set it on 2 wood blocks.

    b. From the backside of the housing, carefully tap the mechanical seal out of the housing.

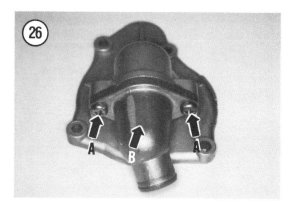

8. Apply clean engine oil to the outer surfaces of the new parts to be installed and to the inner surface of the housing. This will make installation easier.

9. Tap the oil seal, then the bearing into the housing using a socket of the appropriate size to fit the bearing outer race. Tap the bearing in until it seats.

10. Install a new oil seal and mechanical seal. Tap them in until they are completed seated.

11. If removed, install a new O-ring onto the shaft, then install the impeller and pin.

12. Apply clean engine oil to the shaft and install the shaft and impeller into the mechanical seal (**Figure 30**) and through the bearing at the other end.

13. Install the E-clip (**Figure 29**) securing the shaft into the water pump housing. Make sure the E-clip is properly seated in the shaft groove.

14. Rotate the impeller and shaft and make sure it rotates freely with no binding.

Installation

Refer to **Figure 22** for this procedure.

1. Install the thermostat into the connector (**Figure 18**). Push it in until it seats completely. Make sure the rubber sealing surface of the thermostat is not damaged during installation.

2. Install the water pump connector (B, **Figure 26**) onto the water pump cover and install the screws (A, **Figure 26**). Tighten the screws securely and evenly.

3. Install the water pump and new gasket into the crankcase.

4. Rotate the water pump housing until the mounting holes are aligned with the crankcase holes (**Figure 31**).

5. Install the Phillips screws (**Figure 25**) securing the water pump assembly to the crankcase and tighten securely.

9

6. Apply some cold grease into the groove in the backside of the water pump cover and install a new O-ring seal (**Figure 32**).

> *CAUTION*
> *Do not install the cover nor any fasteners until the assembly is completely seated against the crankcase. Do not try to force the assembly into place with the mounting bolts and nut as both the oil pump and the water pump may be damaged.*

7. Slide the cover over the threaded stud in the crankcase and push the water pump cover onto the crankcase until it seats completely. Make sure the O-ring seal is still in place.

8. Install the front upper bolt (A, **Figure 23**) securing the water pump cover. Tighten the bolt finger-tight at this time. It should be tightened later, after the cover and its bolts are installed.

9. Replace the water pump inlet hose if it is starting to deteriorate or is damaged.

10. Install the water pump inlet hose onto the connector and onto the fitting on the frame. Move the clamps into position and tighten securely.

11. Install the trim cover onto the water pump and install the bolts (A, **Figure 16**) and acorn nut (B, **Figure 16**). Tighten the bolts and nut securely in a crisscross patter. Be sure to tighten the bolt installed in Step 8.

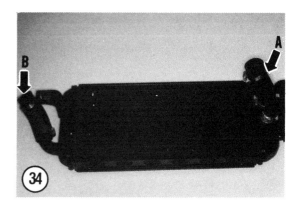

12. Refill the cooling system as described under *Coolant Change* in Chapter Three.

13. Start the bike and check for leaks.

HOSES

Hoses deteriorate with age and should be replaced periodically or whenever they show signs of cracking or leakage. To be safe, replace the hoses every 2 years. The spray of hot coolant from a cracked hose can injure the rider and passenger. Loss of coolant can also cause the engine to overheat causing damage.

Whenever any component of the cooling system is removed, inspect the hose(s) and determine if replacement is necessary.

Replacement

NOTE
*To replace both short sections of hose
that run between the cylinder heads and
the cylinders (**Figure 33**), one of the
cylinders must be removed. Refer to*

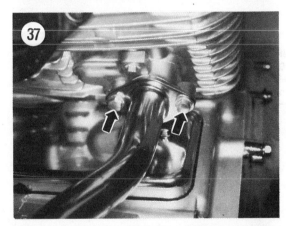

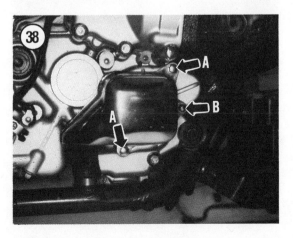

*Cylinder Head and Cylinder Removal
in Chapter Four.*

1. Drain the cooling system as described under
Coolant Change in Chapter Three.

*NOTE
The radiator upper and lower hoses are
very short and also very stiff. The working area around the frame upper hose is
very limited, therefore it is suggested
that the radiator first be removed from
the frame. Replace the hoses while the
radiator is removed from the frame.*

2. Remove the radiator as described in this chapter.
3. After the radiator is removed, perform the following:
   a. Loosen the clamping screw of the upper hose
      clamp. Move the clamp back onto the hose and
      off the neck of the radiator, then remove the
      upper hose (A, **Figure 34**) from the radiator.
   b. Loosen the clamping screw of the lower hose
      clamp. Move the clamp back onto the hose and
      off the neck of the radiator, then remove the
      lower hose (B, **Figure 34**) from the radiator.
4. To remove the water pump outlet hose, perform
the following:
   a. Remove the battery case (A, **Figure 35**) as
      described under *Battery Case Removal/Instal-
      lation* in Chapter Eight.

*NOTE
Figure 36 and **Figure 37** are shown
with the engine removed for clarity.*

   b. Loosen the clamping screw (**Figure 36**) on the
      water pump outlet hose fitting at the back of
      the crankcase. Move the clamp back onto the
      hose and off the neck of the fitting, then remove
      the hose (B, **Figure 35**) from the crankcase
      fitting.
   c. Remove the bolts (**Figure 37**) securing the
      metal coolant pipe to the rear cylinder.
   d. Move the metal coolant pipe (C, **Figure 35**)
      away from the cylinder.
   e. Remove the metal coolant pipe and rubber hose
      assembly from the engine and frame.
5. To remove the water pump inlet hose, perform
the following:
   a. Remove the bolts (A, **Figure 38**) and acorn nut
      (B, **Figure 38**) securing the water pump trim
      cover, then remove the trim cover.

b. Loosen the clamping screw on the water pump inlet hose clamps. Move the clamps back onto the hose and off the neck of the fitting on the frame rail and water pump connector.

c. Remove the hose (**Figure 39**) from both fittings.

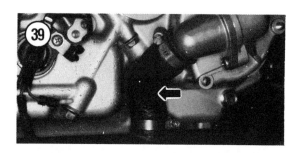

6. Install the new hoses along with the correct type of hose clamp. Tighten the clamps securely, but not so tight that the clamps cut into the new hose.

7. When installing the water pump outlet hose onto the rear cylinder, install a new O-ring seal (**Figure 40**) into the receptacle in the cylinder and apply a light coat of clean engine oil to the O-ring.

8. Install all of components that were removed.

9. Refill the cooling system with the recommended type and quantity of coolant. Refer to *Coolant Change* in Chapter Three.

10. Start the engine and check for leaks.

Table 1 COOLING SYSTEM SPECIFICATIONS

Coolant capacity	1.7 liters (1.8 U.S. qt. [1.5 Imp. qt.])
Radiator cap relief pressure	75-105 kPa (10.7-14.9 psi)
Thermostat begins to open	73.5-76.5° C (164.3-1169.7° F)
Valve lift	Minimum of 6 mm (0.24 in.) @ 90° C (194° F)

CHAPTER TEN

FRONT SUSPENSION AND STEERING

This chapter describes repair and maintenance procedures for the front wheel, front forks and steering components.

Front suspension torque specifications are covered in **Table 1**. **Tables 1-3** are located at the end of this chapter.

NOTE
Where differences occur relating to the United Kingdom (U.K.) models they are identified. If there is no (U.K.) designation relating to a procedure, photo or illustration it is identical to the United States (U.S.) models.

FRONT WHEEL

Removal

NOTE
The front brake disc is mounted on the left-hand side of the front wheel on 1985-1987 models (VS700) and mounted on the right-hand side of the front wheel on 1988-on models (VS750). This procedure is shown on a 1988 model.

CAUTION
Care must be taken when removing, handling and installing a wheel with a disc brake rotor. The rotor is relatively

*thin in order to dissipate heat and to minimize unsprung weight. The rotor is designed to withstand tremendous rotational loads, but can be damaged when subjected to side impact loads. If the rotor is knocked out of true by a side impact, a pulsation will be felt in the front brake lever when braking. The rotor is too thin to be trued and must be replaced with a new one. Protect the rotor when transporting a wheel to a dealer or tire specialist for tire service. Do **not** place a wheel in a car trunk or pickup bed without protecting the rotor from side impact.*

1. On 1987-on models, remove the front axle trim cap (**Figure 1**) from each fork leg.

2. On 1985 and 1986 models, remove the cotter pin and the front axle nut from the right-hand side.

3. Loosen the front axle pinch bolt (**Figure 2**).

4A. On 1987 models, loosen the front axle from the fork leg.

4B. On 1988-on models, loosen the front axle (**Figure 3**) from the right-hand fork leg.

5. Place wood blocks under the footpeg assembly to support the bike securely with the front wheel off the ground.

6. Remove the speedometer cable (**Figure 4**) from the speedometer gear box.

7A. On 1985 and 1986 models, withdraw the front axle.

7B. On 1987-on models, completely unscrew the axle from the right- or left-hand fork leg and remove the axle.

8. Pull the wheel down and forward and remove the wheel from the front fork and the brake caliper.

NOTE
Insert a piece of vinyl tubing or wood in the caliper in place of the brake disc. That way if the brake lever is inadvertently squeezed, the piston will not be forced out of the cylinder. If this does happen, the caliper may have to be disassembled to reseat the piston and the system will have to be bled. By using the wood, bleeding the brake is not necessary when installing the wheel.

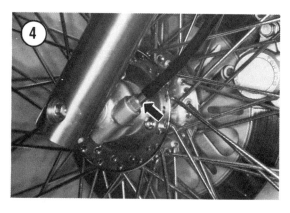

9. Remove the spacer (**Figure 5**) from the brake disc side of the hub.

10A. On 1985-1987 models, remove the spacer and speedometer gear box from the other side of the hub.

10B. On 1988-on models, remove the speedometer gear box from the other side of the hub.

> *CAUTION*
> *Do not set the wheel down on the disc surface as it may get scratched or warped. Set the sidewalls on 2 wood blocks (**Figure 6**).*

Installation

1. Make sure the axle bearing surfaces of the fork sliders and axle are free from burrs and nicks.

2. Install the spacer (**Figure 5**) into the brake disc side of the hub.

3. Align the tangs of the speedometer drive gear (**Figure 7**) with the notches in the front hub and install the speedometer gear box. Make sure the gear box seats completely. If the speedometer components do not mesh properly, the wheel hub components will be too wide for installation.

4. On 1985-1987 models, install the spacer on top of the speedometer gear box.

5. Position the wheel, inserting the brake disc into the caliper carefully to prevent damage to the brake pads.

6. Apply a light coat of grease to the front axle. Insert the front axle through the fork leg, speedometer gear box and the wheel hub.

7. Make sure that spacer (**Figure 8**) is still in place on the brake disc side of the wheel.

8A. On 1985 and 1986 models, install the front axle, then install the front axle nut, but do not tighten it.

8B. On 1987-on models, screw the axle into the right-or left-hand fork leg, but do not tighten it.

9. Slowly rotate the wheel and install the speedometer cable into the speedometer housing (**Figure 4**). Position the speedometer housing and cable so that the cable does not have a sharp bend in it.

10. Tighten the front axle, or axle nut, to the torque specification listed in **Table 1**.

11. Remove the wood block(s) from under the footpeg assembly.

12. With the front brake applied, push down hard on the handlebars and pump the forks several times to seat the front axle.

10

13. Tighten the front axle pinch bolt (**Figure 2**) to the torque specification listed in **Table 1**.

14. After the wheel is completely installed, rotate it several times to make sure that it rotates freely. Apply the front brake as many times as necessary to make sure all brake pads are against the brake disc correctly.

15. On 1987-on models, install the front axle trim cap (**Figure 1**) into each fork leg.

Inspection

1. Remove any corrosion from the front axle with a piece of fine emery cloth. Clean axle with solvent, then wipe the axle clean with a lint-free cloth.

2. Check axle runout. Place the axle on V-blocks and place the tip of a dial indicator in the middle of the axle (**Figure 9**). Rotate the axle and check runout. If the runout exceeds 0.25 mm (0.010 in.), replace the axle; do not attempt to straighten it.

3. Check rim runout as follows:
   a. Remove the tire from the rim as described in this chapter.
   b. Measure the radial (up and down) runout of the wheel rim with a dial indicator as shown at A, **Figure 10**. If runout exceeds 2.0 mm (0.08 in.), check the wheel bearings.
   c. Measure the axial (side to side) runout of the wheel rim with a dial indicator as shown at B, **Figure 10**. If runout exceeds 2.0 mm (0.08 in.), check the wheel bearings.
   d. If the wheel bearings are okay, wire wheels can be trued as described under *Wire Wheel Spoke Adjustment* in this chapter. Cast wheels cannot be serviced, but must be replaced.
   e. Replace the front wheel bearings as described under *Front Hub* in this chapter.

4. Inspect the wheel rim (**Figure 11**) for dents, bending or cracks. Check the rim and rim sealing surface for scratches that are deeper than 0.5 mm (0.01 in.). If any of these conditions are present, replace the rim (wire wheels) or wheel (case wheels).

Speedometer Gear Box Inspection and Lubrication

> *NOTE*
> *The speedometer gear box is a sealed assembly and no replacement parts are*

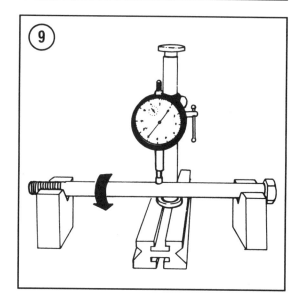

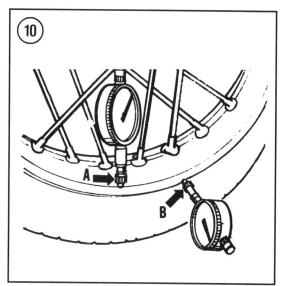

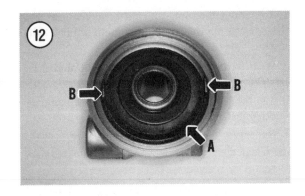

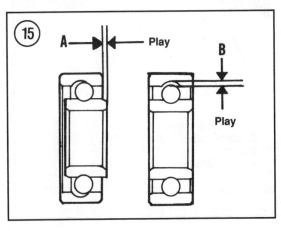

available. If any part of the gear box is defective the entire assembly must be replaced.

1. Remove the front wheel as described in this chapter.

2. Inspect the oil seal (A, **Figure 12**) for leakage.

3. Inspect the tangs (B, **Figure 12**) of the speedometer drive gear for wear or damage.

4. Inspect the notches (**Figure 13**) in the front hub for wear or damage. Repair the hub or replace the wheel.

5. Install the front wheel as described in this chapter.

FRONT HUB

Inspection

Inspect each wheel bearing prior to removing it from the wheel hub.

CAUTION
Do not remove the wheel bearings for inspection purposes as they will be damaged during the removal process. Remove wheel bearings only if they are to be replaced.

1. Perform Steps 1-4 of *Disassembly* in the following procedure.

2. Turn each bearing by hand. Make sure bearings turn smoothly.

3. Inspect the play of the inner race (**Figure 14**) of each wheel bearing. Check for excessive axial play (A, **Figure 15**) and radial play (B, **Figure 15**). Replace the bearing if it has an excess amount of free play.

4. On non-sealed bearings, check the balls for evidence of wear, pitting or excessive heat (bluish tint). Replace the bearings if necessary; always replace as a complete set. When replacing the bearings, be sure to take your old bearings along to ensure a perfect matchup.

NOTE
Fully sealed bearings are available from many bearing specialty shops. Fully sealed bearings provide better protection from dirt and moisture that may get into the hub.

10

Disassembly

Refer to the following illustrations for this procedure:

    a. **Figure 16**: wire wheel.

    b. **Figure 17**: cast wheel.

1. Remove the front wheel as described in this chapter.

2. Remove the spacer (**Figure 5**) from the brake disc side of the hub.

3A. On 1985-1987 models, remove the spacer and speedometer gear box from the other side of the hub.

3B. On 1988-on models, remove the speedometer gear box (**Figure 18**) from the other side of the hub.

4. If necessary, remove the bolts (**Figure 19**) securing the brake disc and remove the disc.

5. Before proceeding further, inspect the wheel bearings as described in this chapter. If they must be replaced, proceed as follows.

6. To remove the right- and left-hand bearings and distance collar, insert a soft aluminum or brass drift into one side of the hub.

7. Push the distance collar over to one side and place the drift on the inner race of the lower bearing.

8. Tap the bearing out of the hub with a hammer, working around the perimeter of the inner race.

9. Repeat for the bearing on the other side.

10. Clean the inside and the outside of the hub with solvent. Dry with compressed air.

Assembly

1. On non-sealed bearings, pack the bearings with a good quality bearing grease. Work the grease in between the balls thoroughly; turn the bearing by hand a couple of times to make sure the grease is distributed evenly inside the bearing.

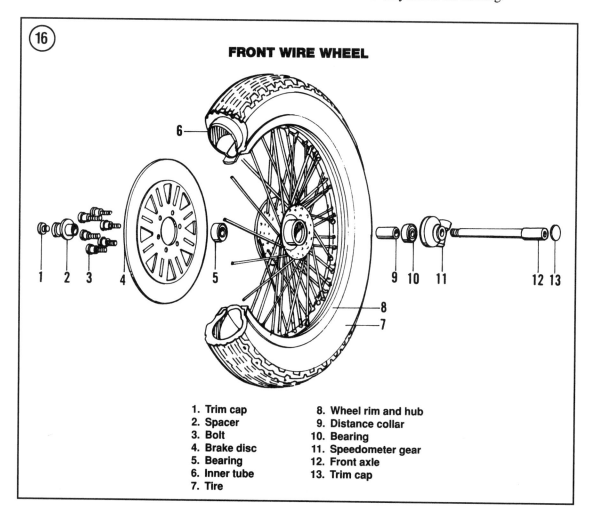

FRONT WIRE WHEEL

1. Trim cap
2. Spacer
3. Bolt
4. Brake disc
5. Bearing
6. Inner tube
7. Tire
8. Wheel rim and hub
9. Distance collar
10. Bearing
11. Speedometer gear
12. Front axle
13. Trim cap

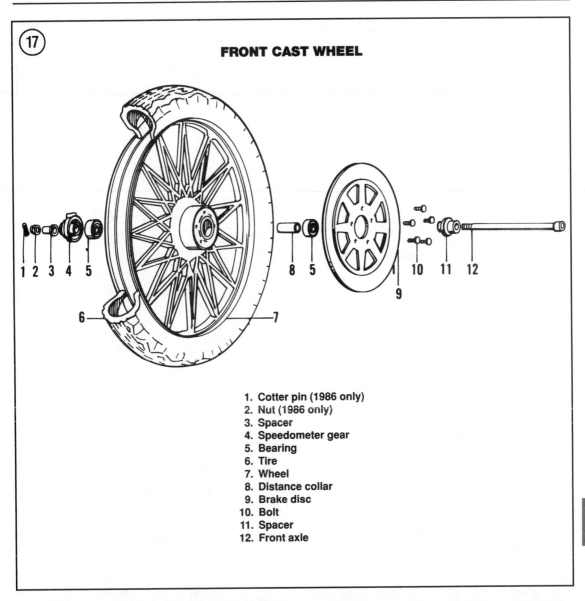

FRONT CAST WHEEL

1. Cotter pin (1986 only)
2. Nut (1986 only)
3. Spacer
4. Speedometer gear
5. Bearing
6. Tire
7. Wheel
8. Distance collar
9. Brake disc
10. Bolt
11. Spacer
12. Front axle

10

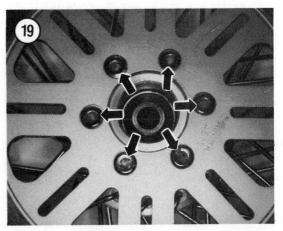

2. Blow any dirt or foreign matter out of the hub prior to installing the bearings.

CAUTION
Install non-sealed bearings with the single sealed side facing outward. Tap the bearings squarely into place and tap on the outer race only. Do not tap on the inner race or the bearing might be damaged. Be sure that the bearings are completely seated.

3A. A special Suzuki tool set-up (Suzuki part No. 09924-84510) can be used to install the wheel bearings as follows:

a. Install the right-hand bearing into the hub first.

b. Set the bearing with the sealed side facing out and install the bearing installer as shown in **Figure 20**.

c. Tighten the bearing installer (**Figure 21**) and pull the right-hand bearing into the hub until it is completely seated. Remove the bearing installer.

d. Turn the wheel over (right-hand side up) on the workbench and install the distance collar.

e. Set the left-hand bearing with the sealed side facing out and install the bearing installer as shown in **Figure 22**.

NOTE
*Suzuki does not specify what "a slight clearance" is equivalent to. The important thing is that the 2 parts are **not** pressed up against each other.*

f. Tighten the bearing installer and pull the left-hand bearing into the hub until there is *a slight clearance* between the inner race and the distance collar.

g. Remove the bearing installer.

3B. If special tools are not used, perform the following:

a. Tap the right-hand bearing squarely into place and tap on the outer race only. Use a socket (**Figure 23**) that matches the outer race diameter. Do not tap on the inner race or the bearing might be damaged. Be sure that the bearing is completely seated (**Figure 14**).

b. Turn the wheel over (right-hand side up) on the workbench and install the distance collar.

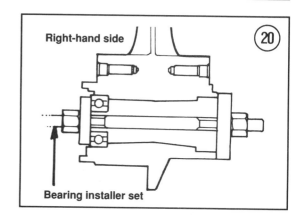
Right-hand side — Bearing installer set

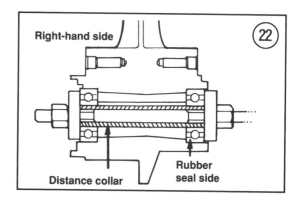
Right-hand side — Distance collar — Rubber seal side

c. Use the same tool set-up and drive in the left-hand bearing.

4. If the brake disc was removed, perform the following:

   a. Apply red Loctite (No. 271) to the brake disc bolts prior to installation.

   b. Install the brake disc and bolts (**Figure 19**). Tighten to the torque specifications listed in **Table 1**.

5. Install the spacer (**Figure 5**) into the brake disc side of the hub.

6. Align the tangs of the speedometer drive gear (**Figure 7**) with the notches in the front hub and install the speedometer gear box. Make sure the gear box seats completely. If the speedometer compo-nents do not mesh properly the hub components of the wheel will be too wide for installation.

7. On 1985-1987 models, install the spacer on top of the speedometer gear box.

8. Install the front wheel as described in this chapter.

WHEELS

Wheel Balance

An unbalanced wheel is unsafe. Depending on the degree of unbalance and the speed of the motorcycle, the rider may experience anything from a mild vibration to a violent shimmy which may even result in loss of control.

The weights are attached to the wheel spokes or to the rim on cast wheels. Weight kits are available from motorcycle dealers. Before you attempt to balance the wheel, check to be sure that the wheel bearings are in good condition and properly lubricated. The wheel must rotate freely.

NOTE
When balancing the wheels do so with the brake disc attached. The brake disc rotates with the wheel and will affect the balance.

1. Remove the wheel as described in this chapter or Chapter Ten.

2. Mount the wheel on a fixture such as the one shown in **Figure 24** so it can rotate freely.

3. Give the wheel a spin and let it coast to a stop. Mark the tire at the lowest point (**Figure 25**).

4. Spin the wheel several more times. If the wheel keeps coming to rest at the same point, it is out of balance.

5A. On cast wheels, tape a test weight to the upper (or light) side of the wheel.

5B. On wire wheels, attach a test weight to the upper (or light) side of the wheel at the spoke or tape a test weight (**Figure 26**) to the rim.

6. Experiment with different weights until the wheel, when spun, comes to a rest at a different position each time.

7. Remove the test weight and install the correct size weight.

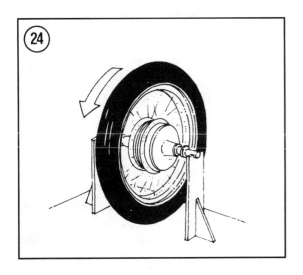

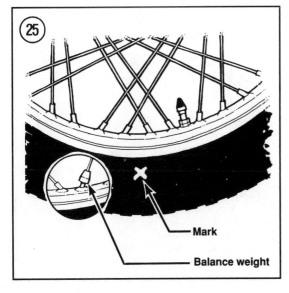

Mark

Balance weight

10

Wire Wheel
Spoke Adjustment

Spokes loosen with use and should be checked periodically. If all appear loose, tighten all spokes on one side of the hub, then tighten all spokes on the other side with a spoke wrench. One-half to one turn should be sufficient; do not overtighten.

After tightening the spokes, check the rim runout to make sure you haven't pulled the rim out of shape. One way to check rim runout is to mount a dial indicator to the front fork or swing arm so that it bears on the rim.

If you don't have a dial indicator, fabricate the tester shown in **Figure 27**. Adjust the position of the bolt until it just clears the wheel rim. Rotate the wheel and note whether the clearance between the bolt and the rim increases or decreases. Mark the tire with chalk or crayon in areas that produce significantly large or small clearances. Clearance must not change by more than 2 mm (0.08 in.).

To pull the rim out, tighten the spokes which terminates on the same side of the hub (**Figure 28**). In most cases, only a small amount of adjustment is necessary to true a rim. After adjustment, rotate the wheel and make sure another area has not been pulled out of true. Continue adjusting and checking until the runout does not exceed 2 mm (0.08 in.).

TIRES

Tire Safety

After installing new tires on the bike, break them in correctly. Remember that a new tire has relatively poor adhesion to the road surface until it is broken in properly. Don't subject a new tire to any high speed riding for at least the first 60 miles (100 km).

Even after the tires are broken in properly, always warm them up prior to the first ride of the day. This will lessen the possibility of loss of control of the bike. If you have purchased a tire brand other than those originally installed by the factory, maintain the correct tire inflation pressure recommended by *that tire manufacturer* and not those listed in **Table 2** located in Chapter Three. **Table 2** is for original equipment tires only.

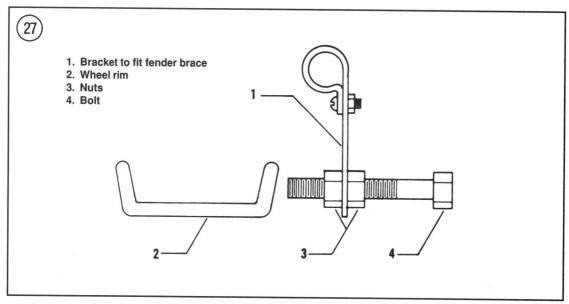

1. **Bracket to fit fender brace**
2. **Wheel rim**
3. **Nuts**
4. **Bolt**

**Tubeless Tires
(Cast Wheels Only)**

WARNING
Do not install an inner tube inside a tubeless tire. The tube will cause an abnormal heat buildup in the tire.

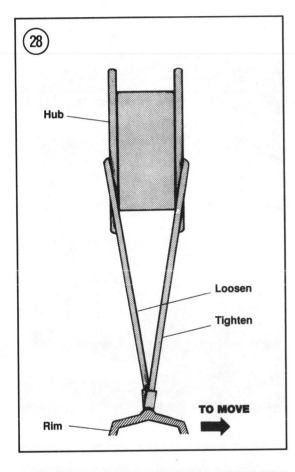

Tubeless tires have the word "TUBELESS" molded into the tire sidewall and the rims have "SUITABLE FOR TUBELESS TIRES," "TUBELESS TIRE APPLICABLE," or equivalent cast into them.

NOTE
Tube type tires have the word "TUBE TYPE" (Figure 29) molded into the tire.

When a tubeless tire is flat, it should be removed from the rim to inspect the inside of the tire and to apply a combination plug/patch from the inside. Don't rely on a plug or cord repair applied from outside the tire. They might be okay on a car, but they're too dangerous on a motorcycle.

After repairing a tubeless tire, don't exceed 50 mph (80 kph) for the first 24 hours. Never race on a repaired tubeless tire. The patch could work loose from tire flexing and heat.

TIRE CHANGING

The wheels can easily be damaged during tire removal. Special care must be taken with tire irons when changing a tire to avoid scratches and gouges to the outer rim surface. Insert scraps of leather between the tire iron and the rim to protect the rim from damage. The stock wire wheels are designed for use with tube type tires while the stock cast wheels are designed for use with tubeless tires.

When removing a tubeless tire, take care not to damage the tire beads, inner liner of the tire or the wheel rim flange. Use tire levers or flat handled tire irons with rounded ends.

NOTE
This procedure applies to both tube type and tubeless tires. Where differences occur regarding inner tube removal and installation they are identified.

Removal

1. If you are going to reinstall the existing tire, mark the valve stem location on the tire (**Figure 30**) so the tire can be installed in the same position for easier balancing.

2. Remove the valve stem core to deflate the tire. On tube type tires, unscrew the locknut (**Figure 31**) from the valve stem.

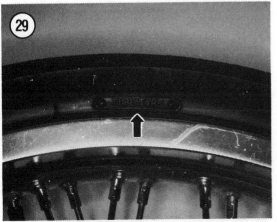

10

3. Press the entire bead on both sides of the tire into
the center of the rim. Make sure the tire is broken
loose around the entire perimeter of the wheel.

4. Lubricate the beads with soapy water.

5. Insert the tire iron under the bead next to the valve
(**Figure 33**). Force the bead on the opposite side of
the tire into the center of the rim and pry the bead
over the rim with the tire iron.

6. Insert a second tire iron next to the first to hold
the bead over the rim. Then work around the tire with
the first tire iron, prying the bead over the rim. On
tube type tires, be careful not to pinch the inner tube
with the tire irons.

7. On tube type tires, remove the valve from the hole
in the rim and remove the inner tube from the tire.

8. Stand the tire on end or turn it over. Insert the tire
iron between the second bead and the side of the rim
that the first bead was pried over (**Figure 34**). Force
the bead on the opposite side from the tire iron into
the center of the rim. Pry the second bead off the rim,
working around as with the first. Remove the tire
from the rim.

9. Inspect the rim as described in this chapter.

Tire and Rim Inspection

1. Wipe off the inner surfaces of the wheel rim.
Clean off any rubber residue or any oxidation.

2. On tubeless tires, if a can of pressurized tire
sealant was used for a temporary fix of a flat, thoroughly clean off all sealant residue from the rim

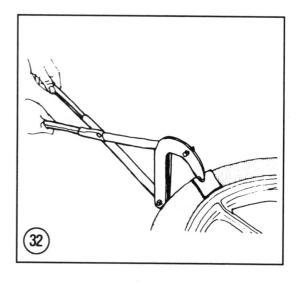

surfaces. Any remaining residue will present a problem when reinstalling the tire and achieving a good seal of the tire bead against the rim.

3. On cast wheels, inspect the rim inner flange. Smooth any scratches on the rim-to-tire sealing surface with emery cloth. If a scratch is deeper than 0.5 mm (0.020 in.), the wheel should be replaced.

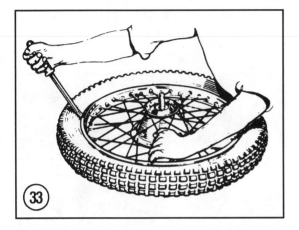

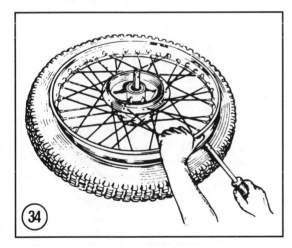

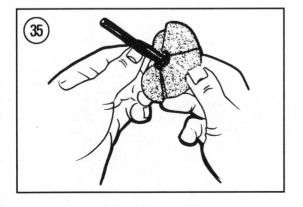

WARNING
*Carefully consider whether a tire should be patched or replaced. If there is any doubt about the quality of the existing tire, **replace it with a new one**. Don't take a chance on a tire failure at any speed.*

4. If a tire is going to be patched, thoroughly inspect the tire.

5. On tubeless tires, if any one of the following are observed, do not repair the tire; *replace it with a new one:*

   a. A puncture or split whose total length or diameter exceeds 6 mm (0.24 in.).
   b. A scratch or split on the side wall.
   c. Any type of ply separation.
   d. Tread separation or excessive abnormal wear pattern.
   e. Tread depth of less than 1.6 mm (0.06 in.) in the front tire or less than 2.0 mm (0.08 in.) in the rear tire on original equipment tires. Aftermarket tires tread depth minimum may vary.
   f. Scratches on either sealing bead.
   g. The cord is cut in any place.
   h. Flat spots in the tread from skidding.
   i. Any abnormality in the inner liner.

5. On tubeless tires, do not relay on a plug or cord patch applied from outside the tire. Use a combination plug/patch (**Figure 35**) applied from inside the tire. Apply the plug/patch, following the instructions supplied with the patch kit.

6. On tubeless tires, inspect the valve stem seal. Because rubber deteriorates with age, it is advisable to replace the valve stem when replacing the tire.

7. Inspect the valve stem hole in the rim. Remove any dirt or corrosion from the hole and wipe dry with a clean cloth.

Installation

1. A new tire may have balancing rubbers inside. These are not patches and should not be disturbed or removed.

2. On tube type tires, if the wheel was serviced, check that the spoke ends do not protrude through the nipples into the center of the rim. If they do they will puncture the inner tube. File off any protruding spoke ends.

3. On tube type tires, make sure the rubber rim tape is in place with the rough side toward the rim.

10

4A. On tube type tires, install the tube valve stem core into the tube valve. Place the tube into the tire and inflate it just enough to round it out. Too much air will make installing the tire difficult and too little air will increase the chances of pinching the tube with the tire irons.

NOTE
Step 4B relates to metal valve stems on tubeless tire only.

4B. On tubeless tires, install a new valve stem as follows:

a. Insert the new valve stem into the rim.

b. Install the nut and tighten with your fingers only. Do not use pliers and overtighten the nut as it may distort the rubber sealing grommet that could result in an air leak.

c. Hold onto the nut and install and tighten the locknut securely.

d. Inspect the valve stem core rubber seal for hardness or deterioration. Replace the valve stem core if necessary.

5. If the tire was completely removed, lubricate both beads of the tire with soapy water. If only one side was removed, lubricate the exposed rim bead.

6. When installing the tire onto the rim make sure the correct tire, either front or rear is installed onto the correct wheel and also that the direction arrow (**Figure 36**) faces the direction of wheel rotation.

7. If remounting the old tire, align the mark made in Step 1, *Removal* with the valve stem. If a new tire is being installed, align the colored spot near the bead (indicating a lighter point on the tire) with the valve stem.

8. If the tire was completely removed from the rim, place the backside of the tire into the center of the rim (**Figure 37**). The lower bead should go into the center of the rim and the upper bead outside. Work around the tire in both directions (**Figure 38**). Use a tire iron for the last few inches of bead (**Figure 39**).

9. Press the upper bead into the rim opposite the valve stem. Pry the bead into the rim on both sides of the initial point with a tire iron, working around the rim to the valve (**Figure 40**).

10. On tube type tires, wiggle the valve stem to be sure the tube is not trapped under the tire bead. Set the valve squarely in the rim hole before screwing on the valve stem nut.

11. Check the bead on both sides of the tire for even fit around the rim.

12. Bounce the wheel several times, rotating it each time. This will force the tire beads against the rim flanges. After the tire beads are in contact with the rim evenly, inflate the tire to seat the beads.

13. On tubeless tires, place an inflatable band around the circumference of the tire. Slowly inflate the band until the tire beads are pressed against the

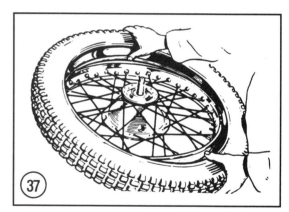

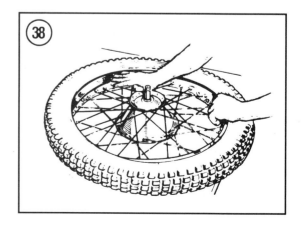

rim. Inflate the tire enough to seat it, deflate the band and remove it.

WARNING
In the next step inflate the tire to approximately 10-15% over the recommended inflation pressure. Do not exceed this pressure as the tire could burst causing severe injury. Never stand directly over a tire while inflating it.

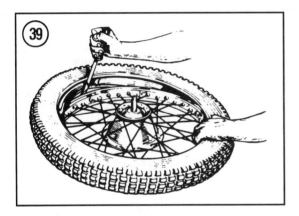

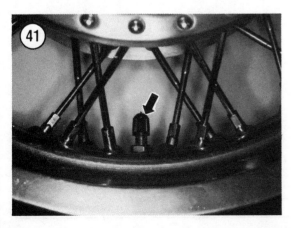

14. After inflating the tire, check to see that the beads are fully seated and that the tire rim lines are the same distance from the rim all the way around the tire. If the beads won't seat, deflate the tire and re-lubricate the rim and beads with soapy water.

15. Re-inflate the tire to the required pressure listed in **Table 2**. Install the valve stem cap (**Figure 41**). Always make sure to install the cap as the cap prevents small pebbles and dirt from collecting in the valve stem; this could allow air leakage or result in incorrect tire pressure readings.

16. Balance the wheel as described in this chapter.

WARNING
If you have repaired a tire, do not ride the bike any faster than 50 mph (80 km/h) for the first 24 hours. It takes at least 24 hours for a patch to cure. Also **never** *ride the bike faster than 80 mph (130 km/h) with a repaired tire.*

TIRE REPAIRS

Patching a tube or tubeless tire on the road is very difficult. A can of pressurized tire sealant may inflate the tire and seal the hole, although this is only a temporary fix. On tubeless tires, the beads must be against the rim for this method to work. Another solution is to carry a spare inner tube that could be installed and inflated. This will enable you to get to a service station where the tire can be correctly repaired.

Suzuki (and the tire industry) recommends that the tubeless tire be patched from the inside. Use a combination plug/patch applied from the inside the tire (**Figure 35**). Do not patch the tire with an external type plug. If you find an external patch on the tire, it is recommended that it be patch-reinforced from the inside Due to the variations of material supplied with different tubeless tire repair kits, follow the instructions and recommendations supplied with the repair kit.

HANDLEBAR

Handlebar Assembly Removal/Installation

Refer to the following illustrations for this procedure:

a. **Figure 42**: Handlebars.

10

b. **Figure 43**: Steering stem (1985-1987).

c. **Figure 44**: Steering stem (1988-on).

NOTE
*If it is not necessary to remove the components from the handlebar for service, perform this procedure. If component removal is necessary, refer to the **Disassembly/Assembly** in the following procedure.*

1. Remove the fuel tank as described under *Fuel tank Removal/Installation* in Chapter Seven.

2. Disconnect the brake light switch electrical connector from the brake lever.

3. Disconnect the starter interlock switch electrical connector from the clutch lever.

CAUTION
Cover the surrounding area with a heavy cloth or plastic tarp to protect it from accidental spilling of clutch and brake fluid. Wash any spilled clutch or brake fluid off any painted or plated surface immediately, as it will destroy the finish. Use soapy water and rinse thoroughly.

4. Remove the trim cap (**Figure 45**) from the Allen bolts.

5. Remove the Allen bolts (**Figure 46**) securing the handlebar upper holders.

6. Remove the upper holders and the handlebar assembly.

7. Move the handlebar assembly back and rest it on the frame.

8. Secure the handlebar assembly so the clutch and brake master cylinder reservoirs remain in the upright position. This is to minimize loss of hydraulic fluid and to keep air from entering into the clutch and brake system. It is not necessary to remove either hydraulic line.

9. Install by revering these removal steps, noting the following:

   a. Tighten the Allen bolts to the torque specification listed in **Table 1**. Tighten the front bolts first then the rear so there is a slight gap at the rear between the handlebar upper and lower holders (**Figure 47**).

   b. Check the throttle operation. If necessary, adjust the throttle operation as described in Chapter Three.

WARNING
*After installation is completed, make sure the brake lever does not come in contact with the throttle grip assembly when it is pulled on fully. If it does the brake fluid may be low in the reservoir; refill as necessary. Refer to **Front Disc Brakes** in Chapter Eleven.*

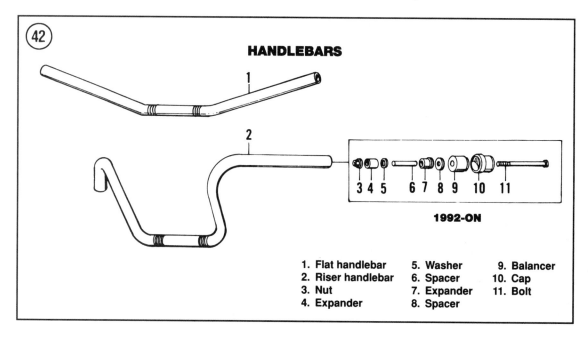

HANDLEBARS

1992-ON

1. Flat handlebar
2. Riser handlebar
3. Nut
4. Expander
5. Washer
6. Spacer
7. Expander
8. Spacer
9. Balancer
10. Cap
11. Bolt

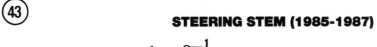

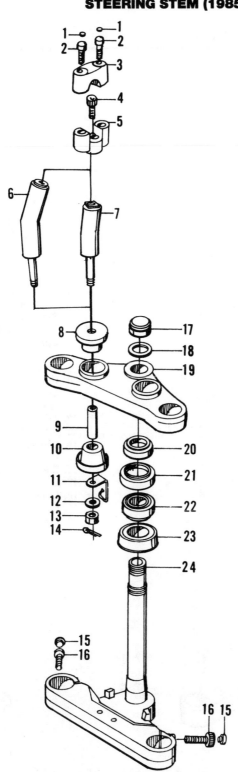

STEERING STEM (1985-1987)

1. Trim cap
2. Allen bolt
3. Handlebar upper holder
4. Allen bolt
5. Handlebar lower holder
6. Extension
7. Extension
8. Upper rubber cushion
9. Spacer
10. Lower rubber cushion
11. Clamp
12. Washer
13. Nut
14. Cotter pin
15. Trim cap
16. Allen bolt
17. Steering stem cap nut
18. Washer
19. Upper fork bridge
20. Steering stem nut
21. Dust seal
22. Upper bearing
23. Lower bearing
24. Steering stem

10

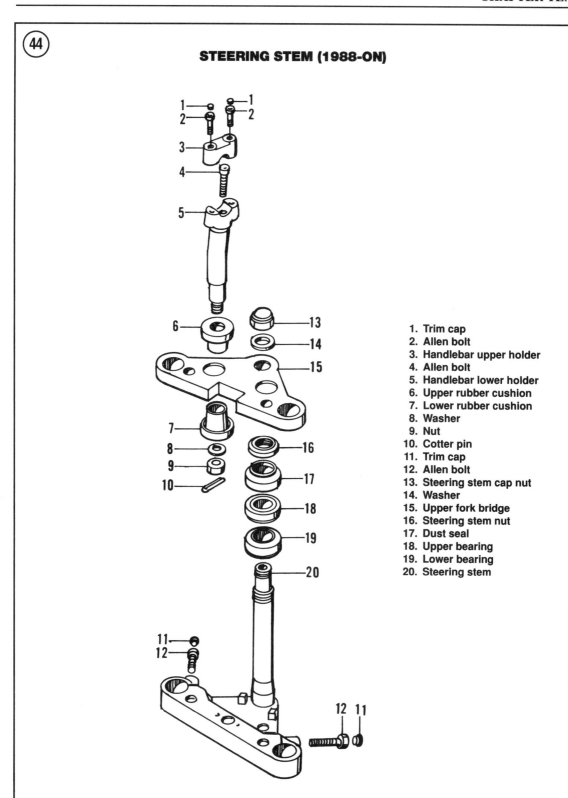

STEERING STEM (1988-ON)

1. Trim cap
2. Allen bolt
3. Handlebar upper holder
4. Allen bolt
5. Handlebar lower holder
6. Upper rubber cushion
7. Lower rubber cushion
8. Washer
9. Nut
10. Cotter pin
11. Trim cap
12. Allen bolt
13. Steering stem cap nut
14. Washer
15. Upper fork bridge
16. Steering stem nut
17. Dust seal
18. Upper bearing
19. Lower bearing
20. Steering stem

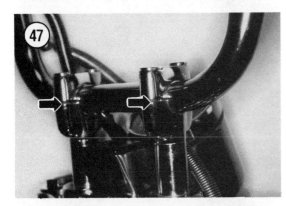

Handlebar and Component Removal/Installation

Refer to the following illustrations for this procedure:

    a. **Figure 42**: Handlebars.
    b. **Figure 43**: Steering stem (1985-1987).
    c. **Figure 44**: Steering stem (1988-on).

NOTE
If it is necessary to remove the components from the handlebar for service, perform this procedure. If component removal is not necessary, only the removal of the handlebar assembly; refer to the preceding procedure.

Right-hand side of handlebar

1. Remove the screws securing the right-hand handlebar switch assembly (**Figure 48**) together.

2. Partially remove the upper half and disconnect the throttle cable from the throttle assembly. Carefully lay the throttle cable over the fender or back over the frame. Be careful that the cable does not get crimped or damaged.

3. Remove the screw (**Figure 49**) securing the engine stop switch electrical connector to the switch assembly.

4. Disconnect the brakelight switch electrical connector (A, **Figure 50**) from the brake switch.

5. Remove the lower half of the right-hand switch assembly (B, **Figure 50**) from the handlebar.

6. Unscrew the rear view mirror (C, **Figure 50**) from the master cylinder.

10

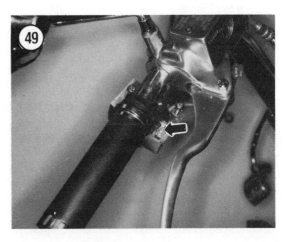

7. Remove the clamping bolts and clamp (D, **Figure 50**) securing the front brake master cylinder to the handlebar.

CAUTION
Cover the surrounding area with a heavy cloth or plastic tarp to protect it from accidental spilling of brake fluid. Wash any spilled brake fluid off any painted or plated surface immediately, as it will destroy the finish. Use soapy water and rinse thoroughly.

8. Remove the front brake master cylinder from the handlebar. Tie the front brake master cylinder to the frame and keep the reservoir in the upright position. This is to minimize loss of brake fluid and to keep air from entering into the brake system. It is not necessary to remove the hydraulic brake line.
9. On 1992-on models, remove the long screw securing the right-hand balance set and remove all parts from the end of the handlebar.
10. Slide the throttle assembly (E, **Figure 50**) from the handlebar. Carefully lay the throttle cable over the fender or back over the frame. Be careful that the cable does not get crimped or damaged.
11. Remove the components from the left-hand side of the handlebar.
12. To remove the handlebar from the fork bridge, perform the following:
  a. Remove the trim cap (**Figure 45**) from the Allen bolts.
  b. Remove the Allen bolts (**Figure 46**) securing the handlebar upper holders.
  c. Remove the upper holders and the handlebar assembly.
  d. Move the handlebar assembly back and rest it on the frame.
13. Install by reversing these removal steps, noting the following:
  a. Apply a light coat of multipurpose grease to the throttle grip area on the handlebar prior to installing the throttle grip assembly.
  b. Tighten the front brake master cylinder clamping upper bolt first, then tighten the lower bolt. Tighten the clamping bolts to the torque specification listed in **Table 1**.

WARNING
After installation is completed, make sure the brake lever does not come in contact with the throttle grip assembly

*when it is pulled on fully. If it does the brake fluid may be low in the reservoir; refill as necessary. Refer to **Front Disc Brakes** in Chapter Eleven.*

  c. Adjust the throttle operation as described in Chapter Three.
  d. Tighten the handlebar mounting Allen bolts to the torque specification listed in **Table 1**. Tighten the front bolts first then the rear so there is a slight gap at the rear between the handlebar upper and lower holders (**Figure 47**).

Left-hand side of handlebar

1. Disconnect the starter interlock switch electrical connector (A, **Figure 51**) from the clutch lever.
2. Unscrew the rear view mirror (B, **Figure 51**) from the clutch master cylinder.

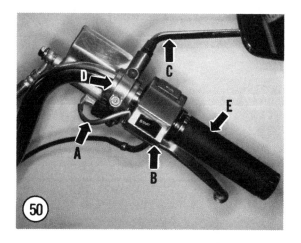
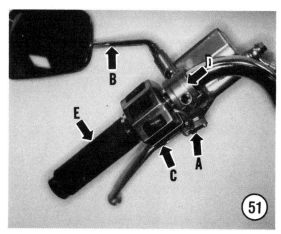

3. Remove the screws securing the left-hand handlebar switch assembly (C, **Figure 51**) together and remove the upper half of the switch.

4. Disconnect the all switch electrical connectors from the left-hand switch assembly. Remove the lower half of the switch from the handlebar.

5. Remove the clamping bolts and clamp (D, **Figure 51**) securing the clutch master cylinder to the handlebar.

CAUTION
Cover the surrounding area with a heavy cloth or plastic tarp to protect it from accidental spilling of hydraulic fluid. Wash any spilled brake fluid off any painted or plated surface immediately, as it will destroy the finish. Use soapy water and rinse thoroughly.

6. Remove the clutch master cylinder from the handlebar. Tie the master cylinder to the frame and keep the reservoir in the upright position. This is to minimize loss of hydraulic fluid and to keep air from entering into the clutch system. It is not necessary to remove the hydraulic brake line.

7. On 1992-on models, remove the long screw securing the right-hand balance set and remove all parts from the end of the handlebar.

8. Slide the hand grip assembly (E, **Figure 51**) from the handlebar.

9. Remove the components from the right-hand side of the handlebar.

10. To remove the handlebar from the fork bridge, perform the following:

    a. Remove the trim cap (**Figure 45**) from the Allen bolts.

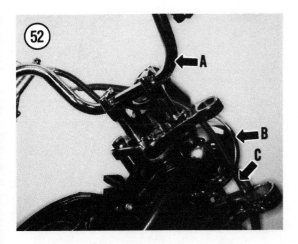

    b. Remove the Allen bolts (**Figure 46**) securing the handlebar upper holders.

    c. Remove the upper holders and the handlebar assembly.

    d. Move the handlebar assembly back and rest it on the frame.

11. Install by reversing these removal steps, noting the following:

    a. Tighten the clutch master cylinder clamping upper bolt first, then tighten the lower bolt. Tighten the clamping bolts to the torque specification listed in **Table 1**.

    b. Tighten all mounting bolts to the torque specification listed in **Table 1**.

STEERING HEAD AND STEM

Disassembly

Refer to the following illustrations for this procedure:

    a. **Figure 43**: Steering stem (1985-1987).

    b. **Figure 44**: Steering stem (1988-on).

1. Remove the front wheel as described in this chapter.

2. Remove the handlebar assembly (A, **Figure 52**) as described in this chapter.

3. Remove the front forks as described in this chapter.

4. Disconnect the electrical connector from the horn, headlight, speedometer and indicator light assembly.

5. Remove the headlight assembly (B, **Figure 52**) as described under *Headlight Housing Removal/Installation* in Chapter Eight.

6A. On 1985-1987 models, remove the clamping screws and disconnect the front brake and clutch master cylinder hydraulic hoses from (C, **Figure 52**) the lower fork bridge.

6B. On 1988-on models, perform the following:

    a. Remove the union bolt and disconnect the hydraulic brake line from both the front brake master cylinder and clutch master cylinder.

    b. Carefully withdraw the hydraulic hoses (C, **Figure 52**) through the holes in both the upper and lower fork bridges. Cover the end of the hoses with a reclosable plastic bag and tie the loose end up to the frame.

10

7. Remove the steering stem cap nut and washer (A, **Figure 53**).

8. Remove the upper fork bridge (B, **Figure 53**).

9. Loosen the steering stem nut (C, **Figure 53**). To loosen the nut, use a large drift and hammer or use the easily improvised tool shown in **Figure 54**.

10. Hold onto the lower end of the steering stem assembly and remove the steering stem nut.

11. Remove the dust seal from the top of the headset.

12. Lower the steering stem assembly down and out of the steering head. Don't worry about catching any loose steel balls as the steering stem is equipped with assembled ball bearings.

13. Remove the upper bearing from the top of the headset area of the steering head portion of the frame.

Inspection

1. Clean the bearing races in the steering head and the bearings with solvent.

2. Check the welds around the steering head for cracks and fractures. If any are found, have them checked by a Suzuki dealer or a competent frame shop.

3. Check the balls for pitting, scratches or discoloration indicating wear or corrosion. Replace them in sets if any are bad.

4. Check the races for pitting, galling and corrosion. If any of these conditions exist, replace the races as described in this chapter.

5. Check the steering stem for cracks, damage or wear. If damaged in any way replace the steering stem.

Steering Stem Assembly

Refer to the following illustrations for this procedure:

    a. **Figure 43**: Steering stem (1985-1987).

    b. **Figure 44**: Steering stem (1988-on).

1. Make sure the steering head outer races are properly seated.

2. Apply an even complete coat of wheel bearing grease to the steering head outer races (**Figure 55**) and to both bearings.

3. Install the upper bearing into the steering head.

4. Install the steering stem into the head tube and hold it firmly in place.

5. Install the dust seal onto the top of the headset.

6. Install the steering stem nut (C, **Figure 53**) and tighten it to the torque specification listed in **Table 1**.

7. Turn the steering stem from lock-to-lock 5-6 times to seat the bearings.

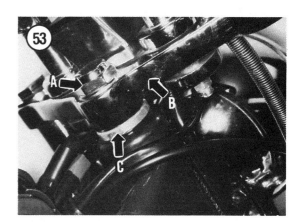

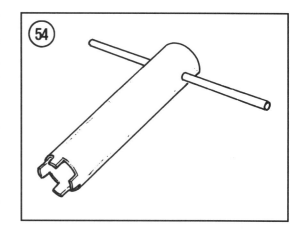

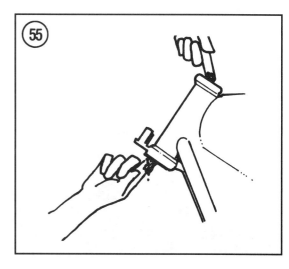

8. Loosen the steering stem nut 1/4 turn (**Figure 56**), then retighten so that *no play can be detected in the steering stem.*

9. Move the steering stem back and forth from side-to-side (**Figure 57**). The steering stem should move freely from side-to-side with no looseness or stiffness. If necessary, repeat Step 6 and Step 8 and readjust the steering stem nut.

10. Install the upper fork bridge (B, **Figure 53**).

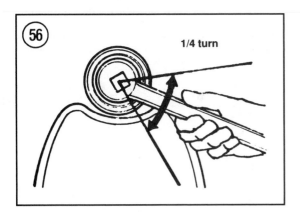

1/4 turn

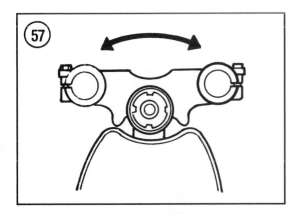

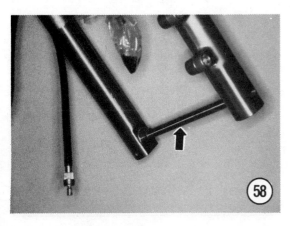

11. Install the washer and the steering stem cap nut (A, **Figure 53**). Tighten the cap nut only finger-tight at this time.

NOTE
Steps 12-15 must be performed in this order to assure proper upper and lower fork bridge to fork alignment.

12. Temporarily slide the fork tubes into position until they bottom out in the stops in the upper fork bridge.

13. Temporarily install the front axle into the fork legs (**Figure 58**) and tighten securely.

14. Tighten the *lower* fork bridge bolts to the torque specification listed in **Table 1**.

15. Tighten the steering stem cap nut to the torque specification listed in **Table 1**.

16. Remove the front axle, loosen the lower fork bridge bolts and slide the front fork tubes down and out.

17A. On 1985-1987 models, reposition the front brake and clutch master cylinder hydraulic hoses (C, **Figure 52**) onto the lower fork bridge and install the clamps and screws. Tighten the screws securely.

17B. On 1988-on models, perform the following:

    a. Remove the reclosable plastic bag from the loose end of the front brake and clutch hoses.

    b. Carefully insert the hydraulic hoses (C, **Figure 52**) through the holes and rubber grommets in both the upper and lower fork bridges.

    c. Attach the hydraulic brake line onto both the front brake master cylinder and clutch master cylinder. Refer to Chapter Five (Clutch) and Chapter Twelve (Brakes) for the correct procedure for reattaching the hydraulic hoses, then bleed the systems as described in the appropriate chapters.

18. Install the headlight assembly as described in Chapter Eight.

19. Reconnect the electrical connector to the horn, headlight, speedometer and indicator light assembly.

20. Install the front forks as described in this chapter.

21. Install the handlebar assembly (A, **Figure 52**) as described in this chapter.

22. Install the front wheel as described in this chapter.

10

STEERING HEAD BEARING RACES

The headset and steering stem bearing races are pressed into the headset portion of the frame. The races are easily bent, so they should not be removed unless they require replacement.

Headset Bearing Race
Removal/Installation

1. Remove the steering stem as described in this chapter.

2A. A special Suzuki tool set-up (Suzuki bearing outer race remover part No. 09941-54911, steering bearing remover/installer part No. 09941-74910) can be used to remove the headset bearing race as follows:

   a. Install the outer race remover (A, **Figure 59**) into one of the outer races.
   b. Insert the bearing remover (B, **Figure 59**) into the backside of the outer race remover.
   c. Tap on the end of the bearing remover with a hammer (C, **Figure 59**) and drive the bearing outer race out of the steering head. Remove the special tool from the outer race.
   d. Repeat for the bearing outer race at the other end of the headset.

2B. If the special tools are not used, perform the following:

   a. Insert a hardwood stick or soft punch into the head tube and carefully tap the outer race out from the inside (**Figure 60**).
   b. After it is started, work around the outer race in a crisscross pattern so that neither the race nor the head tube is damaged.

3A. A special Suzuki tool set-up (Suzuki bearing installer part No. 09941-34513) can be used to install the headset bearing race as follows:

   a. Position the outer races into the headset and just start them into position lightly with a soft-faced mallet. Just tap them in enough to hold them in place until the special tool can be installed.
   b. Position the bearing installer (**Figure 61**) into both of the outer races.
   c. Tighten the nuts on the bearing installer and pull the outer races into place in the headset. Tighten the nuts until both bearing outer races are completely seated in the head set and is flush with the steering head surface.

   d. Remove the special tool.

3B. If the special tools are not used, perform the following:

   a. Position one of the outer races into the headset and just start it into position lightly with a soft-faced mallet. Just tap it in enough to hold it in place.
   b. Tap the outer race in slowly with a block of wood, a suitable size socket or piece of pipe (**Figure 62**). Make sure that the race is squarely

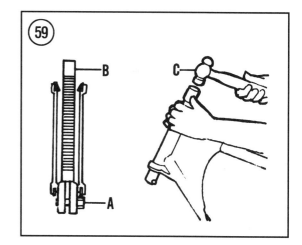

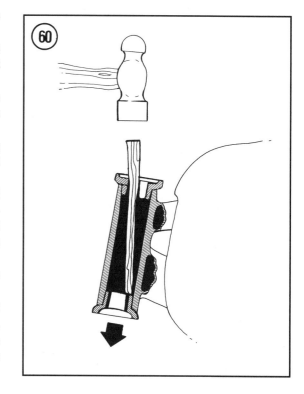

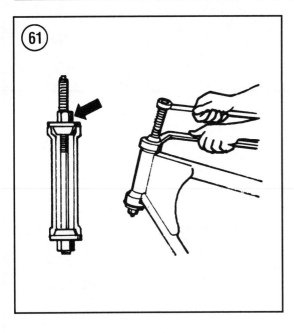

seated in the headset race bore before tapping it into place. Tap the race in until it is flush with the steering head surface.

c. Repeat for the other outer race.

Steering Stem Lower Bearing Removal/Installation

1. Install the Suzuki special tool (bearing remover part No. 09941-84510) (A, **Figure 63**) onto the steering stem assembly (B, **Figure 63**).

2. Tighten the upper bolt (C, **Figure 63**) and withdraw the lower bearing from the steering stem.

3. Remove the special tool and the lower bearing from the steering stem.

4. Install the lower bearing on the steering stem and slide it down onto the top of the shoulder at the base of the steering stem.

5. Install the Suzuki special tool (steering stem bearing installer, part No. 09941-74910) (A, **Figure 64**) on top of the lower bearing (B, **Figure 64**).

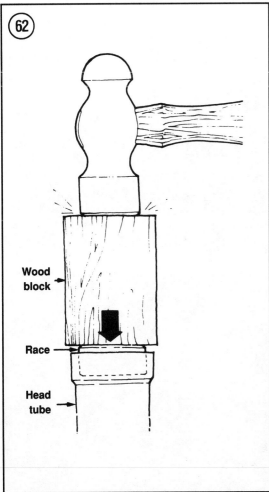

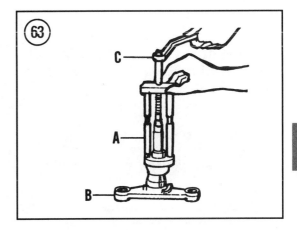

10

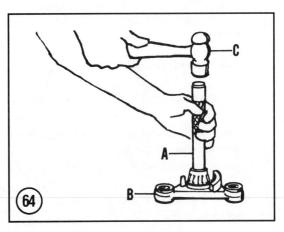

6. Using a hammer (C, **Figure 64**), carefully tap on the bearing installer and drive the lower bearing into place.

7. Remove the bearing installer.

8. Make sure it is seated squarely and is all the way down.

FRONT FORKS

Front Fork Service

Before suspecting major trouble, drain the front fork oil and refill with the proper type and quantity fork oil; refer to *Front Fork Oil Change* in Chapter Three. If you still have trouble, such as poor damping, a tendency to bottom or top out or leakage around the rubber seals, follow the service procedures in this section.

To simplify fork service and to prevent the mixing of parts, the legs should be removed, serviced and installed individually.

Removal/Installation

1. Remove the fork cap bolt (**Figure 65**) and on 1987-on models, the spacer from the top of the fork tube.

> *NOTE*
> *Insert a piece of vinyl tubing or wood in the caliper in place of the brake disc. That way if the brake lever is inadvertently squeezed, the piston will not be forced out of the cylinder. If this does happen, the caliper may have to be disassembled to reseat the piston and the system will have to be bled. By using the wood, bleeding the brake is not necessary when installing the wheel.*

2. Remove the brake caliper as follows:
   a. Loosen, then remove the bolts (A, **Figure 66**) securing the brake caliper assembly to the front fork.
   b. Remove the caliper assembly (B, **Figure 66**) from the brake disc.

3. Remove the front wheel (C, **Figure 66**) as described in this chapter.

4. Remove the screws securing the front fender to the front forks.

> *NOTE*
> *The Allen bolt at the base of the slider has been secured with a thread locking agent and is often very difficult to remove because the damper rod will turn inside the slider. It sometimes can be removed with an air impact driver. If you are unable to remove it, take the fork tubes to a dealer and have the bolts removed.*

5. If the fork assembly is going to be disassembled, slightly loosen (just break it loose) the Allen bolt at the base of the slider, using an Allen wrench . If the bolt is loosened too much, fork oil may start to drain out of the slider.

6. Remove the Allen bolt (A, **Figure 67**) securing the front turn signal mounting bracket to the front fork tube.

7. Loosen the lower fork bridge bolt (B, **Figure 67**).

The fork leg also goes through the directional signal mounting bracket as well as the upper and lower fork bridges. Remember this while sliding the fork tube in and out of the fork bridges.

8. Slide the fork tube from the upper fork bridge.

9. Hold onto the directional signal mounting bracket (A, **Figure 68**) and lower the fork assembly (B, **Figure 68**) out of the lower fork bridge (C, **Figure 68**). It may be necessary to rotate the fork tube slightly while pulling it down and out. Tie the directional signal assembly to the frame with a Bungee cord.

10. Keep the fork assembly in the upright position to avoid spilling fork oil out through the top of the fork tube.

11. Install by reversing these removal steps, noting the following:

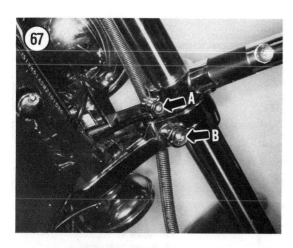

a. Align the front directional signal mounting bracket locating tab with the notch in the lower fork bridge. Tighten the bolt securely.

b. Install the fork tube until it bottoms against the stop in the upper fork bridge. Tighten the fork cap bolt finger tight.

c. Install the front axle into both fork sliders (**Figure 58**) to assure correct alignment between both fork assemblies.

d. Tighten the lower fork bridge bolt to the torque specifications listed in **Table 1**.

e. On models so equipped, install the spacer.

f. Install the fork cap bolt to the torque specifications listed in **Table 1**.

g. Remove the front axle from both fork sliders.

Disassembly

Refer to **Figure 69** during the disassembly and assembly procedures.

1. Remove the fork spring, turn the fork assembly upside down and drain the fork oil into a suitable container. Pump the fork several times by hand to expel most of the remaining oil. Dispose of the fork oil properly.

NOTE
*If you recycle your engine oil, do **not** add the fork oil to the engine oil because the recycler will probably not accept the mixed oil.*

2. Clamp the slider in a vise with soft jaws.

NOTE
The Allen bolt has been secured with Loctite and is often very difficult to remove because the damper rod will turn inside the slider. It sometimes can be removed with an air impact driver. If you are unable to remove it, take the fork tubes to a Suzuki dealer and have the bolts removed.

3. If not loosened during the fork removal sequence, loosen the Allen bolt on the bottom of the slider as follows:

a. Reinstall the fork spring and on 1987-on models, the spacer into the fork tube.

b. Install the fork top cap and tighten securely.

c. Loosen the Allen bolt (**Figure 70**) located at the bottom of the slider.

10

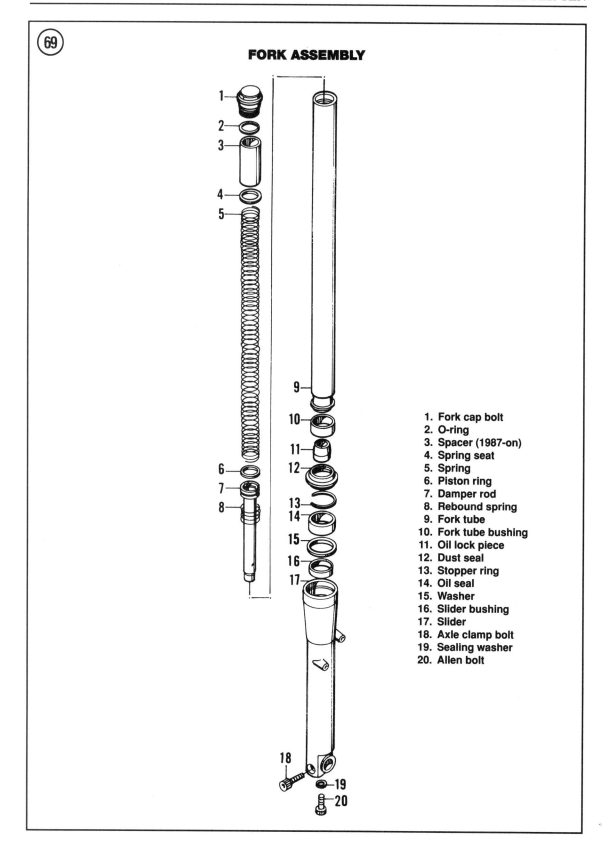

FORK ASSEMBLY

1. Fork cap bolt
2. O-ring
3. Spacer (1987-on)
4. Spring seat
5. Spring
6. Piston ring
7. Damper rod
8. Rebound spring
9. Fork tube
10. Fork tube bushing
11. Oil lock piece
12. Dust seal
13. Stopper ring
14. Oil seal
15. Washer
16. Slider bushing
17. Slider
18. Axle clamp bolt
19. Sealing washer
20. Allen bolt

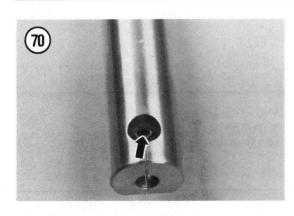

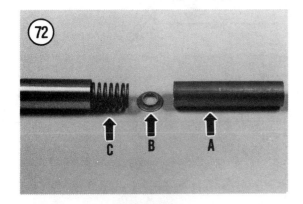

NOTE
If you have the special Suzuki tools used for fork disassembly, loosen the Allen bolt in Step 11.

4. Remove the Allen bolt and gasket from the slider.

5. Hold the upper fork tube in a vise with soft jaws and loosen the fork cap bolt.

WARNING
Be careful when removing the fork cap bolt as the spring is under pressure. Protect your eyes accordingly.

6. Remove the fork cap bolt (**Figure 71**) from the fork tube.

7A. On 1985 and 1986 models, remove the spring seat and the fork spring.

7B. On 1987-on models, remove the spacer (A, **Figure 72**), spring seat (B, **Figure 72**) and the fork spring (C, **Figure 72**).

8. Remove the dust seal trim cap (**Figure 73**) from the slider.

9. Remove the dust seal (**Figure 74**) from the slider.

10. Remove the stopper ring (**Figure 75**) from the slider.

10

11. If the Allen bolt was not loosened before, use special Suzuki tools and perform the following:

    a. Install the attachment "D" (part No. 09940-34561) onto the "T" handle (part No. 09940-34520) as shown in **Figure 76**.

    b. Insert this special tool setup into the fork tube (**Figure 77**) and index it into the hex receptacle in the top of the damper rod to hold the damper rod in place.

    c. Using an Allen wrench, loosen then remove the Allen bolt and washer from the base of the slider.

NOTE
On this type of fork, force is needed to remove the fork tube from the slider.

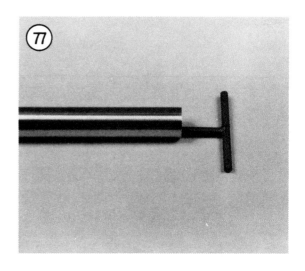

12. Install the fork tube in a vise with soft jaws.

13. There is an interference fit between the bushing in the fork slider and the bushing on the fork tube. In order to remove the fork tube from the slider, pull hard on the fork tube using quick in-and-out strokes (**Figure 78**). Doing so will withdraw the bushing, washer and the oil seal from the slider.

NOTE
It may be necessary to slightly heat the area on the slider around the oil seal prior to removal. Use a rag soaked in hot water; do not apply a flame directly to the fork slider.

14. Withdraw the fork tube from the slider.

NOTE
Do not remove the fork tube bushing unless it is going to be replaced. Inspect it as described in this chapter.

15. Remove the oil lock piece from the damper rod.

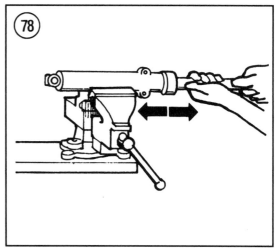

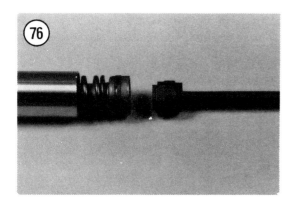

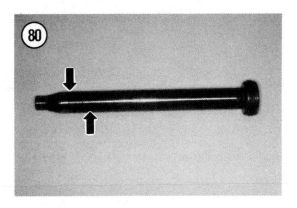

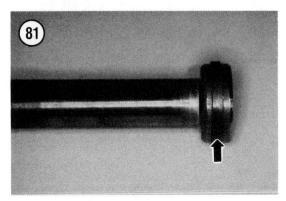

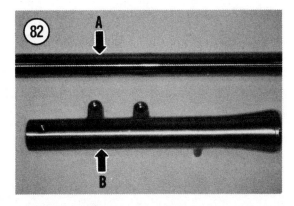

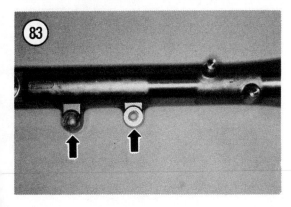

16. Remove the damper rod and rebound spring from the slider.

17. Inspect the components as described in this chapter.

Inspection

1. Thoroughly clean all parts in solvent and dry them. Check the fork tube for signs of wear or scratches.

2. Check the damper rod for straightness. **Figure 79** shows one method. The damper rod should be replaced if the runout is 0.2 mm (0.008 in.) or greater.

3. Make sure the oil holes (**Figure 80**) in the damper rod are clear. Clean out if necessary.

4. Inspect the damper rod and piston ring (**Figure 81**) for wear or damage. Replace as necessary.

5. Check the fork tube (A, **Figure 82**) for straightness. If bent or severely scratched, it should be replaced.

6. Check the slider (B, **Figure 82**) for dents or exterior damage that may cause the upper fork tube to stick. Replace if necessary.

7. Inspect the brake caliper mounting bosses (**Figure 83**) on the slider for cracks or other damage. If damaged, replace the slider.

8. Inspect the slider (**Figure 84**) and fork tube bushings (**Figure 85**). If either is scratched or scored they

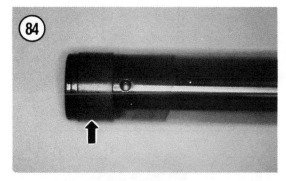

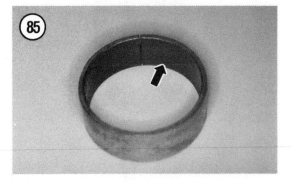

10

must be replaced. If the Teflon coating is worn off so that the copper base material is showing on approximately 3/4 of the total surface, the bushing must be replaced. Refer to **Figure 86**. Also check for distortion on the washer; replace as necessary.

9. Inspect the fork cap bolt threads in the fork tube (**Figure 87**) for wear or damage. Clean up with the appropriate size metric tap if necessary.

10. Inspect the fork cap bolt threads (**Figure 88**) for wear or damage. Clean up with the appropriate size metric die if necessary.

11. Inspect the oil seal seating area (**Figure 89**) in the slider for damage or burrs. Clean up if necessary.

12. Inspect the gasket on the Allen bolt (**Figure 90**); replace if damaged.

13. Measure the un-compressed length of the fork spring (not rebound spring) as shown in **Figure 91**. If the spring has sagged to the service limit

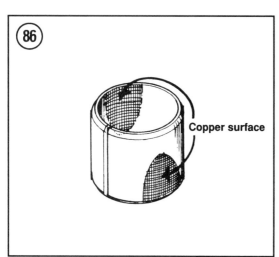

Copper surface

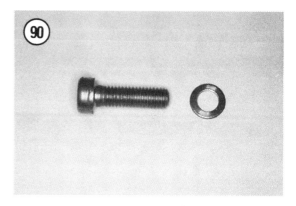

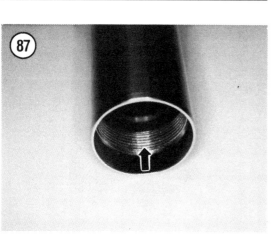

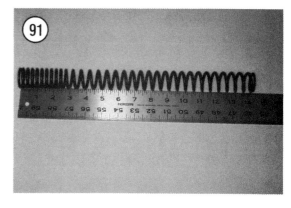

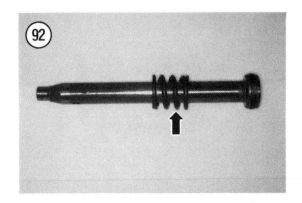

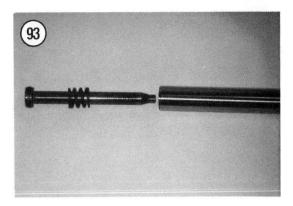

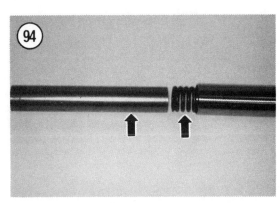

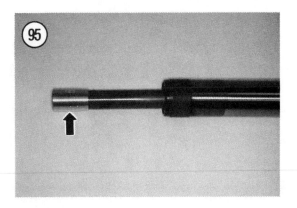

dimensions listed in **Table 4** the spring must be replaced.

14. Any parts that are worn or damaged should be replaced. Simply cleaning and reinstalling unserviceable components will not improve performance of the front suspension.

Assembly

1. Coat all parts with fresh SAE 10W fork oil prior to installation.

2. Install the rebound spring onto the damper rod (**Figure 92**) and insert this assembly into the fork tube (**Figure 93**).

3. Temporarily install the fork spring, spring seat and on 1987-on models the spacer (**Figure 94**) and fork cap bolt to hold the damper rod in place. Tighten the fork cap bolt securely.

4. Install the oil lock piece onto the damper rod (**Figure 95**).

5. Install the upper fork assembly into the slider (**Figure 96**).

6. Make sure the gasket (**Figure 97**) is on the Allen bolt.

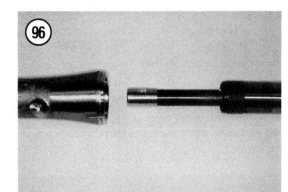

10

7. Apply blue Loctite (No. 242) to the threads of the Allen bolt prior to installation. Install it in the fork slider and tighten to the torque specification listed in **Table 1**.

8. Slide the fork slider bushing (A, **Figure 98**) and the washer (B, **Figure 98**) down the fork tube and rest it on top of the fork slider.

9. Install the new oil seal as follows:

   a. Coat the new seal with fresh SAE 10W fork oil.

   b. Position the seal with the open groove facing upward and slide the oil seal (C, **Figure 98**) down onto the fork tube.

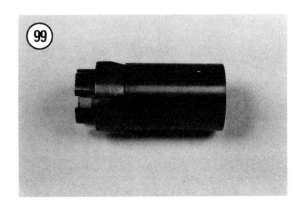

> *NOTE*
> *The following Suzuki special tool (**Figure 99**) is very expensive. If you work on a lot of different bikes this special tool is a must for your tool box. It is adjustable and will work on almost all Japanese fork assemblies (including Japanese "Showa" forks equipped on some late model Harley Davidsons).*

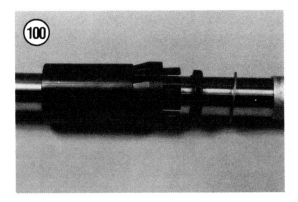

   c. Slide the Suzuki special tool Front Fork Oil Seal Installer (part No. 09940-50112) down the fork tube (**Figure 100**).

   d. Drive the seal into the slider with Suzuki special tool (**Figure 101**).

   e. Drive the oil seal in until the groove in the slider can be seen above the top surface of the oil seal (**Figure 102**).

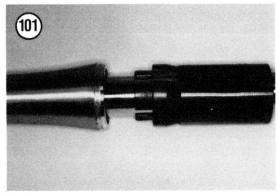

10. Slide the stopper ring (**Figure 103**) down the fork tube.

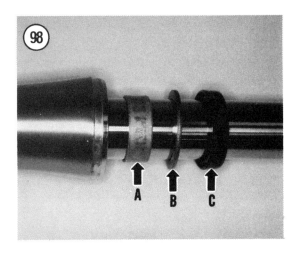

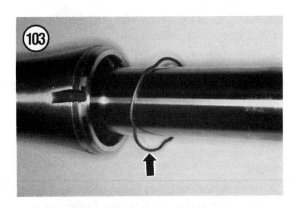

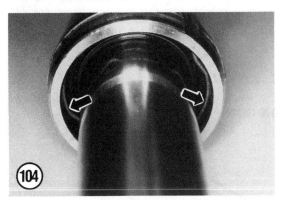

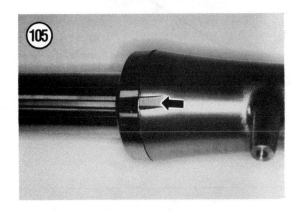

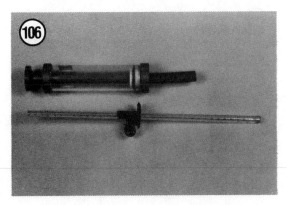

11. Install the stopper ring and make sure it is completely seated in the groove in the fork slider (**Figure 104**).

12. Install the dust seal (**Figure 74**) into the slider. Press it in until it is completely seated.

13. Install the dust seal trim cap (**Figure 73**) onto the slider. Index it into the groove in the slider (**Figure 105**).

14. Unscrew the fork cap bolt, then remove the fork spring, spring seat and on 1987-on models the spacer from the fork tube.

> *NOTE*
> *Suzuki recommends that the fork oil level be measured, if possible, to ensure a more accurate filling.*

> *NOTE*
> *To measure the correct amount of fluid, use a plastic baby bottle. These bottles have measurements in milliliters (ml) on the side.*

15. Compress the fork completely.

16. Add the recommended amount of SAE 10W fork oil to the fork assembly listed in **Table 3**.

17. Hold the fork assembly as close to perfect vertical as possible.

18. Use an accurate ruler or the Suzuki oil level gauge (part No. 09943-74111), or equivalent (**Figure 106**), to achieve the correct oil level listed in **Table 3**. Refer to **Figure 107**.

10

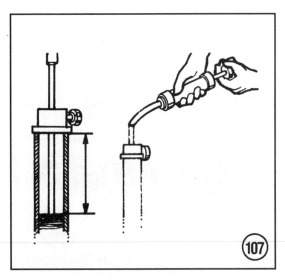

NOTE
*An oil level measuring devise can be made as shown in **Figure 108**. Position the lower edge of the hose clamp the specified oil level distance up from the small diameter hole. Fill the fork with a few ml's more than the required amount of oil. Position the hose clamp on the top edge of the fork tube and draw out the excess oil. Oil is sucked out until the level reaches the small diameter hole. A precise oil level can be achieved with this simple device.*

19. Allow the oil to settle completely and recheck the oil level measurement. Adjust the oil level if necessary.

20. Install the fork spring with the closer wound coils (**Figure 109**) going in last.

21. Inspect the O-ring seal (**Figure 110**) on the fork cap bolt; replace if necessary.

22. Do not install the spring seat, spacer (1987-on models) or the top fork cap bolt at this time. Hold the fork assembly upright so the fork oil will not drain out.

23. Install the fork assemblies as described in this chapter.

24. After the fork assembly has been installed; install the spring seat, and on 1987-on models, the spacer.

25. Install the top fork cap bolt and tighten to the torque specification listed in **Table 1**.

26. Repeat this procedure for the other fork assembly.

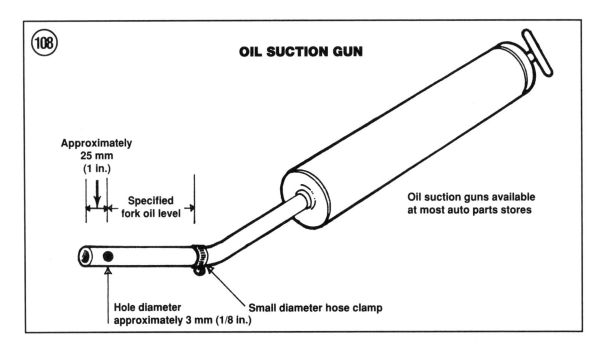

(108)

OIL SUCTION GUN

Approximately
25 mm
(1 in.)

Specified
fork oil level

Oil suction guns available
at most auto parts stores

Hole diameter
approximately 3 mm (1/8 in.)

Small diameter hose clamp

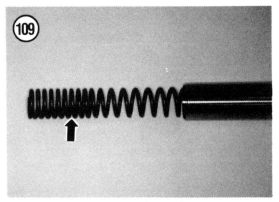

(109)

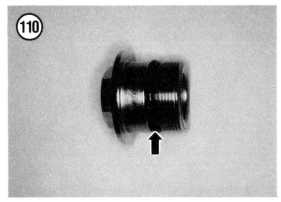

(110)

Table 1 FRONT SUSPENSION TIGHTENING TORQUES

Item	N·m	ft.-lb.
Front axle	36-52	26-37.5
Front axle nut	36-52	26-37.5
Front axle pinch bolt		
1985-1991	15-25	11-18
1992-on	18-28	13-20
Brake disc bolts	15-25	11-18
Handlebar upper holder Allen bolts	12-20	8.5-14.5
Master cylinder clamp bolts		
(brake and clutch)	5-8	3.5-6.0
Steering stem		
Nut	40-50	29-36
Cap nut	60-100	43.5-72.5
Fork cap bolt	25-30	18-21.5
Fork bridge lower clamp bolts	20-30	14.5-21.5
Fork slider Allen bolt	15-25	11-18

Table 2 TIRE INFLATION PRESSURE (COLD)*

	Tire Pressure				
	Front			Rear	
Load	psi	kPa		psi	kPa
Solo riding	28	200		32	225
Dual riding	32	225		36	250

* Tire inflation pressure for factory equipped tires. Aftermarket tires may require different inflation pressure.

10

Table 3 FORK OIL CAPACITY AND DIMENSIONS

Front fork oil capacity (each fork leg)		
1985-1989		
Right-hand fork	358 ml	12.1 oz.
Left-hand fork	370 ml	12.5 oz.
1990-1991		
U.S.	383 ml	13.4 oz.
U.K. and Canada	394 ml	13.8 oz.
1992-1993	386 ml	13.5 oz.
1994	412 ml	14.5 oz.
Front fork oil level dimension		
1985-1989	153 mm	6.02 in
1990-1991		
U.S. and U.K.	175 mm	6.89 in.
Canada	187 mm	7.36 in.
1992-1993		
U.S., Canada and U.K.	178 mm	7.01 in.
1994	177 mm	6.97 in.
Fork oil type	SAE 10W fork oil	

Table 4 FRONT SUSPENSION SPECIFICATIONS

Item	Wear limit
Front axle runout	0.2 mm (0.01 in.)
Front wheel rim runout	
Radial	2.0 mm (0.08 in.)
Axial	2.0 mm (0.08 in.)
Front fork spring free length limit	
1985-1986	563 mm (22.2 in.)
1987	360.8 mm (14.20 in.)
1988-on	348.3 mm (13.71 in.)
Fork oil	
Capacity per leg	
1985-1986	3.37 ml (11.4 U.S. oz. [11.9 Imp. oz.])
1987	3.55 ml (12.0 U.S. oz. [12.5 Imp. oz.])
1988-on	4.13 ml (14.0 U.S. oz. [14.5 Imp. oz.])
Oil level each leg	
1985-1986	144 mm (5.67 in.)
1987	117.4 mm (4.62 in.).
1988-on	124.3 mm (4.89 in.)

CHAPTER ELEVEN

REAR SUSPENSION AND FINAL DRIVE

This chapter includes repair and replacement procedures for the rear wheel and rear suspension components. Tire changing and wheel balancing are covered in Chapter Ten.

Refer to **Table 1** for rear suspension torque specifications. **Table 1** is located at the end of this chapter.

REAR WHEEL

Removal/Installation

1. Block up the engine so that the rear wheel clears the ground.
2. Completely unscrew the rear brake adjusting nut (**Figure 1**).

3. Depress the brake pedal and remove the brake rod, or cable, from the pivot joint in the brake arm. Remove the pivot joint from the brake arm, then install the pivot joint and the adjusting nut onto the brake rod to avoid misplacing them.

4. To remove the brake torque link from the brake panel, perform the following:

   a. Remove the cotter pin from the bolt (A, **Figure 2**).

   b. Remove the bolt, nut and washer.

   c. Swing the brake arm down and out of the way.

5. On models equipped with a brake cable, disconnect the cable from the receptacle (B, **Figure 2**) on the brake panel.

6. On 1985 and 1986 models, remove the cotter pin from the rear axle nut. Discard the cotter pin. Never reuse a cotter pin because the ends could break off allowing the cotter pin to fall out.

7. On 1987-on models, remove the rear axle trim cap (**Figure 3**).

NOTE
The rear axle may be installed from either side.

8. Remove the rear axle nut and washer (**Figure 4**).
9. Insert a drift or screwdriver into the hole in the end of the rear axle and withdraw the axle (**Figure 5**). Don't lose the spacer (**Figure 6**) from the right-hand side between the brake panel and the swing arm.
10. Slide the wheel to the right to disengage it from the hub drive splines and remove the wheel.

Inspection

Measure the axial and radial runout of the wheel with a dial indicator as shown in **Figure 7**. The maximum axial and radial runout is 2.0 mm (0.08 in.). If the runout exceeds this dimension, check the wheel bearing condition.

If the wheel bearings are okay, the wheel will have to be replaced, as it cannot be serviced. Inspect the wheel for signs of cracks, fractures, dents or bends. If it is damaged in any way, it must be replaced.

WARNING
Do not try to repair any damage to an alloy wheel (models so equipped) as it will result in an unsafe riding condition.

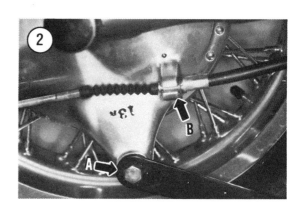

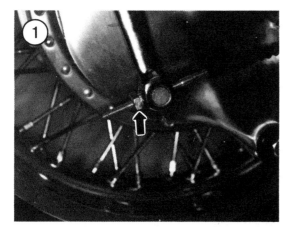

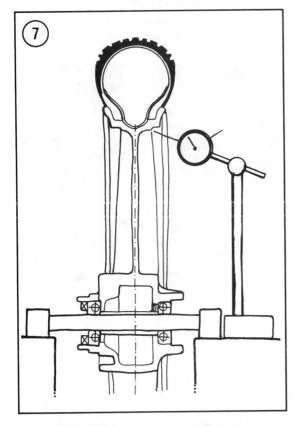

Check axle runout as described under *Rear Hub Inspection* in this chapter.

Installation

1. Apply a light coat of grease (lithium based NLGI No. 2 grease with molybdenum disulfide) to the final driven flange spline and to the rear wheel ring gear (**Figure 8**).

2. Loosen the final drive case mounting nuts.

3. Position the rear wheel so that the splines of the final driven flange and the final drive align. Slowly move the wheel back and forth and push the wheel to the left until it completely seats.

4. Position the spacer (**Figure 6**) on the right-hand side between the brake panel and the swing arm.

5. Insert the rear axle (**Figure 5**) from either side and install the axle nut washer and nut (**Figure 4**). Tighten the nut only finger-tight at this time.

6. To install the brake torque link, perform the following:

    a. Swing the brake arm up and into position.

    b. Install the bolt, washer and nut. Tighten the bolt and nut to the torque specification listed in **Table 1**.

    c. Install a new cotter pin and bend the ends over completely.

7. Insert a drift into the hole in the axle to keep the axle from turning.

8. Tighten the rear axle nut to the torque specifications listed in **Table 1**.

9. On 1985 and 1986 models, install a new cotter pin and bend the ends over completely.

10. On 1987-on models, install the trim cap (**Figure 3**) covering the rear axle nut.

11. Tighten the final drive gear case nuts to the torque specification listed in **Table 1**.

12. After the wheel is installed, completely rotate it and apply the brake several times to make sure it rotates freely and that the brake works properly.

13. Adjust the rear brake free play as described in Chapter Three.

REAR HUB

Inspection

    Inspect each wheel bearing prior to removing it from the wheel hub.

CAUTION
Do not remove the wheel bearings for inspection because they will be damaged during removal. Remove wheel bearings only if they are to be replaced.

1. Perform Step 1 and Step 2 of *Disassembly* in this chapter.

2. Turn each bearing by hand (**Figure 9**). Make sure the bearings turn smoothly.

3. On non-sealed bearings, check the balls for evidence of wear, pitting or excessive heat (bluish tint). Replace the bearings if necessary; always replace as a complete set. When replacing the bearings, be sure to take your old bearings along to ensure a perfect matchup.

NOTE
Fully sealed bearings are available from many bearing specialty shops. Fully sealed bearings provide better protection from dirt and moisture that may get into the hub.

4. Check the axle for wear and straightness. Use V-blocks and a dial indicator as shown in **Figure 10**. If the runout is 0.2 mm (0.01 in.) or greater, the axle should be replaced.

5. Inspect the splines of the final driven flange. If any are damaged the flange must be replaced.

Disassembly

Refer to the following illustrations for this procedure:

    a. **Figure 11**: rear wire wheel.

    b. **Figure 12**: rear cast wheel.

1. Remove the rear wheel as described in this chapter.

2. Pull straight up and remove the brake panel assembly from the hub.

3. Straighten the locking tabs on the lockwashers (A, **Figure 13**) then loosen and remove the bolts (B, **Figure 13**).

4. Remove the lockwashers (C, **Figure 13**) and thrust washers (D, **Figure 13**). Remove all 3 sets.

5. Pull straight up and remove the final driven flange from the hub.

6. Remove the O-ring seal (**Figure 14**) from the rear hub.

7. Before proceeding further, inspect the wheel bearings as described in this chapter. If they must be replaced, proceed as follows.

8. To remove the right- and left-hand bearings and distance collar, insert a soft aluminum or brass drift into one side of the hub.

9. Push the distance collar over to one side and place the drift on the inner race of the lower bearing.

10. Tap the bearing out of the hub with a hammer, working around the perimeter of the inner race. Remove the distance collar.

11. Repeat for the other bearing.

12. Clean the inside and the outside of the hub with solvent. Dry with compressed air.

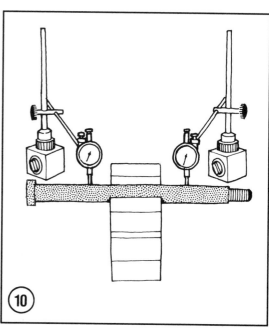

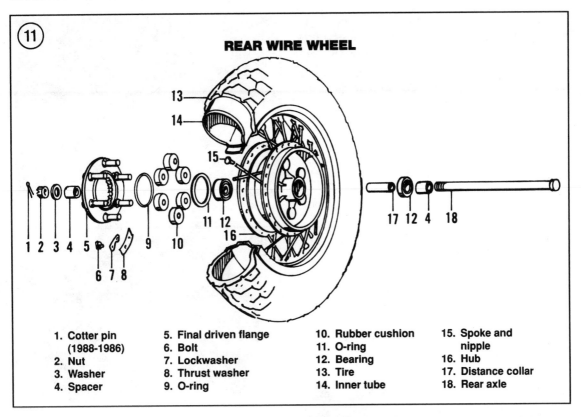

REAR WIRE WHEEL

13
14
15
11 12
16
17 12 4 18
1 2 3 4 5 9 10
6 7 8

1. Cotter pin (1988-1986)	5. Final driven flange	10. Rubber cushion	15. Spoke and nipple
2. Nut	6. Bolt	11. O-ring	16. Hub
3. Washer	7. Lockwasher	12. Bearing	17. Distance collar
4. Spacer	8. Thrust washer	13. Tire	18. Rear axle
	9. O-ring	14. Inner tube	

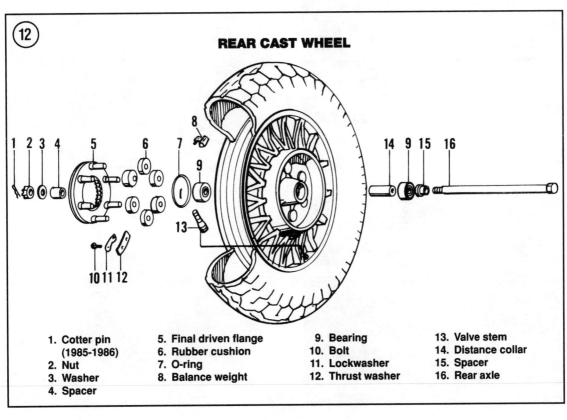

REAR CAST WHEEL

8
1 2 3 4 5 6 7 9 14 9 15 16
13
10 11 12

1. Cotter pin (1985-1986)	5. Final driven flange	9. Bearing	13. Valve stem
2. Nut	6. Rubber cushion	10. Bolt	14. Distance collar
3. Washer	7. O-ring	11. Lockwasher	15. Spacer
4. Spacer	8. Balance weight	12. Thrust washer	16. Rear axle

11

13. Clean the inside and the outside of the final driven flange with solvent. Dry with compressed air.

14. Inspect each rubber cushion (**Figure 15**) for wear or deterioration. Replace if necessary.

15. Inspect the final driven flange as follows:

    a. Inspect the inner splines (**Figure 16**) for wear or missing teeth.

    b. Inspect the studs (**Figure 17**) for cracks or damage.

    c. Inspect the flange (**Figure 18**) for cracks or warpage.

    d. Replace the driven flange if any of these areas are damaged.

Assembly

1. On non-sealed bearings, pack the bearings with a good quality bearing grease. Work the grease in between the balls thoroughly; turn the bearing by hand a couple of times to make sure the grease is distributed evenly inside the bearing.

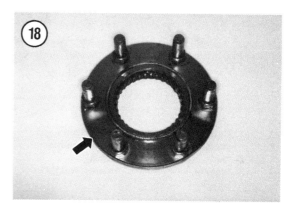

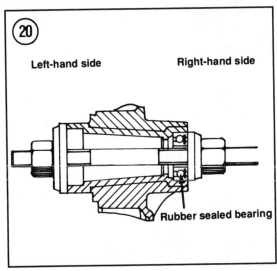

Left-hand side   Right-hand side

Rubber sealed bearing

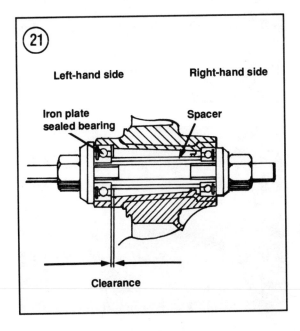

Left-hand side   Right-hand side

Iron plate
sealed bearing   Spacer

Clearance

2. Blow any dirt or foreign matter out of the hub prior to installing the bearings.

CAUTION
*Install non-sealed bearings with the single sealed side facing outward (**Figure 19**).*

3. Pack the hub with multipurpose grease.

4A. A special Suzuki tool set-up (Suzuki part No. 09924-84510) can be used to install the wheel bearings as follows:

    a. Install the right-hand bearing into the hub first.

    b. Set the bearing with the sealed side facing out and install the bearing installer as shown in **Figure 20**.

    c. Tighten the bearing installer and pull the bearing into the hub until it is completely seated. Remove the bearing installer.

    d. Turn the wheel over (left-hand side up) on the workbench and install the distance collar.

    e. Set the bearing with the sealed side facing out and install the bearing installer as shown in **Figure 21**.

    f. Tighten the bearing installer and pull the bearing into the hub until there is a small amount of clearance between the inner race and the distance collar. Suzuki does not specify this clearance, just make sure they do not touch.

    g. Remove the bearing installer.

4B. If special tools are not used, perform the following:

    a. Tap the left-hand bearing squarely into place and tap on the outer race only. Use a socket (**Figure 22**) that matches the outer race diameter. Do not tap on the inner race or the bearing might be damaged. Be sure that the bearing is completely seated.

11

b. Turn the wheel over (right-hand side up) on the workbench and install the distance collar.

c. Use the same tool set-up and drive in the right-hand bearing.

5. Install a new O-ring seal (**Figure 14**) into the groove in the hub. Coat the O-ring with multipurpose grease.

6. Install the final driven flange (**Figure 23**) into the rear hub. Push it down until it is completely seated in the rear hub (**Figure 24**).

7. Install the 3 thrust washers (D, **Figure 13**) into the locking ring in the final driven flange.

8. Install new lockwashers (C, **Figure 13**).

9. Apply red Loctite (No. 271) to the bolts prior to installation, then install the bolts (B, **Figure 13**).

10. Tighten the bolts to the torque specification listed in **Table 1**.

11. Bend up the locking tab (A, **Figure 13**) against a flat of each bolt.

12. Install the brake panel assembly into the hub.

13. Install the rear wheel as described in this chapter.

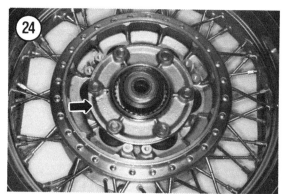

FINAL DRIVE UNIT, DRIVE SHAFT AND UNIVERSAL JOINT

Removal

NOTE
The rear wheel can remain in place after the rear axle and spacers are removed. The procedure shown leaves the rear wheel in place.

1. Remove the rear axle and spacers as described in *Rear Wheel Removal* in this chapter.

2. Drain the final drive unit oil as described in Chapter Three.

3. Remove the upper and lower mounting nuts and washers (**Figure 25**), then remove the left-hand shock absorber.

NOTE
*In **Figure 26** only 2 of the nuts and washers are shown. Be sure to remove all 3 nuts and washers.*

4. Remove the nuts and washers (**Figure 26**) securing the final drive unit to the swing arm.

5. Pull the final drive unit and drive shaft straight back (**Figure 27**) until it is disengaged from the splines on the universal joint.

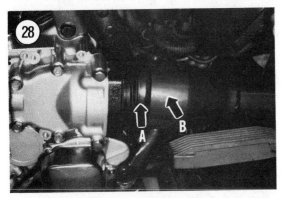

6. Loosen the clamping band (A, **Figure 28**) securing the rubber boot to the swing arm and move the rubber boot away from the swing arm.

7. Remove the screw securing the swing arm trim panel (B, **Figure 28**) and remove the panel.

8. Pull the universal joint (**Figure 29**) toward the rear and disengage it from the bevel gear drive unit.

9. Carefully pull the universal joint out through the swing arm opening (**Figure 30**) and remove it.

Final Drive Unit and
Drive Shaft Inspection

The final drive unit requires a considerable number of special Suzuki tools for disassembly and assembly. The price of all of these tools could be more than the cost of most repairs or seal replacement by a dealer.

All of the internal components of the final drive unit are shown in **Figure 31**.

1. Check that the bearing case flange bolts (**Figure 32**) are in place and are tight.

2. Inspect the splines on the final driven ring gear (**Figure 33**). If they are damaged or worn, the ring gear must be replaced.

NOTE
*If these splines are damaged, also inspect the splines (**Figure 34**) on the rear wheel final driven flange, which may also need to be replaced.*

3. If removal is necessary, carefully pull the drive shaft (**Figure 35**) from the final drive unit, using a circular motion.

4. Inspect the splines on the universal joint end of drive shaft (**Figure 36**). If they are damaged or worn, the drive shaft must be replaced. If these splines are damaged, also inspect the splines on the universal joint; it may also need to be replaced.

5. Inspect the splines on the final drive unit end of drive shaft. If they are damaged or worn, the drive shaft must be replaced. If these splines are damaged, also inspect the splines in the final drive unit; it may also need to be replaced.

6. Check the threads on the threaded studs (**Figure 37**) for wear or thread damage. If necessary, clean the threads with an appropriate size metric die.

7. Check that gear oil has not been leaking from either the ring gear side (**Figure 38**) or pinion joint side (**Figure 39**) of the unit. If there are traces of oil

11

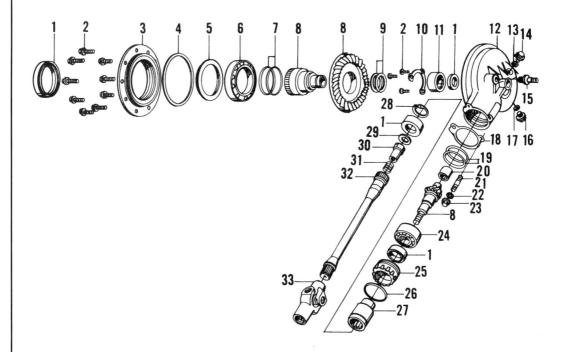

FINAL DRIVE UNIT

1. Oil seal
2. Bolt
3. Bearing case
4. O-ring
5. Bearing plate
6. Bearing
7. Shims
8. Final bevel gear set
9. Shims
10. Bearing retainer plate
11. Needle bearing
12. Final gear case
13. O-ring
14. Oil fill cap
15. Threaded stud
16. Drain cap
17. O-ring
18. Bearing stopper plate
19. Shims
20. Needle bearing
21. Threaded stud
22. Washer
23. Cap nut
24. Bearing
25. Bearing stopper
26. O-ring
27. O-ring
28. Circlip
29. Washer
30. Special nut
31. Spring
32. Drive shaft
33. Universal joint

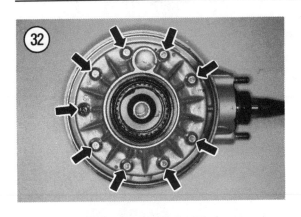

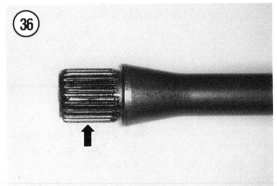

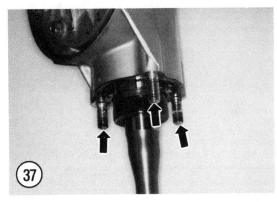

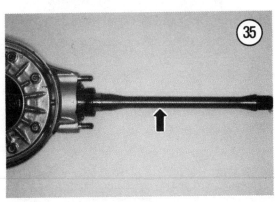

11

leakage, take the unit to a dealer for oil seal replacement.

Universal Joint Inspection

1. Clean the universal joint in solvent and thoroughly dry with compressed air.
2. Inspect the universal joint pivot points for play (**Figure 40**). Rotate the joint in both directions. If there is noticeable side play the universal joint must be replaced.
3. Inspect the splines at each end of the universal joint. Refer to **Figure 41** and **Figure 42**. If they are damaged or worn, the universal joint must be replaced.

> *NOTE*
> *If these splines are damaged, also inspect the splines in the final drive unit and the engine output shaft; they may also need to be replaced.*

4. Apply a light coat of molybdenum disulfide grease (NGLI No. 2) to both splined ends.

Installation

1. Apply a light coat of molybdenum disulfide grease (NGLI No. 2) to the splines at each end of the universal joint.
2. Position the universal joint with the short end (**Figure 43**) going in first toward the drive shaft.
3. Carefully push the universal joint in through the swing arm opening (**Figure 30**).
4. Align the splines and push the universal joint (**Figure 29**) forward and engage it with the bevel gear drive unit. Push the universal joint in until it seats completely.
5. If removed, install the drive shaft onto the final drive unit. Using a soft-faced mallet, tap on the end of the drive shaft to make sure the drive shaft is completely seated into the final drive unit splines.
6. Apply a light coat of molybdenum disulfide grease (NGLI No. 2) to the splines of the drive shaft.
7. Install the final drive unit and drive shaft into the swing arm (**Figure 44**). Insert your fingers into the opening in the drive shaft to hold the rear end of the universal joint up to accept the drive shaft.
8. Slowly push the final drive unit forward and mesh the drive shaft with the universal joint. It may be necessary to slightly rotate the final driven spline

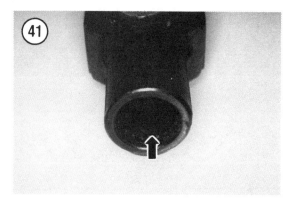

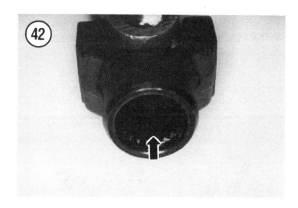

back and forth to align the splines of the drive shaft and the universal joint.

9. Push the final drive unit all the way forward (**Figure 45**) unit it is seated correctly.

10. Install the final drive unit's mounting nuts and washers only finger-tight at this time. Do not tighten

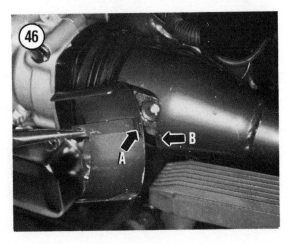

the nuts until the rear wheel and rear axle are in place.

11. Hook the tab (A, **Figure 46**) on the trim panel on the backside opening of the swing arm (B, **Figure 46**) and install the trim panel (B, **Figure 28**) and screw. Tighten the screw securely.

12. Install the rubber boot onto the swing arm. Make sure it is correctly installed and tighten the clamping bolt securely. This is necessary to keep out dirt and water.

13. Install the rear axle, spacers and the rear wheel as described in this chapter.

14. Tighten the final drive unit nuts to the specifications listed in **Table 1**.

15. Install the shock absorber and the upper and lower washers and nuts. Tighten to the torque specifications listed in **Table 1**.

16. Refill the final drive unit with the correct amount and type of gear oil. Refer to Chapter Three.

SWING ARM

In time, the needle bearings will wear and will have to be replaced. The condition of the bearings can greatly affect handling performance and if worn parts are not replaced they can produce erratic and dangerous handling. Common symptoms are wheel hop, pulling to one side during acceleration and pulling to the other side during braking.

Refer to **Figure 47** for this procedure.

Removal

1. Remove the rear wheel as described in this chapter.

2. Remove the final drive unit, drive shaft and universal joint as described in this chapter.

NOTE
*It is not necessary to remove the shock absorber unit, just pivot the unit up and out of the way (**Figure 48**).*

3. Remove the lower mounting bolt and nut (**Figure 49**) securing the right-hand shock absorber.

4. Remove the trim cap (**Figure 50**) from the right-hand side covering the pivot bolt nut.

5. Grasp the rear end of the swing arm and try to move it from side to side in a horizontal arc. There should be no noticeable side play. If play is evident

11

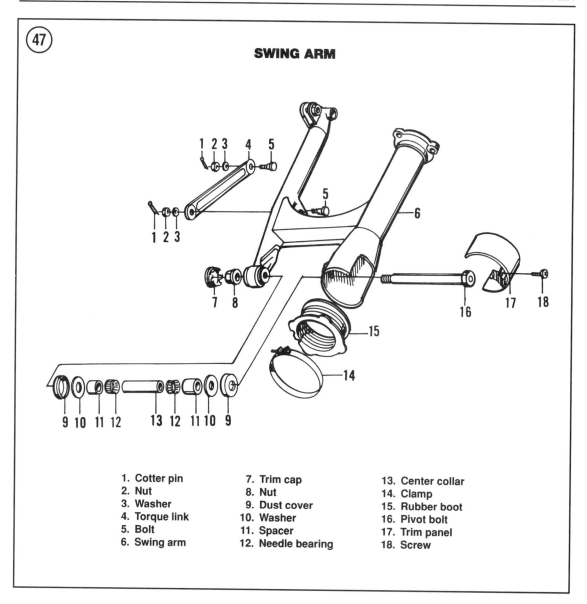

47

SWING ARM

1. Cotter pin
2. Nut
3. Washer
4. Torque link
5. Bolt
6. Swing arm
7. Trim cap
8. Nut
9. Dust cover
10. Washer
11. Spacer
12. Needle bearing
13. Center collar
14. Clamp
15. Rubber boot
16. Pivot bolt
17. Trim panel
18. Screw

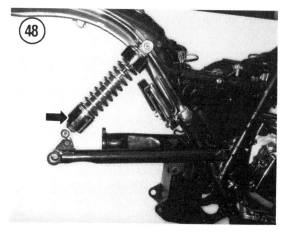

48

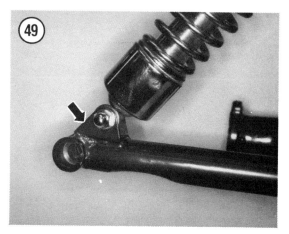

49

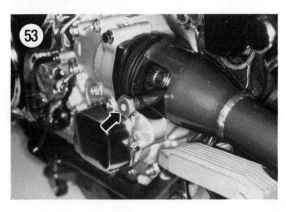

and the pivot bolt nut is tightened correctly, the bearings should be replaced.

6. Hold onto the pivot bolt and loosen, then remove the pivot bolt nut (**Figure 51**).

7. Using a long drift, carefully tap the pivot bolt (**Figure 52**) out toward the left-hand side.

8. Have an assistant hold onto the swing arm and withdraw the pivot bolt (**Figure 53**) from the swing arm and frame.

9. Pull back on the swing arm, free it from the frame and remove it from the frame.

Inspection

1. Check the welded sections on the swing arm for cracks or fractures (**Figure 54**).

2. Inspect the final drive unit mounting bolt holes (**Figure 55**) in the swing arm. If the holes are elongated or worn, replace the swing arm.

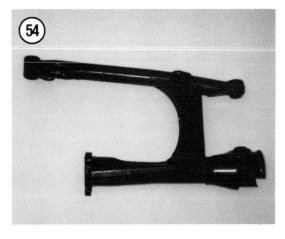

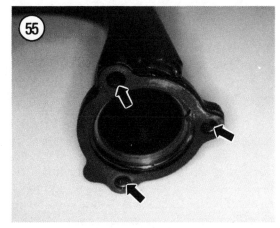

11

3. Inspect the right-hand shock absorber mounting bracket and pivot hole (**Figure 56**) on the swing arm. If the hole is elongated or worn, replace the swing arm.

4. Inspect the swing arm pivot points for wear or damage. Refer to **Figure 57** for the right-hand side or **Figure 58** for the left-hand side.

5. Inspect the rear axle mounting boss for wear or damage (**Figure 59**).

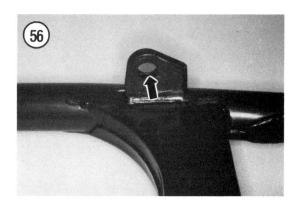

Installation

1. Make sure the needle bearing dust cover (**Figure 60**) is in place on each side of the frame.

2. Position the swing arm into the mounting area of the frame. Align the holes in the swing arm with the holes in the frame. Make sure both dust covers are still in place. Reposition if necessary.

3. Apply a light coat of molybdenum disulfide grease to the pivot bolt.

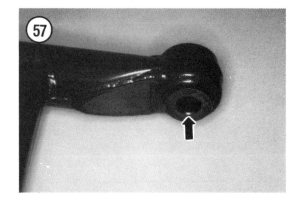

4. Install the pivot bolt (**Figure 53**) from the left-hand side and push it all the way through the swing arm and frame.

5. Install the pivot bolt washer and nut (**Figure 51**). Tighten the nut to the torque specifications listed in **Table 1**.

6. Move the swing arm up and down several times to make sure all components are properly seated.

7. Install the trim cap (**Figure 50**) over the pivot bolt nut.

8. Install the final drive unit, drive shaft and universal joint as described in this chapter.

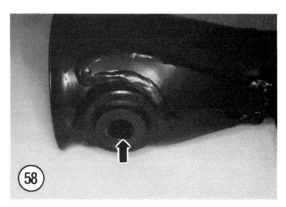

9. Install the rubber boot onto the swing arm. Make sure it is correctly installed and tighten the clamping bolt securely. This is necessary to keep out dirt and water.

10. Attach the lower end of the right-hand shock absorber to the swing arm and tighten the bolt and nut to the torque specification listed in **Table 1**.

11. Install the rear wheel as described in this chapter.

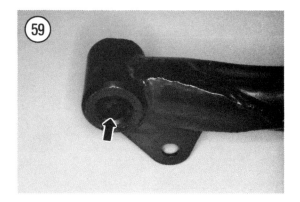

Bearing Replacement

The swing arm needle bearings are installed in the frame at each side. Whenever a needle bearing is removed from the frame it must be discarded. Never reinstall a bearing that has been removed.

The bearing must be removed with special tools that are available from a Suzuki dealer. The special tools are as follows.

    a. Bearing remover: part No. 09921-20210.

    b. Slide hammer weight: part No. 09930-30102.

1. Remove the swing arm as described in this chapter.

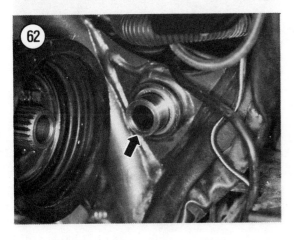

2. Remove the dust seal and washer (**Figure 60**) from each side of the frame.

3. Remove the spacer from each bearing. Refer to **Figure 61** for the right-hand side or **Figure 62** for the left-hand side.

CAUTION
Do not try to remove the needle bearings without the use of these special tools as the bearing mounting receptacle in the frame may be damaged. If damaged, the new needle bearings will not be properly aligned and the swing arm will not pivot correctly.

4. Insert the bearing remover into the needle bearing and attach it to the backside of the bearing. Attach the slide hammer and weight to the bearing remover.

5. Using the slide hammer, slowly withdraw the needle bearing from the frame receptacle. Discard the needle bearing.

6. Repeat Step 4 and Step 5 for the other bearing. Discard this needle bearing also.

7. Remove the center collar from the frame pivot area.

8. Thoroughly clean out the inside of the frame pivot area with solvent and dry with compressed air.

9. Apply a light coat of molybdenum disulfide grease to all parts before installation.

CAUTION
Never reinstall a needle bearing that has been removed. During removal it becomes slightly damaged and is no longer true to alignment and will create an unsafe riding condition.

NOTE
Either the right- or left-hand needle bearing can be installed first.

10. Position the new needle bearing with the markings facing outward.

11. To install the new needle bearing, place the bearing over the bearing receptacle in the frame and drive the needle bearing into place slowly and squarely.

12. Install the center collar, then repeat Step 10 and Step 11 for the other bearing.

11

13. Make sure both bearings are properly seated. Refer to **Figure 63** for the right-hand side or **Figure 64** for the left-hand side.

14. Apply molybdenum disulfide grease to the new needle bearings

15. Apply molybdenum disulfide grease to the spacers and install the spacer into each bearing. Refer to **Figure 61** for the right-hand side or **Figure 62** for the left-hand side. Push the spacers all the way in until they are seated (**Figure 65**).

16. Apply molybdenum disulfide grease to the dust seals and washers. Install a washer into each dust seal.

17. Install the dust seal and washer (**Figure 60**) onto each side of the frame.

18. Install the swing arm as described in this chapter.

SHOCK ABSORBERS

The shock absorbers are spring controlled and hydraulically dampened. Spring preload can be adjusted by rotating the spring lower seat at the base of the spring *clockwise* to increase preload and *counterclockwise* to decrease it.

NOTE
Use the wrench furnished in the factory
tool kit.

Both spring lower seats must be indexed on the same detent. The shocks are sealed and cannot be rebuilt. Service is limited to removal and replacement of the hydraulic unit.

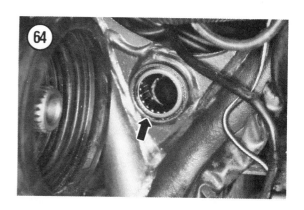

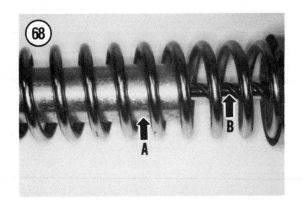

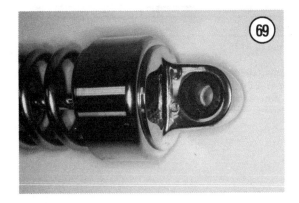

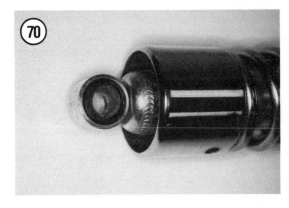

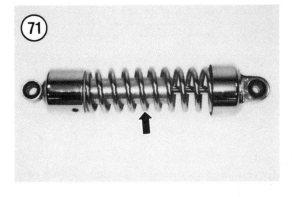

Removal/Installation

Removal and installation of the rear shocks is easier if done separately. The remaining unit will support the rear of the bike and maintain the correct relationship between the top and bottom shock mounts.

> *NOTE*
> *Some prefer to remove the seat (A, **Figure 66**) as a precaution to avoid damage to the seat should a tool slip while removing the shock absorber upper nut.*

1. Block up the engine so that the rear wheel clears the ground. Tie the front of the motorcycle down to remove weight from the rear wheel.
2. Adjust both shocks to their softest setting, completely *counterclockwise*.
3. On models so equipped, remove the trim cap from the upper mount.
4. On the right-hand side, remove the upper nut and washer (B, **Figure 66**) and the lower bolt, nut and washers (C, **Figure 66**) securing the shock absorber to the frame and to the swing arm.
5. On the left-hand side, remove the upper and lower nuts and washers (**Figure 67**) securing the shock absorber to the frame and to the final drive unit.
6. Pull the unit straight off the upper mount and remove it.
7. Install by reversing these removal steps. Tighten the upper and lower mounting nut or bolt to the torque specifications listed in **Table 1**.

Preliminary Inspection

1. Check the damper unit (A, **Figure 68**) for leakage and make sure the damper rod (B, **Figure 68**) is straight.

> *NOTE*
> *The damper unit cannot be rebuilt; it must be replaced as a unit.*

2. Inspect the rubber bushings in the upper (**Figure 69**) and lower (**Figure 70**) joints for wear or deterioration. If damaged, replace the shock absorber as they cannot be replaced.
3. Inspect the spring (**Figure 71**) for wear, damage or sagging. If damaged, replace the shock absorber as the spring cannot be replaced.

11

Table 1 REAR SUSPENSION TIGHTENING TORQUES

Item	N·m	ft.-lb.
Rear axle nut	60-96	43.5-69.5
Brake torque rod bolt and nut	20-30	14.5-21.5
Final driven flange bolts	8-12	6-8.5
Shock absorber mounting nuts		
Upper and lower	20-30	14.5-21.5
Swing arm pivot bolt and nut	50-80	36-58
Final drive unit		
Mounting nuts	35-45	25.5-32.5
Bearing case flange bolts	20-26	14.5-19.0

Table 2 REAR SUSPENSION SPECIFICATIONS

Item	Wear limit
Rear axle runout	0.2 mm (0.01 in.)
Rear wheel rim runout	
Radial	2.0 mm (0.08 in.)
Axial	2.0 mm (0.08 in.)
Swing arm pivot shaft runout	0.30 mm (0.012 in.)

CHAPTER TWELVE

BRAKES

The brake system on all models consists of a single disc on the front wheel and a drum brake on the rear. This chapter describes repair and replacement procedures for all brake components.

Table 1 contains the brake system torque specifications and **Table 2** contains brake system specifications. **Tables 1-2** are located at the end of this chapter.

DISC BRAKES

The disc brake is actuated by hydraulic fluid and is controlled by a hand lever that is attached to the front master cylinder. As the brake pads wear, the brake fluid level drops in the reservoir and automatically adjusts for wear.

When working on hydraulic brake systems, it is necessary that the work area and all tools be absolutely clean. Any tiny particles of foreign matter and grit in the caliper assembly or the master cylinder can damage the components. Also, sharp tools must not be used inside the caliper or on the piston. If there is any doubt about your ability to correctly and safely carry out major service on the brake components, take the job to a Suzuki dealer or brake specialist.

NOTE
*If you recycle your old engine oil **never** add used brake fluid to the old engine oil. Most oil retailers who recycle old oil will not accept the oil if contaminated with other fluids (fork oil, brake fluid or any other type of petroleum based fluids).*

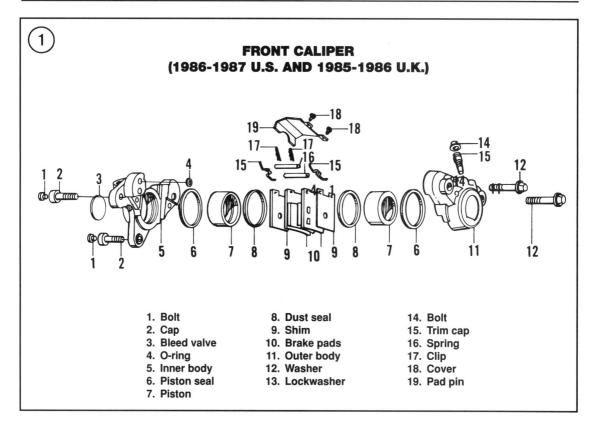

FRONT CALIPER
(1986-1987 U.S. AND 1985-1986 U.K.)

1. Bolt	8. Dust seal	14. Bolt
2. Cap	9. Shim	15. Trim cap
3. Bleed valve	10. Brake pads	16. Spring
4. O-ring	11. Outer body	17. Clip
5. Inner body	12. Washer	18. Cover
6. Piston seal	13. Lockwasher	19. Pad pin
7. Piston		

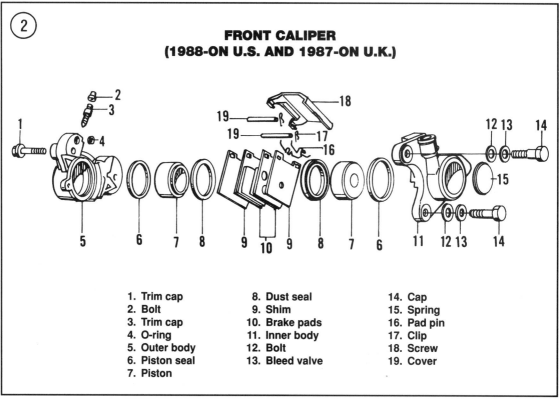

FRONT CALIPER
(1988-ON U.S. AND 1987-ON U.K.)

1. Trim cap	8. Dust seal	14. Cap
2. Bolt	9. Shim	15. Spring
3. Trim cap	10. Brake pads	16. Pad pin
4. O-ring	11. Inner body	17. Clip
5. Outer body	12. Bolt	18. Screw
6. Piston seal	13. Bleed valve	19. Cover
7. Piston		

Consider the following when servicing the disc brake system.

1. Disc brake components rarely require disassembly, so do not disassemble them unless necessary.

> *WARNING*
> *Do not intermix silicone based (DOT 5) brake fluid as it can cause brake component damage leading to brake system failure.*

2. Use only DOT 3 or DOT 4 brake fluid from a sealed container.

3. Do not allow disc brake fluid to contact any plastic, painted or plated surfaces or surface damage will occur.

4. Always keep the master cylinder reservoir and spare cans of brake fluid closed to prevent dust or moisture from entering. If moisture enters the brake fluid it would result in brake fluid contamination and brake problems.

5. Use only disc brake fluid (DOT 3 or DOT 4) to wash parts. Never clean any internal brake components with solvent or any other petroleum base cleaners.

6. Whenever *any* component has been removed from the brake system the system is considered "opened" and must be bled to remove air bubbles. Also, if the brake feels "spongy," this usually means there are air bubbles in the system and it must be bled. For safe brake operation, refer to *Bleeding the System* in this chapter.

> *CAUTION*
> *Do not use solvents of any kind on the brake system's internal components. Solvents will cause the seals to swell and distort. When disassembling and cleaning brake components (except*

brake pads) use new DOT 3 or DOT 4 brake fluid.

> *WARNING*
> *When working on the brake system, do **not** inhale brake dust. It may contain asbestos, which can cause lung injury and cancer. Wear a face mask that meets OSHA requirements for trapping asbestos particles, and wash your hands and forearms thoroughly after completing the work.*

FRONT BRAKE PAD REPLACEMENT

There is no recommended mileage interval for changing the friction pads in the disc brakes. Pad wear depends greatly on riding habits and conditions. The pads should be checked for wear every 6 months and replaced when the wear indicator reaches the edge of the brake disc. To maintain an even brake pressure on the disc, always replace both pads in the caliper at the same time.

Disconnecting the hydraulic brake hose from the brake caliper is not necessary for brake pad replacement. Disconnect the hose only if the caliper assembly is going to be removed.

> *CAUTION*
> *Check the pads more frequently when the wear line approaches the disc. On some pads the wear line is very close to the metal backing plate. If pad wear happens to be uneven for some reason the backing plate may come in contact with the disc and cause damage.*

Front Brake Pad Replacement

Refer to the following illustrations for this procedure:

    a. **Figure 1**: U.S. 1986-1987, U.K. 1985 and 1986.

    b. **Figure 2**: U.S. 1988-on, U.K. 1987-on.

1. Remove the dust cover (**Figure 3**) from the brake caliper.

2. Remove the clips securing both pad pins.

3. Withdraw both pad pins and remove the pad springs.

4. Withdraw both brake pads and shims from the caliper assembly.

12

5. Check the brake pad friction surface (**Figure 4**) for oil contamination or fraying. Check the pad plates for cracks or other damage. If the brake pads appear okay, measure the friction thickness with a Vernier caliper. Replace the pads as a set if the friction thickness is worn to the service limit listed in **Table 2** or less.

> *WARNING*
> *The brake pads must be replaced as a set. When servicing the front brakes, both the left- and right-hand brake pads must be replaced at the same time to maintain brake effectiveness*

6. Clean the pad recess and the end of the pistons with a soft brush. Do not use solvent, a wire brush or any hard tool which would damage the cylinders or pistons.

7. Carefully remove any rust or corrosion from the disc.

8. Lightly coat the end of the pistons, the backs of the new pads (*not* the friction material), and the shims with disc brake lubricant.

> *NOTE*
> *When purchasing new pads, check with your dealer to make sure the friction compound of the new pad is compatible with the disc material. Remove any roughness from the backs of the new pads with a fine-cut file; blow them clean with compressed air.*

9. When new pads are installed in the caliper, the master cylinder brake fluid level will rise as the caliper pistons are repositioned. Perform the following:

    a. Clean the top of the master cylinder of all dirt and foreign matter.

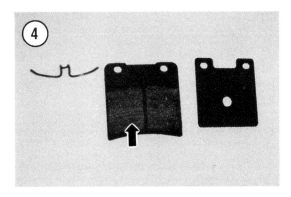

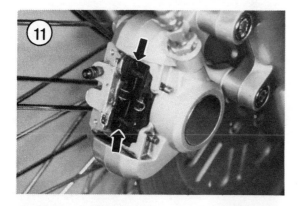

b. Remove the screws securing the cover (**Figure 5**). Remove the cover and the diaphragm from the master cylinder and slowly push the caliper pistons into the caliper. Constantly check the reservoir to make sure brake fluid does not overflow. Remove brake fluid, if necessary, before it overflows.

c. The pistons should move freely. If they don't and there is evidence of them sticking in the cylinder, the caliper should be removed and serviced as described in this chapter.

10. Push the caliper pistons in all the way to allow room for the new pads.

11. Position a shim against the back of each brake pad and install the spring to hold the 2 parts together.

12. Install the inboard pad (**Figure 6**) into the caliper. Push it all the way down until it stops (**Figure 7**).

13. Install the outboard pad into the caliper (**Figure 8**). Push it all the way down until it stops (**Figure 9**).

14. Partially install both pad pins (**Figure 10**).

15. Push the ends of the outboard pad spring down, then push both pad pins through the shim and outboard brake pad. Make sure the spring ends are below both pad pins. This is necessary for proper brake operation.

16. Push the ends of the inboard pad spring down, then push both pad pins through the shim and inboard brake pad. Make sure the spring ends are below both pad pins (**Figure 11**). This is necessary for proper brake operation.

17. Rotate both pad pins until the clip holes (**Figure 12**) are facing up, then push both pad pins in until they stop.

18. Use needlenose pliers and install the clip (**Figure 13**) into the hole in the upper pad pin. Push the clip in until it seats completely on the pad pin.

12

19. Install the remaining clip (**Figure 14**) into the hole in the lower pad pin. Push the clip in until it seats completely on the pad pin.

20. Install the dust cap (**Figure 3**). Make sure it snaps into place otherwise it will fly off when you hit the first bump in the road.

21. Block up under the engine, then tie the back of the bike down or have an assistant sit on the pillion seat to raise the front wheel off the ground.

22. Spin the front wheel and activate the front brake lever as many times as it takes to refill the cylinders in the caliper and correctly locate the brake pads.

> *WARNING*
> *Use brake fluid clearly marked DOT 3 or DOT 4 from a sealed container. Other types may vaporize and cause brake failure. Always use the same brand name; do not intermix as many brands are not compatible. Do not intermix silicone based (DOT 5) brake fluid as it can cause brake component damage leading to brake system failure.*

23. Refill the master cylinder reservoir, if necessary, to maintain the correct fluid level as seen through the viewing port (**Figure 15**) on the side. Install the diaphragm and cover. Tighten the screws securely.

> *WARNING*
> *Do not ride the motorcycle until you are sure the brakes are operating correctly with full hydraulic advantage. If necessary, bleed the brake as described under **Bleeding the System** in this chapter.*

24. Bed the pads in gradually for the first 10 days of riding by using only light pressure as much as possible. Immediate hard application will glaze the new friction pads and greatly reduce the effectiveness of the brake.

FRONT BRAKE CALIPER

Removal

Refer to the following illustrations for this procedure:
   a. **Figure 1**: U.S. 1986-1987, U.K. 1985 and 1986.
   b. **Figure 2**: U.S. 1988-on, U.K. 1987-on.

It is not necessary to remove the front wheel in order to remove the caliper assembly.

> *CAUTION*
> *Do not spill any brake fluid on the front fork or front wheel. Wash off any spilled brake fluid immediately, as it will destroy the finish. Use soapy water and rinse completely.*

1. Clean the top of the master cylinder of all dirt and foreign matter.

2. If the caliper assembly is going to be disassembled for service, perform the following:

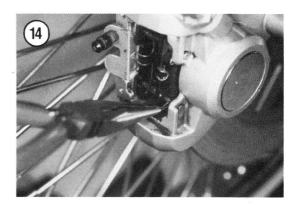

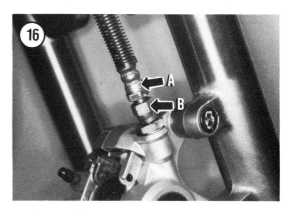

NOTE
By performing Step 2, compressed air may not be necessary for piston removal during caliper disassembly.

a. Remove the brake pads as described in this chapter.

CAUTION
Do not allow the pistons to travel out far enough to come in contact with the brake

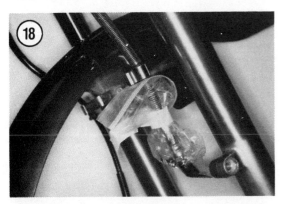

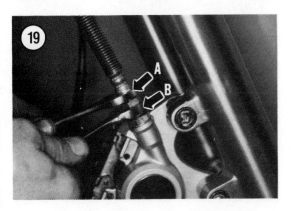

disc. If this happens the pistons may scratch the disc during caliper removal.

b. Slowly apply the brake lever to push the pistons part way out of the caliper assembly for ease of removal during caliper service.

3. Loosen the screws securing the master cylinder cover (**Figure 5**). Slightly loosen the cover and the diaphragm. This will allow air to enter the reservoir and allow the brake fluid to drain out more quickly in the next step.

4. Hold onto the brake hose fitting (A, **Figure 16**) with an open-end wrench. Loosen the brake hose adaptor nut (B, **Figure 16**) securing the brake hose to the caliper assembly.

5. Remove the brake hose (A, **Figure 17**) and sealing washer from the brake hose adaptor nut and let the brake fluid drain out into the container. Dispose of this brake fluid—never reuse brake fluid.

6. Loosen, then remove the bolts (B, **Figure 17**) securing the brake caliper assembly to the front fork.

7. Remove the caliper assembly (C, **Figure 17**) from the brake disc.

8. Place the loose end of the brake hose in a reclosable plastic bag (**Figure 18**) to prevent brake fluid from dribbling out.

Installation

1. Carefully install the caliper assembly onto the disc being careful not to damage the leading edge of the brake pads.

2. Install the bolts (B, **Figure 17**) securing the brake caliper assembly to the front fork and tighten to the torque specifications listed in **Table 1**.

3. Install the brake hose (A, **Figure 17**) and new sealing washer onto the caliper.

4. Screw the brake hose into the brake hose adaptor nut on the caliper.

5. Hold onto the brake hose fitting (A, **Figure 19**) with an open-end wrench. Tighten the brake hose adaptor nut (B, **Figure 19**) securing the brake hose to the caliper assembly. Tighten the brake hose adaptor nut securely.

6. Remove the master cylinder top cover and diaphragm.

WARNING
Use brake fluid clearly marked DOT 3 or DOT 4 from a sealed container. Other types may vaporize and cause

12

brake failure. Always use the same brand name; because some brands are not compatible. Do not intermix silicone-based (DOT 5) brake fluid as it can cause brake component damage leading to brake system failure.

7. If removed, install the brake pads as described in this chapter.

8. Tie the back of the bike down or have an assistant sit on the pillion seat to raise the front wheel off the ground.

9. Spin the front wheel several times and activate the front brake lever as many times as it takes to refill the cylinders in the caliper and correctly locate the pads.

10. Refill the master cylinder reservoir. Install the diaphragm and cover. Do not tighten the screws at this time.

11. Bleed the brake as described under *Bleeding the System* in this chapter.

> *WARNING*
> *Do not ride the motorcycle until you are sure that the brakes are operating properly.*

Front Caliper Rebuilding

Refer to the following illustrations for this procedure:

   a. **Figure 1**: U.S. 1986-1987, U.K. 1985 and 1986.

   b. **Figure 2**: U.S. 1988-on, U.K. 1987-on.

1. Remove the caliper and brake pads as described in this chapter.

2. Remove the caliper housing bolts (**Figure 20**) securing the caliper inner body to the caliper outer body.

3. Separate the 2 caliper bodies.

4. Remove the O-ring seal (**Figure 21**) from the caliper inner body. Discard this O-ring seal as it must be replaced every time the caliper is disassembled.

5. Remove the dust seal (**Figure 22**) from each piston and discard both seals.

> *NOTE*
> *If the pistons were partially forced out of the caliper body during removal, Steps 6-8 may not be necessary. If the piston or caliper bore is corroded or very dirty, additional compressed air*

may be necessary to completely remove the pistons.

6. Place a shop cloth or piece of soft wood over the end of the piston.

7. Perform this step over and close to a workbench top. Hold the caliper body with the pistons facing away from you.

> *WARNING*
> *In the next step, the piston may shoot out of the caliper body like a bullet. Keep*

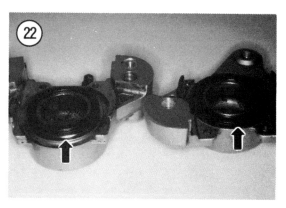

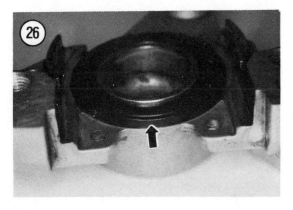

*your fingers out of the way. Wear shop gloves and apply air pressure gradually. Do **not** use high pressure air or place the air hose nozzle directly against the hydraulic line fitting inlet in the caliper body. Hold the air nozzle away from the inlet allowing some of the air to escape.*

8. Apply the air pressure in short spurts to the hydraulic fluid passageway or brake hose inlet (**Figure 23**) and force the piston out. Use a service station air hose if you don't have an air compressor.

CAUTION
In the following step, do not use a sharp tool to remove the dust and piston seals from the caliper cylinders. Do not damage the cylinder surface.

9. Use a piece of plastic or wood and carefully push the piston seal (**Figure 24**) in toward the caliper cylinder and out of its grooves. Remove the piston seal from both caliper halves and discard both seals.
10. Inspect the caliper as described in this chapter.

NOTE
Never reuse the old dust seals or piston seals. Very minor damage or age deterioration can make the seals useless.

11. Coat the new dust seals and piston seals with fresh DOT 3 or DOT 4 brake fluid.
12. Carefully install the new pistons seals in the grooves in each caliper cylinder. Make sure the seals are properly seated in their respective grooves (**Figure 24**).
13. Coat the pistons and caliper cylinders with fresh DOT 3 or DOT 4 brake fluid.
14. Position the pistons with the open sends facing out toward the brake pads and install the pistons into the caliper cylinders. Push the pistons in until they bottom out (**Figure 25**).
15. Install a new dust seal (**Figure 22**) onto each piston. Make sure it seats properly on the piston and caliper (**Figure 26**).
16. Install a new O-ring seal (**Figure 21**) onto the caliper inner body.
17. Assemble the 2 caliper bodies and install the caliper housing bolts (**Figure 20**). Tighten the bolts to the torque specification listed in **Table 1**.
18. Install the caliper and brake pads as described in this chapter.

12

Front Caliper Inspection

1. Inspect the piston seal groove in each caliper body (**Figure 27**) for damage. If damaged or corroded, replace the caliper assembly.

2. Inspect each caliper body (**Figure 28**) for cracks or damage. Replace the caliper assembly if either is damaged.

3. Inspect the hydraulic fluid passageway (**Figure 29** and **Figure 30**) at the end of the caliper body and in the passageway in the base of the piston bore (**Figure 31**). Make sure they are clean and open. Apply compressed air to the openings and make sure they are clear. Clean out if necessary with fresh brake fluid.

4. Inspect the cylinder walls (**Figure 32**) and the pistons (**Figure 33**) for scratches, scoring or other damage. If either is rusty or corroded, replace either the pistons or the caliper assembly.

5. Measure the cylinder bore with a bore gauge or vernier caliper (**Figure 34**). Replace the brake caliper if the inside diameter(s) are worn to the service limit dimension listed in **Table 2** or greater.

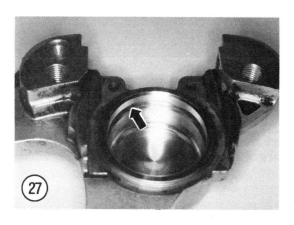

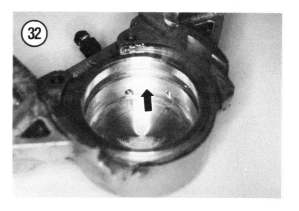

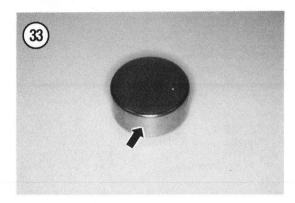

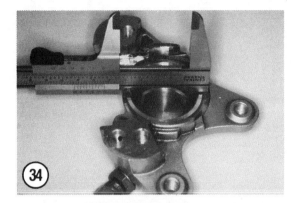

6. Measure the outside diameter of the pistons with a micrometer or vernier caliper (**Figure 35**). Replace the brake piston(s) if the outside diameter(s) are worn to the service limit dimension listed in **Table 2** or less.

7. Inspect the caliper mounting bolt hole threads on the outer body (**Figure 36**) for wear or damaged. Clean up with a suitable size metric tap or replace the caliper assembly.

8. Inspect the caliper housing bolt holes on the outer body (**Figure 37**). If worn or damaged, replace the caliper assembly.

9. Remove the bleed screw (**Figure 38**). Make sure it is clean and open. Apply compressed air to the opening and make sure it is clear. Clean out if necessary with fresh brake fluid.

10. Remove the brake hose adaptor nut (**Figure 39**) from the caliper body. Make sure it is clean and open. Apply compressed air to the opening and make sure it is clear. Clean out if necessary with fresh brake fluid. Make sure the opening in the caliper is clean and open.

11. If serviceable, clean the caliper bodies with rubbing alcohol and rinse with clean brake fluid.

12

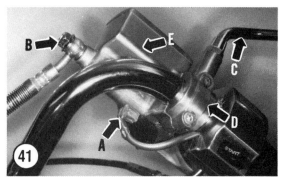

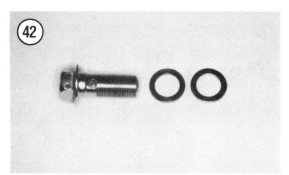

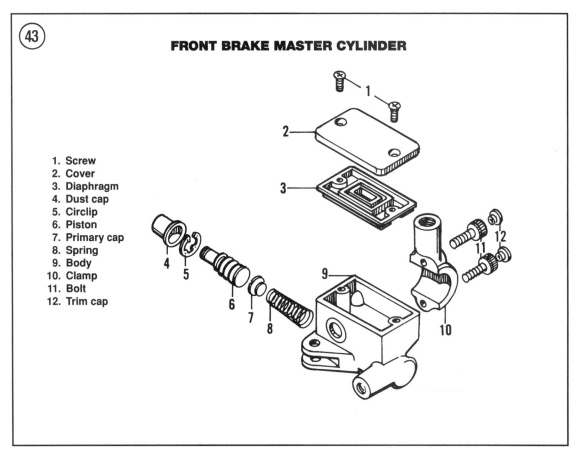

FRONT BRAKE MASTER CYLINDER

1. Screw
2. Cover
3. Diaphragm
4. Dust cap
5. Circlip
6. Piston
7. Primary cap
8. Spring
9. Body
10. Clamp
11. Bolt
12. Trim cap

FRONT MASTER CYLINDER

Removal/Installation

> *CAUTION*
> *Cover the surrounding areas with a heavy cloth or plastic tarp to protect them from accidental brake fluid spills. Wash brake fluid off any painted or plated surfaces or plastic parts immediately, as it will destroy the finish. Use soapy water and rinse completely.*

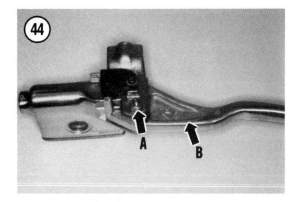

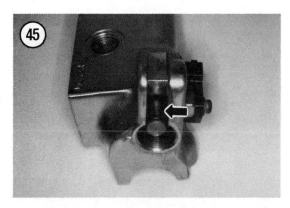

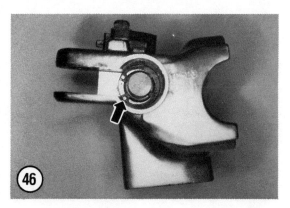

1. Clean the top of the master cylinder of all dirt and foreign matter.
2. Remove the screws securing the cover (**Figure 40**). Remove the cover and the diaphragm.
3. If you have a shop syringe, draw all of the brake fluid out of the master cylinder reservoir.
4. Disconnect the brake light switch electrical connector (A, **Figure 41**) from the brake switch.
5. Place a shop cloth under the union bolt to catch any spilled brake fluid that will leak out.
6. Unscrew the union bolt (B, **Figure 41**) securing the brake hose to the master cylinder. Don't lose the sealing washer on each side of the hose fitting. Tie the loose end of the hose up to the handlebar and cover the end to prevent the entry of moisture and foreign matter.
7. Unscrew the rear view mirror (C, **Figure 41**) from the master cylinder.
8. Remove the clamping bolts and clamp (D, **Figure 41**) securing the master cylinder to the handlebar.
9. Remove the master cylinder (E, **Figure 41**) from the handlebar.
10. Install by reversing these removal steps, noting the following:
    a. Install the master cylinder, clamp and bolts. Tighten the upper bolt first, then the lower to the torque specification listed in **Table 1**.
    b. Place a sealing washer on each side of the brake hose fitting (**Figure 42**) and install the union bolt.
    c. Tighten the union bolt to the torque specification listed in **Table 1**.
    d. Bleed the front brakes as described under *Bleeding the System* in this chapter.

Disassembly

Refer to **Figure 43** for this procedure.
1. Remove the master cylinder as described in this chapter.
2. Remove the bolt and nut (A, **Figure 44**) securing the hand lever and remove the lever (B, **Figure 44**).
3. Remove the rubber dust boot (**Figure 45**) from the area where the hand lever actuates the piston assembly.
4. Using circlip pliers, remove the internal circlip (**Figure 46**) from the body.
5. Remove the piston assembly (**Figure 47**) and the spring.

12

6. If necessary, remove the screw (A, **Figure 48**) securing the brake light switch to the master cylinder and remove the switch assembly (B, **Figure 48**).

Inspection

1. Clean all parts in fresh brake fluid.
2. Inspect the body cylinder bore (**Figure 49**) surface for signs of wear and damage. If less than perfect, replace the master cylinder assembly. The body cannot be replaced separately.
3. Measure the cylinder bore with a bore gauge. Replace the master cylinder if the inside diameter is worn to the service limit dimension listed in **Table 2** or greater.
4. Make sure the passage (**Figure 50**) in the bottom of the master cylinder body is clear. Clean out if necessary.
5. Inspect the piston contact surfaces (A, **Figure 51**) for signs of wear and damage. If less than perfect, replace the piston assembly.
6. Check the end of the piston (**Figure 52**) for wear caused by the hand lever. If worn, replace the piston assembly.
7. Measure the outside diameter of the piston with a micrometer (**Figure 53**). Replace the piston assembly if the outside diameter is worn to the service limit dimension listed in **Table 2** or less.
8. Replace the piston assembly if either the primary (B, **Figure 51**) or secondary cups (C, **Figure 51**) require replacement. The cups cannot be replaced separately.
9. Check the hand lever pivot lugs (**Figure 54**) on the master cylinder body for cracks or elongation. If damaged, replace the master cylinder assembly.

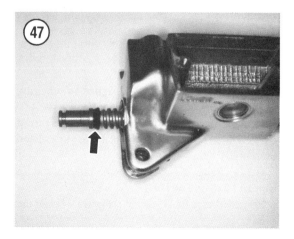

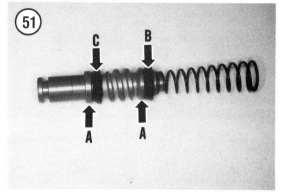

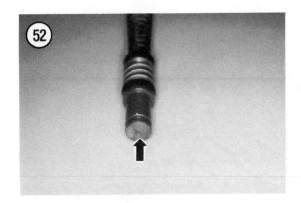

10. Inspect the pivot hole in the hand lever. If worn or elongated the lever must be replaced.

11. Inspect the threads in the bore (**Figure 55**) for the union bolt. If worn or damaged, clean out with a metric thread tap or replace the master cylinder assembly.

12. Inspect the O-ring seal on the hose connector. If starting to harden or deteriorate, replace the O-ring.

Assembly

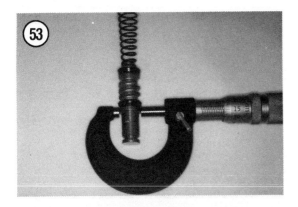

1. Soak the new cups in fresh brake fluid for at least 15 minutes to make them pliable. Coat the inside of the cylinder bore with fresh hydraulic fluid prior to the assembly of parts.

> *CAUTION*
> *When installing the piston assembly, do not allow the cups to turn inside out as they will be damaged and allow brake fluid leakage within the cylinder bore.*

2. Position the spring with the tapered end going in last, facing toward the primary cup on the piston (**Figure 56**).

3. Install the spring, primary cup and piston assembly into the cylinder (**Figure 47**). Push them in until they bottom out.

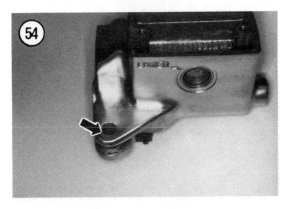

4. Install the circlip (**Figure 46**) and slide in the rubber boot (**Figure 45**).

5. Install the hand lever, the bolt and nut and tighten securely.

6. If removed, install the brake light switch and screws to the master cylinder. Tighten the screw securely.

12

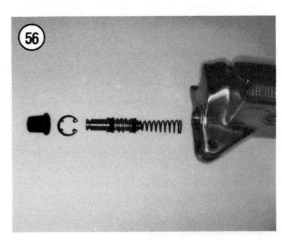

7. Install the master cylinder as described in this chapter.

FRONT BRAKE HOSE REPLACEMENT

Suzuki recommends replacing the brake hose every four years or when it shows signs of cracking or damage.

Removal/Installation

> *CAUTION*
> *Cover the surrounding area with a heavy cloth or plastic tarp to protect them from accidental brake fluid spills. Wash brake fluid off any painted or plated surfaces or plastic parts immediately, as it will destroy the finish. Use soapy water and rinse completely.*

1. Remove the cap from the bleed screw (**Figure 57**) on the front caliper.

2. Attach a piece of hose to the bleed screw and place the loose end in a container.

3. Open the bleed screw and operate the master cylinder lever to pump the brake fluid out of the master cylinder, the brake hose and the caliper assembly. Operate the lever until the system is clear of brake fluid.

4. Clean the top of the master cylinder of all dirt and foreign matter.

5. Remove the screws securing the cover (A, **Figure 58**). Remove the cover and the diaphragm.

6. If you have a shop syringe, draw all of any residual brake fluid from the master cylinder reservoir.

7. Unscrew the union bolt (B, **Figure 58**) securing the brake hose to the master cylinder. Don't lose the sealing washer on each side of the hose fitting.

8. At the brake caliper, hold onto the brake hose fitting (A, **Figure 59**) with an open-end wrench. Loosen the brake hose adaptor nut (B, **Figure 59**) securing the brake hose to the caliper assembly.

9. Remove the brake hose and sealing washer from the brake hose adaptor nut and let the brake fluid drain out into the container. Dispose of this brake fluid—never reuse brake fluid.

10. Unhook the brake hose from the clamp on the right-hand fork leg.

11. Pull the brake hose assembly up through the lower fork bridge (**Figure 60**) and the upper fork bridge (**Figure 61**) and remove the brake hose from the frame.

12. Install new hoses, sealing washers and union bolts in the reverse order of removal while noting the following:

   a. Be sure to install new sealing washers (**Figure 42**) and in their correct positions.

   b. Hold onto the brake hose fitting (A, **Figure 62**) with an open-end wrench. Tighten the brake

hose adaptor nut (B, **Figure 62**) securing the brake hose to the caliper assembly. Tighten the brake hose adaptor nut securely.

   c. Tighten the fittings and union bolts to the torque specifications listed in **Table 1**.

   d. Bleed the brake as described under *Bleeding the System* in this chapter.

FRONT BRAKE DISC

Removal/Installation

1. Remove the front wheel as described in Chapter Ten.

> *NOTE*
> *Place a piece of wood or vinyl tube in the caliper in place of the disc. This way, if the brake lever is inadvertently squeezed the pistons will not be forced out of the cylinders. If this does happen, the caliper might have to be disassembled to reseat the pistons and the system will have to be bled. By using the wood or vinyl tube, bleeding the system is not necessary when installing the wheel.*

> *CAUTION*
> *Do not set the wheel down on the disc surface, as it may get scratched or warped. Set the wheel on 2 blocks of wood (**Figure 63**).*

2. Remove the speedometer housing (**Figure 64**) from the left-hand side.

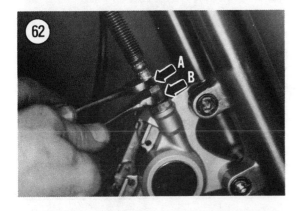

12

3. Turn the wheel over and remove the side collar (**Figure 65**) from the right-hand side.

4. Remove the bolts (**Figure 66**) securing the brake disc to the hub and remove the disc.

5. Install by reversing these removal steps, noting the following:.

    a. Apply blue Loctite (No. 271) to the disc mounting bolts prior to installation.

    b. Tighten the disc mounting bolts to the torque specifications listed in **Table 1**.

Inspection

It is not necessary to remove the disc from the wheel to inspect it. Small marks on the disc are not important, but radial scratches deep enough to snag a fingernail reduce braking effectiveness and increase brake pad wear. If these grooves are found, the disc should be replaced.

1. Measure the thickness of the disc at several locations around the disc with a micrometer (**Figure 67**) or vernier caliper. The disc must be replaced if the thickness in any area is less than that specified in **Table 2**.

2. Make sure the disc bolts are tight prior to running this check. Check the disc runout with a dial indicator as shown in **Figure 68**. Slowly rotate the wheel and watch the dial indicator. If the runout exceeds that listed in **Table 2** the disc(s) must be replaced.

3. Clean the disc (**Figure 69**) of any rust or corrosion and wipe clean with lacquer thinner. Never use an oil-based solvent that may leave an oil residue on the disc.

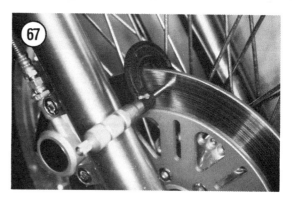

BLEEDING THE SYSTEM

This procedure is not necessary unless the brakes feel spongy, there has been a leak in the system, a component has been replaced or the brake fluid has been replaced.

1. Remove the dust cap from the bleed valve (**Figure 70**) on the caliper assembly.

2. Connect a piece of clear tubing to the bleed valve on the caliper assembly.

CAUTION
Cover the wheel with a heavy cloth or plastic tarp to protect it from the accidental spilling of brake fluid. Wash any brake fluid off of any plastic, painted or

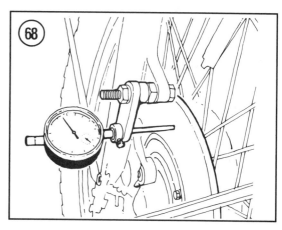

plated surface immediately; as it will destroy the finish. Use soapy water and rinse completely.

3. Clean the top cover or cap of the master cylinder of all dirt and foreign matter.

4. Remove the screws securing the cover (**Figure 71**). Remove the cover and the diaphragm.

5. Fill the reservoir almost to the top lip; install the diaphragm and the cover, or cap, loosely. Leave the cover, or cap, in place during this procedure to prevent the entry of dirt.

6. Place the other end of the tube into a clean container.

7. Fill the container with enough fresh brake fluid to keep the end submerged.

> *WARNING*
> *Use brake fluid from a sealed container marked DOT 3 or DOT 4 only (specified for disc brakes). Other types may vaporize and cause brake failure. Do not intermix different brands or types as they may not be compatible. Do not intermix a silicone based (DOT 5) brake fluid as it can cause brake component damage leading to brake system failure.*

> *NOTE*
> *During this procedure, it is very important to check the fluid level in the brake master cylinder reservoir often. If the reservoir runs dry, you'll introduce more air in the system which will require starting over.*

8. If the master cylinder was drained, it must be bled first as follows:

    a. Remove the union bolt (A, **Figure 72**) and hose from the master cylinder.

    b. Slowly apply the brake lever (B, **Figure 72**) several times while holding your thumb over the opening in the master cylinder and perform the following:

    c. With the lever applied, slightly release your thumb pressure. Some of the brake fluid and air bubbles will escape.

    d. Apply thumb pressure and pump lever once more.

    e. Repeat this procedure until you can feel resistance at the lever.

9. Quickly reinstall the hose, sealing washers and the union bolt. Refill the master cylinder.

12

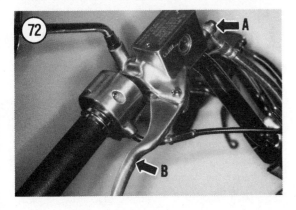

10. Tighten the union bolt and pump the lever again and perform the following:

   a. Loosen the union bolt 1/4 turn. Some brake fluid and air bubbles will escape.

   b. Tighten the union bolt and repeat this procedure until no air bubbles escape.

11. Tighten the union bolts to the torque specification listed in **Table 1**.

12. Slowly apply the brake lever several times as follows:

   a. Pull the lever in and hold it in the applied position.

   b. Open the bleed valve about one-half turn. Allow the lever, or pedal, to travel to its limit.

   c. When this limit is reached, tighten the bleed valve.

13. As the fluid enters the system, the level will drop in the reservoir. Maintain the level to just about the top of the reservoir to prevent air from being drawn into the system.

14. Continue to pump the lever and fill the reservoir until the fluid emerging from the hose is completely free of bubbles.

NOTE
Do not allow the reservoir to empty during the bleeding operation or more air will enter the system. If this occurs, the entire procedure must be repeated.

NOTE
If you are having trouble getting all of the bubbles out of the system, refer to the Reverse Flow Bleeding at the end of this section.

15. Hold the lever in, tighten the bleed valve, remove the bleed tube and install the bleed valve dust cap.

16. If necessary, add fluid to correct the level in the reservoir.

17. Install the diaphragm and the cover.

18. Test the feel of the brake lever, or pedal. It should be firm and should offer the same resistance each time it is operated. If it feels spongy, it is likely that there is still air in the system and it must be bled again. When all air has been bled from the system and the fluid level is correct in the reservoir, double-check for leaks and tighten all fittings and connections.

WARNING
Before riding the bike, make certain that the brakes are operating correctly. Spin the front wheel and apply the lever several times. The wheel must come to a complete stop each time.

19. Test ride the bike slowly at first to make sure that the brakes are operating properly.

Reverse Flow Bleeding

This bleeding procedure can be used if you are having a difficult time freeing the system all of bubbles.

Using this procedure, the brake fluid will be forced into the system in a reverse direction. The fluid will enter the caliper, flow through the brake hose and into the master cylinder reservoir. If the system is already filled with brake fluid, the existing fluid will be flushed out of the top of the master cylinder by the new brake fluid being forced into the caliper. Siphon the fluid from the reservoir, then hold a shop cloth under the master cylinder reservoir to catch any addition fluid that will be forced out.

A special reverse flow tool called the EZE Bleeder is available or a home made tool can be fabricated for this procedure.

To make this home made tool, perform the following:

NOTE
The brake fluid container must be plastic—not metal. Use vinyl tubing of the correct inner diameter to ensure a tight fit on the caliper bleed valve.

   a. Purchase a 12 oz. (345 ml) *plastic* bottle of DOT 3 or DOT 4 brake fluid.

   b. Remove the cap, drill an appropriate size hole and adapt a vinyl hose fitting onto the cap.

   c. Attach a section of vinyl hose to the hose fitting on the cap and secure it with a hose clamp. This joint must be a tight fit as the plastic brake fluid bottle will be squeezed to force the brake fluid out past this fitting and through the hose.

   d. Remove the moisture seal from the plastic bottle of brake fluid and screw the cap and hose assembly onto the bottle.

1. Remove the dust cap from the bleed valve (**Figure 70**) on the caliper assembly.

2. Clean the top cover of the master cylinder of all dirt and foreign matter.

3. Remove the screws securing the cover (**Figure 71**). Remove the cover and the diaphragm.

4. Attach the vinyl hose to the bleed valve on the caliper. Make sure the hose is tight on the bleed valve.

5. Open the bleed valve and squeeze the plastic bottle forcing this brake fluid into the system.

NOTE
If necessary, siphon brake fluid from the reservoir to avoid overflow of fluid.

6. Observe the brake fluid entering the master cylinder reservoir. Continue to apply pressure from the tool, or bottle, until the fluid entering the reservoir is free of all air bubbles.

7. Close the bleed valve and disconnect the bleeder or hose from the bleed valve.

8. Install the dust cap onto the bleed valve on the caliper.

9. At this time the system should be free of bubbles. Apply the brake lever and check for proper brake operation. If the system still feels spongy, perform the typical bleeding procedure in the beginning of this section.

REAR DRUM BRAKE

Pushing down on the brake foot pedal pulls the rod, or cable, pulling the brake arm that in turn rotates the camshaft. This forces the brake shoes out into contact with the brake drum.

Pedal free play must be maintained to minimize brake drag and premature brake wear and maximize braking effectiveness. Refer to Chapter Three for complete adjustment procedure.

Disassembly

Refer to **Figure 73** for this procedure.

WARNING
*When working on the brake system, do **not** inhale brake dust. It may contain asbestos, which can cause lung injury and cancer. Wear a face mask that meets OSHA requirements for trapping asbestos particles, and wash your hands and*

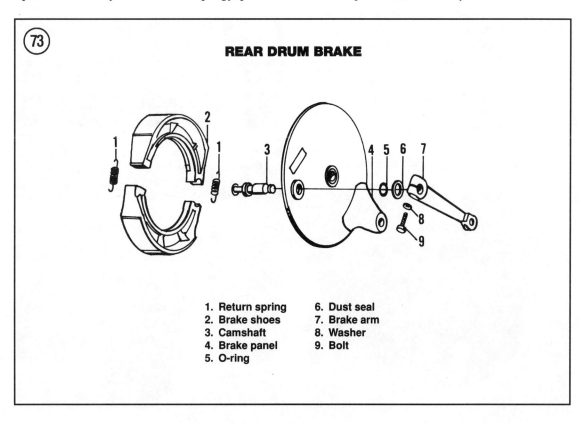

REAR DRUM BRAKE

1. Return spring
2. Brake shoes
3. Camshaft
4. Brake panel
5. O-ring
6. Dust seal
7. Brake arm
8. Washer
9. Bolt

12

*forearms thoroughly after completing
the work.*

1. Remove the rear wheel as described in Chapter
Eleven.

2. Pull the brake assembly straight up and out of the
brake drum.

3. Carefully pull up on both brake shoes in a V-for-
mation (**Figure 74**) and remove the brake shoes and
return springs as an assembly.

4. Disconnect the return springs from the brake
shoes.

5. If necessary, remove the bolt (**Figure 75**) securing the brake arm and remove the brake arm, spring,
washer and O-ring. Withdraw the camshaft from the
backing plate.

Inspection

1. Thoroughly clean and dry all parts except the
brake linings.

2. Check the contact surface of the drum for scoring
(**Figure 76**). If there are grooves deep enough to
snag your fingernail the drum should be reground.

3. Measure the inside diameter of the brake drum
(**Figure 77**). If the measurement is greater than the
service limit listed in **Table 2**, either the rear hub or
the rear wheel must be replaced.

4. If the drum can be turned and still stay within the
maximum service limit diameter, the linings will
have to be replaced and the new ones arced to
conform to the new drum contour.

5. Measure the brake lining thickness with a vernier
caliper (**Figure 78**). They should be replaced if the

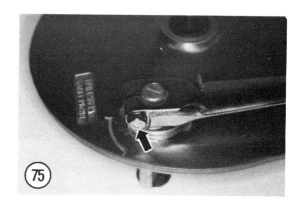

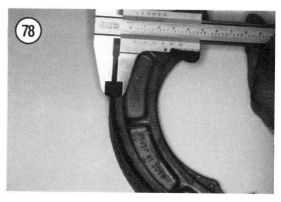

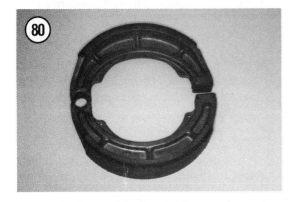

lining portion is worn to the service limit dimension or less. Refer to specifications listed in **Table 2**.

6. Inspect the linings (**Figure 79**) for imbedded foreign material. Dirt can be removed with a stiff wire brush. Check for any traces of oil or grease; if they are contaminated they must be replaced.

7. Inspect the brake shoe assemblies (**Figure 80**) for wear, cracks or other damage. Replace as a set if necessary.

8. Inspect the cam lobe and pivot pins (**Figure 81**) for wear or corrosion. Minor roughness can be removed with fine emery cloth.

9. Inspect the backing plate (**Figure 82**) for wear, cracks or other damage. Replace if necessary.

10. Inspect the rear axle bushing (**Figure 83**) in the backing plate for wear, scoring or other damage. Replace the backing plate if necessary; the bushing cannot be replaced.

11. Inspect the brake shoe return springs for wear. If they are stretched, they will not fully retract the brake shoes. Replace as necessary.

Assembly

1. If removed, grease the camshaft with a light coat of molybdenum disulfide grease. Install the cam into the backing plate from the backside.

2. From the outside of the backing plate install a new O-ring and washer onto the camshaft.

3. Install the spring and the camshaft. When installing the brake arm onto the camshaft, align the gap in the arm with the dimple on the camshaft (A, **Figure 84**).

4. Index the spring onto the brake arm (B, **Figure 84**) as shown.

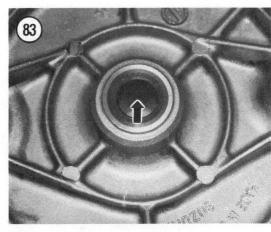

12

5. Install and tighten the bolt to the torque specification listed in **Table 1**.

6. Grease the camshaft and pivot post (**Figure 81**) with a light coat of molybdenum disulfide grease; avoid getting any grease on the brake backing plate where the brake linings may come in contact with it.

7. Assemble the return springs onto the brake shoes.

8. Hold the brake shoes in a "V" formation with the return springs attached (**Figure 74**) and snap them into place on the brake backing plate. Make sure they are firmly seated on it (**Figure 85**).

9. Install the brake panel assembly into the brake drum.

10. Install the rear wheel as described in Chapter Eleven.

11. Adjust the rear brake as described in Chapter Three.

REAR BRAKE PEDAL AND LINKAGE

Removal/Installation (Rod Type)

Refer to **Figure 86** for this procedure.

NOTE
The brake pedal and rod link No. 2 are attached to the footpeg assembly and come off as an assembly. All other components of the rear brake pedal assembly are attached to the frame. The 2 different assemblies are covered separately in this procedure.

Brake pedal

1. Place wood block(s) under the engine to support the bike securely. The sidestand is part of the front footpeg assembly and cannot be used to support the bike.

2. Remove the clips from the bolts securing the front footpeg assembly to the frame.

3. Remove the bolts and lower the footpeg assembly down.

4. Remove the cotter pin, washer and pivot pin, then unhook the rod link No. 2 from the brake pedal link No. 2 arm.

5. Remove the cotter pin, washer and pivot pin securing the rod link No. 2 to the brake pedal link No. 1 arm. Remove the rod link No. 2.

6. Remove the cotter pins, washers and pivot pins securing the rod link No. 1 to the brake pedal link No. 1 arm and to the brake pedal. Remove the rod link No. 1.

7. Remove the cotter pin and cap securing the brake pedal to the pivot post on the footpeg assembly and remove the brake pedal.

8. Install by reversing these removal steps, noting the following:

    a. Apply clean engine oil to all pivot areas prior to installing any parts and again after all parts have been installed.

    b. Always install new cotter pins—never reuse a cotter pin as the ends may break off and the cotter pin could fall out disabling the brake system.

    c. Tighten the bolts securing the footpeg assembly to the torque specification listed in **Table 1** and install the clips on the 2 outboard bolts on each side.

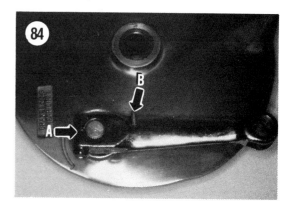

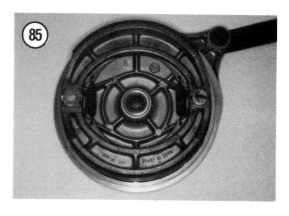

Brake pedal linkage

1. Place wood block(s) under the engine to support the bike securely. The sidestand is part of the front footpeg assembly and cannot be used to support the bike.

2. Remove the clips from the bolts securing the front footpeg assembly to the frame.

3. Remove the bolts and lower the footpeg assembly down.

4. Remove the exhaust system for the front cylinder as described under *Exhaust System Removal/Installation* in Chapter Seven.

5. Remove the battery case as described under *Battery Case Removal/Installation* in Chapter Eight.

6. Remove the regulator/rectifier as described under *Regulator/Rectifier Removal/Installation* in Chapter Eight.

7. Completely unscrew the adjustment nut (**Figure 87**) on the brake rod.

8. Push down on the brake pedal and remove the brake rod from the pivot joint in the brake arm. With the spring still in place on the rod, install the pivot joint onto the brake rod and reinstall the adjustment nut to avoid misplacing the small parts.

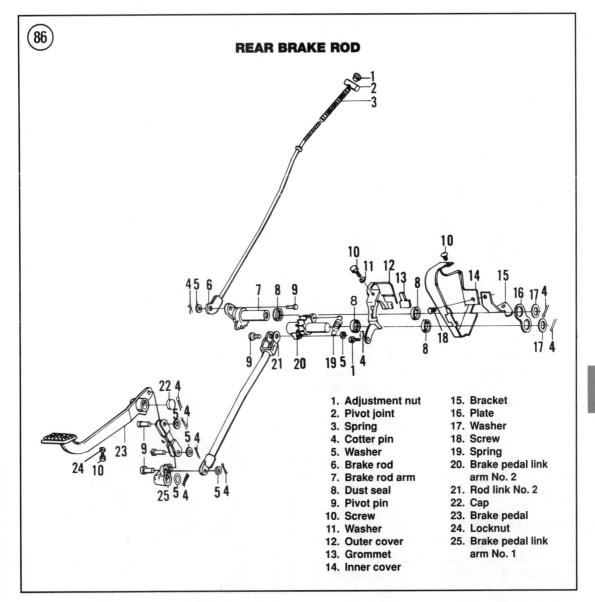

REAR BRAKE ROD

1. Adjustment nut
2. Pivot joint
3. Spring
4. Cotter pin
5. Washer
6. Brake rod
7. Brake rod arm
8. Dust seal
9. Pivot pin
10. Screw
11. Washer
12. Outer cover
13. Grommet
14. Inner cover
15. Bracket
16. Plate
17. Washer
18. Screw
19. Spring
20. Brake pedal link arm No. 2
21. Rod link No. 2
22. Cap
23. Brake pedal
24. Locknut
25. Brake pedal link arm No. 1

12

9. Remove the cotter pin, washer and pivot pin, then unhook the rod link No. 2 from the brake pedal link No. 2 arm.

10. Remove the bolts and washers securing the outer cover and remove the outer cover.

11. Unhook the springs (A, **Figure 88**) from the brake rod arm and brake pedal link No. 2 arm.

12. Remove the cotter pin, washer and pivot pin, then unhook the brake pedal rod (B, **Figure 88**) from the brake rod arm (C, **Figure 88**). Remove the brake rod arm from the frame.

13. To remove the brake rod arm and the brake pedal link No. 2 arm from the frame, perform the following:

    a. Remove the cotter pins (A, **Figure 89**), washers (B, **Figure 89**) and the plate (C, **Figure 89**) from the backside of the pivot pins.

    b. Withdraw the brake rod arm and the brake pedal link No. 2 arm from the frame receptacles.

14. Install by reversing these removal steps, noting the following:

    a. Apply clean engine oil to all pivot areas prior to installing any parts and again after all parts have been installed.

    b. When installing the brake rod arm and the brake pedal link No. 2 arm into the frame receptacles; align the punch mark on both parts. This is necessary for proper brake operation.

    c. Always install new cotter pins—never reuse a cotter pin, because the ends may break off allowing the cotter pin to fall out, disabling the brake system.

    d. Tighten the bolts securing the footpeg assembly to the torque specification listed in **Table 2** and install the clips on the 2 outboard bolts on each side.

    e. Adjust the rear brake as described in Chapter Three.

Removal/Installation (Cable Type)

Refer to **Figure 90** for this procedure.

1. Place wood block(s) under the engine to support the bike securely. The sidestand is part of the front footpeg assembly and cannot be used to support the bike.

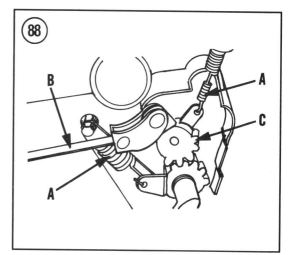

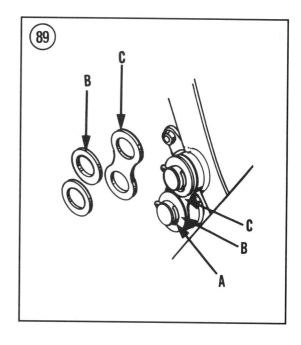

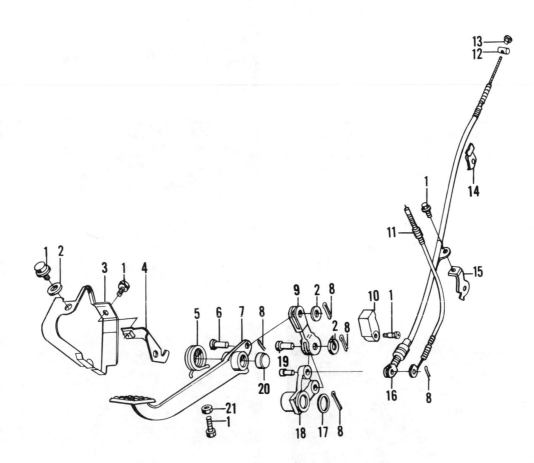

REAR BRAKE CABLE

1. Bolt
2. Washer
3. Cover
4. Bracket
5. Spring
6. Pivot pin
7. Brake pedal
8. Cotter pin
9. Brake pedal link
10. Pad
11. Brake light switch cable
12. Pivot joint
13. Adjustment nut
14. Clamp
15. Clamp
16. Brake pedal cable
17. Washer
18. Brake pedal arm
19. Pivot pin
20. Cap
21. Locknut

2. Completely unscrew the adjustment nut (**Figure 87**) on the end of the brake cable.

3. Push down on the brake pedal and remove the brake rod from the pivot joint in the brake arm. Install the pivot joint onto the brake cable and reinstall the adjustment nut to avoid misplacing the small parts.

4. Remove the brake cable from the receptacle (**Figure 91**) on the brake panel.

5. Remove the bolts and washers securing the cover (**Figure 92**) and remove the cover.

6. Disconnect the brake light switch return spring (**Figure 93**) from the brake light switch cable.

7. Slide the rubber boot (**Figure 94**) off the end of the brake light switch cable.

8. Loosen the locknut (**Figure 95**) and remove the brake light switch cable and the brake panel cable assembly to the frame mounting tab (A, **Figure 96**).

9. Remove the bolt (B, **Figure 96**) securing the brake pedal cable assembly to the frame. Remove the brake light switch cable and the brake panel cable assembly from the frame mounting tab.

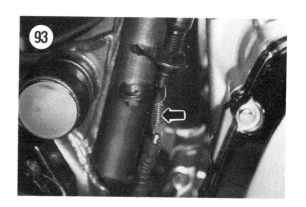

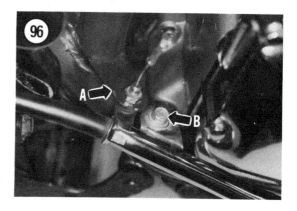

10. Remove the clips from the bolts securing the front footpeg assembly (**Figure 97**) to the frame. Lower the footpeg assembly from the frame.

11. To remove the brake rod arm and the brake pedal link No. 2 arm from the frame, perform the following:

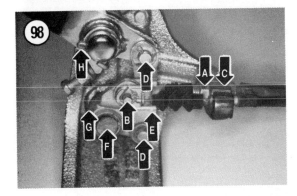

a. Loosen the locknut (A, **Figure 98**) on the brake panel cable.

b. Remove the cotter pin (B, **Figure 98**) securing both cables to the brake pedal arm.

c. Disconnect the cables from the receptacles (C, **Figure 98**) on the footpeg assembly. Remove both cables.

d. Remove both cotter pins and washers (D, **Figure 98**) securing the brake pedal link and remove the brake pedal link (E, **Figure 98**).

e. Remove the cotter pin and washer (F, **Figure 98**) securing the brake pedal arm and remove the brake pedal arm (G, **Figure 98**).

f. Remove the cotter pin and cap (H, **Figure 98**) securing the brake pedal and remove the brake pedal and spring.

12. Install by reversing these removal steps, noting the following:

a. Apply clean engine oil to all pivot areas prior to installing any parts, then oil pivots again after all parts have been installed.

b. Always install new cotter pins—never reuse a cotter pin as the ends may break off and the cotter pin could fall out disabling the brake system.

c. Tighten the bolts securing the footpeg assembly to the torque specification listed in **Table 2** and install the clips on the 2 outboard bolts on each side.

d. Adjust the rear brake as described in Chapter Three.

12

Table 1 BRAKE SYSTEM TIGHTENING TORQUES

Item	N•m	ft.-lb.
Front master cylinder		
Clamping bolts	5-8	3-6
Union bolt	20-25	14-18
Front caliper		
Bleed valve	6-9	4.5-6.5
Mounting bolts	18-28	13-20
Housing assembly bolts	15-20	11-14.5
Brake disc bolts	15-25	11-18
Rear drum brake arm bolt	5-8	3.5-6.0
Front footpeg assembly bolts	15-25	11-18

Table 2 BRAKE SYSTEM SPECIFICATIONS

Item	Specifications	Wear limit
Front master cylinder		
Cylinder bore ID	15.870-15.913 mm (0.6248-0.6265 in.)	—
Piston OD	15.827-15.854 mm (0.6231-0.6242 in.)	—
Front caliper		
Cylinder bore ID	38.180-38.256 mm (1.5031-1.5061 in.)	—
Piston OD	38.098-38.148 mm (1.4999-1.5019 in.)	—
Front brake disc		
Thickness	4.8-5.2 mm (0.189-205 in.)	4.5 mm (0.18 in.)
Disc runout	—	0.3 mm (0.012 in.)
Rear brake		
Drum I.D.	—	180.7 mm (7.11 in.)
Lining thickness	—	1.5 mm (0.06 in.)

CHAPTER THIRTEEN

BODY AND FRAME

This chapter contains removal and installation procedures for all body panels and frame components.

SEATS

Rider's Seat
Removal/Installation

Refer to **Figure 1** for this procedure.

1. Remove the right-hand frame side cover as described in this chapter.

2. Remove the bolt, lockwasher and washer (A, **Figure 2**) at the front on each side.

3. Pull up on the front of the seat (B, **Figure 2**) and move the seat toward the front to disengage it from the rear retaining bracket on the pillion seat.

4. Partially remove the seat. Carefully remove the sidestand check relay (**Figure 3**) from the base of the seat.

5. Remove the seat assembly.

6. To install, move the seat onto the frame and reinstall the sidestand check relay into the base of the seat. Make sure the relay is secured correctly.

7. Insert the seat's rear tab under the retaining bracket on the pillion seat. Push the seat back and make sure the tab is located correctly under the bracket.

> ### WARNING
> *After the seat is installed, pull up on it firmly to make sure it is securely locked in place. If the seat is not correctly locked in place it may slide to one side or the other when riding the bike. This*

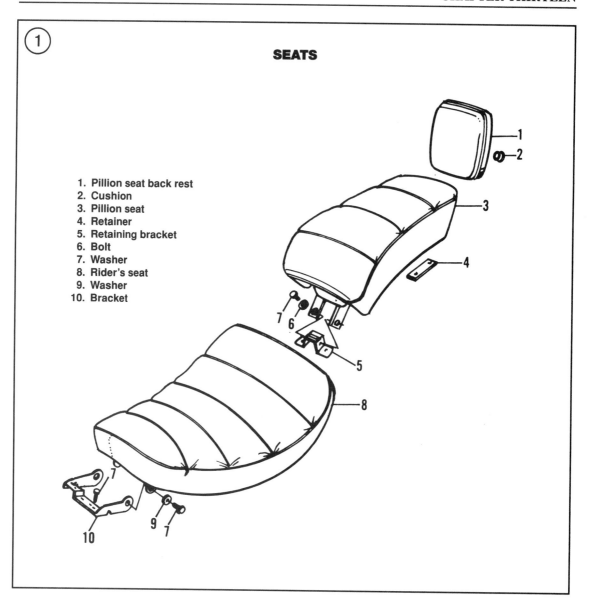

SEATS

1. Pillion seat back rest
2. Cushion
3. Pillion seat
4. Retainer
5. Retaining bracket
6. Bolt
7. Washer
8. Rider's seat
9. Washer
10. Bracket

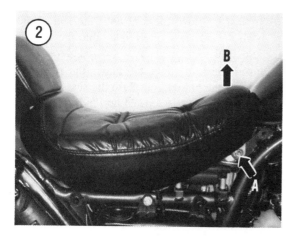

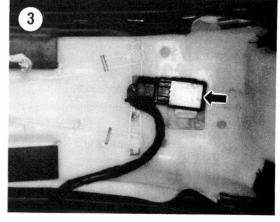

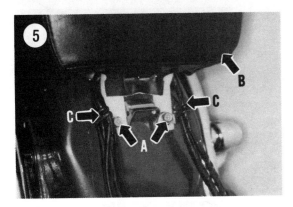

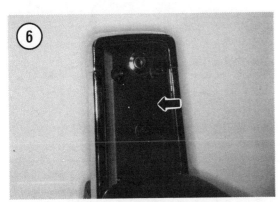

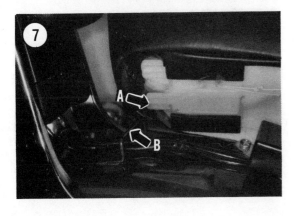

could lead to the loss of control and a possible accident.

8. Push the front of the seat down and align the front mounting bolt holes with the mounting bracket on the frame. Install the washer, lockwasher and bolt (**Figure 4**) on each side and tighten securely.

9. Install both frame side covers as described in this chapter.

Pillion Seat and Backrest Removal/Installation

Refer to **Figure 1** for this procedure.

1. Remove the rider's seat as described in this chapter.

2. Remove the bolts, lockwashers and washers (A, **Figure 5**) securing the pillion seat and retaining bracket to the rear fender.

3. Pull up on the seat toward the front and remove the seat assembly (B, **Figure 5**) from the rear retaining loop on the rear fender.

4. If necessary, carefully pull on both sides of the backrest and disengage it from the locating bosses on the tool box cover on the rear handle.

5. If removed, install the backrest onto the locating bosses on the tool box cover (**Figure 6**) on the rear handle. Move it from side to side to make sure it is secure.

6. Install the seat and insert the seat's locating tab (A, **Figure 7**) under the retaining loop (B, **Figure 7**) on the rear fender. Push the seat back and make sure the tab is located correctly under the loop.

7. Push the front of the seat down and align the front mounting bracket holes with the mounting holes in the fender. Be careful not to trap any of the electrical wires (C, **Figure 5**) under the mounting bracket. Install the washers, lockwashers and bolts (**Figure 5**) and tighten securely.

8. Install the rider's seat as described in this chapter.

FRAME SIDE COVERS

Removal/Installation

1. On the right-hand side only, perform the following:

    a. Remove the bolt and washer (**Figure 8**) securing the frame side cover to the frame rail at the front.

13

b. Carefully pull the front section of the frame side cover off the mounting posts at locations shown in **Figure 9** and remove the cover.

2. On the left-hand side only, perform the following:

a. Remove the rider's seat as described in this chapter.

b. Remove the screw (A, **Figure 10**) securing the frame side cover to the bracket between the fuel pump and fuse panel.

c. Carefully pull the front section of the frame side cover off the mounting posts at locations shown in B, **Figure 10** and remove the cover.

3. Install by reversing these removal steps, noting the following:

a. Make sure the rubber cushions are in place in the mounting brackets on the backside on both frame side covers.

b. On the right-hand side only, make sure the rubber cushion and metal collar are in place in the front mounting hole of the cover.

c. Tighten all screws securely.

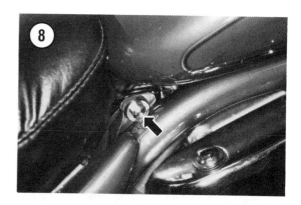

FRAME HEAD SIDE COVERS

Removal/Installation

1. Remove the fuel tank as described in Chapter Seven.

2. Remove the screws securing the left-hand frame head side cover (**Figure 11**).

3. Pull the cover straight off the frame and remove it.

4. Repeat for the other cover if necessary.

FOOTPEGS

Front Footpeg Assembly
Removal/Installation

Refer to **Figure 12** for this procedure.

> *NOTE*
> *The front footpeg assembly (**Figure 13**) cannot be completely removed from the frame without first removing the rear brake pedal assembly from the footpeg assembly.*

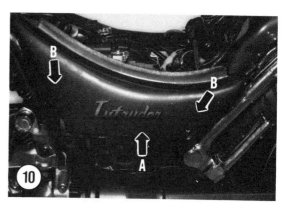

1. Remove the rear brake pedal assembly (**Figure 14**) from the front footpeg assembly as described

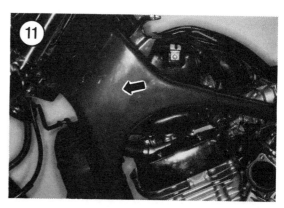

FRONT FOOTPEG ASSEMBLY

WITH BRAKE ROD

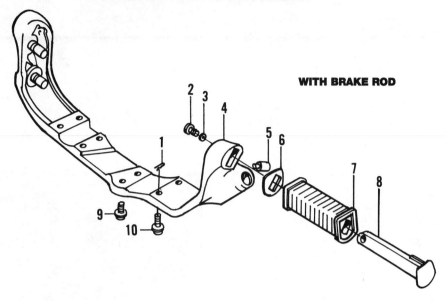

1. Clip
2. Bolt
3. Washer
4. Footpeg bracket
   (with brake rod)
5. Special bolt

6. Spring washer
7. Rubber pad
8. Armature
9. Bolt
10. Bolt (with hole
    for clip)

11. Footpeg bnracket
    (with brake cable)
12. Rubber pad
13. Plate
14. Bracket
15. Bolt

WITH BRAKE CABLE

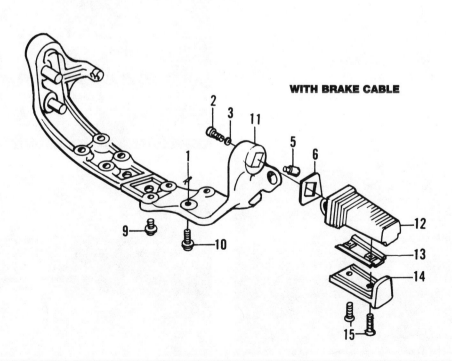

13

under *Rear Brake Pedal and Linkage Removal/Installation* in Chapter Twelve.

2. Remove the screws (**Figure 15**) securing the sidestand check switch to the footpeg assembly and remove the switch.

3. Remove the footpeg assembly.

4. To remove the individual footpeg from the assembly, perform the following:

   a. Remove the inner bolt (**Figure 16**) and the outer bolt (A, **Figure 17**) securing the footpeg.

   b. Remove the footpeg (B, **Figure 17**) from the assembly.

5. Install by reversing these removal steps, noting the following:

   a. Tighten the mounting bolts to 15-25 N•m (11-18 ft.-lb.) and install the clips (**Figure 18**) on the 2 outboard bolts on each side.

   b. Make sure all electrical connectors are free of corrosion and are tight.

Rear Footpeg
Removal/Installation

Refer to **Figure 19** for this procedure.

1. Remove the bolt (A, **Figure 20**) securing the footpeg to the mounting tab on the frame

2. Remove the footpeg (B, **Figure 20**) and shim from the frame.

3. Don't lose the spring and the steel ball detent.

4. Install by reversing these removal steps, noting the following:

   a. Make sure the shim is installed correctly.

   b. Tighten the mounting bolt securely.

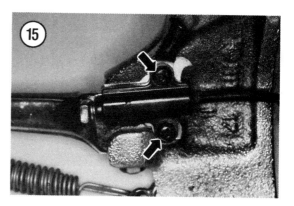

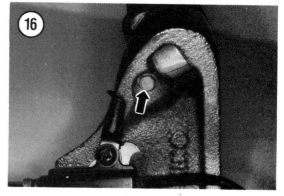

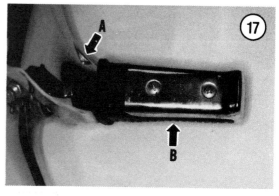

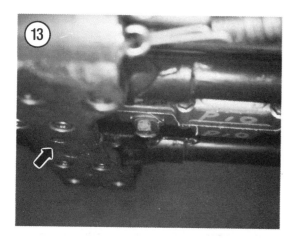

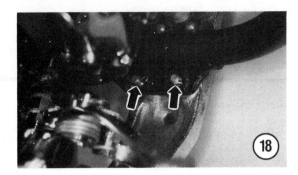

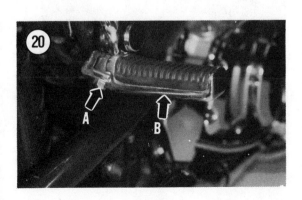

REAR FOOTPEG

1. Rubber pad
2. Plate
3. Footpeg bar
4. Steel ball
5. Bolt
6. Bolt
7. Shim
8. Bracket
9. Shoulder bolt

SIDESTAND

Removal/Installation

1. Place wood block(s) under the engine to support the bike securely.

2. Remove the trim cap (**Figure 21**) from the mounting bolt.

NOTE
Figure 22 is shown with the front foot-peg assembly removed from the frame for clarity. The sidestand can be removed without removing the footpeg assembly.

3. Use vise-grip pliers and disconnect the return springs (A, **Figure 22**) from the pin on the sidestand.

4. Remove the nut (B, **Figure 22**) from the bolt securing the sidestand to the front footpeg assembly.

5. Withdraw the bolt and remove the sidestand and shim from the footpeg assembly.

6. Install by reversing these removal steps, noting the following:

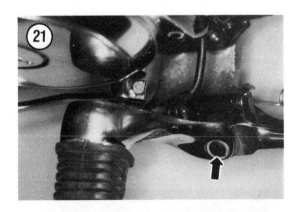

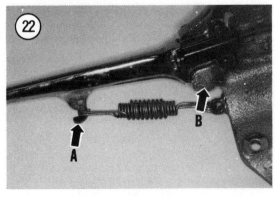

13

a. Apply a light coat of multipurpose grease to the pivot points on the footpeg assembly, the sidestand and pivot bolt prior to installation.

b. Tighten the bolt and nut securely. Install the trim cap onto the bolt head.

FRONT FENDER

Removal/Installation

1. Remove the front wheel (A, **Figure 23**) as described in Chapter Ten.
2. Remove the bolts securing the front fender (B, **Figure 23**) and the front brake caliper brake hose bracket (C, **Figure 23**) and speedometer cable bracket to the front forks.
3. Remove the front fender (B, **Figure 23**).
4. Install by reversing these removal steps, noting the following:

a. Be sure to install the speedometer bracket and front brake hose bracket to the fork assemblies along with the front fender.

b. Tighten all mounting bolts securely.

FRAME

The frame does not require routine maintenance. However, it should be inspected immediately after any accident or spill.

Component Removal/Installation

1. Remove the seats, frame head side covers, frame side covers and fuel tank.
2. Remove the engine as described in Chapter Four.
3. Remove the front wheel, steering stem and front forks as described in Chapter Ten.
4. Remove the speedometer and headlight case as described in Chapter Eight.
5. Remove the rear wheel, shock absorber and swing arm as described in Chapter Eleven.
6. Remove the front and rear fenders.
7. Remove the radiator as described in Chapter Nine.
8. Remove the battery as described in Chapter Three and the battery case as described in Chapter Eight.
9. Remove the wiring harness.
10. Remove the steering head races from the steering head tube as described in Chapter Ten.

11. Inspect the frame for bends, cracks or other damage, especially around welded joints and areas that are rusted.
12. Assemble by reversing these removal steps.

Stripping and Painting

Remove all components from the frame. Thoroughly strip off all old paint. The best way is to have it sandblasted down to bare metal. If this is not possible, you can use a liquid paint remover and steel wool and a fine, hard wire brush.

CAUTION
The fenders, frame head side covers, frame side covers and fuel tank are all metal. Do not sandblast these items as the gauge of the metal is thinner and may be damaged in the process.

When the frame is down to bare metal, have it inspected for hairline and internal cracks. Magnaflux is the most common and complete process.

Make sure that the paint primer that you use is compatible with the type of paint you are going to use for the finish color. Spray on one or two coats of primer as smoothly as possible. Let it dry thoroughly and use a fine grade of wet sandpaper (400-600 grit) to remove any flaws. Carefully wipe the surface clean and then spray a couple of coats of the final color. Use either lacquer or enamel base paint and follow the manufacturer's instructions.

A shop specializing in painting will probably do the best job. However, you can do a surprisingly good job with a good grade of spray paint. Spend a few extra dollars and get a good grade of paint as it

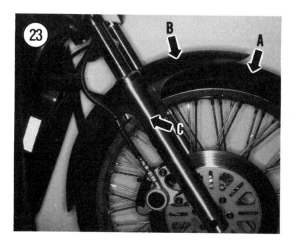

will make a difference in how good it looks and how long it will stand up.

When a good idea to shake the can and make sure the ball inside the can is loose when you purchase the can of paint. Shake the can as long as is stated on the can. Then immerse the can **upright** in a pot or bucket of **warm** water (not hot—not over 120° F).

WARNING

*Higher temperatures could cause the can to burst. Do **not** place the can in direct contact with any flame or heat source.*

Leave the can in the water for several minutes. When thoroughly warmed, shake the can again and spray the frame. Be sure to get into all the crevices where there may be rust problems. Several light mist coats are better than one heavy coat. Spray painting is best done in temperatures of 70-80° F (21-26° C); any temperature above or below this will cause problems.

After the final coat has dried completely, at least 48 hours, any overspray or orange peel may be removed with a *light* application of Dupont rubbing compound (red color) and finished with Dupont polishing compound (white color). Be careful not to rub too hard or you will go through the finish.

Finish off with a couple coats of good wax prior to reassembling all the components.

It's a good idea to keep the frame touched up with fresh paint if any minor rust spots or scratches appear.

13

INDEX

A

Alternator 255-261

B

Ball bearing replacement 26-29
Basic hand tools 13-19
Battery 50-54
   charging system 251-254
   electrical cable connectors 54-55
   installation, new 54
   negative terminal 251
Brakes 381-410
   bleeding the system 194-196, 398-401
   disc brakes 381-383
   front brake caliper 386-393
   front brake disc 397-398
   front brake hose replacement 396-397
   front brake pad replacement 383-386
   front master cylinder 393-396
   problems 41
   rear brake pedal and linkage 404-409
   rear drum brake 401-404
Break-in 167

C

Camshaft 109-110
Carburetor
   adjustments 235-237
   assembly 220-222
   fuel pump 241-243
   fuel shutoff valve and filter 240-241
   fuel tank 238-240
   operation 219-220
   service 220, 222-235
   throttle cable replacement 237-238
   troubleshooting 41
Circuit breaker 306
Cleaning solvent 23-24
Clutch 39, 172-197
   bleeding the system 194-196
   hydraulic system 182-183

   master cylinder 183-190
   slave cylinder 190-194
   starter 276-278
Cooling fan, shroud and fan duct 313-314
Cooling system check 310
Crankcase 151-161
Crankcase breather system (U.S. only) 243
Crankshaft and connecting rods 161-167
Cylinder head and cylinder 114-125

E

Electrical system 250-308
   alternator 255-261
   battery cable connectors 54-55
   battery negative terminal 251
   charging system 251254
   circuit breaker 306
   connectors 251
   components 294-305
   electric starter 267-276
   electrical connectors 251
   fuses 305-306
   lighting system 279-285
   problems 39-41
   starter clutch and gears 276-278
   starter relay 278-279
   starter system 250-251, 265-267
   switches 285-294
   transistorized ignition system 261
   voltage regulator/rectifier 254-255
   wiring diagrams 306, 423-439
Engine 91-171
   break-in 167
   camshaft 109-110
   checks 35-37
   crankcase 151-161
   crankshaft and connecting rods 161-167
   cylinder head and cylinder 114-125
   front cylinder head cover
     and camshaft 96-102
   lubrication 38-39
   noises 38

Engine (cont.)
  oil pump 141-142
  performance 37-38
  pistons and piston rings 135-141
  primary drive gear 142-147
  principles 91
  rear cylinder head cover and camshaft. . 102-109
  removal and installation 93-96
  rocker arm assemblies 111-114
  secondary gear assembly 147-151
  servicing in frame 91-93
  valves and valve components 125-135
Evaporative emission control system
  (California models only) 243-245
Exhaust system 245-247
Expandaple supplies 12
External gearshift mechanism 198-203

F

Fasteners 6-10
Final drive unit, drive shaft and
  universal joint 368-373
Frame and body 411-419
  footpegs 414-416
  front fender 418
  head side covers 414
  seats 411-413
  sidestand 417-418
  side covers 413-414
Front suspension and steering 41, 323-360
  front forks 348-358
  front hub 327-331
  front wheel 323-327
  handlebar 337-343
  steering head and stem 343-346
  steering head bearing races 346-348
  tires 332-333
  tires, changing 333-337
  tires, repairs 337
  wheels 331-332
Fuel, emission control and
  exhaust systems 219-249
    assembly 220-222
    carburetor adjustments 235-237
    crankcase breather system (U.S. only) 243
    evaporative emission control system
      (California models only) 243-245
    exhaust system 245-247
    fuel pump 241-243
    fuel shutoff valve and filter 240-241

  fuel tank 238-240
  operation 219-220
  service 220, 222-235
  throttle cable replacement 237-238
Fuses 305-306

G

Gasket remover 12

H

Handlebar 337-343
Hoses and hose clamps 309-310, 320-322

I

Instruments, troubleshooting 35
Internal gearshift mechanism 213-218

L

Lighting system 279-285
Liquid cooling system 309-322
  cooling fan, shroud and fan duct 313-314
  cooling system check 310
  hoses 320-322
  hose and hose clamps 309-310
  pressure check 310
  radiator 310-313
  thermostat and housing 314-316
  water pump 316-320
Lubricants 10-11
Lubrication, maintenance and tune-up 44-90
  battery 50-54
  battery, installation new 54
  battery, electrical cable connectors 54-55
  periodic lubrication 55-63
  periodic maintenance 63-76
  pre-checks 48
  routine checks 44-48
  service intervals 48-49
  tires and wheels 49-50
  tune-up 76-88

M

Maintenance, periodic 63-76
Manual organization 1-2
Master cylinder 183-190
  front 393-396
Mechanic's tips 24-26

14

O

Oil pump 141-142
Oil seals. 29-30
Operating requirements 35

P

Parts replacement 6
Pistons and piston rings 135-141
Pre-checks. 48
Precision measuring tools. 19-22
Pressure check. 310
Primary drive gear 142-147

R

Radiator. 310-313
Rear brake pedal and linkage 404-409
Rear cylinder head cover and
    camshaft 102-109
Rear drum brake 401-404
Rear suspension and final drive 361-380
    final drive unit, drive shaft and
        universal joint 368-373
    rear hub. 363-368
    rear wheel 361-363
    shock absorbers 378-379
    swing arm 373-378
Riding safety 30
Rocker arm assemblies 111-114
Routine checks 44-48
RTV gasket sealant 11

S

Safety first. 2-3
Seats 411-413
Secondary gear assembly 147-151
Service engine in frame 91-93
    hints 3-5
    intervals 48-49
Shock absorbers 378-379
Sidestand. 417-418
Slave cylinder 190-194
Special tools 22-23
Starter
    clutch and gears 276-278
    relay 278-279
    system. 265-267
Steering head and stem 343-346
Steering head bearing races 346-348

T

Supplies, expendable 12
Swing arm. 373-378
Switches 285-294

Thermostat and housing 314-316
Threadlock 11-12
Throttle cable replacement 237-238
Tires 49-50, 332-333
    changing. 333-337
    repairs. 337
Tools
    basic hand. 13-19
    precision measuring 19-22
    special. 22-23
Torque specifications 6
Transistorized ignition system 261-265
Transmission. 39, 203-213
    external gearshift mechanism 198-203
    internal gearshift mechanism. 213-218
Troubleshooting 34-43
    brake problems. 41
    carburetor 41
    clutch 39
    electrical problems 39-41
    engine checks 35-37
    engine lubrication. 38-39
    engine noises 38
    engine performance 37-38
    engine principles 91
    excessive vibration. 41
    front suspension and steering. 41
    instruments 35
    operating requirements. 35
    transmission 39
Tune-up. 76-87

V

Valves and valve components. 125-135
Vibration. 41
Voltage regulator/rectifier. 254-255

W

Water pump. 316-320
Wheels
    rear hub. 363-368
    rear 361-363
Wiring diagrams 423-439

WIRING DIAGRAMS

1986 VS700 (U.S. and Canada)

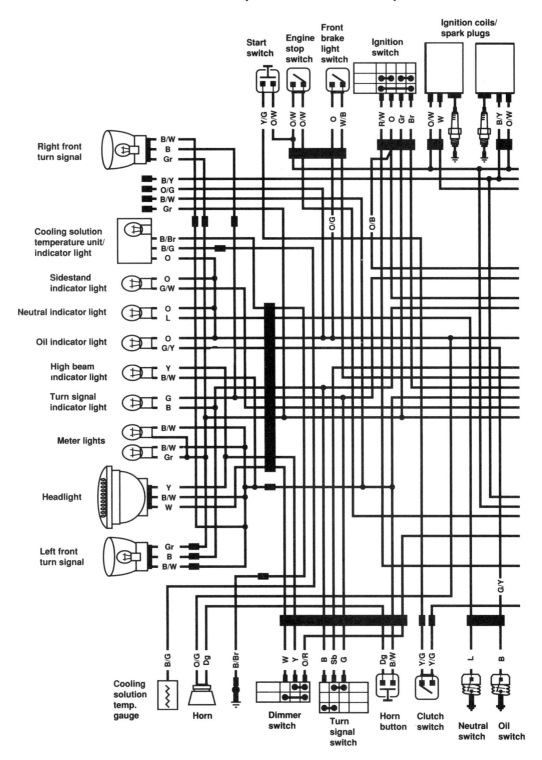

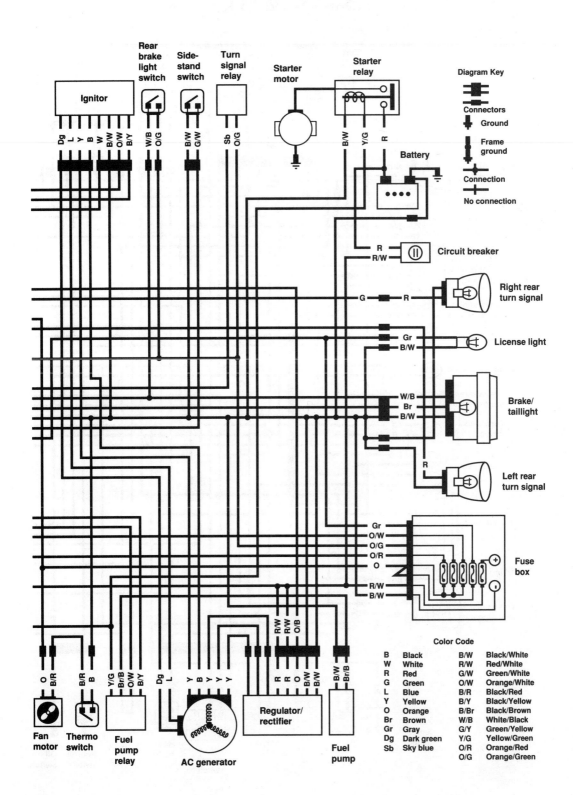

1986 VS700 (U.K.)

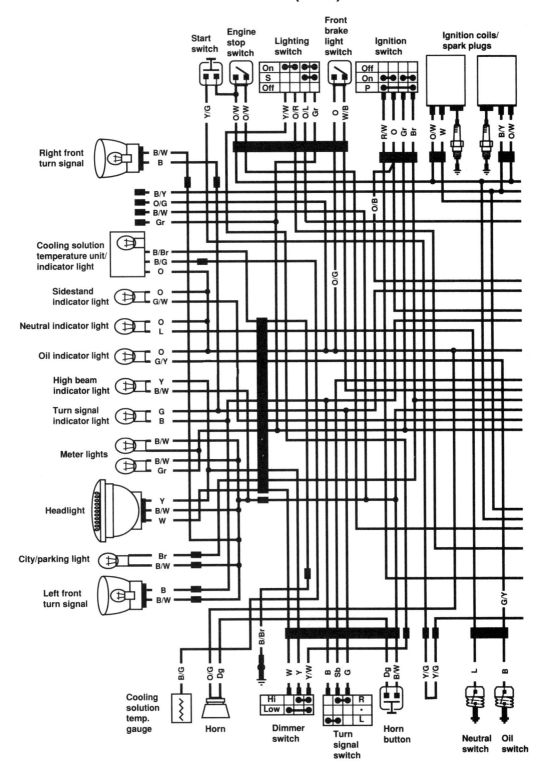

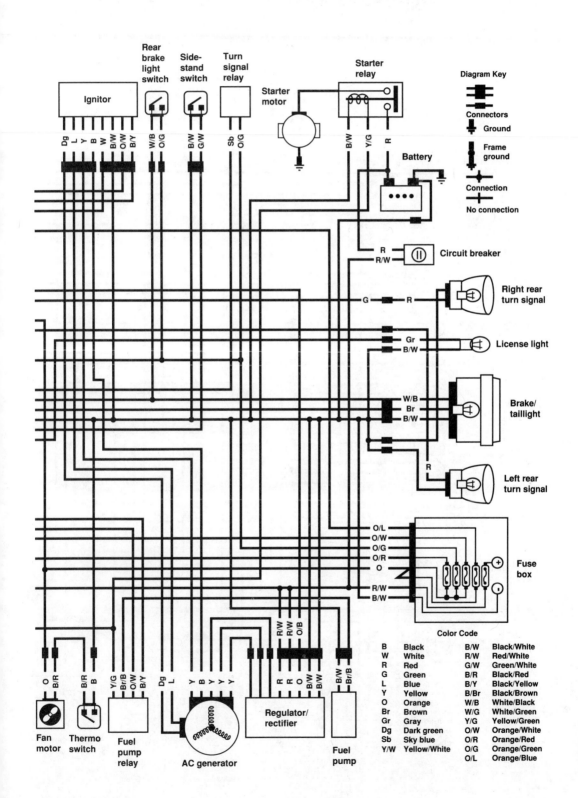

1987 VS700 (U.S. and Canada)

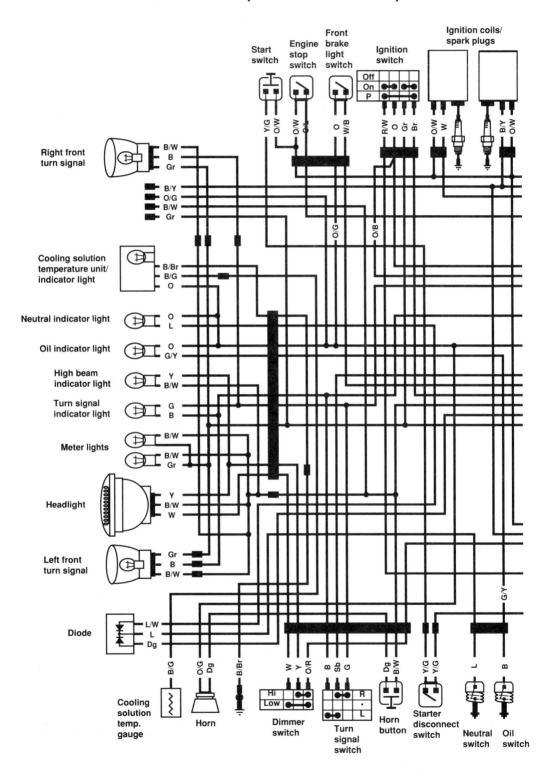

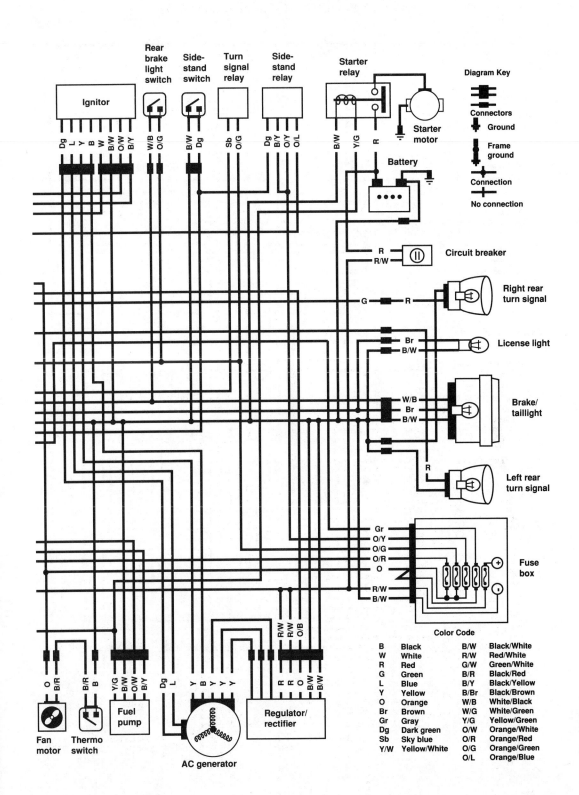

1987 VS700 (U.K.)

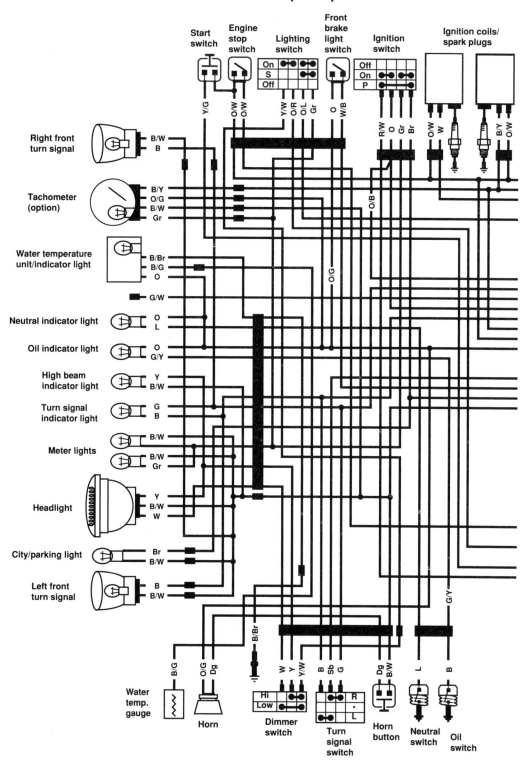

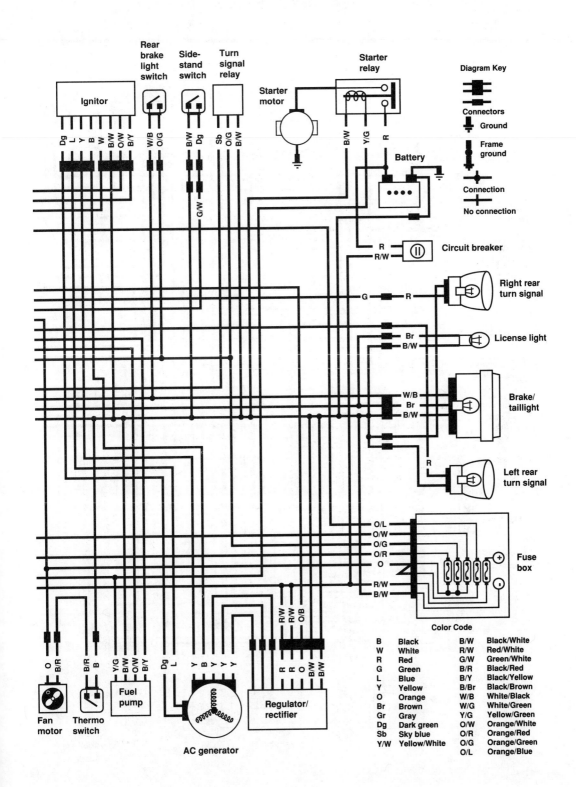

Diagram Key

Connectors

Ground

Frame ground

Connection

No connection

Color Code

B	Black	B/W	Black/White
W	White	R/W	Red/White
R	Red	G/W	Green/White
G	Green	B/R	Black/Red
L	Blue	B/Y	Black/Yellow
Y	Yellow	B/Br	Black/Brown
O	Orange	W/B	White/Black
Br	Brown	W/G	White/Green
Gr	Gray	Y/G	Yellow/Green
Dg	Dark green	O/W	Orange/White
Sb	Sky blue	O/R	Orange/Red
Y/W	Yellow/White	O/G	Orange/Green
		O/L	Orange/Blue

15

1988-1991 VS750 (U.S. and Canada)

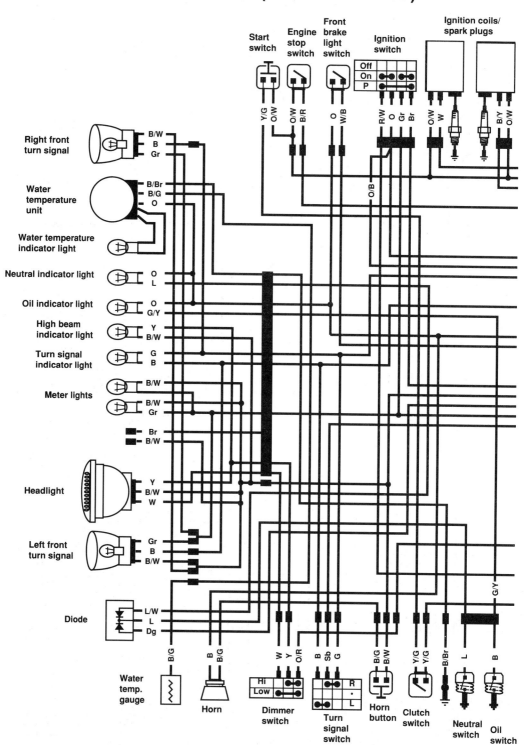

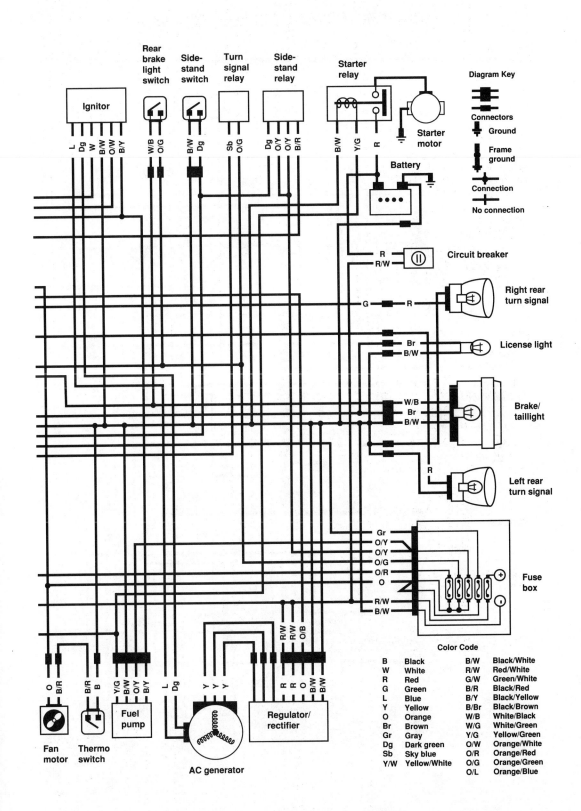

1988-1991 VS750 (U.K.)

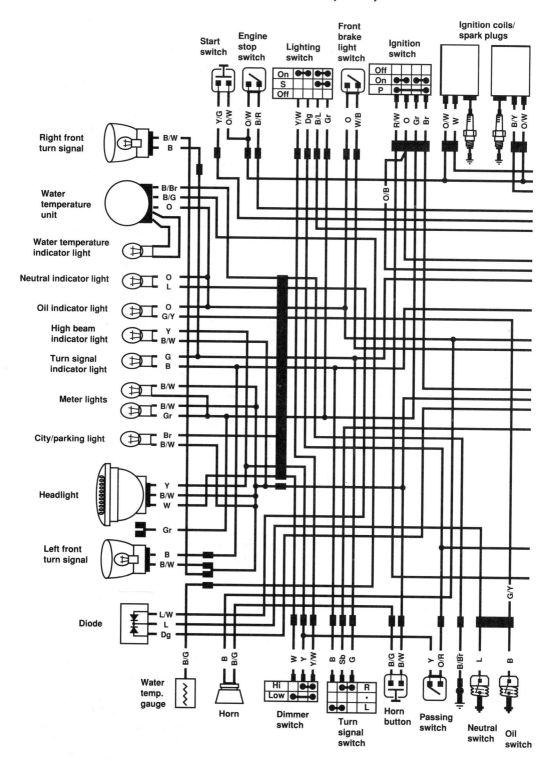

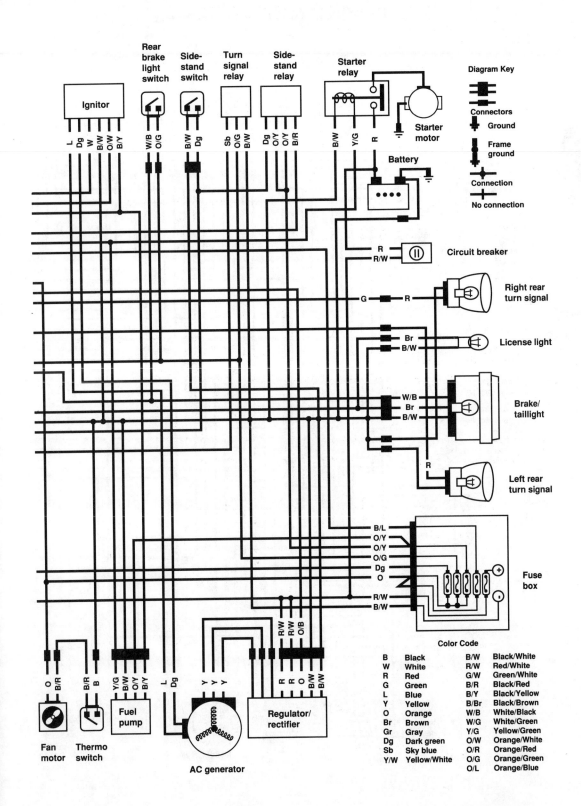

1992-ON VS800 (U.S. and Canada)

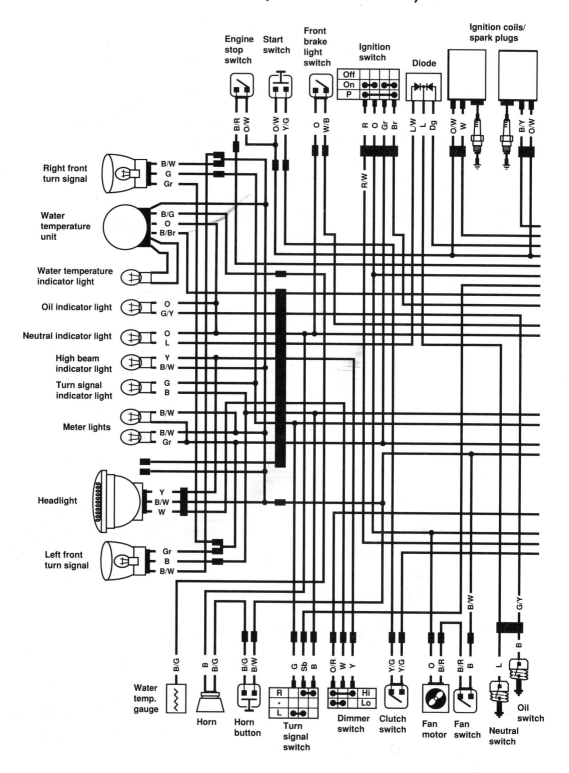

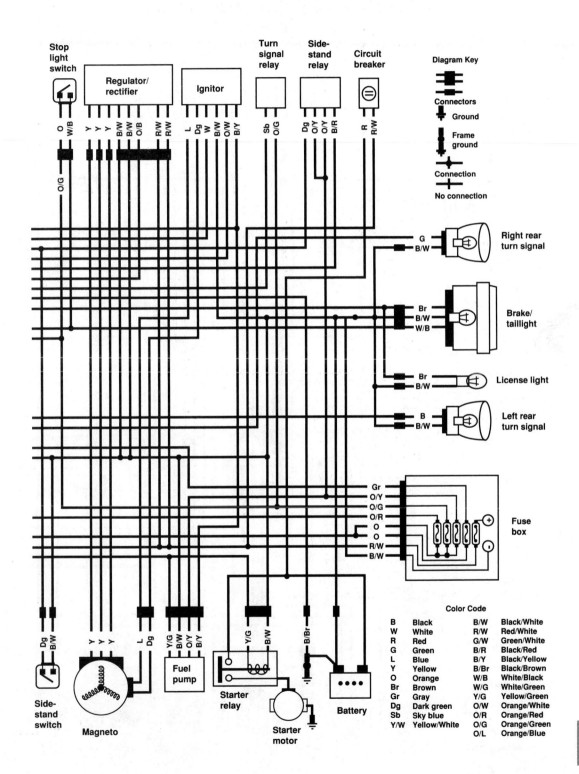

1992-ON VS800 (U.K.)

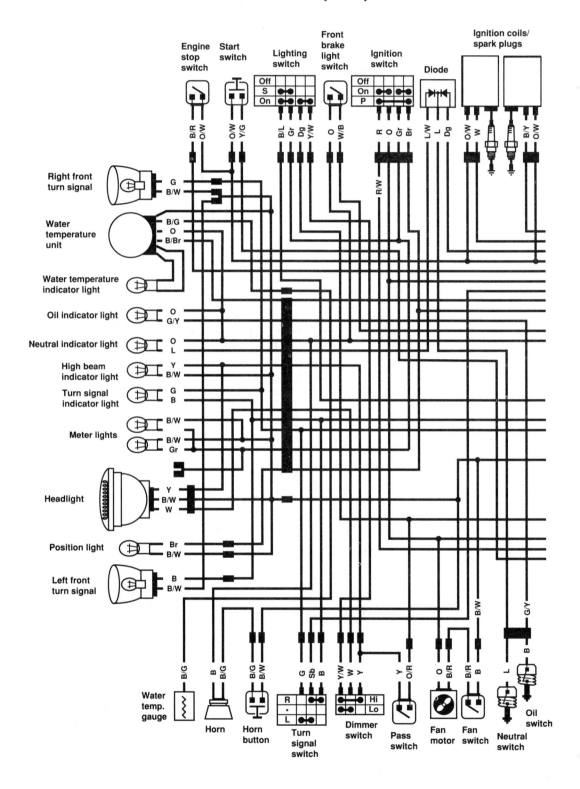

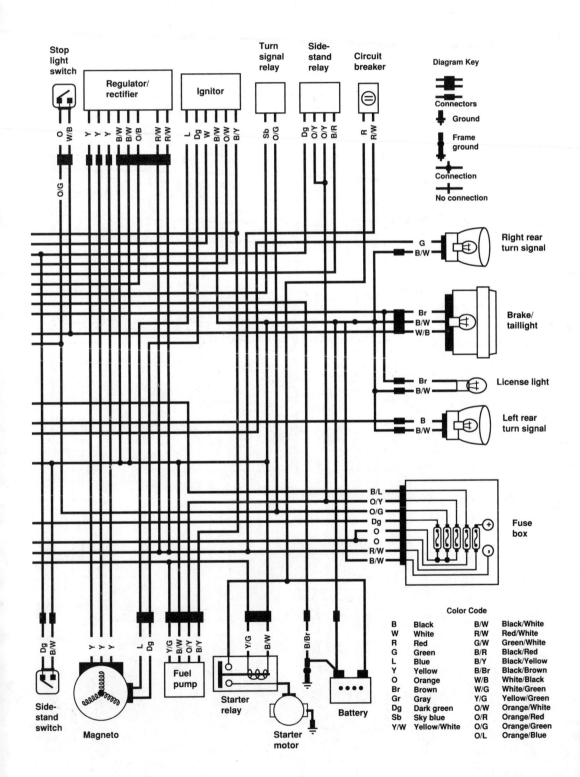

Stop light switch

Regulator/ rectifier

Ignitor

Turn signal relay

Side-stand relay

Circuit breaker

Diagram Key

Connectors

Ground

Frame ground

Connection

No connection

Right rear turn signal

Brake/ taillight

License light

Left rear turn signal

Fuse box

Side-stand switch

Magneto

Fuel pump

Starter relay

Starter motor

Battery

Color Code

B	Black	B/W	Black/White
W	White	R/W	Red/White
R	Red	G/W	Green/White
G	Green	B/R	Black/Red
L	Blue	B/Y	Black/Yellow
Y	Yellow	B/Br	Black/Brown
O	Orange	W/B	White/Black
Br	Brown	W/G	White/Green
Gr	Gray	Y/G	Yellow/Green
Dg	Dark green	O/W	Orange/White
Sb	Sky blue	O/R	Orange/Red
Y/W	Yellow/White	O/G	Orange/Green
		O/L	Orange/Blue

15

NOTES